Black Iconography and Colonial (re)production at the ICC

This book explores the reproduction of colonialism at the International Criminal Court (ICC) and examines international criminal law (ICL) vs the black body through an immersive format of art, music, poetry, and architecture and post-colonial/critical race theory lens.

Taking a multi-disciplinary approach, the book interrogates the operationalisation of the Rome Statute to detail a Eurocentric hegemony at the core of ICL. It explores how colonialism and slavery have come to shape ICL, exposing the perpetuation of the colonial, and warns that it has ominous contemporary and future implications for Africa. As currently envisaged and acted out at the ICC, this law is founded on deceptive and colonial ideas of 'what is wrong' in/with the world. The book finds that the contemporary ICL regime is founded on white supremacy that corrupts the law's interaction with the African. The African is but a unit utilised by the global elite to exploit and extract resources. From time to time, these alliances disintegrate with ICL becoming a retaliatory tool of choice. What is at stake is power, not justice. This power has been hierarchical with Eurocentrism at the top throughout modern history. Colonialism is seen not to have ended but to have regerminated through the foundation of the 'independent' African state. The ICC reproduces the colonial by use of European law and, ultimately, the over-representation of the black accused. To conclude, the book provides a liberated African forum that can address conflicts in the content, with a call for the end of the ICC's involvement in Africa. The demand is made for an African court that utilises non-colonising African norms which are uniquely suited to address local conflicts.

Multidisciplinary in nature, this book will be of great interest to students and scholars of international criminal law, criminal justice, human rights law, African studies, global social justice, sociology, anthropology, post-colonial studies, and philosophy.

Stanley Mwangi Wanjiru is a London based lawyer and theorist. He holds a PhD in International criminal law from Sussex University, LLM(Distinction), LLB (Hons) and BA(Hons). Mwangi was called to the Bar (England and Wales) by the Inner Temple in 2004 after his Vocational Course (BVC) at the College of Law, London. Mwangi focuses on the interaction between the law and the black citizen. His research areas are in decolonising theories, critical legal theories, constitutionalism, public international law international economic law, and international criminal law. He currently teaches Law at University of Kent and is a visiting lecturer in constitutional, administrative, and human rights law at the City University London. Previously and parallel to his work in the law, Mwangi has worked in community projects and safeguarding both internationally and in the UK.

Directions and Developments in Criminal Justice and Law

The ways in which crime is constructed in society are of time-honoured interest to criminologists across the globe. The ever-changing landscape of what is criminal and what is not affects scholars and policymakers in their approach to the body of law defining prohibited conduct, how that law evolves, and the modes by which it is administered. Rule of law cannot exist without a transparent legal system, strong enforcement structures, and an independent judiciary to protect against the arbitrary use of power. Critical consideration of the mechanisms through which societies attempt to make the rule of law a reality is essential to understanding and developing effectual criminal justice systems. The *Directions and Developments in Criminal Justice and Law* series offers the best research on criminal justice and law around the world, offering original insights on a broadly defined range of socio-legal topics in law, criminal procedure, courts, justice, legislation, and jurisprudence. With an eye toward using innovative and advanced methodologies, series monographs offer solid social science scholarship illuminating issues and trends in law, crime, and justice. Books in this series will appeal to criminologists, sociologists, and other social scientists, as well as policymakers, legal researchers, and practitioners.

7 **Biosecurity, Economic Collapse, the State to Come**
Political Power in the Pandemic and Beyond
Christos Boukalas

8 **Black Iconography and Colonial (re)production at the ICC**
(In)dependence Cha Cha Cha?
Stanley Mwangi Wanjiru

9 **Criminal Justice Responses to Domestic Abuse in Northern Ireland**
Ronagh J.A. McQuigg

https://www.routledge.com/Directions-and-Developments-in-Criminal-Justice-and-Law/book-series/DDCJL

Black Iconography and Colonial (re)production at the ICC

(In)dependence Cha Cha Cha?

Stanley Mwangi Wanjiru

Routledge
Taylor & Francis Group
LONDON AND NEW YORK

First published 2023
by Routledge
4 Park Square, Milton Park, Abingdon, Oxon OX14 4RN

and by Routledge
605 Third Avenue, New York, NY 10158

Routledge is an imprint of the Taylor & Francis Group, an informa business

British Library Cataloguing-in-Publication Data
A catalogue record for this book is available from the British Library

Library of Congress Cataloging-in-Publication Data
Names: Wanjiru, Mwangi, author.
Title: Black iconography and colonial (re)production at the ICC : (in)dependence cha cha cha? / Mwangi Wanjiru.
Description: Abingdon, Oxon ; New York, NY : Routledge, 2023. | Series: Directions and developments in criminal justice and law | Includes bibliographical references and index.
Identifiers: LCCN 2022021020 (print) | LCCN 2022021021 (ebook) | ISBN 9781032302553 (hbk) | ISBN 9781032302560 (pbk) | ISBN 9781003304173 (ebk)
Subjects: LCSH: International Criminal Court. | Discrimination in criminal justice administration. | Intercultural communication. | Eurocentrism. | Racism. | Stereotypes (Social psychology)
Classification: LCC HV7419 .W36 2023 (print) | LCC HV7419 (ebook) | DDC 364.089—dc23/eng/20220810
LC record available at https://lccn.loc.gov/2022021020
LC ebook record available at https://lccn.loc.gov/2022021021

ISBN: 978-1-032-30255-3 (hbk)
ISBN: 978-1-032-30256-0 (pbk)
ISBN: 978-1-003-30417-3 (ebk)

DOI: 10.4324/9781003304173

Typeset in Times New Roman
by codeMantra

To my maternal grandmother Wangari Kimani who passed on to *ngomi* in December 2016. Thank you for the *Mau Mau* history. To my maternal grandfather Kimani wa Mutugu Karugo and his friends who were disappeared by the British in 1952, may this be in your memory.

My Mother Wanjiru Kimani, a true free thinker, thank you. To my countless family members, cousins by the dozens, thank you all for the support.

Contents

Preface

In this book, I interrogate the operationalisation of the Rome Statute through a post-colonial/CRT lens to detail a Eurocentric hegemony at the core of ICL. This hegemony excludes slavery and colonialism, the largest genocides known to humankind, as the foundations of not just contemporary ICL, but the crimes litigated by ICL. By asking if Africa has become a testing site for ICL, my research shows that this omission translates to the fact that the influences of these two events in the contemporary 'impunity' discourse are conveniently discarded. Consequently, until very recently few scholars saw ICC's involvement in Africa as the reincarnation of colonialism. I join an increasing minority of scholars focusing on how these two events have come to shape International Criminal Law. My research exposes this perpetuation of the colonial and warns that it has ominous contemporary and future implications for Africa. As currently envisaged and acted out at the ICC, this law is founded on deceptive and colonial ideas of 'what is wrong' in/with the world. As it was in days gone by, this is often identified as the 'tribal 'conflicts'' emanating from Africa. What must be 'cured' is the 'impunity' of a small elite and then neo-liberal nirvana would be achieved.

What is at stake however is power, not justice. We find that this power is hierarchical with Eurocentrism at the top, where it has remained throughout modern history. Colonialism is seen not to have ended but to have regerminated through the foundation of the 'independent' African state. The ICC is firmly located at the contemporary neo-liberal phase of that hegemony where African states are entangled in the straitjacket of treaties such as the Rome Statute, with dire consequences for their self-determination. The ICC reproduces the colonial by use of European law, and the over-representation of the black accused. The iconography of the black accused/victim cements a biased legal industrial complex already well established in the west. The African via the ICL offers this emerging complex a ready market with the black body yet again becoming a commodity.

At the end, I find that the contemporary ICL regime is founded on white supremacy that corrupts the law's interaction with the African. In the atomisation that follows, the African is but a unit utilised by the global elite to exploit and extract wealth from the continent. From time to time, these alliances disintegrate with ICL becoming a retaliatory tool of choice.

To end this subjugation, a liberated African forum that can address conflicts on the continent is enunciated here with a call for the speedy end of ICC's involvement in Africa. The demand is made for the supremacy of an African Court that utilises non-colonising African norms which are uniquely suited to address local conflicts.

Acknowledgements

There are countless people who encouraged and inspired this book and therefore it is impossible to list everyone on this one page. Special mention however to Dr Charlotte Skeet and Dr Michael Kearney for your patience, support, and guidance.

Thanks to my editor Lydia de Cruz, Medha Malaviya, and the entire team at Routledge for your support.

Abbreviations

ACHPR	African Charter on Human and Peoples' Rights
ACJHR	African Court of Justice and Human Rights
ACtHPR	African Court on Human and Peoples' Rights
ADR	Alternative Dispute Resolution
AU	African Union
BLM	Black Lives Matter
CAR	Central African Republic
CJS	Criminal Justice System
CRT	Critical Race Theory
FPLC	*Forces Patriotiques pour la Libération du Congo*
HRW	Human Rights Watch
ICC	International Criminal Court
ICL	International Criminal Law
ICRC	International Committee of the Red Cross
ICTR	International Criminal Tribunal for Rwanda
ICTY	International Criminal Tribunal for the Former Yugoslavia
IEL	International Economic Law
IFIs	International Financial institutions
IMF	International Monetary Fund
IPR	Intellectual Property Rights
MLC	Movement for the Liberation of Congo
MNE	Multinational Enterprise
MNE	Multi-National Enterprise
NGO	Non-Governmental Organisation
NSGJ	National Service of *Gacaca* Jurisdictions
OAU	Organisation of African Unity
OTP	Office of the Prosecutor
SAPs	Structural Adjustment Programmes
SCSL	Special Court for Sierra Leone
TAR	*Tribunale Amministrativo Regionale* (the Regional Administrative Tribunal)
TRC	Truth and Reconciliation Commission
TWAIL	Third World Approaches to International Law

UDHR	Universal Declaration of Human Rights
UNDP	United Nations Development Programme
UN	United Nations
UPC	Union des Patriotes Congolais
WTO	World Trade Organisation

1 Introduction

Source: Frankline McMahony, Bobby Seale at the Conspiracy Trial 1968 (Wikimedia/ Commons).

DOI: 10.4324/9781003304173-1

Standpoint

I write as a black man. I use my black standpoint in this book to capture the stifling epistemic racism that I argue pervades neo-liberalism and International Criminal Law (ICL). The overarching theme here is the need to decolonialise ICL to counter the status quo of epistemic racism[1] existing for example in relation to the International Criminal Court (ICC) vis-à-vis Africa. 'Black' in the sense I apply it encompasses not only an identity, but also a methodology and a cultural, political pose/positioning. It is therefore crucial that in the whole of this work, the term is understood in that context and with the understanding of the politics of identity. Interchangeably, I use black and African as the same and synonymous in this political sense although I understand there are Africans who are not black and black people who are not African. Blackness is a descriptive construct that has been used in the West as both a degrading and empowering term to describe those with African ancestry. It has been used as a racialised demarcation by those in power for the purpose of social stratification and domination.[2] This term has been re-signified by people of African ancestry and others as an affirmative political marker and, in many contexts, a declaration of African heritage.[3] To avoid the risk of over-generalisation, I would warn the reader that the term has various localised meanings beyond this generalised application. For example, in Australia the term has often been used derogatively to describe aboriginal people, but I have recently observed that aboriginal activists have started to use 'black' in the wider political sense during their BLM protests.[4] However, in the context of this book and the wider decolonising/post-colonial, discourses there is a broad context in which the notion of blackness as political and conceivably historical self-understanding can be explored. Amongst the authors I will explore in this book, it is widely understood that there are commonalities in the experiences of blackness that transcend 'citizenships,' geographical and national borders. The authors explored here recognise the perpetual effects on the black body from its contact with the European in days of slavery, colonialism, and contemporary neo-liberalism. Therefore, I look at the contact between Africa and the ICC within this progression of servitude and place it in the contemporary (neo-liberal phase) of the new enslavement which if not visibly physical, is in my view metaphysical.

As a black African lawyer in London, my understanding of these issues informs my engagement with the law generally as well as the wider contemporary global geopolitical issues. I have also been greatly influenced by the black liberation movement in its historical entirety as well as many anti-colonial movements globally, particularly those in south and central America. What I mean in short is that, presented with the same legal conundrums as the situations before the ICC, my understanding of 'what the problem is' is informed by all my experiences as a black lawyer of Kenyan origins working and living in a major colonial city, London. Consequently therefore, while my 'black' movement approach enlightens my view of the ICC and criminal law generally, it may be the case that a white lawyer's understanding of the same may be different because of, amongst other factors, their gaze being shaded by their whiteness. This dichotomy is important because I would argue that when blackness matters as an analytical category, the research outcomes must always lead to efforts to change the status quo. Consequently, materials on post-colonialism, TWAIL and southern epistemologies are analysed and applied in this book because I have an interest in helping to shape discourses around blackness, thereby joining the already impressive list of 'discourse setters' in the black community, including writers, activists and academics engaged in public discussions around community issues. Bringing on board my own lived experiences means that, as a researcher, I integrate my own standpoint into my analysis in a direct way which adds to the validity of the work through my unique reflections on my position as both a black/African lawyer and a researcher. I have found it rather frustrating that of the many TWAIL researchers reviewed so far, none has used their own standpoint as black lawyers in looking at the position of race in relation to the ICC. Although as noted earlier, there is an increasing minority of researchers looking at race and the ICL, one is still left with no option other than to argue that the majority of ICL researchers and the ICC are reluctant to identity race as the most important factor at the ICC, given that all most all the cases at the ICC have been against black men.

My own interest in this area of law was born out of observing the Charles Taylor trial.[5] For example, I was fascinated by the dynamics between a white bench and a black British lawyer who was counsel to Charles Taylor. It was clear to me then that the bench struggled to come to terms with being challenged by a black lawyer and consequently the lawyer became the court's target as he was viewed as being disrespectful for challenging judicial biases, which led to the counsel being sanctioned by the tribunal. One of the memorable flash points was when the defence request to file a case summary was denied because the bench deemed it late. But for a keen observer, what was interesting and relevant perhaps to my discussions on iconography later in Chapter 4, was the prosecution's insistence on having the model Naomi Campbell give evidence about receiving a few dirty diamond pebbles as a gift from Mr Taylor. One would have thought tracing the diamonds to their European traders would have been better evidence, but I digress.[6]

I do not claim uniqueness in the standpoint I take in this work because it has been used by many black activists/authors, particularly in the black consciousness movement, but taking this approach in a critique of the ICC from the perspectives of 'black' liberation thought is a unique contribution that I offer to this specific area of scholarship. As the reader will see in my discussion in Chapter 2 regarding TWAIL, often the authors explored display the anger and frustrations of the international legal system that produces injustices, but they seem afraid to suggest a break away from this system. Makau Mutua for example suggested the twinning of TWAIL and

CRT in confronting the inequalities but did not suggest any actual outcome of such twinning.[7] More recently Thuo Gathii has also suggested this joining of forces between TWAIL and CRT but failed to put forward the need for that force to destruct Eurocentric hegemony – all he would like is for the 'lens to be widened' into tracing issues of race in international law.[8] Because of this paralysis, I endorse the radical thinking in Fanon's work[9] and the practical suggestions given by De Sousa[10] of doing away completely with Eurocentricity, especially when dealing with issues particular to Africa. I advocate this decolonisation because, uniquely, I link the racist tendencies of the law in colonial states like the UK and the USA, for example, with the developments at the ICC *vis-à-vis* Africa. My standpoint is influenced by many black liberated thought figures including Dedan Kimathi,[11] Patrice Lumumba,[12] Kwame Nkrumah,[13] Audre Lorde,[14] Steve Biko,[15] Ngugi wa Thiongo,[16] Langston Hughes,[17] Frantz Fanon, Miles Davis,[18] Maya Angelou,[19] James Baldwin,[20] Toni Morrison,[21] Fela Kuti,[22] Thomas Sankara,[23] Bob Marley,[24] and Jah Fakoly.[25] I would however consider WEB du Bois as the 'father' of the modern day black standpoint because, as early as 1903 with the seminal work *The Souls of Black Folk*,[26] he was able to articulate what later authors like James Baldwin and, lately, Cornel West[27] would build on; that black people must always be conscious of how they view themselves, as well as being conscious of how the world views them. In addition, it is not just black authors who have unashamedly applied a standpoint perspective because others, including Adrienne Rich, did not shy away from inhabiting space in the world and being open and honest about their positions, interests, and points of contention.[28] This way of approaching research is seen by Patricia Lather as a practice towards self-emancipation.[29] She does not see any conflicts with objectivity for a researcher to aim for their self-liberation or that of the persons who are the subject of their research.[30] Lather sees the particularity of the researcher's race, class or gender as giving them a unique validity due to their experiences as members of these subgroups in what she calls 'catalytic validity'[31] because they are committed to mobilising towards the group's emancipation.

Audre Lorde, in her influential collection of essays *Sister/Outsider* highlighted the importance of self-positioning in terms of identifying one's own social marginalisation or relation to systems of oppression, but also in building connections among other groups and connecting oneself to the others' stories and struggles. Most poignant though was her understanding that the oppressed cannot use the oppressor's 'standpoint' to achieve their freedoms.[32] I draw on such inspiration to critique the problem I have identified in the overall ICL/post-colonialism discourse which variously identifies international law as reproducing the colonial but neither offers an alternative nor demands an end to what is seemingly unbalanced treatment of African states at the ICC, for example. I will explore my suggested alternative(s) in Chapter 6, but it is worth noting that Africa had already demonstrated its own capacities to deal with (post)conflicts as seen in Rwanda with the

Gacaca model. The example set in Rwanda is not taken up by the international community as a routine process to resolve conflicts in Africa and the latest attempt by Africa to set up its own court is deemed nefarious. I argue that Africa should litigate its own crimes and disputes and that those arguing otherwise have hidden agendas as it is now widely acknowledged that there is "no value neutral science because at its best it is unrealizable, at worst self-deceptive, and is being replaced by social sciences based on explicit ideologies."[33] Other thinkers have argued on similar lines and called for freedom to replace implicit interests with explicit ones because it is logically impossible to claim that knowledge is interest free.[34]

At the end of my research, I formed the view that in relation to ICL authorship in general and the ICC in particular, the idea that an Africa based court should not oversee African cases is 'the' nefarious standpoint given all the historical considerations described in this thesis and by many authors in this area. The current international legal regime is governed to a large extent by western scholarly work and it is my contention that the ICC is perpetuating a knowledge production industry using African bodies. This 'knowledge' industrial complex where the western legal author/researchers' foundational norm system excludes and does not liaise, consider, or work in concert with African/southern value system(s) only produces alienated, half-baked and fantastic truths about Africa.[35] More importantly in this respect, research in relation to Africa has to be towards support for Africa being self-sustaining in all aspects, including law. There should be resistance to the status quo where the 'technologies' generated from this research on African bodies are 'owned' by the western authors and their political backers. This is because, as we see at the ICC, the power that emanates from this 'ownership' or even the technologies themselves are not shared with the African who provided the data and who is on the receiving end of those technologies.[36] John Heron remarked that in order to protect citizens from being manipulated and managed, people as autonomous beings have the moral right to take part in decision making on knowledge production that affects them. Their capacity for self-determination should be promoted by sharing the power which accrues from both the generation and application of the resulting technologies.[37]

It is therefore important for the reader to note that I use epistemology regularly in its broader context of knowledge and the value system around how the knowledge is produced and where it comes from.[38] The intention here is to include 'other' ways/forms of exploring and being aware that the idea of 'discourse setter'[39] should not be limited to academia because this in my view only represents a very limited, and at times elitist type of black narrative of experience and may reinforce subjugation rather than liberate.[40] This is because I posit that it would be self-destructive for the Eurocentric and neo-liberal university to promote a truly universal epistemology as De Sousa suggests bourgeois narratives are inherently non-progressive because of their origins.[41] In this regard, I draw inspirations from academic sources as well as art, music and oral narratives from my community and therefore take a multi-disciplinary approach in that sense by moving beyond law. I use art, poetry and music for inspiration and in Chapter 4, for example, I explore architecture to show the effects of the contact between the black body and a Eurocentric law more vividly and how this helps in the performance of power relations in legal contexts. 'Space' is seen here not only in terms of physical orientation but also in terms of social, political, and economic context. The law is seen through looking at the 'theatre' where it is practiced, as reproducing a modernity that is colonial and promoting a neo-liberalism that perpetuates subjugation. In this respect, I have no choice but to see the law as a space that extends old geographical colonial fields. In this regard, I have had to reflect on who is the end user of my work outside the law department. I therefore have had to decide from whose perspective I will adopt my analytical references and whose symbols and systems of meanings I will attempt to describe. This requires an overt political positioning which I appreciate will make some uncomfortable, although my research shows that political positioning in most writing on southern epistemology is becoming the norm.[42]

Post-Colonial and Critical Race Theories

I will explore neo-colonial theory in its wider context and in relation to the ICC in chapters two and will therefore not detail it here except to note that the anti-racist stance and the black standpoint taken here is not informed by one specific school of post-colonial thought but is inspired by many thinkers who conceptualise colonial relations as continuing rather than fundamentally having ended. Drawing inspiration from Fanon, law is not only seen as having a direct racist impact on the black accused/wider community but it also acts as one of Fanon's zones of being and nonbeing,[43] whereby the ICL fraternity continuously present contemporary western notions of human rights as 'the' solution to the political inequality and historical oppression of various groups on the basis not only of nationality, but also of the strong social demarcations of race and ethnicity.[44]

In addition, CRT as a movement is a grouping of thinkers, activists and scholars involved in the exploration of and commitment to changing the dynamics of race, racism, and power. The movement does not divert from 'traditional' civil rights and minorities discourses but contextualises these same issues using a wider perspective that includes politics, economics, history and. as we see in this book, law amongst others. A major distinction between the current crop of CRT activists and our predecessors is the urgent need for and the refusal of the incremental progress that has been promised but never delivered by 'neutral' constitutionalism. We see the liberal order underpinned by constitutionalism including equality theory, legalistic language/reasoning, and enlightenment as largely contributory to and part of a nefarious hegemony that needs to be overthrown.[45] The main assumption about race in this discourse is that racism is best understood as a set of ideologies, rather than an individual system of belief. Interpersonal racism must have a context and it is this context that gives racism its coherence.[46] The context, then, can be understood as societal racism – comprised of attitudes that are wide reaching and can manifest themselves in individual and institutional behaviour.[47] One of the most appropriate frameworks for investigating racism on a structural level is using the tools of ethnography to explore experiences of 'everyday racism,' including descriptions of 'vicarious experiences of racism' and reconstructing these experiences in an analytical sense which provides the best window into understanding racist behaviour.[48] The reasoning behind this is that those who experience racism in their daily lives notice patterns and are able to highlight 'micro manifestations' of racism. They are able to offer considerable insight to those attempting to understand bigger structural patterns.[49]

And therefore, instead of merely suggesting that the ICC is selective in targeting Africa, I explore the mind-boggling silence by the neo-liberalist human rights industry towards the unbalanced nature of this justice system. At the beginning of my research in 2016–2017, of the 23 cases in nine situations which had been brought before the ICC, all were from Africa and all 32 individuals who had been indicted at that stage were African.[50] Although there are current investigations in Israel/Palestine, Georgia, Afghanistan, and Bangladesh/Myanmar, by April 2019, the Court had issued indictments against only 45 individuals, all of them Africans.[51] I see this over-representation as the inherent characteristic of a racist criminal justice system and argue that it occurs by design rather than by mistake.

While this over-representation is a reproduction of local CJS at an international level, the fact that no other situations apart from those in Africa have been litigated so far at the ICC means that Africa is being used to operationalise the ICC bureaucracy and as a testing field for the Rome Statute. I also contend that the ICC has become wholly aligned with the justice systems in the USA and UK where the over-representation of the black accused has been variously described as institutional racism, as discussed later in Chapters 4 and 5. I explore the idea of Africa as a testing ground for the Rome Statute and the resulting reproduction of laws from a post-colonial and critical race perspective and investigate whether the ICC could be viewed as a colonial institution, as claimed by many in Africa and elsewhere.[52]

Since I make the link between local racist tendencies in the UK and the USA criminal justice systems and what is occurring at the ICC in relation to Africa, it is important to note that it is in this CRT manner of understanding structural/institutional racism that I employ Ava DuVernay's documentary '13th.'[53] The reader will notice that I employ art in various forms throughout the book to make this an immersive volume, hence the deliberate use of a documentary as a source. Once the reader has watched and engaged with the issues explored in the documentary, discussions of black body and criminal justice systems become more vivid and, hopefully, the explorations of iconography in Chapter 4 become even more clearer. And therefore, I use '13th' first to show how art can be used as a critique method/device that shows CRT in practice; second to explore and show the industrial complex that I explore in the book more vividly and bring to life the iconography of the black accused.

To bring out the issues of race at the ICC more clearly, I detail the origins of the campaign against the ICC by African states using the situation in Kenya as an example. The African cases discussed here, including the Kenyatta case, are used to test my hypotheses rather than the cases themselves being 'the' subject of my study. I use the Kenyatta and Gbagbo cases, for example, to highlight the continuation of colonialism and the iconographic consequences of such cases in local political contexts. I also show how the elite use international spaces for their power contests rather than as vehicles towards 'global' justice or peace. In addition, I use the Bemba and Mahdi cases to explore the 'testing' of the Rome Statute and the reproduction of pre-existing international laws. The Kenyatta case led to some countries in Africa, including Burundi and South Africa, starting the process to withdraw from the ICC and to the AU passing a non-binding resolution for all member states to withdraw from the Rome Statute, with Burundi finally withdrawing from the Rome Statute in October 2017.[54]

I argue that the ICC is founded on the adaption of European law in its widest meaning to include common law and civil law, as I will explore later, but also in terms of epistemology. This, I argue, contributes to the coloniality at the heart of the ICC. I emphasise that the ICC ignores the fact that the epistemological foundations of such law are racist in nature especially in relation to/in colonised states.[55] Defenders of the ICC and academic researchers have so far mostly looked at how the court should function better and critique of bias has mainly been addressed through appointing more African court employees, including judges.[56] However, I argue that it is valid to hypothesise that Africa is a testing site for the Rome Statute and other associated ICC practices because the African subject and African conflicts are central and crucial for the operation of the court given that all but a few cases emanate from Africa. I trace this to practices inherited from slavery and colonialism and further argue that neo-liberalisation of the law means that, yet again, the black body becomes a tool for exploitation through the current ICL regime.

The black body, represented here by Africa, is seen as the site where these 'liberating' western shenanigans have necessarily occurred since the slavery days, but also along the same lines as Ann Sagan's arguments that siting criminality and victimhood on the African subject is

> ...crucial to the self-identity of the ICC because it corroborates the court's cosmopolitan and liberal narratives...These representations are consequently institutionalised in the operation of the court, which

> encourages the repeated indictment of African subjects at the ICC and the reproduction of the criminal—victim dichotomy in the representation of African subjects in the discourse of international criminal law.[57]

This structural racism within international bodies has recently also been noted by the UN Special Rapporteur on racism who reported that the historic racial injustices of slavery and colonialism remain largely outside the process of accountability for today but nevertheless "require restitution, compensation, satisfaction, rehabilitation and guarantees of non-repetition."[58] Significantly for this book, the rapporteur said that failure to redress the racism of slavery and colonialism leads to the racially discriminatory effects of structures of inequality and subordination.[59]

I argue that this focus on crimes located in Africa by the ICC is not a mistake but is the default of the 'international' law's design as Africa is demarcated permanently in the Eurocentric imagination as the site for crime and Europe as the site for justice. Kamari Clarke goes further and suggests that this manner of understanding justice promotes inequalities and also that institutions such as the ICC should be seen as founded on white supremacy.[60] Inadvertently, the idea of white supremacy at the heart of the ICC is eloquently and rather tragically expounded by a senior African employee of the court; Eboe-Osuji, the president of the ICC, while commenting on the then escalating dispute between the ICC and the USA said, "It is surprising from such a renowned bastion of liberal democracy...it is something you expect from certain kinds of countries...but you don't expect that from the United States."[61] This dispute emanated from the ICC's attempt to investigate the US personnel's crimes in Afghanistan which had led to the US government sanctioning the prosecutor. The ICC has become a colonialising tool in the sense that it instrumentalises Mr Oboe-Esuji's stated dichotomy as a discursive contrast between the horrors which may be controlled through the construction of an international justice system and the spread of a contemporary form of 'civilisation' through the universalisation of the Rule of Law. This manner of looking at law produces lasting iconographies of not only a barbaric Africa, but also the saviour west. The victim must, however, always be black and most often female, which prompted me to look at the cases presented from a post-colonial/CRT perspective.

Following in the footsteps of other decolonial theorists like Fanon, I use my standpoint and lived experiences of racism in the UK and life more generally in a similar manner to that explored by Fanon in *Black Skin, White Mask*[62] where the creation of racialised subjectivity is seen as a real consequence of colonialism, grounded in stories and history. Second, I apply Fanon in the manner he suggested in the *Wretched of the Earth*,[63] with an unequivocal stand against colonialism and support of revolutionary action(s) of all kinds to liberate Africa(ns) from the stranglehold of the European. In this regard, I address whether the ICC has colonial foundations and whether it acts like a colonial institution in its dealing with African states. I then utilise literature from critical race theory to analyse how this way of dealing with Africa continues and mirrors inherent biases within domestic law towards the 'black body' in colonial states themselves, such as the UK and USA.[64]

However, to set some limits, it is important to acknowledge from the outset that ample research already exists on the ICC as an institution and I am not proposing to repeat it here as it does not form part of my research focus, but I have engaged with the ICC in relation to the Kenya cases in Chapter 3. My research is not focused on the chronology of the ICC's involvement with Africa, nor is it research on the general functioning of the ICC. That kind of academic work has been well undertaken by various authors, including William Schabas who engages with the ICC from its inception to its operational principles.[65] I use William Schabas and others to gain an understanding of the background although, unlike them, I concentrate more on the epistemological questions arising from ICC's interaction with Africa because it is my view that most authors reviewed, including Schabas, have not engaged with the epistemological challenges facing the ICC in Africa. In addition, I have reviewed research by others, such as Yuval Shany, who have looked at the effectiveness of international courts, including the ICC.[66] In my view, Shany is among many authors who take an approach that focuses on why the tribunals, including the ICC, are not 'functioning' as they should but does not look at the foundational 'thinking' behind the ICC as I do here.

I locate discussions on the ICC in the wider historical context and argue that the ICC's focus on Africa continues the pattern of writing global memories. It also hinders recording of actual memories because it presupposes that atrocities against humanity began with World War II, conveniently ignoring slavery and colonialism, which not only sets the coloniser free for those crimes but in turn presents the coloniser as the saviour. The irony of this narrative is played out in the Kenyan cases because, while the post-war conventions against war crimes were being adopted, the British state was committing atrocities in Kenya during the *Mau Mau* uprising.[67] Later, while the Kenyan cases were being litigated at The Hague, the British state was fighting to avoid responsibilities for those atrocities committed during its colonial rule of Kenya at the High Court in London in a case brought by the *Mau Mau* veterans.[68]

In this case, a group of survivors who included my maternal grandmother, brought a case against the UK government for the atrocities committed in Kenya during the peasants' revolution that led to the collapse of the colonial settler government. During the hearing, evidence was presented of mass atrocities authorised by the British government including mass murders, rapes, disappearances, and population displacements which would in my view be captured by the Rome Statute if they were happening today but should nonetheless have been captured by precedent set at Nuremberg.[69] In my view, the *Mau Mau* case is notable also for the silence with which it was treated by the Eurocentric ICL commentators, particularly the NGO/

victims industry. This I argue is because the narrative it provided was not the orthodox ICL story of the African woman needing a white saviour and protection from her brothers but one with agency and in solidarity with her brothers, a freedom fighter, willing to take on the might of the British state for justice with no help from white people who were the perpetrators this time around.

The manner of re-thinking international law I advocate is being applied by more and more scholars who are looking beyond the mere fact of political 'independence' and including neo-colonialism to explore the epistemological foundations of the colonial state as well as the interrogation of how international bodies perpetuate those philosophies. My work re-emphasises the premise that the rumour of the death of the colonial state is exaggerated. The colonial state lives through neo-liberal economic relationships as well as through international bodies such as the ICC. As we shall see later, this proposition is not new as it continues arguments by others, including Fanon and Nkrumah, but what is ground-breaking however is my exploration of whether Africa is being used as a testing site for international criminal law theories as well as whether Africa can and should provide a *grundnorm* to counter the hegemony of a Eurocentric universality.

The immediate scholarly impact of this book is my contention that Africa has become a site for testing, reproduction, and instrumentation of the Rome Statute and, in the process, mirroring colonialism. In doing so, I make a distinctive and major contribution to the specific area of International Criminal Law because most of the literature available on the ICC and Africa discourse shows that little if any research has been undertaken so far looking at the current impasse and using a combination of post-colonial and CRT perspective. In addition, the application of a standpoint perspective in the study of the ICC v Africa phenomenon is ground-breaking. Further, it is clear from my research that although there is an increasing critique of ICL, there are few authors, particularly black authors, looking at the epistemologies that underscore the ICC's engagement with Africa. Finally, I have recognised the hesitation by many critiques of the status quo to provide a clear alternative and therefore, in this book I propose that ICC's involvement in Africa should be wound down in a considered and pragmatic manner in preparation for the arrival of the African Court. This pragmatic end of ICC's occupation of Africa should not mean the end of ICC's involvement with the rest of the world but entails a gradual and then hastened transferring of skills and technologies to the African Court by the ICC.

Art and Other Ways of 'Looking'

One of the main critiques I have faced from reviewers is that my standpoint perspective makes this work non-legal and tautological. I have also noticed that the mainstream is uncomfortable with being directly confronted with alternative views on the 'international' nature of law. Bianchi noted this tendency of the hegemony to discard critique as other and not technically legal enough.[70] It is therefore important to note that my work falls within wider qualitative methods that examine the *why* and *how* of decision making, not just *what, where, when*, or *who*.[71] A qualitative researcher uses a wider lens of considering multiple sources of 'hard data' and the focus is to explore the totality of the situation in order to understand the presenting problem/phenomenon.[72] The research may begin with a grounded theory approach with the researcher having no previous understanding of the problem at hand; or the study may commence with propositions and proceed in a scientific and empirical way throughout the research process.[73] I chose qualitative methods precisely because of their capacity to allow a wider approach which was not restricted to the use of one approach and allowed me to take a multi-disciplinary approach allowing room for this project to evolve organically.

In this sense I suggest that if my work was a piece of music, it would be Jazz, allowing for improvisation of either the vocals or instruments or both while borrowing from many musical traditions. I have for example used purposive samples in looking at the Kenyatta, Bemba, and Mahdi cases to better understand a phenomenon[74] in our case, the suggested coloniality of the ICC and the Africa v ICC impasse. I have also used other methods and sources including observations, texts, films, pictures, and other materials.[75] I considered archival research more appropriate and encompassing than interviews in addressing what evolved to be a much wider topic than originally envisaged and therefore studies of historical items, photographs, public and official documents, in addition to images in the media and literature fields became in my view a suitable source of data specific to my topic.[76] Other sources of data included documents, reports, academic texts, academic articles, newspapers, music, and other art forms including graphics and photography.

The second and more focused level in understanding my work is that, as legal research, it is not doctrinal. My work did not, as doctrinal research would have done, involve systematic analysis of the Rome Statute or the legal principles and propositions contained in that statute. I was not just researching the law by emphasising substantive law, rules, doctrines, concepts, and judicial pronouncements of the ICC. And finally, this was not a research based on legal propositions, judicial pronouncement of the ICC and other conventional legal material revealing the legislative intent, policy and history of the rule or doctrine.[77] On the contrary, my research falls within the wider socio-legal approach exploring the actual interaction of the law with the individual and the society. In this respect, the synergies between CRT and socio-legal theory are immense because both perspectives focus on the exercise of power and analyse how power dynamics affect human relationships in the social and political spheres.[78]

As opposed to doctrinal approaches, my research studied what is actually taking place in practice rather than focusing on the law in the 'texts.' For example, it investigates ICL in action and the actions of the ICC as an institution within Africa, and cases such as the situation in Kenya in relation to global power relations, which a doctrinal analysis does not allow.[79] Rather than focusing on case law and statutes, this approach gathers data wherever it is appropriate to a particular investigation and explores the social and political factors that influence the operation of the law in question.[80] In our case, my research focused on "the various cultural, economic and political consequences of the selective enforcement of different laws by the ICC as an institution, including the basis on which discretion is being exercised in practice."[81] This focusing and interrogating is done from a post-colonial as well as a CRT perspective. Applying CRT, for example, allows me to use my standpoint as a black-African lawyer practicing in England and using my lived experiences of race and law to both motivate and inform the direction of my research while at the same time acknowledging my biases towards a truly decolonised law.

One of the unique ways I have endeavoured to interrogate the law through the CTR/decolonisation prism is by using art. The reader is at various points in this book invited to engage with art, music and poetry. In using art in the critique of the law, I am linking to a well-established culture in the black liberation movement(s) to critique power using art. Art in protest/revolution serves many purposes, including creating annoyance, sensitising, and educating. Music is particularly useful in entertaining the cadre to keep them motivated/inspired. Most significantly however, art can act as a historical reservoir for posterity, a library. In most black communities, especially in the cities, graffiti against the authorities has always thrived. Using art to critique law enforcement is an integral part of an urban black resistance movement. *Fuck tha Police*![82] was not just a protest anthem but also inspired by numerous urban graffiti of a similar nature. Art has also been more targeted and deliberate in its attack on law's mistreatment of black people and one piece in particular resonates with my discourse on decolonisation and hegemony. In 1971, the New York State Police massacred about 39 prisoners and hostages after prisoners took control of the Attica prison in protest against racist practices by the prison authorities. As is the norm, no police officers were held accountable for those deaths. In response, Faith Ringgold created *United States of Attica* which I regard as one of the most poignant protest pieces detailing America's atrocities all over the world.[83]

This piece by Ringgold is mentioned here for its engagement with America's hegemony and for its reference to Pan-Africanism as a mode of protest, an idea that is antithetical to racism. Ringgold was not alone in the use of art as protest. Emory Douglas not only documented the black liberation but also poignantly focused on the role of women in the Black Panther Movement. Emory's work not only deals with localised freedom fights, but also links these to a global need for uprising(s). While exploring the icon of the black woman as a victim in Chapter 5 of this book for example, I am reminded of his 1969 work depicting a black woman in all her glory with a rifle on her back, and brandishing a spear.[84] Through this, Douglas highlighted the central role of female revolutionaries-all over the colonised spaces.

Through Art, African women have engaged with the 'atomisation' of their bodies and have also used art to depict the ideas of exploitation that I explore later in Chapter 5. Ingrid Mwangi for example uses her own body to explore the idea of Africa as the 'dark' continent and by extension the exploitation of the female form.[85] In addition, another Kenyan-Artist, Wangechi Mutu, is renowned for her 'distortionist' and at times surreal depiction of the African female form.[86] Through her work, Wangechi uses various mediums, including collage, video, performance, and sculpture, and investigates themes of gender, race, and colonialism. Her most visited theme is the hyper-objectification of black female bodies and she has used an otherworldly nature to reiterate the fictitious nature of society's depictions of black women.

Chapters

In Chapter 2, I critically explore literature on post-colonialism, decolonisation, neo-colonialism, law and imperialism, and TWAIL. This is done to define key concepts, contextualise my research and identify the gaps in the literature which this book intends to bridge. In Chapter 3, I place the ICC in the neo-liberalism phase of a continuum of colonialism. I interrogate the ongoing disquiet amongst African states with the ICC within this neo-liberalism context by tracing Africa's initial enthusiasm to the prevailing neo-liberalist orthodoxy of the 1990s–2000s and the subsequent disappointments. Within this continuum, I therefore argue that the Rome Statute and 'rule of law' in general should be viewed as anti-revolution(s) as it does not distinguish between the oppressor and the oppressed's fight for freedom(s) and should therefore be seen as a tool to maintain the exploitative, Eurocentric hegemony. I then look at the Kenyan cases as a sample for discussion to contextualise this neo-liberalism discourse. I chose the Kenyan cases mainly because of my familiarity with the local situation and because of what I argue was 'the iconographic' nature of the Kenyatta case which ties in with my discourse on legal iconography in Chapter 4.

In Chapter 4, I explore the over-representation of the black accused at the ICC and how this relates to slavery and colonialism and significantly, what iconography is produced by such over-representation. Here, the colonial is not only seen as present in the ICL's victim/criminal dichotomies, but also in the reproduction of the colonial via the Eurocentric legal architecture including courthouse construction, courtroom design and use of language. The over-representation of the black accused at the ICC reproduces colonial ideas that equate the African male with murder and plunder. The predominance of the male accused reproduces patterns already seen in the USA and the UK where the black male is over-represented in the criminal justice system. The chapter also discusses how the elite, including African elite, utilise the emerging iconography for their power-seeking endeavours.

In Chapter 5, I show the demarcation of Africa as the 'site' of what I would term as awfulness, which allows Africa to become the site where the Rome Statute is tested, operationalised, and instrumentalised. Because this is the first time the Rome Statute is applied, Africa becomes the testing site, but it is also acting as a replication site for already existing international norms in areas including rape, cultural destruction, and victim participation. In *Bemba,*[87] for example, I explore how the testing of Article 28 of the Rome Statute is carried out as well as the reproduction of war rape jurisdiction. In *Mahdi,*[88] I discuss the testing of Article 8 of the Rome Statute as well as the reproduction of plea bargains at the ICC. I also discuss the expansion of victim participation and how this affects the accused's right to fair trial as well as justice for the victims. In summary, I explore how the ICC variously presents its decisions as 'ground-breaking' although in effect they are a regurgitation of old laws. This presentation as 'new,' I argue, is partly a sign that the ICC recognises its connections with a tainted coloniality but it is also a common ploy in neo-colonialism to hoodwink critics and to stymie calls for change.

Before concluding this book, I proceed to provide viable solutions to the identified coloniality of the ICC through highlighting southern alternatives in Chapter 6. I explore *Ubuntu* as an already existing normative legal foundation that should anchor alternative(s) to the prevailing Eurocentric ICL and, more importantly, I suggest it should inform the emerging African court. In this regard, I showcase *Gacaca* courts as an Africa-centric model based on *Ubuntu* which has already been used to deal with 'international crimes' in Rwanda. The reason I proceed to suggest solutions is mainly because, as indicated above, I adopted a methodology and a standpoint that critiques the current ICL regime as a reproduction of the colonial and this requires me to provide an alternative that I view as liberating in the manner suggested by Fanon who argued that intellectuals in the anticolonial movement must play a crucial role in creating a truly independent alternative.

Notes

1 For a further exploration of the term see for example Ramón Grosfoguel, 'Epistemic Islamophobia, and Colonial Social Sciences' (2010) 8 (2) *Human Architecture: Journal of the Sociology of Self-Knowledge* 29–38.

2 Ian F. Haney Lopez, 'The Social Construction of Race: Some Observations on Illusion, Fabrication, and Choice' (1994) 29 *Harvard Civil Rights–Civil Liberties Law Review* 1; Ian Haney-Lopez, *White by Law: The Legal Construction of Race* (New York University Press 2006).

3 For a discussion on Negritude see for example Rabaka Reiland, *The Negritude Movement: WEB Du Bois, Leon Damas, Aime Cesaire, Leopold Senghor, Frantz Fanon, and the Evolution of an Insurgent Idea* (Lexington Books 2015).

4 See Ian Keen (ed.), *Being Black: Aboriginal Cultures in 'Settled' Australia* (Aboriginal Studies Press 1994).
5 *Prosecutor v. Charles Ghankay Taylor, SCSL-03-1-T,* Special Court for Sierra Leone, 18 May 2012.
6 For the shenanigans in Charles Taylor's case, see Charles Jalloh Chernor. 'Charles Taylor' in William Schabas (ed.), *The Cambridge Companion to International Criminal Law* (CUP 2016) 312–332; Very relevant to my exploration of imagery in Chapters 4 and 5, see the attempts to pit Ms Campbell vs a contemporary white woman in popular imagination in, for example, 'Mia Farrow contradicts Naomi Campbell' *The Guardian*, 9 August 2010.
7 Makau Mutua, 'Critical Race Theory and International Law: The View of an Insider-Outsider' (2000) 45 *Villanova Law Review* 841.
8 Gathii James Thuo, 'Writing Race and Identity in a Global Context: What CRT and TWAIL Can Learn from Each Other' (2020) 67 *UCLA Law Review* 1610–1650.
9 See more generally Leo Zeilig, *Frantz Fanon: The Militant Philosopher of Third World Revolution* (Bloomsbury Publishing 2015).
10 Boaventura de Sousa Santos, *The End of the Cognitive Empire* (Duke University Press 2018).
11 Leader of the *Mau Mau* peasants' revolution who was murdered and buried in unmarked grave by the British. See Ngugi wa Thiong'o and Micere Githae Mugo, *The Trial of Dedan Kimathi* (Waveland Press 2013).
12 See more generally, Georges Nzongola-Ntalaja, *Patrice Lumumba* (Ohio University Press 2014).
13 Ama Biney, *The Political and Social Thought of Kwame Nkrumah* (Springer 2011).
14 Audre Lorde, *The Master's Tools Will Never Dismantle the Master's House* (Penguin 2018).
15 See particularly Steve Biko, *I Write What I Like: Selected Writings* (University of Chicago Press 2015).
16 Ngugi wa Thiong'o has had a major influence in my upbringing and influenced me at an early age into looking at my own education in a different light. See Ngugi wa Thiong'o, *Decolonising the Mind: The Politics of Language in African Literature* (East African Publishers 1992).
17 Langston Hughes, *The Collected Poems of Langston Hughes* (Vintage 2020).
18 Miles Davis, *Kind of Blue* (Columbia 1959). While this is arguably 'the' Jazz album of all time, my inspiration from this is more in the manner described by Prof Cornel West (note 27 below); that of improvisations and the necessity of pragmatism towards resolving social justice issues including those of racism.
19 Maya Angelou, *Maya Angelou: The Complete Poetry* (Hachette 2015).
20 See James Baldwin, *Sonny's Blues* (Ernst Klett Sprachen 2009) and James Baldwin and Raoul Peck, *I Am Not Your Negro: A Major Motion Picture* (directed by Raoul Peck Vintage 2017).
21 Toni Morrison, *A Mercy* (Random House 2008). Although her previous works are all immensely informative on black experience during and after slavery, this book surpasses all with its exploration of America's sense of exceptionalism.
22 Fela Kuti, *Zombie* (Polydor 1977) is a classic commentary on the post-colonial African state.
23 For four years between 1983 and 1987, Sankara led a socialist revolution in Bukina Faso, before being assassinated. See Thomas Sankara, *Thomas Sankara Speaks: The Burkina Faso Revolution 1983–87* (2nd edn, Pathfinder 2007).
24 Bob Marley, *Uprising* (Tuff Gong/Island 1980), the all-time revolutionary's soundtrack?

26 Tiken Fakoly is an artist from Ivory Coast who details the evils of colonialism in his music that I have used in the following chapters. See an exploration of his music in Olivier Bourderionnet, 'Displacement in French/Displacement of French: The Reggae and R'n'B of Tiken Jah Fakoly and Corneille' (2008) 4 (39) *Research in African Literatures* 14–23 and Kassoum Kourouma, 'Reggae et politique en Afrique: le mythe du paradis perdu' (2019) 23 *Recherches Africaines* 17–29.

26 WEB du Bois, *The Souls of Black Folk; Essays and Sketches* (A G McClurg 1903).

27 See Miriam Strube and Cornel West, 'Pragmatism's Tragicomic Jazzman: A Talk with Cornel West' (2013) 58 (2) *Amerikastudien / American Studies* 291–301.

28 See Adrienne Rich, 'Split at the Root: An Essay on Jewish Identity' in Adrienne Rich (ed.), *Blood, Bread, and Poetry: Selected Prose 1979–1985* (WW Norton & Company 1994)110.

29 Patricia Lather, *Getting Smart: Feminist Research and Pedagogy with/in the Post-modern* (Psychology Press 1991) 50–69.

30 Ibid.

31 Ibid., 68.

32 Audre Lorde, 'The Master's Tools Will Never Dismantle the Master's House' in *Sister Outsider: Essays and Speeches* (Crossing Press 1984) 110–113.

33 Mary Hesse, *Revolutions and Reconstructions in the Philosophy of Science* (Harvester Press 1980) 247.

34 Reinharz Shulamit, *"Feminist Distrust: Problems of Context and Content in Sociological Work" Exploring Clinical Methods for Social Research* (Sage 1985) 153–172.

35 John Heron, *Experiential Research* (British Postgraduate Medical Federation 1981) 29.

36 Ibid., Technologies to be understood here both in its simplest meaning of knowledge and in the Foucauldian sense of governmentality. See generally Thomas Lemke, *Foucault, Governmentality, and Critique* (Routledge 2015).

37 John Heron (note 35) 30.

38 This is done in the manner suggested by Boaventura de Sousa Santos, *Epistemologies of the South: Justice against Epistemicide* (Routledge 2015).

39 On discourse theory more generally, see Margaret Wetherell Stephanie Taylor and Simeon J. Yates (eds), *Discourse Theory and Practice: A Reader* (Sage 2001).

40 See a wider discussion on this topic in Julie Cupples and Ramón Grosfoguel (eds), *Unsettling Eurocentrism in the Westernized University* (Routledge 2018).

41 Boaventura de Sousa Santos, 'Public Sphere and Epistemologies of the South' (2012) 37 (1) *Africa Development* 43–67.

42 De Sousa Santos (note 41) suggests that this form of intellectual activism is key to global equalities.

43 Frantz Fanon, *Black Skin White Masks* (Pluto Press 1952) 2; More generally see Lewis R. Gordon, *What Fanon Said: A Philosophical Introduction to His Life and Thought* (Fordham University Press 2015).

44 See for example Walter Mignolo, Who Speaks for the 'Human' in Human Rights? (2009) 5 (1) *Hispanic Issues on Line* 7–24.

45 Richard Delgado and Jean Stefancic, *Critical Race Theory: An Introduction* (Vol. 20, New York University Press 2017) 3.

46 Philomena Essed, *Understanding Everyday Racism: An Interdisciplinary Theory* (Vol. 2, Sage 1991) 3.

47 Ibid.

48 Ibid.

49 Ibid., 20.

50 International Criminal Court, 'Cases,' available at https://www.icc-cpi.int/Pages/defendantswip.aspx accessed 11 April 2019).
51 Ibid.
52 See for example an exploration of this and wider alternatives discussed in Albert Isaac Olawale, *"Back to the Future: Rethinking Alternatives to External Intervention in African Conflicts." Indigenous Knowledge Systems and Development in Africa* (Palgrave Macmillan 2020) 171.
53 Ava DuVernay, *"13th" A Netflix Original Documentary* (Kandoo Films 2016).
54 'Burundi Becomes First Nation to Leave International Criminal Court' *The Guardian*, 27 October 2017.
55 See Walter D. Mignolo and Catherine E. Walsh, *On Decoloniality: Concepts Analytics Praxis* (Duke University Press 2018).
56 See for example Josephine J. Dawuni, 'African Women Judges on International Courts: Symbolic or Substantive Gains' (2018) 47 *The University of Baltimore Law Review* 199.
57 Ann Sagan, 'African Criminals/African Victims: The Institutionalised Production of Cultural Narratives in International Criminal Law' (2010) 39 (1) *Millennium* 8–9.
58 UN General Assembly, Report of the Special Rapporteur on contemporary forms of racism, racial discrimination, xenophobia and racial intolerance, 21 August 2019 Report A/74/321.
59 Ibid.
60 Kamari Maxine Clarke, 'Negotiating Racial Injustice-How International Criminal Law Helps Entrench Structural Inequality' (24 July 2020), available at https://www.justsecurity.org accessed 18 October 2020.
61 Jason Burke, 'Head of International Criminal Court Accuses US of Acting Unlawfully' *The Guardian* (London 24th June 2010).
62 Frantz Fanon, *Black skin, White Masks* (trans. Charles Lam Markmann, Grove 1967).
63 Frantz Fanon, *The Wretched of the Earth* (Penguin 2001).
64 For an exploration of CJS racial biases in the USA see Ta-Nehisi Coates, *Between the World and Me* (Text Publishing 2015) and Ava DuVernay, *"13th" A Netflix Original Documentary* (Kandoo Films 2016). For the UK see Liz Fekete, 'Lammy Review: Without Racial Justice, Can There Be Trust?' (2018) 59 (3) *Race & Class* 75–79.
65 William A. Schabas, *An Introduction to the International Criminal Court* (5th edn, Cambridge University Press 2017).
66 Yuval Shany, *Assessing the Effectiveness of International Courts* (Oxford University Press 2014).
67 Caroline Elkins, *Imperial Reckoning: The Untold Story of Britain's Gulag in Kenya* (Macmillan 2005).
68 *Ndiki Mutua & Others -v- The Foreign and Commonwealth Office [2012] EWHC 2678 (QB).*
69 Caroline Elkins, 'Alchemy of Evidence: Mau Mau, the British Empire, and the High Court of Justice' (2011) 39 (5) *The Journal of Imperial and Commonwealth History* 731–748.
70 Andrea Bianchi, *International Law Theories; An Inquiry into Different Ways of Thinking* (Oxford University Press 2016) 28.
71 Robert Bogdan and Steven Taylor, 'Looking at the Bright Side: A Positive Approach to Qualitative Policy and Evaluation Research (1987) 13 (2) *Qualitative Sociology* 183–192.
72 Ibid.
73 Ibid.

74 Julie-Ann Racino, *Policy, Program Evaluation, and Research in Disability: Community Support for All* (Psychology Press 1999).
75 Savin-Baden Maggi and Claire Howell Major, *Qualitative Research: The Essential Guide to Theory and Practice*. (Routledge 2013).
76 Steven Taylor J. and Robert Bogdan, *Introduction to Qualitative Research Methods: The Search for Meanings* (2nd edn, John Wiley and Sons 1984).
77 Vijay M. Gawas, 'Doctrinal Legal Research Method a Guiding Principle in Reforming the Law and Legal System Towards the Research Development (2017) 3 (5) *International Journal of Law Volume* 128–130.
78 Pamela Davies, Peter Francis, and Victor Jupp, *Doing Criminological Research* (Sage 2011) 173.
79 Michael Salter and Julie Mason, *Writing Law Dissertations: An Introduction and Guide to the Conduct of Legal Research* (Pearson Education 2007) 126.
80 Philip A. Thomas (ed.), *Socio-legal Studies* (Dartmouth Publishing 1997) 99.
81 Michael Salter and Julie Mason (note 79).
82 N.W.A (1988), *Fuck tha Police*, in the Album: *Straight Outta Compton* (1988) Ruthless/Priority.
83 Faith Ringgold, *United States of Attica* 1972. This is one of the most poignant protest pieces, a poster detailing America's atrocities all over the world.
84 Emory Douglas, *Afro-American Solidarity with the Oppressed People of the World* (1969).
85 Ingrid Mwangi, *Static Drift* (2001).
86 Sarah Jane Cervenak, 'Like Blood or Blossom: Wangechi Mutu's Resistant Harvests' (2016) 42 (2) *Feminist Studies* 392–425.
87 *Bemba, ICC, ICC-01/05-01/08 424*. Decision Pursuant to Article 61(7)(a) and (b) of the Rome Statute, PTCH II, 3. 7. 2009, §438. Hereinafter referred to as Bemba, Decision Pursuant to Article 61(7)(a) and (b) of the Rome Statute.
88 *The Prosecutor v. Ahmad Al Faqi Al Mahdi ICC-01/12-01/15*.

2 *(In)dependence Cha Cha Cha!* Post-Colonialism, Situated

Source: © Yinka Shonibare CBE. All Rights Reserved, DACS/Artimage 2022. Image courtesy Stephen Friedman Gallery, London and James Cohan Gallery, New York. Commissioned by the Museum for African Art, Long Island City, NY.

…Si tu me laisses l'uranium
Moi je te laisse l'aluminium
Si tu me laisse tes gisements
Moi je t'aide à chasser les Talibans
Si tu me donnes beaucoup de blé
Moi je fais la guerre à tes côtés
Si tu me laisses extraire ton or
Moi je t'aide à mettre le général dehors

Ils ont partagé Africa
Sans nous consulter!
Sans nous demander!
Sans nous aviser!

Ils ont partagé le monde
*Plus rien ne m'*étonne![1]

DOI: 10.4324/9781003304173-2

Introduction

More and more scholars, including for example Antony Anghie,[2] Anibal Quijano,[3] de Sousa Santos,[4] and Kamari Maxine Clarke,[5] are looking beyond the mere fact of political 'independence' as well as the widely discussed neo-colonialism to the epistemological foundations of the colonial state[6] and the interrogation of how international bodies such as the ICC perpetuate those philosophies. This chapter and indeed the book as a whole, is based on the premise that the rumour of a dead colonial state is exaggerated; the colonial state is alive and well.[7] My overall thesis is that the colonial state lives through neo-liberal economic relationships, including through organisations such as the International Criminal Court. As we shall see below, this proposition is not new as it continues arguments by others, including Fanon[8] and Nkrumah,[9] but what I suggest is ground-breaking in my approach is the linking of these colonialism/post-colonial discourses to the exploration of whether Africa is being used as a testing site for international criminal law and, towards the end of this book, whether Africa can and should provide an alternative *grundnorm* to counter the hegemony of a Eurocentric universality.

The claim I make in this chapter, and indeed in the whole book, is that Africa has become the testing and reproduction ground for ICL. I therefore use this chapter to situate the book within the wider discourses on post-colonialism by engaging with the literature on neo-colonialism, law and imperialism, and TWAIL. I also engage with general philosophical ideas on law including a cosmopolitanism that demarcates Africa as the site for victims and criminals of the 'international' kind and hence my idea of a testing site. In this chapter and elsewhere in the book, I explore some ideas by authors in this area of scholarship in order to contextualise and frame the key discourses and theoretical ideas as well as to inform my research.[10] This manner of engagement is encouraged in grounded research where it is common practice for researchers to be familiar with contemporary work in their area of study before embarking on their own explorations.[11] It may be important however to note that the approach I take contradicts the 'orthodoxy' of grounded theory as initially envisaged.[12] This is because of the multifaceted/multidimensional nature of my arguments which use a combination of many methods/methodologies and approaches, although grounded theory allows for this flexibility as research areas become more complex and multidisciplinary.[13] In addition to grounding my research, my engagement with other scholarly literature had several other aims; first, it provided direction in the construction of my research theories and methodology as well as forming part of my research data collection and it helped set the scope of my project thereby enabling me to avoid stretching the boundaries and to remain within a certain framework. Second and related to the idea of scope, understanding the relevant scholarly work helped situate my own work within that wider scholarship and compare/contrast my own findings with/in this wider perspective. Finally, engaging with other authors forms a part of the research on the overall hypothesis and helps in articulating a critical analysis of my findings. Specifically, the literature shows how African (southern) states, despite their façade of 'independence,' are still controlled by their colonial masters.

What the literature reviewed shows is that even before the Rome Statute, post-colonial thinkers were already looking at how international institutions like the ICC are used by western nations to influence their ex-colonies. There is ample evidence from literature to suggest that it was widely accepted by scholars in this area that colonialism had in most cases not ended with the cessation of territorial occupations. The literature also showed a pattern that emerges even from the earlier literature on this field; that there was a division amongst southern scholars and western scholars, post-capitalist scholars and Marxist scholars on how to resolve what was already becoming a heated debate in the later 1960s and 1970s, especially on the proliferation of wars to promote capitalism as a global hegemony. In Africa we see those early debates being started by Fanon and Nkrumah and later taken up by scholars such as Ngugi wa Thiong'o. In addition, I point out that apart from in academic literature, these arguments have continued in other forms of decolonialisation expressions, particularly in music.

These debates inform my ICC and Africa discourse, because in the early days and until very recently, no research had been undertaken looking at Rome Statute v Africa through the lenses advocated by Nkrumah and Ngugi, for example. Although it is now an emerging area of research, more interrogation is needed, especially using a combination of post-colonial and Critical Race Theory as I attempt to do in this book. This area of law is fast moving and so, between summer 2017 when I commenced my research and 2022, there have been various developments in TWAIL scholarship and there are several scholars undertaking similar explorations. What my research has shown however is that, so far, there is little authorship addressing race issues at the ICC in more depth, as I do here. Related to this is the overwhelming domination of the 'Eurocentric canon' in the ICL arena, although my review revealed the emergence of a more vocal TWAIL authorship. This emerging alternative means that the Eurocentric hegemony is facing a challenge, especially because in the past, ICL in Africa had become accepted with minimal critique particularly the epistemologies that established the ICC's engagement with Africa.

This chapter begins with a section on "Post-colonialism" with a discourse on neo-colonialism and post-colonialism which defines key concepts and aids in understanding the wider issues explored in the book. The section on "Post-Colonial ICL Authorship?" explores the emerging TWAIL discourses on post-colonialism and international law. These two sections detail the arguments made by different authors regarding the way institutions such as the ICC are a means by which the colonial states still exert control over their 'former' colonies. These sections situate my arguments within this wider decolonisation discourse, particularly the emerging counter-hegemony discourses amongst TWAIL scholars. In the sections "Fuck/Empire" and

"Twail and Critical Race Theory," I engage with some of the authors who deal with ICL/ICC as empire as well as with emerging synergies between post-colonial theory and Critical Race Theory before applying those theories to interrogate whether the ICC could be viewed as a colonial institution. These two sections extend the arguments already detailed in previous sections to show, for example in "Fuck/Empire," that although African states are 'independent' they are forever in the 'waiting room' of civilisation and, therefore, "Twail and Critical Race Theory" makes the argument that synergies between citizens in these countries and the global 'others' need to be formed to confront this 'otherisation' in the spheres of global economics and international law.

Post-colonialism

In this section, I explore key concepts including colonialism, imperialism, post-colonialism, neo-colonialism, and decoloniality theories. This is done with the aim of situating my work within the wider area(s) of scholarship. To lay the foundations for the ensuing discourse, I apply colonialism and imperialism interchangeably to mean the same thing, although I acknowledge that authors have variously defined them as two distinct terms. The orthodox understanding of colonialism used to initially be in relation to 'settler' takeover of territories and the subsequent transfer of European legal structures, but I prefer Horvath's straightforward definition of colonialism as a practice of domination and imperialism as the manner in which one country exercises this domination over another, whether directly through occupation or indirectly through other means.[14] I argue for example that there is little difference between physically occupying African states and epistemologically occupying them through language and/or law. Therefore, occupying countries physically is in the wider epistemological sense similar to, but obviously not same as, occupying their 'way of doing things' for example law or government. Understanding law in this 'epistemological occupation' sense is crucial for my ensuing discourse because law is the technology through which colonial domination was/is legitimised and transfer of European laws to regions in Africa and Asia, for example, was part of that colonisation.[15]

Post-colonialism, according to Ashcroft and others, is therefore an area of scholarship that explores the aftermath of European colonisation of other peoples and civilisations and it is employed to interrogate the processes and effects of, and reactions to, this colonisation which continues to date in the form of neo-colonialism.[16] Slemon adds that the notion of 'post-colonialism' is utilised to encompass a wide range of scholarly disciplines[17] but I focus mainly on the understanding of post-colonialism as articulated by Frantz Fanon in particular. Fanon's engagement with the idea of post-colonialism explores the puzzle of how Eurocentrism has in days gone by sanctioned colonial behaviour, and still validates it. Because this colonial historicism has Europe/white as the centre and agent(s) of civilisation, it conversely and perpetually frames Africa as being a historically backward place which in turn, and this is relevant to my ICC discourse, allows western countries to act as if it is their historical duty to dominate Africa and the global south at large.[18]

Neo-colonialism is on the other hand only one minimal strand in the broader spectrum of post-colonialism. The term neo-colonialism was coined by Kwame Nkrumah, the first president of independent Ghana who argued that "the essence of neo-colonialism is that the State which is subject to it is, in theory, independent and has all the outward trappings of international sovereignty but, its economic system and thus its political policy is directed from outside."[19] According to Nkrumah, the political life and economies of African countries are perpetually controlled by their (ex)colonial masters. If Nkrumah had foreseen his removal from power, he would perhaps have emphasised the use of armed coups as a popular tool for ex-colonial powers but he was right in that the nefarious colonists continue to exert their power through commerce and also, I add, through the Bretton Woods institutions and, as we see in this book, through agents such as the ICC.[20] Nkrumah was way ahead of his time in his understanding of the colonial state because he was able to connect Wall Street, Multi-National Enterprises MNEs and the colonial states' designs for Africa after they withdrew their European officers from the continent. Significantly for our discourse here, he saw other forms of neo-colonialism exerted using culture and education, trade through MNEs/monopolies, and the terms of trade promoted by the Bretton woods institutions. Because of the unwillingness of Europeans to let go of the benefits accrued from colonisation, they still maintain an unrelenting hold of their (ex)colonies and so neo-colonialism can be taken to cover these and all other forms of 'hidden' control.[21] Nkrumah, in my view, saw the performance nature of the 'saviour' interventionist/ international tribunals like the ICC because he argued that Hollywood had by then started to portray the other as 'savages' and the white soldiers/CIA type as saviours.[22] Significantly for my discourse, Nkrumah identified the ideological underbelly of the new international dispensation and political shenanigans, including murders by Europeans, with the connivance of their local agents. For his sins, Nkrumah was overthrown in what most agree was a CIA backed coup in 1966.[23]

According to Nkrumah, neo-colonialism may be beyond imperialism itself in terms of the dangers it poses to the subjugated as it is the pinnacle of the development of empire building as a process. This is because Nkrumah thought that, at least when it came to imperialism, there was a clearly set out, open and honest agenda of a colony and the coloniser with no mistaking the relationships and power structures, while in the era of neo-colonialism, the agenda remains hidden, at least to the colonised, and this is truly relevant to my later discussion on why African states signed the Rome Statute *enmasse* in which I note that the relationships are presented as equal and balanced. To Nkrumah, the current arrangement means "power without responsibility and exploitation without redress"[24] and, crucially for our discourse, it was his view that during this contemporary relationship, former colonies are heavily manipulated by their (ex)colonial masters, sometimes without their knowledge. Nkrumah thought that this deception meant that the economic relationships between the former colonies and their masters continued to favour the latter because any financial transfers from the west to Africa bizarrely increased financial inequalities between the two. Research has shown for example that, due to trade deficits, loan repayments and other illicit transfers, Africa is a net 'lender' to the west. For example, between 1980 and 2009, Africa was a net creditor to the world to the tune of US$1.4 trillion.[25]

Therefore, neo-colonialism is the process by which past colonial rulers and their allies endeavour to perpetuate and attain positions that allow them to control former colonies. Post-colonial theory engages with the analyses and understanding of the manner in which this is carried out. In simple terms, neo-colonial behaviour could result from post-colonial ways of thinking – although they are not the same. In this regard, I explore where the previously described neo-colonial claims against the ICC stem from. The question I address is this: are there any 'post-colonial reasons' for the feelings of discontent about the ICC? In other words, are the claims made by some African leaders and authors regarding the ICC fuelled by the neo-colonial behaviour of the international court? Before answering this question, it is important to understand what post-colonialism involves and to be able to identify possible post-colonial behaviour.

The first sign of post-colonial behaviour is that past colonial masters continue to portray their countries, states, cultures, and peoples as advanced, more contemporary, more refined than their counterparts in the global south.[26] "Culture is understood to have been wielded by colonialist powers to denigrate the traditions of non-western cultures, and to celebrate the superiority of particular versions of western culture."[27] This may explain in my view, and taking inspiration from Fanon, why some African elite view all western influences, interventions, and ideas as progressive and beneficial to the continent as this way of thinking about Africa became the template post 'independence.' Increasingly therefore, post-colonial theory views the European[28] citizen/mind as still colonised and hence, this colonised mind cannot fathom equality amongst cultures/peoples because the European still suffers from cultural 'brainwashing.'[29] Hence, for the European citizen and his/her/their state, a process of decontamination needs to take place by working "through the embedded modes of reasoning, thinking, and evaluation that secrete assumptions about privilege, normality, and superiority."[30]

However, my standpoint aims at ending this neo-colonialism at the core of ICC and so it belongs with decolonial theories, although I prefer decoloniality as it includes praxis. Decoloniality, according to Walter Mignolo follows, derives from, and responds to coloniality and the ongoing colonial process and condition.[31] It is a form of struggle and survival, an epistemic and existence-based response and practice.[32] This struggle aims to shatter the colonial matrix of power that is made of a combination of the rhetoric of modernity which involves ideas such as progress, development, and growth on one hand, and the logic of coloniality with its dimensions of poverty, misery, and inequality on the other.[33] To break this matrix, the understanding of how modernity and coloniality emerged must be central to any discussion of contemporary global inequalities.[34]

In taking a decolonising pose in relation to ICC for example, my stand challenges the hegemonic perspective which has the tendency to view everything in the global south in the negative. From its modernity and secularism to its democracy and even capitalism, the south is always seen to be deficient, not living up to the standards set by the west.[35] Because I ask that we do away with Eurocentric ICL in Africa, my work should therefore be seen as going beyond the mere rhetorical challenge to Eurocentricity I explore later in relation to TWAIL, and drawing closer to Maldonado-Torres et al's 'decolonial turn' which they see as a philosophical form which goes "beyond the liberal and Enlightened emancipation of rationality, and beyond the more radical Euro-critiques that have failed to consistently challenge the legacies of Eurocentrism and white male heteronormativity."[36]

I take a multi/inter disciplinary approach in my work which means I take, in places, a multifaceted perspective on the topic(s) at hand and use several methods and tools while interacting with a topic. For example, I use a variety of devices such as music, art, and poetry to critique issues such as rape as a war crime in Chapter 5. I chose to interrogate the discourse at hand this way because post-colonial theory itself has enabled "a complex interdisciplinary dialogue in the humanities and through the incorporation of theories as antagonistic as Marxism and Post-culturalism."[37] Therefore, post-colonial theory is not a product of uniform discourse, nor is it a unitary perspective and it may be better understood and explained to mean "multiplicity and heterogeneity."[38] In this multiplicity, my approach should be understood within the emerging post-colonial legal theory approaches in legal studies.[39] In this regard I critique the liberal doctrine's presentation of history as progressing in/through a simple, straight path that inevitably has the global south as still on a route to catching up with the west. Second, in relation to international law, I interrogate the relationship between power and colonial knowledge production and how the assumptions about the other have come to be (re)produced by institutions such as the ICC. Third, I interrogate the question of whether subjects of these liberal institutions, for example the African citizen in relation to the ICC, possess their own agency, including resistance in response to this coloniality.

When one interrogates institutions such as the ICC as colonial entities, it becomes much clearer why, as I detail in Chapter 6, African human rights regimes are not deemed to be good enough or as meeting 'international' standards. This is because societies are seen to be in transition towards a just and modern 'westernised' status and are "sitting in the 'imaginary waiting room of history' before they can claim the right to be modern."[40] This view ultimately triggered the colonial enterprise and is used to justify contemporary interventionist institutions such as the ICC and the wider 'right to intervene' regime.[41] Post-colonial scholarship challenges this idea of linear human progress and disputes that the development of the rule of law as a marker for this progress is such a neat and tidy project. This progress is seen here as a one-sided imposition of a Eurocentric view on the world that is based on 'civilising' notions which have been exclusionist and are now widely challenged, as we see in this book, by scholars from the global south. History as progress is fiction and 'law' is seen here as an instrument for maintaining unbalanced hierarchies of power and as a subjugating and civilising tool of the western powers. It is this space that I inhabit and I interrogate my theory of the Eurocentric ICC as a colonial enterprise meant to perpetuate the commodification and the oppression of the black body. As already indicated, literature shows that I am not alone in this endeavour to explore the Eurocentricity of ICL. In the next section, I look at some of the scholars who engage specifically with the idea(s) of ICL as a continuation of the colonial. We will also see the emerging and urgent need to reshape international law and to undermine this suggested coloniality.

Post-colonial ICL Authorship?

The aim of this section is to explore how other scholars have used the post-colonial/decolonising approaches in interrogating ICL and to what effect. How has the so-called TWAIL explored and dealt with the Eurocentric ICL hegemony? The emerging body of literature dealing with international law as a continuation of the colonial is mostly, though not exclusively, from the so-called Third World Approaches to International Law (hereafter referred as TWAIL) scholars. I say so-called because I protest against the TWAIL categorisation just as I have always detested the categorisation of music from non-European artists as 'world music.' These are terms which are used to 'other' the discourses on law/music and to make them seem outside of the mainstream – not part of the canon. For the authors who accept this term to describe their work, I argue that it is a contradiction in terms for them as legal philosophers to seek a non-colonial legal order and yet accept a hierarchical demarcation that categorises their work as 'other.' Despite my protestations at the name, TWAIL scholars are now widely accepted as 'the' alternative voice in international law.[42]

Makau Mutua is a prominent TWAIL thinker who, for example, sees TWAIL as old and yet new. He argues that TWAIL has various core claims and foundations. To begin with, Mutua defines TWAIL as a collection of school of thought(s) and action(s) by southern academics, policymakers, statesmen, organisations, and states who rally around exposing and eliminating the normative, structural, and institutional subordination of the south by the European west.[43] Second, Mutua says that TWAIL seeks to bring about intellectual and structural conditions that will herald a new form of international law. TWAIL, according to Mutua, is therefore "against white supremacy or any other racial hierarchies and opposes all hegemonic doctrines and practices that foster exploitation and the dehumanization of Third World cultures, communities, and philosophies."[44] While I support this stand, one finds many 'Eurocentric' tendencies in Mutua's musing because, while expounding anti-imperialist thoughts, he simultaneously expresses a 'saviour mentality' as he seems to suggest that the TWAIL elite have a duty to help 'human development' though transforming 'third world' cultures, philosophies, and cultures.[45]

Therefore, Mutua argues that TWAIL is an old idea which has now been given a new momentum by current international realities.[46] Accordingly, TWAIL seeks a genuinely universal framework for international law and rejects the obvious enlightenment project inherent in the western liberalism that underpins international law.[47] The contradictions contained in current hegemony are exposed by TWAIL as unsustainable as the imbalances of power are exposed and racist hierarchies, economic and otherwise, with non-Europeans at the bottom are challenged.[48] The prophesied equality of states is also challenged as a lie and international human rights deemed an imperial project.[49] There is however, in my view, an inherent contradiction in Mutua's position as he seems to accept that there is a hierarchy of scholarship, and therefore epistemologies. It appears at least from their name that TWAIL scholars accept belonging to the third tier in a hierarchy of knowledge production and therefore in that logic, the group is constantly fighting for legitimacy and acceptance by the hegemony. This acceptance contradicts the ideal of eradication of racial hierarchy exposed by Mutua and other 'TWAIL' scholars which will be explored below.

One thing that becomes clear from interrogating literature in this field is the almost complete 'casting away' and lack of consideration of other forms of decolonial discourses apart from 'academic literature.' However, as I indicated earlier, music and other oral traditions have been/and were the prominent decolonial technologies until the very recent decolonial theories explored here. As already stated, occupied peoples have had decolonisation discourses since their contact with the European colonisers. The neat genealogy presented by scholars like Bianchi, tracing the development of TWAIL from the 1950s' 'decolonisation' to the current cohort of scholars, is welcome but risks not acknowledging that current southern scholars continue/build on those early resistance thinkers whose mode of discourse was, for example, oral traditions. As such one should not really talk of phases but of a continuum. However I find Bianchi's use of TWAIL I and TWAIL II useful only in the sense that it differentiates historical periods when each cohort has operated with the technologies available to them at the time. According to Bianchi, the fathers of TWAIL had state sovereignty and self-determination at the core of their thinking. However, this came with the unconditional acceptance of the state-centred system. The state becomes the political form of organisation around which international law revolves.

This wave of TWAIL scholars is named TWAIL I by Bianchi who then proceeds to state that a second wave of TWAIL II scholars arose from the 1990s with the new critical insights into the hierarchical nature of international law. Importantly this new TWAIL generation started interrogating the fact that political independence was not enough and that newly independent states still find themselves economically tied to their erstwhile colonisers in such a manner that they cannot disentangle themselves. Critically also this generation starts to look at international economic law as a continuation of this domination and western-based multinationals start to be seen as the long arm of states that could be used to exercise economic and political control over newly independent states.[50]

Apart from this tracing of neo-colonialism, other scholars like Luis Eslava and Sundhya Pahuja say that TWAIL, rather than being a method, is a political 'coming together' to strategically engage with international law by those with common agendas.[51] I view Pahuja and Eslava as looking at TWAIL as a 'pushback' strategy akin to my 'standpoint' in this book, which involves TWAIL engaging with international law by aligning with the *homo sacer* of this law and articulating the need for reforms (not revolution) to force international law (unsuccessfully) to address the needs of those excluded by this same law.[52] In this sense TWAIL should be seen as directly opposed to fundamental injustices propagated by international law rules and practices. There is an acceptance in this that TWAIL scholars have a set of concerns that need to be heard. These concerns make TWAIL scholars a group "solidly united by a shared ethical commitment to the intellectual and practical struggle to expose, reform, or even retrench those features of the international legal system that help create or maintain the generally unequal, unfair, or unjust global order."[53]

I think categorisations like TWAIL are nefarious in themselves and are meant to 'pigeonhole' authorship both for commercial/marketing purposes, that is to make material sell easily, and to denigrate them at the same time. And so, where do my views fit in in this hierarchy of scholarship? I detect that the mostly white ICL hegemony views authors like me with suspicion, as not qualified enough to be part of the canon and hence the attempt to categorise us as exotic/other. However, if my views must be contained in a box/shelf, it has to be a shelf that has a place for activists in legal scholarship, like many southern authors who see the intellectual engagement with international legal hegemony as a struggle towards equality of thought.[54] Walter Mignolo calls this approach epistemic disobedience which I find more fitting as it resonates more with the resistance/revolution approach I prefer compared to the 'reform' suggested by many TWAIL scholars.[55] A critique of the Eurocentric character of international law as represented by western scholars is at the centre of TWAIL arguments but it is also important to debunk the progress narrative in the discipline, focusing on enquiries to foreground the uninterrupted hegemonic power within international law aimed at subjugating the third world. The domination of others by European countries through colonisation delinks international law from universality and objectivity.[56]

In search for the solution to the dilemma of neo-colonialism, TWAIL scholars argue that international law requires reform to compensate for the unequal treatment of third world countries by the international legal order. Some, like Mohammed Bedjaoui,[57] call for preferential treatments, especially in international trade, while earlier thinkers like Nkrumah[58] and Fanon[59] advocated for the total independence of ex-colonised states and opposed imposition of western laws in their countries. This request for preferential treatment in international law in my view exposes the conflicted attitudes towards international law portrayed by TWAIL scholars because international law is seen as partly to blame for having developed rules that are inconsiderate of the third world and that have been used to exploit both its people and its resources. At the same time, international law principles, such as territorial sovereignty and non-intervention in the domestic affairs of other states, are invariably invoked as a shield against any abuse and interference from western states.[60] However, the southern states' claim of 'equality' amongst the community of nations is mismatched by their calls for 'equalling' policies such as preferential treatment as regards trade, development, and environmental protection.[61]

This need to be seen as 'equal,' particularly in relation to western nations, is problematic in treaties such as the Rome Statute and breeds subsequent disenchantment with international bodies such as the ICC in southern states as they soon find out there is a hierarchy. I see this argument of 'equal' states as problematic because it is an argument that is anti-restitution. If any form of compensation is broached in relation to the colonial past, African states cannot be on equal footing with their ex-colonisers at least in 'legal' terms while negotiating restitutions although they are 'formally' equal as states. This need for preferential treatment has been criticised by Bianchi as an indirect acknowledgement of the backwardness or inferiority of the 'third' world, which has perpetuated the colonial logic of subjection and dependence on western states.[62] To admit that help and preferential treatment are needed is tantamount to conceding that there is no equality and that there can be no parity unless the difference is acknowledged and made up for.[63] Bianchi misses the point on reasons for restitution because we ask for restitution, not so that we can become/develop (to equal white people) but so that they at least acknowledge the benefits accrued to them through slavery and colonialism and to do this by repaying some of the wealth and resources stolen (and continuing to be stolen) from Africa. However, I acknowledge his point on lack of equality as valid. The pro 'development' TWAIL scholars throughout the 1980s and 1990s saw the transformative power of international law and their mainstay was that international law can be reformed to meet third world needs as the prevailing narrative is one of linear progress.[64] To catch up with the west is seen in this school of thought as the aspiration of the third world.[65] Any impediments to development must be removed.

International law is seen as containing an inherent capacity to change as it suffices to modify the content of the law for the desired change to materialise over time.[66]

TWAIL is also seen as engaging at this phase of its development with changing international law-making processes as they campaigned for soft law and about the norm-creating character of certain resolutions causing a shift from the traditional divide between legally binding and non-legally binding norms to a relative vision of normativity that would later open the way for the consolidation of soft law.[67] Through the UN General Assembly, TWAIL also started to question the fairness of the UN system and its rules as well as the lack of neutrality in international law. TWAIL moves away from the official discourse and traditional approaches that tend to separate law and morality.[68] Later on, the hegemonic tendencies of western states are exposed with the emphasising of the 'otherness' of the third world and the fact that international law is made of a plurality and a variety of cultures whose ontology may profoundly differ. Contemporary/current/modern TWAIL is a break away from the traditional view that international law has universal values that are valid across the board for all peoples and countries of the world. Current TWAIL scholars, like for example Makau Mutua as explored above, see international law and colonialism as mutually constitutive, given that the latter has been justified and legitimised by the international legal system. Unlike the earlier TWAIL scholars, such as Mohammed Bedjaoui who was also mentioned above, who were benevolent towards international law and occasionally critical, current TWAIL sees the global south as excluded from the international meaning of 'self' that is blatantly Eurocentric and geared towards exclusion of 'others.'[69] Modern day TWAIL sees the international legal system's claim to universality as a product of a hegemonic design, systematically pursued and cynically fostered by the western world.[70]

Bianchi indicates that in terms of analytical tools, TWAIL use dialectics, dyads, or opposites which lends their scholarship a special flavour and enhanced rhetorical efficacy. The south as opposed to the north, both literally and metaphorically, the coloniser as opposed to the colonised, subjugation to domination, the centre to the periphery and particular to universal. Hence the alleged universality of international law is a myth that deflects attention from the realities of subaltern peoples, whose condition is met with indifference by the international legal system. The blatant lack of justice and the instrumental use of law perpetuate current power structures and permit them to thrive. In a manner that is reminiscent of other approaches to international law, TWAIL often uses dialectics to buttress its critical discourse about international law.[71]

As if he expected otherwise, Bianchi notes that there is also a focus on intellectual rigour, although this leads to the criticism that a new form of intellectual elitism seems to emerge, in which the conversation often becomes highly sophisticated and occasionally too cryptic to follow for the unskilled reader.[72] The TWAIL II scholar is seen to appreciate the importance of knowledge production in the field of international law, and how narratives are formed and strategically used.[73] There is also more attention given to the question of who is in charge of relevant decision-making processes and who gets to decide, not merely in terms of politically relevant decisions taken at international level, but also in relation to the determination of which forms of scholarships are regarded as authoritative. Power and authority stand out as central objects of inquiry.[74] Yet another sensibility is the use of history and historical methodology. By looking at a historically constructed past, with a view to deconstructing its mystifications, and by taking up genealogical inquiries to highlight the contingency of the present,[75] TWAIL II scholars are challenging the conventional wisdom of more traditional investigations into the history of international law, which has been primarily geared towards showing the ineluctability of the present and to drawing legitimacy from the past in justifying current choices of forms of international organisation.[76]

TWAIL literature shows that this movement frequently evolves and encompasses new ideological spaces because in their critique of the Eurocentric Universalism, the current crop of TWAIL scholars, including this author, are moving from the traditional 'third world' focus to draw attention to the 'have-nots' and the disposed of the entire world, and those living in the peripheries and margins of otherwise affluent societies, be they migrant workers, minorities, or indigenous peoples.[77] What matters most is to unveil patterns of dominance and oppression, conditions of subalternity and subjugation.[78] This then leads to a marked difference between TWAIL I and TWAIL II scholars, because the current crop tends to view law as a process that is deeply embedded in society. The eminently political character of law is not denied, but rather directly acknowledged and dealt with.[79] They are aware of the primacy of the political sphere and they tend to give priority to the political dimension over the economic aspects of development as earlier TWAIL scholars did.[80]

Despite the validity of arguments by Bianchi, there are risks in attempting to deal with the history and development of scholarship neatly and chronologically as Bianchi does. The difficulty with Bianchi (who arguably is not a TWAIL scholar but is someone who has written on TWAIL), Mutua and other 'TWAIL' scholars discussed in this section is that they appear to accept the premise that Africans and other colonised peoples began their protest against European enslavement in the 1950s and they concentrate only on the 'written' works by southern thinkers, ignoring a long history of 'oral' traditions which are/were the 'containers' of Africa's organic (traditional) laws.[81] This neat arrangement of history not only provides an escape for crimes committed by colonisers but also does not celebrate victories against colonialism/enslavement before this period because they, for example, ignore the Maroons in the Caribbean and the Mississippi delta as well as the slaves' revolution in Haiti.[82]

Fuck/Empire

> *... how the BRITISH empire had sunk its claws deeper into the land/ had lined its borders with blood/had formed Nigeria/into a factory/to further steal from its people/but said nothing/for the crown had officers/ posted/watching/He waited for the wise ones/at the old clearing/who whispered about empires/as dusk took the sky/that such is their destiny/ to crumble and fall/and even their powerful enemies/time would consume them all*[83]

In this section, I narrow the above discourse(s) to international criminal law and explore how TWAIL scholars are increasingly viewing law as empire. This is to mean law itself is used to dominate others but also that law becomes a 'space' that can be claimed/colonised.[84] It also means that it can therefore be instrumentalised to demarcate/define us vs them in the process of dominating others.[85] Looking at law as empire begins from the premise that international law was entirely the deliberate product of a Eurocentric perspective that was handed over to other peoples and entities outside Europe, when the latter came into contact with the European civilisation.[86] Although Verzijl is to be criticised for propagating the myth of western nations civilising influence or the white man's burden narrative, his comments nonetheless depict the true origins of international law. However, other scholars sought to show the contribution of non-European countries to the development of international law and took issue with the apparent ignorance of some strands of western scholarship that simply ignored the culture, attitudes, and history of Asian and African countries.[87]

Antony Anghie demonstrates how since its inception, international law has been subservient to a logic of imperialism and hegemony by European countries first, and later by the western world more generally.[88] Anghie unveils the imperialist tendency of early international law scholarship. He argues it is by constructing the category of uncivilised peoples in need of trustees, as if they were children in need of a guardian, that the Spanish were entitled to exert their *dominium.*[89] If the 'Indians' were to react, the Spanish would then be justified to use force in self-defence. Violence is then presented as either protective, in the form of humanitarian intervention, or reactive, as legitimate self-defence against the use of force by the others. These narratives are powerful and would soon quickly and pervasively inform international law doctrines and principles in the early stages of the formation of the discipline. The apparent benevolent character of the inclusion of the 'Indians' within the order of European rationality is but a violent assertion of control to transform the 'Indians' and have them behave and look like the rest of the civilised world. The international legal scholarship of the time was as conflicted as it is today in relation to equality of 'races' as earlier anti- Spanish conquest scholars advocated for enslavement of the African instead of the indigenous populations.[90]

In line with this, Anghie further argues the doctrine of positivism with its main pillar as 'sovereignty' has contributed to the further differentiation between civilised countries and uncivilised ones by legitimising the conquest of *terrae nullius* inhabited by uncivilised peoples, and by making sovereignty and government the ultimate test of civilisation. The idea that non-western people were 'lacking' became the predominant perception, and the cultural default setting in relating to them which led to European Law becoming the singular 'universal' law.[91] It is in this sphere where this book becomes important in the search of a different narrative of the 'universal.' The hypothesis supported by the wide-ranging literature reviewed being that there are different sources of the universal rather than the prevailing hegemony of the Eurocentric Law. In the proposed new realm, Africa becomes the author of truly global norms used to litigate disputes in the continent and shared with the world. In my view, this will avoid situations as exemplified by Kenyan cases at the ICC where we witnessed a battle of will between a local elite and their international counterparts where the black body becomes a currency for both sides.

Eurocentric law becoming the hegemony despite southern states becoming 'independent' and law itself becoming 'the' empire has happened with the connivance of the United Nations. This is because the prevailing UN based international system of legal administrative control is aimed at producing global outcomes essentially designed by the west.[92] The existing ICL should be seen as the extension of Michel Foucault's 'governmentality' which is the use of a complex form of power over the population through the use of techniques of measurement, on whose alleged neutrality and objectivity rational institutions and representative systems of government could be built.[93] This use of UN sanctioned power by institutions like ICC reinforce the mechanisms of control and management on non-western societies. By design, self-government and statehood later achieved through the UN system was the product of techniques of management and control developed by the west. Like Derrida's 'mystical foundation of authority'[94] sovereignty was bestowed on newly independent states in a way which the violence of the foundations and the maintenance of Law is justified and silenced retrospectively. The nation state paradigm was enforced on a myriad of different communities in the name of civilisation as understood and practised by the West. Inclusion and integration came at the price of the renunciation of difference.[95] Assimilation took place in a way which 'third' world countries would still regard themselves as 'lacking' even if the formal requisites of statehood had been obtained. Anghie argues that a 'dynamic of difference' reveals the logic that subaltern entity always regards itself as needing to remedy a situation of backwardness and underdevelopment, or to bridge a 'gap' that the very dichotomy between civilised and uncivilised or developed and undeveloped, has created.[96] Pahuja offers a similar account by describing the encounter between rival jurisdictions (European versus the other) and the subsequent displacement of rival laws via the so-called universalisation of international law.[97] This universalisation is accelerated by the state becoming the centre of governance after which, economic growth through the technologies of gross domestic product become the instrument by which promises of equality would be made to everyone. From this perspective, development proceeds to re-characterise rival jurisdictions as undeveloped, and the nation-state 'as the ultimate container of social relations.'[98]

These arguments show the uncomfortable truth that imperialism lives on and that colonialism is inherent in international law. Indeed, the two are mutually constitutive. International law has always been hegemonic; one of the failures of the 'third' world has been to fight within the system and refuse a more radical critique, helping to 'further entrench European hegemony.'[99] And therefore, the end of 'formal' colonisation did not mean a rupture with the past as new and different forms of colonialism have simply replaced the formal bonds of colonial rule by the west. The mere fact of the imposition of statehood and its attributes as the normal form of political organisation, and the education of the people 'to understand community in terms of nationhood,' annihilates difference, and brings about a process of normalisation, intended to spread a western political and institutional model throughout the globe.[100] Statehood then forms the basis of interaction between ex-colonies and former colonisers and then constitute the pillars around which the international legal system revolves which leads others to conclude that even the notion of responsibility to protect, structured as it is along the lines of sovereign power and the failure to exercise it, reveals a patronising and paternalistic attitude held by those who have authority and power towards those who are in need of protection.[101]

As noted earlier, the very notion of development comes to mould perceptions of inadequacy and subalternity against the linear progress narrative that characterises the prevailing approach to development as a way to earn a place in the club of civilised nations.[102] The vocabulary might have changed but the substance of the problem has remained the same. Economic growth and development are seen as benchmarks against which the state's standing is assessed. This becomes the new means of universalising international law in the image of the west, under the guise of parameters perceived to be 'true,' 'historically destined' and/or 'technical,'[103] I discuss the wider 'development' movement as it relates to the ICC vs Africa debate in Chapter 3, but it is noteworthy that the African Charter on Human and Peoples' rights[104] envisages a different form of development than this western view, the African Charter envisaged a holistic view which takes into account African people's distinct identities and must include social justice.[105] For example, in a ruling which was later replicated in the Sustainable Development rhetoric, the African Commission on Human and Peoples' Rights found in the *Endorois*[106] decision that the Kenyan government had violated the Endorois' rights to religious practice, to property, to culture, to the free disposition of natural resources, and to development, under the African Charter

(Articles 8, 14, 17, 21 and 22, respectively) as well as the right to development under the U.N. Declaration on the Right to Development.[107]

Conditionality policies by international monetary institutions and other international organisations ensure that the alleged universal standards of political and economic liberalism are respected and that no one tampers with the expectations of so-called' international community.'[108] Thus the current crop of TWAIL scholars view formal decolonisation as not necessarily a rupture but simply a configuration of a logic of dominance. The vocabulary of hierarchy and difference shifts from race, or nature to a League of Nations/United Nations mandated formal colonial control to the current form of 'development' led hierarchy and control through neo-liberalism with international bodies becoming the new guardians of colonial control. Global governance and its dependence on international bodies/expertise is reminiscent of Foucault's notion of biopower as a model of modern governance.[109]

In a new system of global colonial governance, power is no longer exclusively territorial, but rather operates through sophisticated narratives of economic and technological development. Even the 'newness' of terrorism is capable of being turned into an instrument of western hegemony. Hegemony becomes new colonialism. According to Rajagopal, hegemony is an active process involving the production, reproduction, and the mobilisation of popular consent, which can be constructed by any "dominant group" that takes hold of it and uses it.[110] This legacy of dependence ensures that, "the past remains the present, albeit in a different form, and the historical relationship with Empire continues to inform the way in which the relationships of dominance and subordination, inclusion and exclusion are played out in the contemporary period."[111] Pahuja describes how the process of decolonisation "is not a moment of either/ or, but rather a moment of both/and. That is, international law was neither still imperial nor newly liberatory-and yet it was both."[112] Like the old wine in new bottle(s) this new order is rich with the inheritance of old, clothing ancient power dynamics with the 'universality' of law and its associated institutions.[113] This realisation leaves the TWAIL scholars with the conundrum of how to effectively advance claims of social justice, ensure respect of cultural and political difference, and ultimately, design and bring about a more equitable international legal order.

Thus TWAIL has to interreact in a methodical manner with the international law establishment in order to advocate for the interests of those suffering the transformative violence of neo-liberalism distilled down to the grassroots by institutions such as the IMF, World bank and the ICC.[114] TWAIL must emancipate itself from the 'desire to save the world' which is a continuation of the 'benevolence of Empire.'[115] There is need to leave the Eurocentric nature of international law behind and associated critiques, while pushing this tradition to open up and meet other traditions by fully recognising 'the dignity of the laws of other peoples' are among the most compelling challenges for TWAIL scholars.[116] There is a need to rethink how to reinterpret the strategies of resistance and agency of the poor, while not hiding away from engaging with the politics inherent in international law.

Critically, it is not just TWAIL scholars who see imperialism in international law. Fredrick Cowell for example argues that the Rome Statute is inherently imperialist, as it is...

> predicated on the domination of weaker states and the diminution of their sovereign decision-making capacities. In this light, certain provisions within the ICC Statute can be read as inherently imperialist in that they envisage a legal relationship with states predicated on an ongoing sovereign dominance of the organization over the state.[117]

In addition, the aspirations of the statute would also be founded on inherent imperialism if we consider what the Rome Statute as a

> legal instrument wants the world to look like, not in what way it shapes the world. Those who hold that the anti-imperialist criticism of the ICC is largely political focus too much on the contingent application and operation of the law, forgetting to critically interrogate the world imagined by that law.[118]

In an argument that echoes my overall discourse, Cowell argues that Article 17 on complementarity for example envisages perpetual weak and underdeveloped states.[119] In addition, he argues that Article 13 which gives the UN Security Council the power to refer cases to the Prosecutor is a form of legal imperialism.[120] Given the political nature of international law, perhaps the more concerning is Article 15 which gives the prosecutor a *proprio motu* (i.e. of its own initiative) power to initiate proceedings without referrals from member states or security council.[121] Because the prosecutor is given unlimited powers to define what constitutes 'the most serious of crimes' it leads to improvisation leading to for example new legal doctrines like 'continuing crimes' as seen *in the Situation in the Cote' d'Ivoire*[122] where the Pre-Trial Chamber allowed the Prosecutor to bring charges that went beyond the facts contained in the original referral.[123] Fredrick Cowell like myself goes into specific areas where the Rome Statute/ICC duplicates the colonial. By envisaging Africa as a place of perpetual weak states, one wonders whether the UN system is complacent in maintaining this status quo, to legitimise institutions like ICC and other UN related agencies. As I will explore later in Chapters 3–5, these weak states translate into a ready market for the international interventionist industry leading me to hypothesis the emergence of neo-slavery. By neo-slavery I mean the practises through which the black body, represented here by Africa, is used as a unit for capital/monetary gain. My claim is that international criminal law uses the African body primarily as a measurement(s) unit of its necessity/success. Secondly, this ICL is itself an industry contained within a wider interventionist/development/NGO/UN ecosystem. To survive, this ecosystem feeds on the misery of the black body. I explore this in depth in Chapter 5 as it relates to Rape as a war crime.

Twail and Critical Race Theory

In fidelity to my standpoint, I link the post-colonial, TWAIL and CRT approaches not only to explore what other authors have argued but also to show the possibilities inherent in the alliances of these liberating perspectives. This is because TWAIL scholars like Mutua have seen the importance of the synergies between CRT and TWAIL in decolonising international law. Mutua for example indicates that CRT must work hand in hand with TWAIL because it challenges in a substantial manner systems which allow subjugation, and it focuses on ensuring actual delivery of social justice.[124] Critical for my discourse is the idea that CRT and TWAIL scholars should work together, share ideas, and learn from each other's perspective. In this respect I not only use a CRT standpoint but draw on inspirations from various decolonising approaches especially in Chapter 6 where I look at alternatives to Eurocentrism. Unlike Mutua, I see no difference between CRT and TWAIL, but I agree that since the 'subterranean' issues CRT scholars deal with are global in nature, they should take an international pose to show they also engage fully with this global intersectionality.[125] The cooperation between TWAIL and CRT is not a new phenomenon and therefore Mutua and others should look back to the 1950s and 1960s for clear examples of these interconnectivities.[126] The power of CRT Mutua notes, is that it has created a useful theoretical methodology in studying the struggles of other subordinated groups such as the LGBTQ+ who have successfully used this approach in their campaigns for social justice.[127] Multidimensionality and intersectionality are for example two core innovations by CRT which should be used widely to debunk essentialist constructions. In Chapters 3 and 5 for example I reject the ICL's characterisation of African women as victims and celebrate their role in decolonisation struggles. This is because as Mutua suggests using CRT as an approach offers room for a deeper and nuanced exploration of the use of 'identities as social and legal phenomena.'[128] This is done by helping to deconstruct the many levels of subjugation and help in building emerging multidimensional resistance sites.[129]

This alliance is potent in countering the Eurocentric international law sold as "universal," even though according to Mutua, its European and Christian origins are not contested.[130] Diametrically opposed to this oppression is CRT, which speaks to resistance and liberation, contrary to international law which is used as technology to conquer and dominate.[131] International law cannot be universal, whether it claims it or not, because the birth and infancy stages of international law took place during the Age of the Empire, when Europe colonised most non-European peoples.[132] Empire/colonialism and contemporary neo-liberalism forced 'universalism' down the throats of 'southern' people and their emerging states mainly through international institutions of global governance. It is impossible to divorce racism/white supremacy from this Eurocentric authorship of international law because the last 5 centuries have been a period of the imbedding of this 'universality' of an international legal order whose sole purpose is to maintain European and American hegemony as opposed to its claimed pursuit of equalities.[133]

The ICC over enthusiasm in Africa typifies this imperialism and represents a subtly biased view of what is wrong in the world i.e., what most threatens the international society. As I view it, the threat to international society according to the Eurocentric hegemony, is not the rampant neo-liberalism and ever-increasing inequalities but 'tribal conflicts' in Africa. Once these are resolved presumably via the ICC, neo-liberal nirvana is/will be attained. However, as we shall see in Chapter 3 in relation to development, this nirvana is never strictly defined, and like a mirage disappears when approached. At the same time, there is an increased marketisation of international law as well as the focus on individualism as opposed to structural causation which has led to assigning guilt to an individual for crimes committed by the collective. This *tribunalisation* of African violence has become the hegemonic model for justice which in turn creates a moral/ human rights economy led by NGO's and global elite.[134] My interpretation of *tribunalisation* goes beyond the mere establishment of international courts and tribunals. It means a system where violence in Africa becomes a commodity in the global legal, media, and NGO world where it attains a monetary value meaning its elimination or propagation serves the same purpose. A self-perpetuating industry is created around international bodies like the ICC made of 'experts,' local 'fixers,' international financiers requiring a labyrinth of actors, relationships and systems that feed on the mere existence of violence towards the black body.

The creation of an African ICL market is therefore in my view a continuation of the colonial exploitation of the 'black body' dating back to slavery days which has in turn led to the use of Africa as a test site for the development of ICL doctrines meant to benefit a selected elite. Harnessing the synergies proposed by Mutua, I use the double lens of post-colonialism and CRT to equate this emerging ICC/NGO industrial complex with the legal/prison industrial complex recently described by Ava DuVernay in her acclaimed documentary, 13th.[135] This documentary uses CRT to look at the creation of a prison industrial complex in the USA which DuVernay argues is a continuation of slavery by other means.[136] Overall in this book and particularly in Chapters 4 and 5, I apply this argument to the international criminal law and look at the African cases at the ICC from both a CRT and post-colonial view with the ICC in this hypothesis seen as an industrial complex and a continuity of the colonial project of "otherization" in which Africa is repeatedly and subtly portrayed as a site of a political savagery, a truly dark continent.[137] This leads to interventionist international law led by international tribunals like the ICC for the benefit of a global elite and to the detriment of Africa.

It is therefore appropriate at this point to state that the ICC was founded by the wider 'Responsibility to Protect' school of thought which according to Anne Orford tries to litigate competing claims for authority during revolutions or civil wars.[138] Often, this responsibility has taken violent forms as we have witnessed in Libya, Iraq, Afghanistan, and Syria. Ann Orford says that the dangers of the interventionist approach is that the argument can be seen as simultaneously revolutionary and authoritarian because in simple terms, at any one crisis, there would be one force that has to impose on the other for 'protection' purposes.[139] In this school of thought therefore, the ICC interventions in Africa offer an opportunity for others to perpetually decide what is 'good' for Africa, who needs punishment, and who needs pardoning. One could already see the imperialist thinking at the core of ICC's 'impunity' rhetoric as articulated by Hobbes in Leviathan because for him, there was no room for resistance against the 'commonwealth' because it was necessary to submit to an absolute political authority which should contain the warring religious factions that threatened the commonwealth.[140] A common power to guarantee the protection of citizens was important for Hobbes and he did not seem to mind much where this 'power' accrued its legitimacy from. And hence, in this Hobbes logic, the ICC does not seem to mind that its rhetoric on impunity sounds like the 'civilising' mantra of days gone by, and that its epistemological foundations are colonial.

Overall but particularly in Chapter 4, the current impasse between the ICC and Africa is seen not as an isolated phenomenon, but as exemplifying positive law's treatment of, and engagement with the "black body" so well-articulated in the DuVernay documentary discussed above. Duvernay stipulates that like slavery before it, the current prison industrial complex in the USA is designed to exploit black men and the justice system is designed to ensure the perpetuation of this industry. I apply the same argument here in relation to the emerging ICL complex and contend that we should look at the current ICC/Africa conflict through Agamben's concept of 'bare life.' Agamben describes as "bare life, a life that has no significance beyond the fact of its existence."[141] Agamben shows the distinction between two forms of life; "the life of those who are fortunate enough to be included within the political community, and those who are placed at its margins or outside of it altogether."[142] "Bare life" in my view perfectly describes the irony and cruelty of an international legal order that while preaching universalism of human rights and the benefits of globalisation, has always ruthlessly excluded the African to the margins of global citizenship. The African becomes in this discourse, *'homo sacer'* abandoned and completely excluded from the 'benefits' of the structures of international discourse until of course there is a "crisis" as happened in the Kenyan Situation. Even when included, it is only as a victim who needs saving or a criminal who needs to atone for their impunity.

This idea of crisis brings us back to Schmitt who was an admirer of white supremacy and authoritarianism as he advocated for a state that can defend an "indivisibly similar, entire, unified people."[143] It appears therefore that there may be traces of supremacist ideology in the 'universalist' interventionism which tends to idolise a unified global community. This global community is supposed to exercise sovereignty over nations in times of crisis, but this thinking becomes toxic when one explores Schmitt's idea that the sovereign was the one who could distinguish friends and enemies and was the one able to defend the people against this identified enemy and thereby guarantees the security of those within the state. I would like the reader to have this discourse in mind later in Chapter 3 where I discuss ICC in relation to revolutions. This is because when considering our discourse on the ICC through Schmitt's statement: "Sovereign is he who decides on the state of exception"[144] one finds that the ICC could be a tool to impose on others what they themselves have already rejected. In other words, the rule of law could be the 'thing' people would want to revolt against for its oppressiveness, yet this approach sees the rule of law as the cure to all emergencies. In this regard, the ICC could be seen as usurping sovereignty for example in Kenya, a notion that becomes problematic as it will suppose that there was rule of law at the point of ICC's entry to Kenya, and that the ICC suspended this 'local rule of law' to instigate its own rule of law because as the sovereign, it gained powers to decide that the rule of law must be suspended as Schmitt would have advocated. For Schmitt this was the core element in the exercise of sovereign power because of this inseparable relationship between law and exception.[145] In that regard, was the ICC correct in defining the Kenyan situation as a crisis necessitating its intervention? Because violence had stopped, and a peace agreement signed and implemented at the time of ICC's intervention, the implications become ever more daunting.

The fact that 'the' crisis in Kenya had already passed by the time of ICC's intervention brings us to interrogate the ICC/African situation through Michel Foucault's concept of biopolitics, where in the recent times sovereignty has become mostly concerned with populations.[146] This concept provides a useful way in which states use our biological bodies for political purposes. This idea of biopolitics strongly links to my hypothesis that ICL is using Africa as a testing site for legal theory, and I would therefore suggest that African mere bodies are useful in terms of the numbers game. The ICC and its critics can claim their position is right by either showing how many bodies they are protecting in Africa, or how many bodies are being destroyed by the other side's inaction or action. The ICC's neo-colonial project I argue only survives if it can present itself as new and ground-breaking in this biopolitical sphere. In this respect, I discuss in Chapter 5 that the ICC is seen to be testing the Rome Statute exclusively on Africans and constantly reproduces old laws while presenting them as new. By actively presenting itself and its decisions on rape, and cultural destruction as ground-breaking for example, I argue that the ICC is cognisant of the critiques levelled against it and the claims of imperialism in international law and therefore its efforts to claim particularism.[147]

Martti Koskenniemi has recently interrogated this tendency by the ICC and ICL generally to present itself as new. Koskenniemi argues this pretence *of* "emergence avoids the critique of imperialism because the future it promises is not fixed in any particular institutions or identities; its utopia only shows a horizon that recedes as it is approached."[148] Poignantly for my discourse on the coloniality of the ICC, Koskenniemi posits that this manner of presenting the law hinders interrogations into the ways the ICC acts as a cultural producer because of the projections that the ICC/ICL contain an idealistic inevitability and that it has a critical and constantly emerging nature.[149] By acting in this way, the ICC pretends to be a non-political, universalist entity which therefore can punish acts of impunity because it is untarnished by politics. Discourses such as the ones this text is engaging with, that of the making of/and the history of the criminal subject is not encouraged because the ICC must be seen to be an emerging and transcending idea that is shifting state-based sovereignty towards 'the' cosmopolitan society.[150] And therefore the ICC fits well in the category of agents whose *raison d'être* is to ever 'develop' others towards some ever-shifting utopia. As with the case of developed vs undeveloped, the construction of the criminal does not exist however without its binary opposition. This claim by the ICC of particularism suggests a gap with the past and signals a shift in paradigm from the old to the new which I argue is impossible for an international law body to claim given the history I detailed earlier of the links with Slavery and colonialism. I would not be alone in linking the current ICL regime to Slavery as authors like Emily Haslam[151] have sought to bring slave trade and its legacy into the fold of comprehending the foundations of international criminal law and to debunk the myth of 'Tokyo to Hague' chronology. In what is truly relevant to my discussion here, Haslam depicts an ICL founded by the events at the 'abolitionist' stages of the end of slavery and the subsequent ignored legacies of that process in birthing of the human rights movement and extends to how the ICC defines victims and criminals, particularly in the African context.[152] The ICL iconography I address in Chapter 4 was born during this era as the African with no agency of his/her own became the leitmotif of international law. The abolitionist movement and the ensuing commemoration of that movement depicts, the white saviour, as the only force that defeated slavery. One can already identify the template of the contemporary interventionist ideology in this fixation by the European with the white abolitionists. Although the slave, once 'freed' by the benevolent white person was still not yet fully human. Otherwise, how could the British pay slave owners compensation for owning humans unless they were still seen as chattel?[153]

Overall and in Chapters 3 and 4 in particular, I view the ICC as a neoliberal project with its relentless push towards 'atomisation' of the law in what is a uniquely western capitalist focus on the individual rather than the community. Although at 'independence' African states had been sold the idea that the state is the organ towards self-rule and sovereignty, with the emergence of international institutions like the ICC, this orthodoxy is disrupted. Where previously the state was the custodian of individual freedoms, in the neo-liberal utopia, the state is no longer the custodian of these rights but international institutions like the ICC are to take over this previously 'sovereign' role and thereby safeguard the citizen from their own state as well as from the divisive politics of nationality and ethnicity. The nefarious individual perpetrator becomes the leitmotif at the ICC with the Rome Statute institutionalising and perpetually codifying this simplistic concept of one evil individual spewing violence to the innocent group.[154]

Conclusion

Looking at literature on the wider topic of international law and colonialism, patterns start to emerge that most of the research has focused on international economic law rather than international criminal law although there is an emerging scholarship focusing on ICL as continuation of the colonial and it is here that this research makes an impact in widening the literature in this field.

Secondly, the lasting impression left is better captured by Makau's acceptance that there is a clear contradiction and ambivalence of TWAIL scholars towards international law because there is the tendency to regard international law variously as either the problem or the solution to world's injustices.[155] My work endeavours to avoid the pitfall faced by most TWAIL scholars who are criticised as expounding highly conceptual and elitist ideas that have no relevance to the particular they claim to represent. Particularly important is that I strive to use accessible language whenever possible in this text while maintaining the expected scholarly attitudes in order that my findings and arguments are accessible to many and not just the few in academia because TWAIL scholarly writings are criticised as being "highly sophisticated but hardly comprehensible which limits their audience."[156]

Most importantly though, one notices that until very recently TWAIL was not addressing race as the crucial factor in international criminal law. This fact probably is why TWAIL is ambivalent on a way forward which leads to a constant swing between resistance/revolution and reform to enhance equitableness of the international legal system. This realisation puts this research at the centre of the current TWAIL scholarship opting for resistance and engagement that reconciles opposition to the dark sides of international law with the aspiration to propose agendas for reform and improvement of the international normative system. Literature also showed that there is still residual faith in international law if not its institutions amongst the TWAIL scholars although the challenge is dealing with the politicisation of international law, establishing how and where to engage with it.[157]

This love/hate oscillation by TWAIL scholars leads us to interrogate the hypothesis of Africa as a testing site in detail in Chapter 5 and investigate in

Chapter 6 the possibility for alternative 'southern' norms capable of countering the Eurocentric hegemony. This is in line with my aim of propagating plurality as an alternative to the status quo and the need to look at the possibility that the south can also provide norms that can/should be equally universal. This is because there is the need for scholars to reflect on the fact that international law has always been involved in shaping the world order and it has invariably carried with it methodology and interpretation that would provide the modalities by which such order is shaped. To think critically about international law without providing a way forward is no longer enough as an end by itself particularly if one realises the ideological baggage discussed above. To realise the pervasive effects of international law in everyday life, and to proceed, with sensitivity of an ethnographer, to explore the international sites where international law is made and the local sites where international law is re-embodied and affects the lives of people may be a good reflex in interrogating where the world needs to be reshaped and the international rethought.[158]

We have also seen in this chapter that one of the main reasons why international criminal law is the continuation of the colonial is because it is structured through the 'state' which itself is a colonial legacy. Secondly these 'independent' states inherited and continue to reinforce colonial/Eurocentric laws. Thirdly, the new state had to relate with other states via the emerging UN system(s) of international governance. Former colonial masters highly influence this international system. It is through these unequal international relationships that bodies like the ICC have hijacked the role of the envisaged state to guarantee the rights of its citizen in the mad rush towards the 'global citizen.' The 'global state' must in turn curiously protect the citizen against his own state and his fellow citizens.

Therefore, one cannot interrogate the pervasiveness of international law without exploring how African states became entangled with the Rome Statute via the neo-liberal orthodoxy leading to the current conflict between the ICC and African states or rather the conflict between global elite and African elite. In the following chapter, I detail how neo-liberalism uses the rhetoric of 'development' to entangle African states in treaties and international agreements such as the Rome Statute which are detrimental to their self-determination. Neoliberalism I also argue breeds inequalities leading to conflicts. A vicious cycle is then perpetuated where foreign imposed economic/social/political policies lead to conflicts which then 'require' further foreign interventions. I explore these claims in the context of the push for African states to sign on to international human rights bodies such as the ICC and the subsequent fall out exemplified by the situation in Kenya.

Notes

1 Tiken Jah Fakoly, *Plus rien ne m'étonne* in the album *Coup de Gueule* (Barclay 2004); it is crucial for the reader to note that lyrics are not translated in light of my exploration of the use of languages in colonisation and the loss of urgency and meanings attributed to such translations.

2 Antony Anghie, *Imperialism, Sovereignty, and the Making of International Law* (Cambridge University Press 2005).
3 Anibal Quijano, 'Coloniality of Power and Eurocentrism in Latin America' (2000) 15 (2) *International Sociology* 21.
4 See for example Boaventura de Sousa Santos, *Toward a New Legal Common Sense; Law, Globalization, and Emancipation* (Butterworths 2002).
5 Kamari Maxine Clarke, *Affective Justice: The International Criminal Court and the Pan-Africanist Pushback* (Duke University Press 2019).
6 I use this term regularly to denote states like post 'independent' Kenya but also the colonising states like the UK as my hypothesis is that there has not been any independent African state since slavery/colonialism and current states are Eurocentric states in Africa, the only difference being geography and the skin colour of the elite in power.
7 Paraphrasing Mark Twain quoted in the *New York Journal* 2 June 1897.
8 See Frantz Fanon, *The Wretched of the Earth* (Grove Weidenfeld 1991).
9 Kwame Nkrumah, *Neocolonialism: The Last Stage of Imperialism* (Panaf Books Ltd 1965).
10 Martyn Denscombe, *The Good Research Guide for Small Scale Social Research Projects* (Open University Press 1998) 217.
11 Mark Easterby-Smith, Richard Thorpe and Andy Lowe, *Management Research Methods* (Sage Publications 2002) 46–47.
12 Barney G. Glaser and Anselm L. Strauss, *Discovery of Grounded Theory: Strategies for Qualitative Research* (Routledge 2017).
13 Nick Pidgeon and Karen Henwood, 'Grounded Theory' in Melissa Hardy and Alan Bryman (eds), *Handbook of Data Analysis* (SAGE 2004) 625–648.
14 See in general Ronald J Horvath, 'A Definition of Colonialism' (1972) 13(1) *Current Anthropology* 45–57.
15 Sally E Merry, 'Law and Colonialism' (1991) 25(4) *Law and Society Review* 889–922; John L. Comaroff, 'Colonialism, Culture, and the Law: A Foreword' (2001) 26 *Law & Social Inquiry* 305; Mahmood Mamdani, *Citizen and Subject: Contemporary Africa and the Legacy of Late Colonialism* (Princeton University Press 1996).
16 Bill Ashcroft, Gareth Griffiths and Helen Tiffin, *Post-colonial Studies: The Key Concepts* (Routledge 2013)186–188; See various post-colonial thinkers in Bibhash Choudhury, *Reading Post-colonial Theory; Key Texts in Context* (Routledge 2018); Gaurav Gajanan Desai, Gaurav Desai, and Supriya Nair (eds), *Postcolonialisms: An Anthology of Cultural Theory and Criticism* (Rutgers University Press 2005).
17 Stephen Slemon, *De-scribing Empire: Post-colonialism and Textuality* (Routledge 1994) 16–17.
18 Frantz Fanon, *Black Faces, White Masks* (trans. Charles Lam Markmann, Grove 1967); Frantz Fanon, *The Wretched of the Earth* (Grove Weidenfeld 1991).
19 Kwame Nkrumah, *Neocolonialism: The Last Stage of Imperialism* (Panaf Books Ltd 1965) 10.
20 Ibid.
21 Peter Childs and Patrick Williams, *An Introduction to Post-colonial Theory* (Harlow: Pearson Education 1997).
22 Kwame Nkurumah (note 19) 246.
23 Four More Ways the CIA has meddled in Africa, BBC 16th May 2016.
24 Kwame Nkurumah, *Neocolonialism: The Last Stage of Imperialism* (International Publishers 1966) ix.
25 African Development Bank and Global Financial Integrity (May 2013), Illicit Financial Flows and the Problem of Net Resource Transfers from Africa: 1980–2009, available at http://www.gfintegrity.org/ accessed 9 February 2021.

26 Clive Barnett, 'Postcolonialism: Space, Textuality, and Power' in Stuart C. Aitken and Gill Valentine (eds), *Approaches to Human Geography* (SAGE Publications 2009) 147.
27 Ibid.
28 European in this book should be taken in its widest meaning possible to include political, culture, social, economic, and epistemological connotations of the westerner/coloniser/white and the opposite of the term black as defined earlier. Theorists however do argue that Europe and therefore the European is a product of colonialism as it emerged from the need to differentiate from the colonised. See Gurminder K. Bhambra, 'Postcolonial and Decolonial Dialogues' (2014) 17 (2) *Postcolonial Studies* 115–121.
29 James D. Sidaway, 'Postcolonial Geographies: An Exploratory Essay' (2000)24 (4) *Progress in Human Geography* 591–612.
30 Clive Barnett (note 26).
31 Walter D. Mignolo and Catherine E. Walsh, *On Decoloniality: Concepts, Analytics, Praxis* (Duke University Press 2018) 17.
32 Ibid.
33 Gurminder K. Bhambra, 'Postcolonial and Decolonial Dialogues' (2014) 17 (2) *Postcolonial Studies* 115–121.
34 Ibid.
35 See in general *Aditya Nigam, Decolonizing Theory: Thinking across Traditions* (Bloomsbury Publishing 2020).
36 Maldonado-Torres, Nelson Rafael Vizcaíno, Jasmine Wallace, and Jeong Eun Annabel We, 'Decolonising Philosophy' in Gurminder K. Bhambra, Dalia Gebrial and Kerem Nişancıoğlu (eds), *Decolonising the University* (Pluto Press 2018) 65.
37 Leela Gandhi, *Postcolonial Theory: A Critical Introduction* (Columbia University Press 1998) 3.
38 Antony Kwame Appiah, 'In My Father's House: Africa in the Philosophy of Culture' (1994) 92 (2) *Modern Philology* 267.
39 Alpana Roy, 'Postcolonial Theory and Law: A Critical Introduction' (2008) 29 *Adelaide Law Review* 315.
40 Kwame Appiah (note 38).
41 On the right to intervene and its colonial/empire connotations see Mark Duffield and Vernon Hewitt (eds), *Empire, Development & Colonialism: The Past in the Present* (Boydell & Brewer Ltd 2013).
42 Andrea Bianchi, *International Law Theories; An Inquiry into Different Ways of Thinking* (Oxford University Press 2016) 208; Makau Mutua and Antony Anghie, '"What Is TWAIL?" In Proceedings of the Annual Meeting' (2000) *American Society of International Law* 31–40.
43 Makau Mutua, 'Critical Race Theory and International Law: The View of an Insider-Outsider' (2000) 45 *Villanova Law Review* 841.
44 Ibid., 852.
45 Ibid.
46 Ibid.
47 Ibid.
48 Ibid.
49 Ibid.
50 Mohammed Bedjaoui, *Towards a New International Economic Order* (Holmes & Meier Publishers 1979) 36.
51 Luis Eslava and Sundhya Pahuja, 'Between Resistance and Reform: TWAIL and the Universality of International Law' (2011) 3 *Trade, Law & Development* 103–104.

52 Ibid.
53 Obiora Chinedu Okafor, 'Newness, Imperialism, and International Legal Reform in Our Time; A TWAIL Perspective' (2005) 43 *Osgoode Hall Law Journal* 171, 174–175.
54 See for example Walter D. Mignolo, 'Geopolitics of Sensing and Knowing: On (De) coloniality, Border Thinking, and Epistemic Disobedience (2013) 1 (1) *Confero* 129–150.
55 Walter D. Mignolo, 'Epistemic Disobedience, Independent Thought and Decolonial Freedom' (2009) 26 (6–7) *Theory, Culture & Society* 159–181.
56 Andrea Bianchi, *International Law Theories; An Inquiry into Different Ways of Thinking* (Oxford University Press 2016) 208.
57 Mohammed Bedjaoui, *Towards a New International Economic Order* (note 50).
58 Kwame Nkrumah, *Neocolonialism: The Last Stage of Imperialism* (Panaf Books Ltd 1965).
59 Frantz Fanon, *The Wretched of the Earth* (Grove Weidenfeld 1991).
60 George Abi-Saab, 'The Newly Independent States and the Scope of Domestic Jurisdiction' (1960) 54 *ASIL Proceedings* 84.
61 Ibid.
62 Andrea Bianchi (note 56) 213.
63 Ibid.
64 Gilbert Rist, *The History of Development; From Western Origins to Global Faith* (Zedbooks 1997) 147.
65 Ibid.
66 Mohammed Bedjaoui, *Towards a New International Economic Order* (note 50) 63.
67 Richard Baxter, 'International Law in Her Infinite Variety' (1980) 29 *International & Comparative Law Quarterly* 549 and Christine Chinkin, 'The Challenge of Soft Law: Development and Change in International Law' (1989) 38 *International & Comparative Law Quarterly* 850.
68 Dianne Otto, 'Subalternity and International Law: The Problems of the Global Community and the Incommensurability of Difference' (1996) 5 *Social & Legal Studies* 337, 346.
69 For the wider discussion on the development of international law and imperialism, see here Antony Anghie, *Imperialism, Sovereignty, and the Making of International Law* (Cambridge University Press 2005).
70 Ibid.
71 Andrea Bianchi, *International Law Theories; An Inquiry into Different Ways of Thinking* (note 56) 209.
72 Ibid., 216.
73 Ibid.
74 Ibid.
75 Partha Chatterjee, *The Black Hole of Empire: History of Global Practice of Power* (Princeton University Press 2012).
76 Ibid.
77 Dianne Otto, 'Subalternity and International Law: The Problems of the Global Community and the Incommensurability of Difference' (1996) 5 *Social & Legal Studies* 337, 346.
78 Ibid.
79 Andrea Bianchi (note 56) 217.
80 Ibid.
81 Njabulo B Khumalo, 'From Oral Traditions to Written Records: The Loss of African Entitlement to Self-rule and Wealth' (2019) 7 (1) *Oral History Journal of South Africa* 1–13; Ida Nursoo, 'Indigenous Law, Colonial Injustice and the

Jurisprudence of Hybridity' (2018) 50 (1) *The Journal of Legal Pluralism and Unofficial Law* 56–70.

82 Although Emily Haslam, *The Slave Trade, Abolition and the Long History of International Criminal Law: The Recaptive and the Victim* (Routledge 2019) has attempted to detail the foundation of current international law from the abolitionist era, others have gone even deeper and detailed how the Maroons manoeuvred their freedoms in an age of slavery. See for example Charlton W. Yingling, 'The Maroons of Santo Domingo in the Age of Revolutions: Adaptation and Evasion 1783–1800' (2015) 79 (1) *History Workshop Journal* 25–51.

83 Inua Ellams, 'Fuck/Empire' in *The Actual* (Penned in the Margins 2020) 79.

84 Jose E Alvarez, 'Contemporary International Law: An Empire of Law or the Law of Empire' (2009) 24 *American University International Law Review* 811.

85 Ibid., see also Jean L Cohen, 'Whose Sovereignty? Empire versus International Law' (2004) 18 (3) *Ethics & International Affairs* 1–24; Jean Allain, 'Orientalism and International Law: The Middle East as the Underclass of the International Legal Order' (2004) 17 *Leiden Journal of International Law* 391.

86 Jan Hendrik Willem Verzijl, *International Law in Historical Perspective* (Sijthoff 1968) 435–436.

87 Elias Taslim Olawale and Richard Akinjide (eds), *Africa and the Development of International Law* (Martinus Nijhoff Publishers 1988); and Ram Prakash Anand, *Origin and Development of the Law of the Sea* (Nijthoff 1983).

88 Antony Anghie, *Imperialism, Sovereignty, and the Making of International Law* (Cambridge University Press 2005) 1–12.

89 Ibid., 13–31.

90 One of the earliest Spanish anti-imperialists, Las Casas, advocated ending the enslavement of Indigenous South Americans by importing African slaves instead. See Armando Lampe, 'Las Casas and African Slavery in the Caribbean: a Third Conversion' in David Thomas Orique and Rady Roldán-Figueroa (eds), *Bartolomé de las Casas, O.P.: History, Philosophy, and Theology in the Age of European Expansion* (Brill 2018) 421–436.

91 Antony Anghie (note 88) 32–114.

92 Makau Mutua, 'Critical Race Theory and International Law: The View of an Insider-Outsider' (2000) 45 *Villanova Law Review* 841.

93 Michel Foucault, *Security, Territory, Population: Lectures at the College de France 1977–1978* (Palgrave Macmillan 2007) 108.

94 Jacques Derrida, 'Force of Law: The Mystical Foundation of Authority' (1990) 11 *Cardozo Law Review* 919.

95 Sundhya Pahuja, *Decolonising International Law: Development, Economic Growth and the Politics of Universality* (Cambridge University Press 2013) 5–6.

96 Antony Anghie (note 88) 4.

97 Sundhya Pahuja, 'Laws of Encounter: A Jurisdictional Account of International Law' (2013) 1 *London Review of International Law* 63.

98 Sundhya Pahuja (note 95) 80.

99 Dianne Otto, 'Subalternity and International Law: The Problems of the Global Community and the Incommensurability of Difference' (1996) 5 *Social & Legal Studies* 354.

100 Sundhya Pahuja (note 97) 94.

101 Anne Orford, *International Authority and Responsibility to Protect* (Cambridge University Press 2011).

102 Sundhya Pahuja, *Decolonising International Law* (note 95) 39.

103 Ibid.

104 African Charter on Human and Peoples' Rights (Banjul Charter) adopted 27 June 1981, OAU Doc. CAB/LEG/67/3 rev. 5, 21 I.L.M. 58 (1982), entered into force 21 October 1986.

105 Justice C. Nwobike, 'The African Commission on Human and Peoples' Rights and the Demystification of Second and Third Generation Rights under the African Charter: *Social and Economic Rights Action Centre (SERAC) and the Centre for Economic and Social Rights (CESR) v. Nigeria*' (2005) 1 (2) *African Journal of Legal Studies* 129–146.
106 *Centre for Minority Rights Development (Kenya) and Minority Rights Group International on Behalf of Endorois Welfare Council v. Kenya, 276/2003.*
107 Ibid.
108 Andrea Bianchi, *International Law Theories; An Inquiry into Different Ways of Thinking* (note 56) 222.
109 Michel Foucault, *History of Sexuality, Volume 1 An Introduction* (Vintage 1990) 140.
110 Balakrishnan Rajagopal, *International Law from Below: Development, Social Movements, and the Third World Resistance* (Cambridge University Press 2003) 47, 18.
111 Ratna Kapur, *Erotic Justice; Law and the New Politics of Postcolonialism* (Glass House Press 2005) 22.
112 Sundhya Pahuja, *Decolonising International Law* (note 95) 25.
113 Ibid.
114 Ibid., 8 (Pahuja does not name the institutions, but I name some).
115 Sundhya Pahuja, *Laws of Encounter* (note 97) 96.
116 Ibid., 97.
117 Fredrick Cowell, 'Inherent Imperialism: Understanding the Legal Roots of Anti-imperialist Criticism of the International Criminal Court' (2017) 15 *Journal of International Criminal Justice* 667–687.
118 Ibid.
119 Ibid.
120 Ibid.
121 Ibid.
122 *Decision Pursuant to Article 15 of the Rome Statute on the Authorisation of an Investigation into the Situation in the Republic of Côte d'Ivoire ICC-02/11-14, 3 October 2011, §178–179.*
123 Ibid.
124 Makau Mutua, 'Critical Race Theory and International Law: The View of an Insider-Outsider' (2000) 45 *Villanova Law Review* 841.
125 Ibid.
126 See for example Ruth Reitan, 'Cuba, the Black Panther Party and the US Black Movement in the 1960s' (1999) 21 (2) *Issues of Security, New Political Science* 217–230.
127 Makau Mutua, 'Critical Race Theory and International Law: The View of an Insider-Outsider' (2000) 45 *Villanova Law Review* 841.
128 Ibid.
129 Ibid.
130 Ibid.
131 Ibid.
132 Ibid.
133 Ibid.
134 Kamari Maxine Clarke, *Fictions of Justice: The International Criminal Court and the Challenge of Legal Pluralism in Sub-Saharan Africa* (Cambridge University Press 2009) 4–221.
135 Ava DuVernay, "13th." A documentary (Netflix 2016); Theodore Twidell, '"13th": Ava Duvernay's Stark Exploration of the Mass Incarceration Crisis Facing Black Men' (2017) 6 (1) *Tapestries: Interwoven Voices of Local and Global Identities* 21; Samantha Pereira, 'Mass Incarceration: Slavery Renamed' (2018) 6 (1) *Themis: Research Journal of Justice Studies and Forensic Science* 3.

136 Ibid.
137 Kamari Maxine Clarke (note 134) 36.
138 Anne Orford, *International Authority, and the Responsibility to Protect* (Cambridge University Press 2011) 110.
139 Ibid.
140 Thomas Hobbes, *Leviathan* (J.C.A. Gaskin (ed.), Oxford University Press 2006).
141 Giorgio Agamben, *Homo Sacer: Sovereign Power and Bare Life* (Stanford University 1998) 183.
142 Ibid.
143 Carl Schmitt, *Legality and Legitimacy* (trans. Jeffrey Seitzer, Duke University Press 2004) 28.
144 Carl Schmitt, *Political Theology: Four Chapters on the Concept of Sovereignty* trans. George Schwab (University of Chicago 2005) 5.
145 Carl Schmitt, *The Nomos of the Earth in the International Law of the Jus Publicum Europaeum* (Telos 2003).
146 Michel Foucault, *The Birth of Biopolitics: Lectures at the Collège de France 1978–1979* (Palgrave Macmillan 2008).
147 Preston King, *Thinking Past a Problem: Essays on the History of Ideas* (Routledge 2013) 84.
148 Martti Koskenniemi, 'Legal Cosmopolitanism: Tom Franck's Messianic World' (2003) 35 (2) *New York University Journal of International Law and Politics* 486.
149 Ibid.
150 Ibid.
151 Emily Haslam, *The Slave Trade, Abolition, and the Long History of International Criminal Law: The Recaptive and the Victim* (Routledge 2019).
152 Ibid.
153 See more generally Nicholas Draper, *The Price of Emancipation: Slave-Ownership, Compensation and British Society at the End of Slavery* (Cambridge University Press 2010).
154 Kirsten Ainley, 'Responsibility for Atrocity: Individual Criminal Agency and the International Criminal Court' in John T. Parry (ed.), *Evil, Law and the State: Perspectives on State Power and Violence* (Vol. 24, Rodopi 2006) 143–158.
155 Luis Eslava and Sundhya Pahuja, 'Between Resistance and Reform: TWAIL and the Universality of International Law' (2011) 3 *Trade, Law& Development* 122.
156 Andrea Bianchi, *International Law Theories; An Inquiry into Different Ways of Thinking* (Oxford University Press 2016) 209.
157 Luis Eslava and Sundhya Pahuja (note 155).
158 Andrea Bianchi, *International Law Theories; An Inquiry into Different Ways of Thinking* (Oxford University Press 2016) 226.

3 C’est quoi cette indépendance là? The Neo-liberal ICC

On est fatigué

De danser votre cha-cha-cha là
...50ans de zigzag
Zigzag politique
50ans d’esclavage
Esclave économique

...Les décisions de la BAC
Sont prises à Francfort
Et non Congo

Ça *c’est pas réglo*
Pas du tout rigolo

C’est quoi cette indépendance là?[1]

Introduction

In the previous chapter, I detailed arguments around post-colonialism and neo-colonialism and argued that ICL/ICC is a continuation of the colonial. In this chapter, I develop that argument further and particularly focus on the IEL/development discourses and how these have come to shape Africa’s contemporary international relations, including the signing of ‘human rights’ treaties such as the Rome Statute. Zeroing in on this area of study allows me to narrow the scope and focus of my critique to neo-liberalism which, as I will detail below, is the dominating hegemony. My argument here is that in neo-liberalism’s continuation of ‘developing’ Africa, the ICC becomes simultaneously the ‘stick’ in the pedagogical relationship advocated by one of the universalist/cosmopolitan fathers, Kant, while also confirming the need of this ‘development.’ The wider claim I make here is that ‘development’ is but another gimmick, a governing technology which, because it does not have a fixed/concrete meaning, may be used to suit the hegemony at each given time. The associated claim I also make is that the hegemony not only defines what ‘development’ means for certain states i.e.

DOI: 10.4324/9781003304173-3

defines what the problem is/what makes them backward/uncivilised, but also prescribes the treatment for the supposed backwardness and more importantly, sets 'milestones' by which to measure those states' journeys towards an ever-shifting definition of civilisation/development.

I start by acknowledging that this is a well-researched area and far broader than can be covered in this section. The approach here is not to exhaustively detail the workings of 'law and development'[2] or IEL[3] as a wider topic because that is far broader area of study than I can cover in this one section. The idea here is to set my discourse on a firm footing, especially in relation to how Africa may or may not have been influenced by development/neo-liberalism to become a signatory to the Rome Statute. In this regard therefore, I explore the IEL's drive to have African and other southern states harmonise/standardise their laws and economies in pursuit of the aim to make them investor friendly (developed). This chapter should therefore be read as an expansion of the engagement I had earlier with material on neo-colonialism in Chapter 2, but here I narrow my focus to look at neo-liberalism and to lay foundations for the exploration of Kenyan cases. Exploring neo-liberalism at this stage is important because my overall hypothesis is that the commercialisation of law risks repeating the defining characteristics of slavery of viewing the African as a 'unit' that can be costed, sold. This section also helps us to contextualise the weakening of previously 'successful' neo-colonial/neo-liberal states like Kenya and Côte d'Ivoire and the subsequent consequences of producing what I claim is an ICL industrial complex.

Up to this point, we have in general seen that international law is increasingly being viewed by some authors, especially those from the south, as empire in designer clothing. We have seen, for example, Sundhya Pahuja saying that organising the newly independent communities through the 'state' was a 'trick' played to perpetuate colonial domination not just because the new states retained the colonial structure/character but because of the power dynamics of the UN system. Unlike Chapter 2 where I introduced concepts like neo-colonialism and situated my work in the wider post-colonial discourses, the aim of this chapter is to answer the question, how did we arrive at this point of a conflict between the ICC/Africa? It is only through contextualising the complexities of the contemporary neoliberalism hegemony that one achieves a proper insight into the discussed coloniality of the ICC and in association also appreciates the chronology of the emerging disobedience.

The signing of the Rome Statute by African states should not, in my view be considered in isolation from the prevailing neo-liberal orthodoxy in the 1990s and the drive in most southern states, for example Kenya, to democratise and liberalise: joining/signing international human rights conventions became the 'measure' for being democratic, modern, developed. After exploring how states like Kenya signed the Rome Statute, I interrogate how this romance ended so soon with the emerging conflict between the ICC and

Africa in the section titled 'Trouble in Paradise? Kenya and the Birth of an ICL Crisis.' I selected the situation in Kenya for discussion here to show the suggested coloniality of the ICC, including both the political background that led Kenya to be a signatory to the Rome Statute and then the subsequent politics that led to the fall out between Kenya and the ICC. The exploration of the Kenyan cases in this section highlights the political nature of international criminal law, as well as the risks of targeting just high-profile elites in litigating communal conflicts. I chose the Kenyan example mainly because of my familiarity with the local situation and because of what I argue was the 'iconographic' nature of the case which ties in with my discourse on legal iconography later in Chapter 4. It is therefore appropriate to repeat that the African cases discussed here, including the Kenyan cases, are used to test my hypotheses rather than the cases themselves being 'the' subject of my study.

In the section titles 'Neo-liberalist Coloniality' below, I begin by defining the Kantian idea of cosmopolitanism, not as a full exploration of Kantian philosophy but just to define the term as it relates to my discourse on ICC, universalism, and development. I then explore the idea of 'development' more as a continuation of the neo-colonialism discourses in Chapter 2, in order to lay firm grounds for my claim that the ICC is a neo-liberal institution. The simple claim I make here is that, in order to be deemed 'developed,' African states had little choice but to sign up to human rights treaties such as the Rome Statute in the push for 'rule of law,' which was/is a potent technology utilised by development colonialism. Given the now common disappointments with neo-liberalism, is it a wonder that those African states that signed the Rome Statute in some numbers later became the most prominent critics of the same treaty? This exploration is necessary because my hypothesis is that Africa was not part of the epistemological foundations of the Rome Statute. However, some researchers in this area have argued that the ICC cannot be a hegemonic tool of western countries because African countries played an essential role in its formation.[4] For example, Mandiaye Niang dismisses the critique of the 'universality' of the ICC and argues that the ICC is African in nature because of its membership and operations, including recruitment of African judges, backroom staff and its first female prosecutor.[5] It is apparent that Mandiaye Niang and others who argue this way have not considered structural racism in law but, as I argue in Chapter 4, it is also not uncommon for minorities working for a racist system to knowingly or inadvertently advocate for their employers.

In the section 'Revolution Anyone?' I argue that the claim to universality by ICL should be taken with a pinch of salt because recent examples suggest that those who have taken arms in a necessary revolution against oppression are placed in the same categories as their oppressors, as for example in the latest case of the situation in Palestine.[6] Although the ruling that the ICC can investigate the Israel/Palestinian situation is being celebrated as a path towards justice for the Palestinians, the irony is that those fighting against the occupation will be subjected to the same scrutiny as the occupiers.

The section 'Trouble in Paradise? Kenya and the Birth of an ICL Crisis' argues that the Kenyan cases are an example both of how this neo-liberalism failed in Kenya and, most importantly, of how the effects of that failure have led to the current conflict(s). These cases show how this failure of neo-liberalism is ignored and/or hidden because other convenient explanations such as 'tribal' conflicts for land fit more neatly into the cosmopolitan narrative. The link between neo-liberalism and the ICC is important for two reasons. First, it contributes to making the wider argument that contemporary ICL follows a 'business' model and that the emerging legal industrial complex mirrors the slavery practices of the past and of the USA prison industrial complex already discussed. Second, placing cases, for example the Kenyan ones, in a wider neo-liberal context introduces the reader to the very 'colonial' manner in which the African cases are handled by the ICC. In addition to giving an example of the colonial nature of the ICC's engagement with an African state, this section also acts a precursor to the discourse in Chapter 4 on iconography because of the significance of Kenyatta in Kenya's anti-colonial romance.

Neo-liberalist Coloniality

Before I explore 'development,' neo-liberalism, and African elites' rush to the Hague, it is appropriate to define the term cosmopolitanism which appears regularly in the following chapters and I suppose is the end/*nirvana* of the suggested development. Walter Mignolo indicates that the term comes from the Kantian concept of "cosmopolitanism" which was itself a Eurocentric view of what a cosmo-polis should be.[7]

Kant argues that there is a universal law of morality (moral cosmopolitanism) that is based upon the categorical imperative. This means that moral requirements are based on a standard of rationality, which is "reason's guide to action" for the purpose of discovering a universal law and particularly perpetual peace.[8] In the Kantian vision, individuals have the same challenges as always (everywhere?); however, moral cosmopolitanism, suggested for the purpose of perpetual peace,[9] has influenced the majority of the world's states to put moral principle ahead of national sovereignty.[10] According to this view, law institutions do not change people directly but they can provide a powerful mechanism[11] for promoting moral behaviour through specific penalties.

The link to our 'development' discourse is that according to Kant's doctrine of the universality of moral law, the principle of moral action must be impersonal, objective, and impartial as between one person and another.[12] A moral community (commonwealth) develops from this supposed 'impartiality' of individuals, each of whom must be considered an end and never merely a means in the calculations of others.[13] Simply put, because individuals are objective, reasoning beings, they work for the betterment of this utopian community. But obviously, there is punishment if they deviate. To Kant, this idea is universal, omnipresent, almost God-like (in a white Judeo-Christian sense).

And so, the universal principle of justice is born to conform to this absurd/simplistic idea of human nature because to Kant 'universalisability' is core to his conception of morality.[14] Universality is however to be achieved not organically, but through practical requirements in moral laws that could be legitimately enforced through external coercion.[15] The ICC is the modern tool of coercion, the Rome Statute the universal moral law. This is what Kant perhaps had in mind when he mused about cosmopolitan law in '*Perpetual Peace. A Philosophical Project*.'[16] Kant's ideas were later to become UNDP's rhetoric that "a violation of right on one place of the earth is felt in all"[17] because it seems that modern day universalists have adopted Kant's conclusions that cosmopolitan law must form a 'supplement' to the 'unwritten code' of both state law and international law if the 'public rights of human beings' are to be secured.[18]

Kant did not go unchallenged by other white men of the day as Hegel is seen by many to have been Kant's nemesis through his advocating for the role of the individual in the republic rather than for cosmopolitanism. Whether Hegel was rejecting cosmopolitanism in total and was a nationalist has occupied a good number of brains since.[19] I will not engage with Hegel's critique of Kant.[20] For the purposes of this section, it is however notable that Hegel thought an individual's loyalty should be to his or her state rather than to this cosmopolitanism.[21] Because cosmopolitanism in its modern mutation(s) envisages an international order that takes on functions such as the security of citizens which previously rested in the state, as the ICC does for example, does it not then boil down to Hegel's position on the individual/state relationship? What is the difference between the Kantian state and Hegelian state? While the individual in the Hegelian state is loyal to the state, isn't the cosmopolitan loyal to the universal state? Is the global state not asking for almost unqualified support for its institutions, similarly to a Hegelian model?

But the critique I favour is from those who argue that cosmopolitanism is essentially a banner under which powerful nations conduct wars against their enemies and portray them as enemies of humanity itself.[22] Carl Schmitt made these arguments at Nuremberg, saying that the only distinction between crimes against humanity and crimes for humanity is that the former were committed by Germans and the latter by Americans.[23] More generally, Schmitt maintained that the moralisation of war under a cosmopolitan flag has a close affinity to the totalisation of war, since it turns the enemy into a monster/other which must be annihilated.[24] This attack on the idea of cosmopolitan right alleges the hypocrisy of those powers which usurp it to their own ends and use it to demonise their foes.[25]

Kant was a racist.[26] A conundrum not resolved by literature reviewed is why Kant, with his racist views became an inspiration for the supposed universalist approach in international law post Nuremberg.[27] Shouldn't he have faced the same criticisms for his racist views as Schmitt did for his pro-Nazi stand?[28] Because of Kant's racist views, I find cosmopolitanism/universalism/Eurocentrism guilty of being germinated on racist grounds.[29] According to Emmanuel Eze, non-European people would not have qualified for Kant's cosmopolitanism, which required reason.[30] This was because they were devoid of ethical principles as they lack the capacity for development of "character," and they lacked character presumably because they lacked adequate self-consciousness and rational will, for it is self-reflectivity, the "ego concept" and the rational principled will which make the upbuilding of (moral) character possible through the (educational) process of development of goodness latent in/as human nature.[31]

And this Kantian cosmopolitanism was keen on the 'development' of Africans who can be educated but only as slaves, that is if they allow themselves to be trained.[32] To train the African to submission, Kant, the founding father of equality cosmopolitanism advises the use of a split bamboo cane instead of a whip, so that the 'negro' will suffer a great deal of pains.[33] It needs to be done in this manner because the blood needs to find a way out of the negro's thick skin to avoid festering.[34] The African, according to Kant, deserves this kind of "training" because he or she is exclusively idle, lazy, and prone to hesitation and jealousy, and the African is all these because, for climate and anthropological reasons, he or she lacks "true" (rational and moral) character.[35]

Defending Kant's racism is a scholarly approach as I have discovered.[36] In their text, Thomas Hill and Bernard Boxill, two white men, spend a reasonable amount of time disputing the observations made by Immanuel Eze above, a black man from whose standpoint Kant's ideas were infected by racism.[37] I guess Eze and others like myself should be grateful to these white men for telling us what we should find racist. However, such defenders have no answer to the fact that, for such a venerated philosopher, Kant's research methods on his 'anthropology' were to say the least sketchy. For his evidence he read the cosmopolitan's canon on 'exotic' people/places, Captain James Cook's Voyages (1773).[38] He also hung about the Konigsberg docks to gather seafarers' stories.[39] And so with the help of Captain Cook, Kant developed a deep appreciation of domestic violence to advocate that wives enjoy being beaten by their husbands as a proof of true love. If the beatings do not happen, the woman becomes not just a public property but a bone.[40] I take this to mean that either Kant fancied himself as a canine or saw fellow white men as canines.

Now that we understand that Africans were not part of the humanity envisaged by the father of the universalist *nirvana*, it would be appropriate for me to state that the ICC is part of this project to make the African see/have reason by, as Kant would have wanted, the end of a cane. This caning is done through sanctions and conditionalities as neo-liberalism uses technologies such as adherence to individual human (property) rights as a measure for development. Neo-liberalism, according to David Harvey, entails the state proactively ensuring that market forces are the leading principle in governance.[41] Private property, free trade, and monetisation are crucial, and the state must create by force, if necessary, market conditions where they do not already exist, for example in areas such as education, health, or social security.[42] Once these markets exist, the state must not interfere.[43] In this phase of colonialism, we see that state law enforcement exists for the sole purpose of serving the market. In this section I elaborate how this understanding of the 'state' helps to explain why African states first signed the Rome treaty *en masse*, but have of late come to see the court as problematic.

Out of the 123 countries who are States Parties to the Rome Statute, 33 are African States, 19 are Asian-Pacific States, 18 are from Eastern Europe, 28 are from Latin American and Caribbean States, and 25 are Western European and other States.[44] Researchers such as Yuval Shany have explored why African states enthusiastically signed the Rome Statute establishing the ICC as well as why they seem to have lost their enthusiasm about the Court.[45] As seen in the previous chapter, the discourse by authors such as Yuval and others tends to be from Eurocentric scholars with a general tendency of unmitigated enthusiasm for the ICC. Although an emerging TWAIL scholarship is detailing the colonial nature of international law, most of the literature reviewed in respect to Africa's recent relationship with the ICC tends to hold the view that critiques of the court are ill-founded and the claim of neo-colonialism misplaced.[46]

However, I argue that scholars should explore the interaction between the ICC and Africa through the wider social and legal lenses because only in that way are we able to appreciate the many reasons why nations sign treaties, including geo-political considerations. My conclusion from the literature is that studies in this area of ICL ignore the uniqueness of the African state in relation to post-colonial global power structures and the African state's status within the hierarchy of that power structure. Nonetheless, scholars like Mueller[47] indicate that states like Kenya signed the Rome Statute due to their changing politics and the existing weakness of the rule of law. In Mueller's view, politics play a significant role in states signing treaties and specifically the Rome Statute.[48] Politics also, she argues, played a key role in states wanting to withdraw from the Rome Statute.[49]

This acceptance that politics play a crucial role in international law-making is important in our discourse because international lawyers and the ICC downplay the role of politics in the law[50] and at times seems unprepared to engage with the politics around its operations.[51] While I agree with Mueller on the politics point, her point on 'lack of rule of law' is overstretched, simplistic, and problematic in the context of the overall discourse of 'the need' for colonialism because we have seen that this white peoples' burden to export the 'rule of law' was one of the justifications for colonialism. On the contrary, Kenya signed the Rome Statute during Moi's dictatorship that was famous for its strong-armed 'rule of law'[52] and in that respect, the problem was not lack of but excessive respect for 'law.' Moi's signing of the Rome Statute should not be presented as his (or others') road to Damascus moment, but as a consequence of the prevailing democratisation/development hegemony of the 1990s/2000s.

Part of this political consideration is the need of emerging states to use international treaties to entrench newfound freedoms, particularly 'new democracies.' Moravcsik for example argues that states sign treaties in an attempt to "lock in new democracies, to contain internal threats, and to keep them from reverting to fascism."[53] This argument also needs to be considered in the wider context of the 'democratisation' movement in most African countries in the 1990s and the neo-liberal movement of the 2000s where local activists, with the support of foreign states and international NGOs, pressurised states to sign because they wanted to 'lock in' the hitherto one-party states to an international mechanism. There seems to be a similar argument, but made slightly differently, by others who see states as joining treaties to hoodwink other states to believe that they have undergone change and hoodwink their critics at home into believing that they have reformed and become less despotic, which keeps those critics from agitating for change.[54]

This argument that states sign treaties as a safety net against internal tendencies towards fascism has been discredited by others like Chapman and Chaudoin who argue that it would be against their self-interest for repressive states to do so because states which are despotic would usually be reluctant to ratify the Rome Statute.[55] I tend to disagree with this view because I think, as with greenwashing,[56] states have now become aware of the instrumentalisation of human rights rhetoric and they therefore sign to present the image of being part of the 'civilised us' and therefore not able to torture etc. Meanwhile, some of those states will operate torture complexes like Guantanamo[57] or operate Apartheid-like stop and search laws[58] on a section of their population. A view I find persuasive is that of Tom Ginsburg who argues there are some states that may have ratified the Rome Statute in pursuit of 'victors' justice' rather than justice.[59] I find this more applicable in 'peace building' initiatives because as we see in this book the ICC/ICL often comes into play after the event, for example in the Kenyan cases or indeed in the many cases from Eastern Congo. I will also go further and argue that states use the statute to promote their own domestic political agendas, a discourse I explore further in relation to the ICC and revolutions in the section 'Revolution Anyone?'

Yvonne Dutton on the other hand argues that some states cynically sign sovereignty limiting treaties knowing or hoping that these treaties have no real enforcement power.[60] This is linked to the argument that, due to their grip on power and fear amongst their populations, strong dictatorships are more likely to support the United Nations Convention Against Torture.[61] Mueller however argues that because the Rome Statute has actual legal power, unlike other human rights, this argument does not apply in relation to it.[62] Another linked argument is that governments sign up to these treaties because of local activism.[63] The idea of local activism in the promotion of 'human rights' and 'democracy' is a far wider topic than can be captured here but it is noteworthy that these local 'activists' are seen by some authors as being agents of foreign actors.[64] These domestic activists are seen as necessary in the building of a rights culture in concert with their international partners.[65] This is however the 'industrial complex' I critique in this book because these local actors' role is not to ensure the realisation of African self-reliance but is to "alert Western public opinion and Western Governments."[66]

In agitating for change in this limited manner, all they achieve is to ensure the continuation of the status quo as their repressive /colonial regimes deceitfully sign up to human right treaties to "regain foreign aid, overcome international sanctions, and strengthen their positions in relation to local opposition."[67] It is not clear to me why alerting western governments is seen by local activists as liberating, because all they achieve is cede even more power to the west because not only is the local activist beholden to his/her foreign financier, but their success is measured in terms of how much their countries are tied into more foreign debt/aid. In addition, the local activist is drawn into legitimising a false narrative that human rights are 'foreign' to Africa and is bamboozled into ignoring the role of their foreign financiers in conniving with the same local governing elite (they now pretend to fight) in killing Africa's hopes of true liberation.

However, it is my view that although some states in Africa would have signed up to the Rome Statute for the reasons argued above, there is a uniqueness in African and other southern states in that they have different historical experiences to those of the western ex-colonial masters, principally as victims of colonialism and slavery which, as argued here, continue to date. In this sense, it would be naïve if not intellectually dishonest to suggest that a country like the UK has an equal footing with a country like Kenya in signing the Rome Statute or any other treaty. In this regard, I argue that to characterise earlier enthusiasm for the ICC by Africa as motivated by free will and local agency is to deliberately ignore the prevailing orthodoxy in the 1990s and early 2000s when the agitation for the formation of the ICC was alive.[68] To understand Africa's signing of the Rome Statute in considerable numbers, one must look at the arguments made by the scholars above in the context of the unrelenting pressure put on African states to adopt 'universal' norms in their domestic laws.[69] This was coupled with 'democratisation' and the neo-liberal push to open Africa to foreign investments and lead Africa towards 'development' which in turn was seen to be equal to/or leading to social justice as discussed by Johan Galtung,[70] Amartya Sen,[71] and Stephen Davies[72] amongst others.

Signing up to the Rome Statute cannot therefore be separated from this wider context of countries wanting to be perceived as 'developed,' especially by western donor agencies, and the signing cannot be divorced from the prevailing neo-liberal view of the world at that time. It is important therefore to engage briefly here with the meaning of 'development' as understood from an anti-colonial southern perspective. It is widely accepted that development could be interpreted to mean progress from one stage to another, but it is when the term is applied to communities that it becomes problematic. Esteva explains the distorted adaptation of the word from its biological meanings to current use because the difficulty is that the word reminds some of their undesirable, undignified condition – to develop you first must be seen as underdeveloped in the eyes of the developer.[73] Esteva is just one of the many authors who see the idea of development as synonymous with colonisation. This area of study, including the idea of post-development, is wider than the scope of this book, but I will explore some ideas that link with post-colonialism. Other authors I consider in this section include Arturo Escobar,[74] Frederick Cooper,[75] and David Simon.[76] For the purpose of my arguments in this book, I adapt Esteva's understanding of 'development' in that I see it as equal to colonisation/westernisation/occupation by other means. Any other meanings attributed to the word by 'world governing agencies,' local or otherwise, are in my view meant to bamboozle and hide the real intentions and purposes of the development movement(s).

And therefore, although the term has been used regularly since the 1700s,[77] Frederick Cooper particularly argues that 'development' as understood in modern times was taken to Africa by the French and the British in the 1940s with the aim of making the colonies more productive and 'stable' post-war. European experts were sent to show settler farmers and their workers how to be more productive, and also to reform health and education sectors.[78] Although initially the project was to be overseen by these colonial experts, with the agitation for 'independence' and a willing African elite to take the project forward, it became the 'process' through which colonies could be let free.[79] The blueprint then as now, was to open up Africa for extraction through infrastructures such as railways, with the African lacking in agency where development was done 'to' and 'for' the continent.[80]

The prominence of development as 'the' global template seems to stem from President Truman's idea of 'undeveloped' and by association development in relation to states. To Truman, development is the concept of democratic fair dealing characterised by scientific and industrial growth.[81] It is arguable that, for Truman, the undeveloped meant the ex-colonies who were the 'other' and not like us and we needed to make them like us. To become like us, they needed to industrialise and adopt our type of democracy. In his seminal work on the concept of underdevelopment, Andre Gunder Frank argues that the creation of 'developed and underdeveloped' is a false duality and that underdevelopment as a concept was a deliberate capitalist ploy.[82] In this light therefore, Truman's ideas were not new and he seemed to follow what imperialists like Lord Lugard had promoted; that the west has a moral obligation to bring the blessings of western civilisation to the colonies and put their resources to good use.[83]

This idea of looking at some communities as others who are 'less' than us (European) is found in most literature promoting development as a concept. For example, B.C. Smith goes to a lot of trouble to insist that there should be countries known as 'third world'[84] to differentiate them from the developed world. Wrongly in my view and very crucial to our ICC discourse, Smith in the same breath equates democracy with development and says that globalisation of political values and institutions has "lent credence to the view that there is an inevitable trend towards a universal form of government on which all societies will eventually converge."[85] It is in this Smithian Utopia that institutions like the ICC belong. They form the judicial arm of this new world order.

Therefore, it is my view that African signatories to the Rome Statute saw this/were forced to see it as an act of/and towards development as propagated by the Washington consensus. This neo-liberal push is seen here as a continuation of colonialism by other means. In the past, colonisers were open about their intentions, as exemplified by the notorious Cecil Rhodes and Lord Lugard. However, the Washington consensus meant that imperialists had to come up with new means of accessing resources and markets without annexing territories. Globalisation allows western commercial interests to continuously demand ever more comprehensive concessions, creating ever more favourable conditions for European corporations.[86] This view is shared by many, including Francois Partant[87] and Randall Baker,[88] who argue that development is nothing but a continuation of the west's designs for the rest of the world which have been in place for centuries. In other words,

> formal colonialism came to an end not because the colonial powers had decided to forego the economic advantages it provided but because, in the new conditions, these could now largely be obtained by more politically acceptable and at the same time, as we shall see below, more effective methods.[89]

Important for our discourse is my view that although defining 'development' is controversial enough, measuring it and showing what it looks like is even more so. Literature in this area shows that development has many faces depending on the agent measuring it and the purpose of those measurements. For example, to show that 'development' does work, the Bretton Woods Institutions, NGOs and the larger Washington consensus shifted from the much maligned GDPs, to the Millennium Development Goals (MDG), to their current buzz words 'Sustainable' Development Goals (SDG) measurements.[90] In a nutshell, the current idea is to measure human progress not by monetary wealth alone (GDP) as that has become an inconvenience due to evidence that the rich are getting richer as a result of these policies.[91] Since the 1980s inequalities have widened drastically, with a top 1% wealth share of approximately 40% in 2016 versus 25–30% in the 1980s. In China, Europe, and the United States combined, the top 1% wealth share has increased from 28% in 1980 to 33% today, while the bottom 75% share hovered around 10%. The figures are however incomplete as the top 1%'s wealth is hard to trace due to financial globalisation.[92] In Kenya, the gap between the richest and poorest is alarming with fewer than 0.1% of the population (8,300 people) owning more wealth than the bottom 99.9% (more than 44 million people).[93] The richest 10% of people in Kenya earned on average 23 times more than the poorest 10%.[94] My hypothesis is that the hegemony does not want us to focus on this and hence the shift is to measure human centred outcomes such as reduction of poverty, health, education, and environmental protection.[95] There is still the obsession with measurements and milestones which from a decolonising perspective, is 'the' reason for all the talk on development as the African is always lacking in something; in wealth, health, government, and now clean water and air. And hence the need to intervene. In a nutshell, globalisation of capital through/under the guise of the 'development' mantra means that there is always space for interventionist industries as this globalisation causes havoc in local communities including inequalities, environmental damage and other human rights abuses.

Often, there is no mention in SDG of the elimination of the colonial set ups which hinder organic, local solutions. It is no surprise then that when researchers asked Kenyans what the main cause of inequalities is, colonialism came up as one of the primary reason(s)… "the Kenyan participants were considerably more critical than their white British counterparts, who spoke little of colonialism, and so were effectively oblivious to the role of colonialism in generating contemporary inequalities."[96] This acceptance that all growth is measurable with an indicator also ignores the simple fact that in some areas like health, numbers mean little if anything as they do not measure mental health and community cohesion for example. The key word here is measurements. Neo-liberalists have tended to change their use of language to suit every new moment. Because neo-liberalism faces relentless criticism for focusing on financial indicators, they quickly adapted to 'sustainable goals' as the new language meaning the same, i.e. states with high GDPs (or with help of donor aid) are able in theory to finance health, education, and other 'human' indicators. The example I think of to explain the African states' neo-liberalism conundrum is that of a hamster caged in a treadmill. The hamster is baffled by its lack of progress. It is looking at the whole ordeal from the wrong perspective, it is told. Doesn't it see that it is producing electricity and losing weight? In the meantime, it is given some extra medication to ease the hunger and help inspire a new perspective.

My hamster analogy is perhaps the best way to understand the Washington consensus as it relates to Africa and show why neo-liberalists have never shied away from this obsession with indicators and the reduction of everything to monetary values. This is because Washington consensus is a term that means different things to different commentators, as observed by John Williamson who coined the term in 1989.[97] I use the term in its broader sense and as synonymous with neo-liberalism but Williamson used it to refer to ten principles he thought were necessary in a free-market economy, which included fiscal discipline, reordering public expenditure priorities, tax reform, liberalising interest rates, a competitive exchange rate, trade liberalisation, liberalisation of inward foreign direct investment, privatisation, deregulation and property rights.[98] Williamson has since 1989 attempted to show how his ideas have been misinterpreted but he has also indicated that there are variations in understanding the term that he agrees with including that it refers to the policies the Bretton Woods institutions applied toward their client countries, or perhaps the attitude of the US government plus the Bretton Woods institutions.[99] He however objects to the term being used as a synonym for neo-liberalism or market fundamentalism but says that the term should be understood to mean economic policies which have gained a "consensus in some significant part of Washington, either the US government or the IFIs or both, or perhaps both plus some other group."[100]

'Development' merges with our discourse on the ICC where, apart from the increase in 'purchasing power,' others have equated 'development' to peace.[101] According to this approach, there are two forms of peace; "negative peace, which remains the absence of organized collective violence, and positive peace, which is the existence of values including; Economic growth and development, absence of exploitation, equality and Justice."[102] This idea of positive peace in my view can also be linked to the idea of development as freedom propagated by Amartya Sen who for example argued that development offered women, especially in the poorest nations, the ability to work outside the home.[103] The idea of development as peace is however borrowed from the earlier theories of liberal thinkers like Richard Cobden who argued that free trade and free exchange of thoughts are sufficient means for maintaining peace.[104] The Rome Statute's promise to end global impunity should be understood as motivated by this theory of peace as justice which in my view is a defective perspective as it disregards the many facets of social justice. In a globalised economy, and with the ICC becoming the 'police' arm of the IEL/development agenda, as I argue, it is no wonder that the ICC is occupied with the idea of the absence of violence as a marker for peace. I would however argue that violence must be understood to include the rampant inequalities necessary to maintain a capitalist state.

In my view, the discourse around the ICC and the Rome Statute cannot be divorced from international economic law (IEL) and an almost universal acceptance of the idea of 'development' as well as the wider neo-liberal tendency to standardise and financialise human interactions. The Rome Statute in this perspective forms 'the' strong arm of this neo-liberal world order because states are eager to show their financiers at the World Bank and IMF that they have put in place internationally accepted standards in the areas of human rights, trade and investment liberalisation, economic deregulation and protection of property rights that seem to dominate international law. An international criminal court completed the domination of IEL because proponents of globalisation argue that it is necessary to harmonise rules and standards to create a level playing field. These rules and standards have been applied to all states across the world regardless of their level of economic development. The subsequent appearance of the Rome Statute completes this harmonisation and ensures there is 'peace' which allows for neo-liberalism to take root and that MNEs can prospect for resources in peace.

From my standpoint, the already documented effects of the Washington consensus on African states is a form of racism as their economies are shaped to disadvantage them vis-à-vis the west through a centralised authority which is established for the task of collecting massive amounts of information from the peripheries, analysing and processing this information through a universal discipline such as economics, and constructing an ostensibly universal science, a science by which all societies may be assessed and advised on how to achieve the goal of economic development.[105]

Antony Anghie has indicated that the idea of the rule of law is a part of the larger good/global governance ideology.[106] This good governance comes about because the west, through its vehicles the Bretton Woods institutions, realises that development as a project has attracted valid critique, and hence there is the need for new terminologies like sustainable development goals.[107] All this is happening because, as we see in this section, various scholars have linked development to colonialism and more importantly argued that rights set out in the International Covenant on Economic, Social and Cultural Rights, which include the right to health and education, for example, have been undermined by international financial institutions (IFIs) through their structural adjustment policies (SAPs).[108] Further, many of the African countries which submitted to IFIs' structural adjustment policies are now even worse off than they were initially and are deeper in debt. IFIs have given priority to debt repayment as opposed to the provision of the basic welfare services necessary for survival, leading to situations like that in Tanzania where in 1999, 40% of the people died before the age of 35 and debt payments were six times greater than spending on healthcare.[109] Further, the Articles of Agreement of the Bank, the constituent document of the organisation, require the World Bank to base its lending policies strictly on economic criteria. As such, the Bank is arguably prohibited from taking the human rights record of a particular state into account when deciding whether or not to make a loan to that country.[110] The World Bank becomes the all-powerful leviathan institution, with claws reaching every aspect of a country's policies and practices. There are virtually no aspects of a southern state that are out of reach of this leviathan creature. This, according to Nira Wickremasinghe, changes the global system as it interferes with states' core institutions.[111]

While reshaping/structuring southern economies though SAPs was bad enough, a more insidious way in which IEL creates and maintains western hegemony and injustices is in the sphere of intellectual property rights (IPR).

The 'Agreement on Trade Related Aspects of Intellectual Property Rights' (TRIPS), signed in 1994, is a founding element of the WTO.[112] TRIPS constitutes the most important attempt to establish a global harmonisation of Intellectual Property (IP) protection and enforcement, creating international standards for the protection of patents, copyrights, trademarks and design.[113] This leads to pressure on the poorest states to reform their legal systems as discussed elsewhere in this discourse. The hypocrisy and unfairness of the current requirements on poorer states is that having benefited from a loose IPR regime for over a century, through the WTO industrialised countries are now imposing on poorer countries requirements that they themselves did not have in place until very recently.[114]

While the historical origin of IPRs is colonial,[115] it is in the sphere of protecting the ownership rights of the few over the potential benefits to the many that I think IPRs show their unjust character. IPRs seek to hinder dissemination of the benefits of knowledge, kill off competition and promote protection of an 'owner' who must benefit exclusively, usually from items produced by others or natural resources owned by others. The idea of IPR is usually to promote the impression of scarcity that then leads to higher values, but with the negative consequences for the many.[116] This power can have negative social consequences and can deliver over-arching market power to the holder or owner of such rights. An example of this monopoly power is playing out right now, live on your favourite news channel regarding a few pharma companies and the Covid vaccine. As with Covid vaccines today, another example was the HIV/AIDS epidemic in which pharmaceutical companies for years resisted poor countries' production of generic drugs for distribution at a lower cost to their citizens.[117]

Although the Doha Declaration[118] reaffirmed the flexibility of TRIPS member states in circumventing patent rights for better access to essential medicines, America and European countries still managed to water down its effect on TRIPS.[119] As western countries stockpile vaccines for themselves, today as in the past, the moral question is at what point do rights-based incentives to invest in developing life-saving pharmaceutical products defeat the very purpose of saving lives? In addition, as shown with the example of HIV medications the patent system distorts inventions, especially in pharma industries, because money is to be made from western world diseases, for example heart diseases, which receive more research attention than the diseases affecting poor countries. In the spirit of *Ubuntu*,[120] I would support Marie Jean Condorcet who rejected the notion of intellectual property as a right. Condorcet argued that ideas are not produced by individuals alone as they are the fruit of a collective process of experience. He further argues that granting exclusive property rights concentrates privilege in a small number of hands and is unjust.[121]

To a casual observer, this exploration of TRIPS/IPR may seem out of place in relation to the ongoing discourse on ICL, slavery and colonialism. The reader is however reminded that the ICC is seen here in the context of a colonial global governance in which global resources benefit the west and their allies. And therefore, the 'rule of law'[122] which includes TRIPS becomes synonymous with – and the aim of – this 'development.'[123] This drive to harmonise legal systems has meant that poor countries are asked to reform their legal systems so that they become 'investor friendly' and reduce the cost of doing business.[124] Law in this sense is intended to serve business rather than the wider community, and the protection of investments becomes the primary focus for legal systems and legal procedures initially meant to protect citizens, for example against environmental degradation, are seen as costly to businesses.[125] The argument by Mueller discussed earlier that politics plays 'the' major role in African states' unhappiness with the ICC faces difficulties here because others, such as Faundez, see this imposition of foreign legal doctrines as problematic as it generates local suspicions because those new laws are viewed as tools aimed at undermining indigenous legal culture and identity.[126] In my view, this argument by Faundez suggests that there is always 'organic' local mistrust of foreign interventions and laws even without the agitation of the local elite, and as I explore in Chapter 6, there has always been an uncomfortable co-existence of Eurocentric laws and local indigenous laws in most colonised states.[127] This is because local populations have always understood this imposition of 'rule of law' in 'development' clothes as a repeat of the colonial and despite their states being 'free,' they are only free to the extent that they agree with the dominant neo-liberal orthodoxy.[128] It is noteworthy that the protest against foreign legal doctrines is not just found in 'southern' states as the imposition of foreign laws as an argument is also regularly applied by the USA in relation to its opposition to the ICC. Pro-Brexit[129] agitators in the UK also used this argument which shows how hypocritical western countries are in this regard because they aggressively defend intrusion into their legal systems by foreign ideologies: regarding the ICC discourse, America is a notable example of this as a non-signatory to the Rome Statute for this reason.[130]

Therefore, the enthusiasm shown by African states for the Rome Statute should be seen in the context of a neo-liberal push for uniform legal norms and the equation of lack of violence to peace as discussed above. This push to conform came in the form of the (in)famous conditionalities imposed by Bretton Woods institutions on poorer states. Despite industrialised countries aggressively defending their own sovereignty, encroachment on 'others' sovereignty by IEL is immense. My analyses here are in line with other scholars, such as Faundez, who argues that international law is an inescapable straitjacket for developing countries as the emphasis by the Washington consensus is to lock in policies to safeguard global markets.[131] Second, the imposition of policies from outside means that citizens' democratic will is interfered with. This is especially so in developing states where the IMF and World Bank require as part of 'structural adjustments,'[132] that governments spend less on welfare, including health and education, and push those governments towards 'marketisation' where those services should be provided by the private sector.[133] Sovereignty however is more under threat where failure to toe the line means removal of elected governments from power, as happened in Chile during the 1973 coup.[134] To help remove the socialist government, the World Bank cancelled Chile's loans and credit facilities following successful pressure by the United States but reopened the facilities for the military junta that took over with the help of America.

In the same way, the ICC is a form of contemporary shock therapy because it can become, at least as in the Cote d'Ivoire, a facility to initiate what I would term a *soft coups d'état*, conveniently allowing foreign states to intervene and impose their preferred governments. Thus, the French intervention in Cote d'Ivoire led to the Gbagbo cases at the ICC. Gbagbo was removed from power and transferred to the ICC by French forces after a political-military crisis followed a disputed presidential run-off election between him and his former Prime Minister Alassane Ouattara in November 2010.[135] The dispute escalated to a full-scale armed conflict which ended after Gbagbo's arrest by French soldiers.[136] It is also important to note that Gbagbo himself had come to power following peace initiatives such as the 2007 Ouagadougou Political Agreement after civil war in 2002. Before he was captured by the French, the 'international community' had exhausted other means including financial sanctions to pressure Gbagbo to step aside.[137] Similar arguments were also put forward by a section of the Kenyan political class – that the ICC was being used to pave the way for a preferred candidate to become president.[138]

What comes out clearly from the literature review is that this neoliberalism at the core of international law is propagated by a network of well-funded and organised western NGOs.[139] I will not explore the NGO movement in relation to the ICC in full as it is a much wider topic than the scope here will allow, but it is my argument that the Eurocentric activist/NGO has led to the racist legal outcomes discussed in this book because western NGOs dominated the founding of the ICC and the subsequent legal jurisprudence in areas such as rape, cultural destruction and victim participation which I discuss in Chapter 5. To take just one area as an example, the inclusion of victim participation in the Rome Statute was initially led by France and New Zealand who initially faced objections from Australia, the United Kingdom, and the United States, who argued that the prosecutor should be the sole voice of victims.[140] It is at this point that the NGO movement established itself as a key actor at the ICC because, although victims' participation raised red flags for many who anticipated myriad political and legal complications, the provision was included in the statute as Article 68 with the support from several influential NGOs.[141] The unique participation of NGOs in drafting the Rome Statute and their subsequent role in cases presented at the ICC has immense colonial connotations, as I discussed above. In addition, while NGOs were instrumental in drafting the Rome Statute, they are also crucial in ICC functioning, especially in collection of evidence and witness handling. It is also important to note that NGOs have been major actors in this arena since the birth of the 'development' agenda and their central role in the creation and functioning of the ICC should therefore be seen in this light. In this respect therefore, western NGOs are part of the wider scheme to 'develop' Africa using the Rome Statute. For example, at the core of the ICC is a group of over 2,500 NGOs known as coalition for the ICC and funded by the global north, including funding from other larger NGOs such as the Open Society Institute, the Sigrid Rausing Trust, the Ford and MacArthur Foundations, and the European Union, Australia, New Zealand, Luxembourg, Irish Aid, The Kingdom of Belgium, Denmark, Netherlands, Norway, Sweden, Liechtenstein, Austria, Finland, and Switzerland.[142] Given that we shall see later that the ICC's functions are reportedly hindered by a lack of resources, it is an unresolved conundrum in the literature reviewed that these donors and states are not able to fund the ICC directly to improve its effectiveness, but are able to fund a parallel organisation whose main aim is to ensure that the ICC functions effectively.

The role of NGOs in the wider development industry is not the central theme of this book and it has been well articulated by other authors[143] including those discussed above. I will however suggest here that these organisations do not actively oppose the Washington consensus[144] despite having 'ground level' evidence of the negative impact of neoliberal policies in Africa, Asia and Latin America. It is my view that aid agencies thrive on both the propagation and the failure of the Washington consensus because their *raison d'*être is the ever-present crises of war and poverty. In my view, they perpetuate these crises by actively undermining capacity building in weaker states leading to the necessity for interventionist mechanisms like the ICC where they are again the core actors.[145] They can also be viewed as creations of 'benevolent' colonisers who came to save the natives from themselves. This is a view shared by others, like William Fisher, who argues that these NGOs, many of them based in the west, are to a large extent puppets of western governments' foreign policy.[146] In that sense the NGOs do not really represent the grassroots/'victims' they purport to represent. NGOs in my view become the moderators of a modernity trend that is geared towards a Eurocentric manner of global governance with its ever-encroaching privatisation of common spheres. And in this context, it is useful to view NGOs from a business model perspective because, as businesses, they exist for the sake of their own perpetuation. However, Esteva encourages a new wave of thinking that challenges this uniformity of thought to a return to truly revolutionary 'commons'[147] which would mean accepting other modes of thinking and in my view including southern legal systems in international spheres.

Revolution Anyone?

We see above that the ICC/ICL is the stronger arm of the IEL which has led to the dominance of neo-liberalism globally. This means that the IEL/ICL alliance is naturally anti-revolution. In this section, I will explore whether, due to these neo-liberalist foundations, the emerging industrial complex is keen to strangle local revolutionary actions using the Rome Statute. Earlier, in Chapter 2, I argued that the ICC's interventions in Africa are the cosmopolitan's imposition on others of its perceived world view, particularly in relation to who wages war. I have also argued above that the marriage between the ICL and IEL means that the ICC could be interpreted as the neo-liberal way of sanitising spaces for exploitation in which peace enables MNEs to exploit. In this future-shaping sphere, the Rome Statute, and the ICC's judgments in subsequent cases from Africa mean that the ICC is a tool that is used to maintain the *status quo* in localised politics and should be viewed as anti-revolutionary in that respect. I argue this because in some instances, revolution could be necessary as it was in ending settler colonialism in Ireland,[148] Kenya, Algeria,[149] Cuba,[150] and Zimbabwe[151] to name just a few cases.

The Rome Statute is silent on revolution. However, its operationalisation betrays the anti-revolutionary nature of the statute which is advanced through court judgements. For example the court has ruled that non-state actors are now subject to the Rome Statute, as seen in the *Lubanga*[152] case and other cases, particularly those emanating from Eastern Congo where we see the prevalence of non-state actors being tried at the ICC.[153] My point here is that all revolutionary groups are non-state actors and therefore the prevalence of non-state actors in this legal sphere brings with it the question of: what is the role of the ICC in situations involving a people's revolution? I explore below the implications of its jurisdiction on future revolutions by using two recent examples to discuss my point.

In the first example, Thomas Lubanga Dyilo the leader of *Union des Patriotes Congolais (UPC)* and its military arm the *Forces patriotiques pour la libération du Congo (FPLC)* was found guilty under Article 8(2)(e)(vii) of the Rome Statute for co-perpetrating the crimes of enlisting and conscripting child soldiers and using them to participate actively in hostilities.[154] To place the ensuing discourse in context, it is important to note that it is the Congolese government that requested Lubanga's indictment by the ICC.[155] Note also that the conflict litigated in the Lubanga case involved various local groups as well as foreign countries, including Uganda.[156] It is also an important point that after being convicted at the Hague, Mr. Lubanga, who is now free, went to prison in the DRC, indicating that his country has always had some CJS capacity.[157] It is therefore not clear from the literature reviewed why, despite the many cases emanating from Congo, the ICC has not so far worked with the DRC government to set up local tribunals or support efforts towards a lasting solution to Eastern Congo conflict(s). This leaves one to conclude that the Congo DRC government conveniently uses the ICC to manage its everlasting eastern 'problem.' The regular referral to the ICC by the DRC government needs to be interrogated through this prism because it is wrong in my view for the 'international' community to assume that the central government in Kinshasa represents the interests of *Ituri* citizens as opposed to the Kinshasa elite or MNEs' mining interests in the region.[158] It is also problematic to assume that Lubanga's stated liberation was not geared towards eliminating the well documented exploitation of the region by MNEs for minerals.[159] In this instance we see the state enlisting the ICC to help deal with a political nemesis.

The second example is the dispute between the Israeli state and the ICC which ended with the ICC ruling on 5 February 2021 that the Court has territorial jurisdiction in the territories occupied by Israel since 1967, namely Gaza and the West Bank, including East Jerusalem.[160] This ruling followed the decision on 20 December 2019 by the ICC Prosecutor that following a preliminary examination of the situation in Palestine, all the statutory criteria under the Rome Statute for the opening of an investigation had been met.[161] Consequently and after the objection by the Israeli government, the OTP on 22 January 2020, under Article 19(3) of the Rome Statute, requested the Chamber to make a determination on the scope of the Court's territorial jurisdiction in the situation in the State of Palestine.[162] It is important to detail briefly why this ruling is problematic from a resistance[163] point of view, especially in relation to equating resistance force with occupier's force. The trigger for this ICC decision was a number of incidents surrounding Israel's military activities, including over 2,360 air strikes in the occupied territories after 27 December 2008,[164] killing 1,300 Palestinians and wounding more than 5,000, a third of them children.[165] According to the Israeli government's own reports, the retaliatory attacks by Hamas and other groups consisted of 617 rockets and 178 mortar shells fired into Israel, killing 3 and wounding 182, with nine Israeli soldiers killed inside the Gaza Strip.[166] Following allegations of violations of international law from many complainants, a United Nations Fact Finding Mission on the Gaza Conflict was appointed by the Human Rights Council[167] which reported in September 2009.[168] The Goldstone Report said that both the Israeli military and Palestinian armed groups had violated international humanitarian law by indiscriminately and intentionally targeting civilians.[169] Some of the critical findings against Israel included that the conduct of the Israeli armed forces constituted grave breaches of the Fourth Geneva Convention in respect of wilful killings and wilfully causing great suffering to protected persons and as such gave rise to individual criminal responsibility.[170] It also found that the direct targeting and arbitrary killing of Palestinian civilians was a violation of the right to life.[171] In addition, the arbitrary deprivation of liberty and violation of due process rights, the cases of the detained Palestinian civilians including continuous and systematic abuse, outrages on personal dignity, and humiliating and degrading treatment were contrary to fundamental principles of international humanitarian law.[172] This treatment of civilians constituted the infliction of a collective penalty and amounted to measures of intimidation and terror which breached the Geneva Conventions and constituted a war crime.[173] Regarding Palestinian armed groups, including Hamas, the report found that their expressed intentions to target civilians as reprisals for the fatalities of civilians in Gaza as a result of Israeli military operations, were also contrary to international humanitarian law.[174]

Equating the actions of Hamas with those of the Israeli state is problematic on many fronts but first because one party is fighting against occupation and the other fighting to maintain it. A more significant problem relates to 'fire power' and damage caused by each party to the other's territory. It is for example not possible that Hamas and other Palestinian groups' activities of December 2008 met any war crimes threshold as defined by the Rome Statute. It is debatable too whether the Israeli state actions on that day met the threshold either.[175] If armed struggle is 'prohibited' though the ICC intervention and by conflating the occupier and the freedom fighter, it is my view that the ICC had questioned the Palestinians right to self-determination and was conflict with earlier UN resolutions.[176]

Therefore, despite the recent decision being celebrated as a path towards justice, it is ridden with the complexities I explain above because the ICC would at least in theory have to interrogate both Israel and Palestinian groups on an equal footing. It is even more concerning that, due to Israel's refusal to cooperate, this in practice would mean that the ICC would only be able to investigate actions by Palestinian groups. What is pertinent to my argument here are the submissions made by the Israeli government in these proceedings. The Israeli government's main argument was that the occupied territories are not a 'state' in the meaning of the Rome Statute and therefore the preconditions for the Court's jurisdiction are not met.[177] This argument obviously did not sway the pre-trial chamber to see the world through the Israeli state's perspective because the state wanted to essentially create a vast 'dark' site where no ICL could intervene, particularly because occupied Palestinian territories remain disputed. However, the law once again finds itself in an entanglement of how to distinguish 'good' and 'bad' violence?

Two main issues arise in these two situations. In *Lubanga*, we see the Congolese state using the Rome Statute to potentially crush a revolutionary movement in the Eastern Congo, while in the Israeli-Palestinian case we see the Israeli state not recognising the Rome Statute as it relates to the occupied territories. Second, they both raise a more pertinent issue of equating state violence with revolutionary violence by oppressed groups who may feel the need to take up arms for their own liberation and self-determination. For this reason, the ICC and other international tribunals are not the best suited forum for 'trying' revolutions. This is because, as I have consistently argued in this discourse, ICL interventions prevent local solutions and may in fact not address the real 'crimes' local people are worried about. The most important trial in this respect in my view is, for example, not *Lubanga* and others at the ICC but *International Rights Advocates v. Apple, Microsoft, et al.*[178] brought before a court in the USA, not by the Congolese government, but by local people against MNEs extracting and exploiting their resources. This case is particularly important for our discourse not only because it targets the MNEs who extract resources in conflict zones but more crucially because local people are at the forefront of the action.

Frédéric Mégret concludes that international bodies like the ICJ/ICC are not the best forums for preventing genocide but that having solidarity with grassroot acts of resistance is the key.[179] I say here that local people may have a different view of what crimes/genocides are happening locally because in criticising the international attitudes to the Rohingya atrocities, local activists have noted the lack of support for their long struggles – armed and otherwise against state oppression.[180] They argue that "Instead of treating the Rohingya like helpless lambs to be saved, the task of solidarity is to fight back against the multiplicity of forces upholding the butcher's knife."[181] This view is particularly poignant in relation to situations like Congo where the prominent iconography of the African woman victim is the fodder at the ICC.

This iconography denies her agency, as explained by Ratna Kapur,[182] and breeds an industry around her suffering – hence my argument that ICC is germinating neo-enslavement. This representation of the African woman suppresses the African woman as revolutionary and as a freedom fighting icon, the Wangari Maathais, Mandikezela Madelas of the continent. In Kenya for example, women like my grandmother were shoulder to shoulder with their brothers in the anti-colonial struggles.[183] Women's role in anticolonial struggles in Africa, particularly in South Africa, Kenya, and Nigeria are well documented.[184] In Eastern Nigeria for example, women were the first to start armed revolution against the colonial government.[185] The women organised locally against colonialism including taxation and the behaviour of local colonial warrant chiefs.[186] Their uprising was met with brutal repression by the colonial administration, leading to many deaths amongst the women.[187] However, they succeeded in having the taxation of women stopped and some of the chiefs removed and are viewed by many as the pioneers of Nigeria's liberation movement.[188]

In Kenya, the agitation against colonialism started way before the *Mau Mau* revolution. In fact, Mekatilili wa Menza, a formidable woman, led one of earliest recorded revolts against colonial government in 1913.[189] One could also hypothesise that by challenging their men to rise and fight colonialism, Agikuyu women ignited the *Mau Mau* revolution. This is because in the early 1920s women had already started to organise against the settler government.[190] For example, when Africans heard of the arrest of Harry Thuku, a trade unionist and anti-colonial activist, they gathered at Nairobi's central police station led by a woman, Mary Nyanjiru where they demonstrated and agitated for Thuku's release.[191] Colonial police opened fire, killing many demonstrators according to local people – but about 20 demonstrators according to the police – and Mary Nyanjiru was amongst those killed.[192] The events of that day, like all revolutionary mythology, vary in degrees of dramatisation. One enduring telling of the event is that when Nyanjiru saw that the men were afraid of confronting the colonial police, she admonished them and asked them to wear her dress and give her their trousers![193] Till the end of settler colonialism, the Agikuyu women remained active in the anti-colonial movement and organised themselves around their own political group, Mumbi Central Association (MCA).[194] Like their sisters in Eastern Nigeria described above, it is important to note that MCA not only fought for liberation, but also for economic rights and was for example strongly opposed to women being forced to work in colonial coffee plantations.[195]

I would not hesitate to hypothesise that the reason Kenya became a neo-liberal hell/heaven is the absence of these women in the emerging power structures. While Kenyatta and fellow loyalists were 'detained' and later released as heroes of independence, unknown numbers of 'radical' women (official figures say hundreds) languished in inhumane detention centres from 1952 to 1960.[196] But here I celebrate those women, some of them my grandmother's friends who were never to return to their families. The fighting spirit(s) of Nyanjiru was/were later to inspire other women in Kenya and in February 1992, a group of mothers, later joined by Wangari Maathai brought Nairobi to a standstill when they stripped naked in protest.[197] They were demanding the release of their sons who had been detained by the Moi dictatorship.[198] As with the colonial police before, these women were met with brutal police force[199] but, although not on that day, their sons were eventually released.[200] These women became part of the increasing clamour for democracy which led to the end of Moi's dictatorship.[201]

In its silence on revolutions and in equating revolutionary violence to state violence, I see the ICC and ICL/IEL hegemony as the bourgeois culture and science maintaining their neo-liberalist hubris and hoping, against hope that revolutions will not disrupt their debauchery. In this respect then, is there a justification for violence against the prevailing racist and exploitative international order represented by the ICC and others? I would argue the affirmative, following in the footsteps of others like Georges Sorel[202] and Frantz Fanon.[203] The form of violence advocated here is not the equivalent of the Iraq war, or the Syrian or Libyan wars, which were Eurocentric violence to defeat the armed forces of a state in fixed battle. It is violence that prevents governments from consolidating power through exploitative and racist policies such as we see in Israel and Burma. The ICC, I argue, is used in both Lubanga and the Israel/Palestinian situation to stymie revolutionary awakening by a ruling class willing to use international bodies to maintain their hold on power, with the support of their 'financiers,' to ensure that their interests and those of their masters are not disrupted by revolutions.

International law does however allow violence by white men, in the now much discredited right to intervene/protect regime as we saw in Kosovo, Iraq, and Libya.[204] I mean here that no western state or individual has been held legally accountable for example for the war in Iraq. This form of interventionist violence seems to be in line with a much more conflicted (non) acceptance of violence in Arendt's model where violence is instrumental in nature and,

> is rational to the extent that it is effective in reaching the end that must justify it. And since when we act we never know with any certainty the eventual consequences of what we are doing, violence can remain rational only if it pursues short term goals.[205]

Even in this use of violence, its legitimacy is questionable because its justification loses plausibility the further its intended end recedes into the future.[206] This manner of viewing violence has no room for revolutions as it sees no space for violence in shaping politics or indeed in helping birth new political thought(s). In this sense, Arendt sees revolutions as problematic and, wrongly in my view, as glorifying violence for its own sake because revolutionary violence is arguably no longer political but antipolitical.[207] I would however counter-argue that use of violence to persuade the end of foreign owned capitalist hegemony in Cuba and as a means towards a just/commons led economy did not result in the dystopian perpetual violence of the kind predicted by Arendt, who seemed to suggest that use of violence for political goals leads to these same goals being overwhelmed by the violence which then creates conditions giving rise to new violent ends.[208]

There are obvious contradictions in Arendt's musings on violence and revolution of which others have written more eloquently than can be managed in the space available here.[209] It is however not my intention to endorse her views but those of other thinkers like Fanon and Sorel, who see the necessity of revolutionary violence in obvious instances of oppression. Sorel for example wrote that,

> proletarian violence, carried on as a pure and simple manifestation of the sentiment of class struggle, appears as a very fine and heroic thing; it is at the service of the immemorial interests of civilization...While it is not perhaps the most appropriate method of obtaining immediate material advantages, it may save the world from barbarism.[210]

This kind of violence finds its legitimacy not in state sanctioned law such as Rome Statutes or UN declarations, but in proletarian revolutionary consciousness. Violence in this sense is not used for its own sake, as practised by a Eurocentric state army say in Iraq or Libya, but for a more just future; not to dominate others but to provoke and inspire and to *"mark the separation of classes."*[211] I add that the barbarism Sorel talks about is the kind practised by the old colonialism and new colonialism of the ICC kind; the corrupting, indecent entanglement between zombie old bourgeois and the animated/emerging bourgeois in the global south. When violence is applied here, it is in a preventative and healing sense to borrow medical terms; it cleanses the proletariat/emerging bourgeoisie of their afflictions of neo-liberalist sin and destroys any lingering colonial tendencies.

Sorel's musings on revolution remind me of my maternal grandmother's stories of her exploits during the *Mau Mau* revolution. As one of the many women who took arms against the colonial settler government, she told of their struggles and exploits with pride and nostalgia, comrades' deaths remembered and celebrated, slaughter by the British condemned. My grandmother narrated these stories in the form of Sorel's myths and glorification.[212] In my grandmother's narrations, *Mau Mau* glorious victories were passed on by word of mouth and spread like a 'bush fire' amongst the peasants who took inspiration that it was possible to destroy settler colonialism. This theatrical telling of the revolution continues to inspire a generation of us, the children of *Mau Mau*, as it did back in the 1950s when the *Gikuyu* peasant could imagine, orientate, and motivate herself in a historic struggle with the colonialists. This seems to be what Sorel had in mind when he wrote that "the energy this myth generated would in turn feed the real moment of tactical force, the proletarian strike which dealt the final crippling blow to the bourgeois order, killing capitalist society and its state apparatus in a single moment."[213] I feel it appropriate to use my grandmother's telling of the *Mau Mau* revolution here both in her memory but also because from Kenya to Cuba, Algeria, Zimbabwe and to Ireland, revolutions acted as a future deterrent, a warning to colonisers that there is the possibility it can be re-enacted, while at the same time it feeds our sense of history.[214] This then is the territory Fanon's ideas in *The Wretched of the Earth* occupy as violence in Fanon's sense is the only antidote to the crushing of the subject's agency by the unmediated violence of colonialism.[215] Violence, according to this approach, is not primarily to defeat the colonial army but instead, "it is a function of its therapeutic promise as the participation of empire's victims in counter-violence helps them to claim back their dignity and to heal the psychological wounds inflicted by the settlers."[216]

I would argue that one sees the similarities with Arendt entangled engagement in Benjamin's 'Critique.' Both seem to want a revolution with no violence. Both philosophers, I argue, provide a particularly good analogy of the current ICL/ICC regime and their TWAIL critics who seek to unsuccessfully end a violent past by trying to at least not soil it with the old tendencies of law to be violent.[217] To explore Benjamin's 'Critique' in this one paragraph would be an impossible task, but the simplest explanation is that he gets himself bogged down in a quagmire of word play as he tries to distinguish 'law-making violence' and 'law-preserving' violence.[218] But I think he simply meant that revolutions bring an end to old legal order(s) and help create new legal order and that once the new order is in place, a healthy dose of violence may be necessary to maintain it.

Were both Arendt and Benjamin living today in our shiny neo-liberal reality, they would be engaged in a futile dialogue with phantoms because international or indeed state law is no longer made solely by the state actors, as ghost MNEs (NGOs at the ICC) often capture law making through 'lobbying' (corruption).[219] In my view corruption emanates from the lack of democratic accountability as most lobbyists, but not all, represent businesses and other parties who are not voted for by the people. In the contemporary global space(s) governed by shadowy agents, there is no hope of ending the inheritance of violence of the type these two thinkers were contemplating because it becomes increasingly difficult to identify who is the real fire starter in many situations like the ones litigated at the ICC. As a grandchild of *Mau Mau* revolutionaries, I take heart in the fact that Benjamin seemed to countenance the idea of a revolutionary violence that is 'pure' where the past is gone and the 'new' is guilt free.[220] Although his religious analogies are problematic for me, they suggest that it may be impossible to have new beginnings without shedding some blood.[221] We, the children of *Mau Mau*, however, bear witness that this shedding of blood may not herald a new beginning but just mark the end of the old.[222] What follows is the *never never* land where new possibilities arise, but one cannot celebrate those possibilities due to the ever present neo-colonial zombie(s).

> *I'm here to evoke the spirit of the one who put the country first, above her own personal safety ... She confronted gun-carrying white men who were sworn killers ... Here, she lived in constant naked contact with danger, prepared to lose her life, even the life of her own children ...*
>
> *You fought for what you believed was right, possessed only by your love for our people and the restoration of their dignity ...*
>
> *... Equally big Mama, some of those who sold you to the regime are here! They are crying louder than all of us who cared for You ... Mma you never told me how to treat them when they get here. I am waiting for a signal mama.*
>
> *Mama Nomzamo, all those who said they could not associate with a 'criminal', they are here! Some of them have played prominent roles in your funeral ... Mma, I'm waiting for a signal on how we should treat them ...*
>
> *... We see you in your beautiful suits, betrayers! SELL OUTS! We see you.*[223]

Trouble in Paradise? Kenya and the Birth of an ICL Crisis

What happens to a dream deferred?
Does it dry up
like a raisin in the sun?
Or fester like a sore—
And then run?
Does it stink like rotten meat?
Or crust and sugar over—
like a syrupy sweet?

Maybe it just sags
like a heavy load

Or does it explode?[224]

In my view, there was no better colonial site to birth a crisis of the ICL than Kenya. I use Kenya here for the sole reason that, as an author of Kenyan heritage, I have familiarity with the setting but, as explained earlier, Kenya and Cote d'Ivoire are similar in relation to our ICL/ICC discourse, because in my view they have a remarkably similar post-colonial trajectory. Both countries achieved some semblance of 'progress' after a black elite took power from the colonial officers until the explosion of violence in both countries from the 1990s and the subsequent theatrics at the Hague.[225]

From the pristine white sand beaches, the yearly migration of wild beasts, to the ever smiling and obliging native, Kenya excites the average colonialist like no other space. Drunk with empire nostalgia and inspired by scenes from the white mischief,[226] the European experiences a truly transformative psychosis of the bi-polar kind when engaging with Kenya. The coloniser sees the country as an empty paradise for their taking as described by Karen Blixen,[227] and this empty paradise needs preservation as described by Kuki Gallmann.[228] It is however at the same time a violent dystopia of the Joseph Conrad[229] kind and is depicted as such in films like *The Ghost and the Darkness.*[230] This unhealthy romance makes Kenya a heaven for a myriad of invaders including foreign military, UN bodies, large MNEs, NGOs, and conservationists who see Kenya as an ideal base for their African shenanigans, including and very significantly for our discourse, testing products on the local populations as fictionalised by John le Carre in *The Constant Gardener.*[231] It is this colonial space that the ICC occupies in my view, in concert with the other foreign actors based in Kenya.

The ICC's conflicted 'colonial' attitude towards the country begins with the initial visit by the prosecutor to Kenya. Because the country was in a crisis and people needed saving, the prosecutor spent two days in Nairobi where he had breakfast at the aptly named 'Windsor' hotel, met with the UN officials and political leadership, went for a game drive at the Nairobi National Park, but did not meet any of the victims.[232] In line with the argument of the ICC as a colonial set-up, I argue that the involvement of the ICC to deal with the 2007/2008 post-election violence helped only to rewrite a history where the coloniser again becomes the saviour. Meanwhile colonial atrocities by the British settler government in Kenya remain unpunished and on-going. The eventual collapse of the ICC cases also means the stated aim to end impunity failed and more importantly, as this book shows, the focus on individuals meant that grass roots criminals who committed the actual murders went unpunished.

However, to concentrate the reader's mind on the overall post-colonial discourse, it is necessary at this moment to dispel the widely held view that the violence had its foundations 'solely' in the land distribution that followed Kenya's *madaraka*. Human Rights Watch got it right only when they reported that European settlers confiscated the most fertile agricultural lands, without asking, without permission, and without paying for it.[233] However, HRW got it totally wrong when they speculated that political violence can be traced to this land distribution because instead of land being returned to its original owners, Jomo Kenyatta (the father of President Uhuru Kenyatta) sold it to the highest bidder, mostly his own *Gikuyu* ethnic group.[234] This narrative is sensational and not based on evidence because post-independence land redistribution did not favour the *Gikuyu* public but mostly favoured a small group of colonial government loyalists, white settlers and Kenyatta's friends and not the wider *Gikuyu* community who did not bid for the land.[235] In addition, only limited land was involved in this 'redistribution' as most of the land remained in government's hands as trust land while some settlers retained their vast ranches.[236] Others, like Southall, support this view that this and subsequent land grabbing by the elites led to the latest conflicts.[237] The narrative of land being the cause of the violence is wrong and selective at best because the fact is that widespread political violence was largely unheard of in Kenya until after 1990 when the then president, Arap Moi, instigated inter-ethnic violence in parts of Rift Valley to counter political challenges he was facing from the pro-democracy agitators who were led by prominent Kikuyu politicians,[238] although the prodemocracy movement was itself nationwide.[239] The narrative is wrong in fact because no land was confiscated form the 'evicted' groups and attacks include landless individuals who happened to work in the affected areas including in the informal settlements in Nairobi.[240] The issue of land becomes a convenient 'reason' given by the elite to cover their political machinations, using their ethnic base to gain political leadership.

It is important that this narrative is debunked because it propagates the myth that land ownership after 'independence' in Kenya, South Africa, Zimbabwe, Namibia, Cote d'Ivoire, and other ex-colonies is the 'main' cause of conflict. This toxic narrative is used to show that the coloniser was right that the native cannot be trusted with land ownership. In my view, this narrative is particularly poignant because to begin with, in Kenya, South Africa, Namibia, and Zimbabwe for example, land was not redistributed to the masses after 'independence' and hence the African has not been trusted with his/her/their ancestral land since colonialism. Second, this explanation absolves the ex-colonial states of their responsibilities for the post- 'independence' violence in countries they left in a hurry, including, as I have discussed later in Chapter 4, of their direct interference in these 'new' states. Most of the literature on the events leading to the ICC involvement in Kenya conveniently ignore local elites and western political machinations in Kenya, Congo, and Cote d'Ivoire leading to their respective cases at the ICC as we see explained elsewhere in this book.[241]

Most significantly though, the narrative ignores the effects of the overall economic model adopted by the newly 'independent' Kenyan state. For the purposes of our 'testing' theory, few if any of the literature reviewed has explored the role Kenya (like Chile) played in testing the neo-liberal economics which were later to dominate the world economy. With the help of the American government the Kenyan government adopted neo-liberal, macro-economic policies from 1965, designed to consist of a private, a public, and a cooperatives sector.[242] Until the end of the 1970s these policies led to often-celebrated rapid economic growth and political stability in the country. The reality however is far more disturbing and I suggest these policies laid down the foundations for the conflict litigated later at the ICC because they resulted in a massively unequal society. National wealth remains concentrated in very few hands and there is unbalanced regional growth because, amongst other things, the policies divided the nation into compartments of high potential and low potential areas.[243]

The division into high potential and low potential was part of a simplistic approach in which areas with, for example, agricultural potential received more government support while those with low potential were largely abandoned. This meant that infrastructure and industries were in the high potential areas where agricultural development with its new core of emerging black farmers received strong state support.[244] However these neo-liberalist policies did not go unopposed and the main critique came from Jaramogi Oginga Odinga who censured Kenyatta for ignoring people like my grandmother who formed the core of the *Mau Mau* revolution.[245] Kenyatta's attitudes towards freedom fighters tellingly revealed the direction the post-colonial state would take soon after independence because both politics and the economy were to become increasingly elitist and Eurocentric. For his sins, Odinga was removed from government and later detained by Jomo Kenyatta but he remained a critic of the capitalist state to his death. We can then fast-forward to 2007 and his son Raila Odinga's claim that his election victory was 'stolen' which led to the violence later litigated at the ICC.[246]

It is also important to note that many settlers retained their usually vast tracks of land in Kenya because, as is the case in South Africa and Zimbabwe, the willing buyer/seller policies only benefited the already established local elite and European settlers who had attained citizenship of the 'new' states and were able to access financing from the same fund set up to purchase land for redistribution to local populations.[247] In a twisted story of recolonisation, settlers were then able to eject local people as squatters from their vast land tracts.[248] It is therefore problematic to suggest that the violence was mostly due to land ownership and ethnicity, as the commission formed to investigate the violence claimed,[249] because this narrative ignores the inherent violence of a capitalist economy as well as neo-liberalism's capacity to stoke the political turbulence in which it thrives.

Having put the post-election violence in context, it is important however to note that initially, African governments seemed to welcome the ICC in dealing with conflicts in the continent, starting with Joseph Kony's case in 2003.[250] However, the ICC fall out with Africa began in 2008 when the prosecutor applied for a warrant of arrest for Sudan's President Omar Al-Bashir.[251] Subsequently, Al-Bashir travelled to several African states, including Kenya and South Africa, which refused to arrest him as mandated by the Rome Statute.[252] To maintain my focus on the Kenyan situation, and in order not to digress, I will not engage with the literature or the legalities of the Sudan case as I mention it here for contextual purposes only. I have not identified any literature to show there was a conflict between African states and the ICC prior to the Al-Bashir case.

After Sudan, the other high-profile case that led to the ICC/Africa conflict involved the Kenyan president, Uhuru Kenyatta, and his deputy, William Ruto. The ICC intervened in Kenya from late 2009 when the government failed to set up a mechanism to investigate and try perpetrators of the 2007–2008 post-election violence. The disputing parties agreed to establish a commission[253] that recommended setting up a local tribunal to prosecute violence perpetrators.[254] Kenya's parliament failed to do this and the former UN Secretary General Kofi Annan, who led the mediation process, submitted information containing the names of the main suspects to the ICC in July 2009.[255] It is notable that the list did not include the main protagonists in that election, Mr. Odinga and his opponent, President Mwai Kibaki, and neither has ever been asked to account for their role in that violence. This is even though the ICC, through the Office of the Prosecutor, was monitoring the situation from the beginning of the violence, as Kenya was a signatory to the Rome Statute.[256]

When the Kenyan government failed to set up mechanisms to investigate and try perpetrators of the 2007–2008 post-election violence, the ICC prosecutor announced that he would prosecute six Kenyans, including president Kenyatta and his deputy.[257] The Kenyan government unsuccessfully challenged the admissibility of the cases before the ICC because they argued that local accountability processes had been initiated and therefore the ICC intervention violated the Rome Statute's complementarity principle.[258] The court rejected this argument because Kenya failed to provide evidence showing that this domestic process was happening.[259] This decision was wrong in law in my view because the statute does not give 'timescales' within which local processes should start, but speaks generally of willingness and capacity to prosecute crimes.[260] Finally, the case against Kenyatta collapsed and according to the OTP, the cases collapsed after the Kenyan state refused to cooperate in gathering further evidence and after various OTP witnesses recanted their evidence or failed to appear.[261] However, the court records tell a different story as the judges had already directed the OTP to withdraw or alternatively show that it had met the evidential threshold to justify proceeding to trial.[262]

The fall out that followed both the Sudan and the Kenyan situations led to Burundi and South Africa starting the process to withdraw from the ICC[263] and the AU passing a non-binding resolution for all member states to withdraw from the Rome Statute.[264] I argue that this conflict is because of the 'colonial' relationship between African states and the ICC. This colonial relationship in my view translated into the poor evidential bases for these cases to be brought to trial. There is ample literature attesting to the 'prosecutor without a supervisor,' meaning that the ICC overwhelmingly relies on poor quality evidence despite the pre-trial chamber having oversight of the evidence provided.[265] In the Kenyan cases for example, Judge Christine Van den Wyngaert reprimanded the prosecutor for poor investigation of the president's case.[266] There were grave problems in how evidence was reviewed by the OTP as well as lack of proper oversight.[267] Lack of proper evidence was also a central feature in the *Gbagbo* case with the court raising serious concerns about the evidence provided by the OTP[268] and subsequently acquitting him for lack of evidence.[269] The court is also criticised for lack of local knowledge and use of intermediaries as investigators.[270] However, regarding poor evidence collection and management, the ICC is not alone as other international tribunals have not fared much better. For example, the special tribunal established to prosecute former Khmer Rouge in Cambodia has been plagued by internal strife and government hostility, achieving only one conviction in seven years.[271]

It is my argument that the Kenyan cases collapsed mainly due to this poor evidence gathering and analysis of evidence, despite the prosecutor presenting the failure as largely due to the Kenyan government's failure to cooperate.[272] Moreno-Ocampo the then ICC prosecutor, admitted that the evidence against Kenyatta was not as strong as he would have liked, "but all he had to do for the moment was get through the pretrial hearings. After that, more evidence could be found."[273] Significantly, Ocampo admitted that a militia leader who was instrumental in the violence had admitted his role in the violence but was not charged as he was willing to give evidence against Kenyatta.[274] Should this militia leader not have been on trial as a non-state actor as well? I suggest this manner of witness handling not only led to the cases collapsing but also shows the blasé colonial officer attitude towards the 'black body.' Working with a militia leader who was key to the violence is in my view a good example of OTP's careless witness handling which could have put some of his witnesses at risk. How sure was the OTP that the militia leader was not reporting to a different party? This is significant because literature suggests that many militia members were 'disappeared' in an apparent clean-up operation.[275] Although the case hinged on these witnesses the OTP itself worried about their reliability and Kenyatta's attorney claimed in court that some witnesses tried to extort him in exchange for evidence that could aid the defence.[276]

This poor handling of witnesses in an overly sensitive case seems to have continued even after the cases had collapsed, as shown by Ocampo naming his "protected" witnesses.[277] This led those who worked with the ICC to lose trust in it; "They put a lot of people at risk, living as I do here, the best thing is to keep off someone like Ocampo."[278] It is however in court where glaring gaps in evidence handling and examination were noticeable. The accused Kenyans retained well prepared advocates from reputable London chambers while the prosecutor rather bizarrely decided to cross-examine President Kenyatta himself.[279] Watching the televised proceedings, any average criminal law practitioner would have noticed the prosecutor's poor case preparation or indeed poor prosecutorial skills. I was particularly baffled by Mr. Ocampo's line of questioning when he questioned Mr. Kenyatta about his 'patrimony' which had no relation to matters at hand in a status hearing – which is a mere timetabling formality.[280] Mr. Ocampo's preparations were scant and he refused to delegate to better prepared colleagues.[281] When asked how long it took him to learn about the militia who were the focus of his case, Ocampo replied: "Me? Two hours."[282] Mr. Verini notes that Ocampo's staff were worried but knew protest was pointless.[283] The quality of the prosecution's case and professionalism is in my view a crucial part of ensuring that the accused's right to a fair trial and due process is guaranteed and the victims are not let down by no one being held to account. This poor case handling led to the successful appeal in *Bemba* and was relied on for a claim of damages in *The Prosecutor v. Jean-Pierre Bemba Gombo*. Although this claim for damages was unsuccessful, it is prudent to note that OTP/Trial Chamber failures listed by the claimants include, most worryingly, bribing/paying of witnesses by the OTP, which was a claim made in the Kenyan cases as well.[284] Mr. Ocampo perhaps understood the performance value of his role during the trial and the unacknowledged associated fact that the hearings were less about 'justice' than that performance of power in relation to his black accused.

> *The ICC has been reduced into a painfully farcical pantomime,*
> *a travesty that adds insult to the injury of victims.*
> *It stopped being the home of justice*
> *the day it became the toy of declining imperial powers.*[285]

My argument is that the OTP's attitude towards the accused and the judicial process generally is typical of colonial attitudes but also of how the law deals not only with Africa, but with the black body generally. Albert Bandura for example explains that we get our behaviour from social learning and conditioning in our environment.[286] The non-African prosecutor in this regard acted towards the black accused as he had been trained and conditioned. By non-African, I mean the prosecutor who was obviously a white man and used a Eurocentric legal theory and practice in a Eurocentric institution. This attitude I argue was well represented by the person of the prosecutor in the Kenyan cases as detailed but it also raises a more fundamental obstacle in 'reforming' the ICC. This is because to decolonise the interaction between the ICC and Africa as this book suggests will require all actors in the ICL industrial complex to accept the arguments made here that the ICC draws its structural and jurisdictional inspirations from slavery and colonialism.[287] This means a decolonising of minds at all levels as suggested by Ngugi wa Thiong'o[288] because only then would the prosecutor understand that his actions were only reproducing how a typical colonial officer would have behaved towards an accused African. This is because in looking at, for example, Ocampo's cavalier attitudes in the Kenyan cases, one must consider his 'perspective' as it relates to the genealogy of knowledge with the ICC and the OTP representing the 'truth' and 'knowledge' as known and developed by the Europeans. According to Foucault, what appears to be rational, scientifically sound, and necessary truths are in fact products of historical and social forces as well as a commitment to ethical and political values.[289]

Conclusions

In interrogating the truth as it is presented to us, the critical approach used in this chapter, and indeed in the whole book, has meant questioning traditional (colonial) assumptions about truth and disrupting the deeply held conviction of fixity as an absolute congruence, as Derrida articulated.[290] These colonial attitudes need challenging. However, I am aware of the risks associated with this approach because scholars who have engaged with critique of the ICL say that the apparent successes of the ICTY, in the Charles Taylor case, and in several referrals to the ICC have made critique largely unpopular, prompting suspicion that critique equals endorsing atrocities.[291] In what I have reviewed so far, that critique of the ICC has been concentrated on the effectiveness or strengthening of structures and not on the thought form and assumptions that inform the ICC's interactions with Africa. This for example is the focus of Lionel Nichols' work, the most comprehensive research done on the Kenyan situation so far, which focused on the effectiveness of the OTP and the notion of positive complementarity in Kenya.[292] Because this is a fast-moving area of law, Nichols' research predates the attempts by African states to withdraw from the Rome Statute and, between the beginning of my research in 2016–2017 and now, several authors have looked at the ICC from a critique perspective and Kamari Clarke notably uses a similar approach of advocating for an African centred solution to conflicts in Africa.[293]

My aim in this chapter was to offer an explanation for an often-quoted contradiction that, despite the AU wanting to distance itself from the ICC, it forms the largest signatory block to the Rome Statute. The main reason behind this questioning has been the tendency by authors in this field to separate IEL from ICL and not to consider that they work hand in hand. I have therefore explained that this short lived African romance with the ICC was mainly due to the prevailing neo-liberalist orthodoxy in the 2000s which was geared towards more 'internationalisation' and opening of the continent for foreign investments in the push to become 'developed.' Amongst other things, African states were to democratise and standardise their laws, including signing up to international human rights treaties such as the Rome Statute.

Using examples from Eastern Congo and the Israel/Palestinian conflict, I have linked this signing of the Rome Statute to the debate on whether the Rome Statute allows room for revolutions because with the inequalities bred by the rampant neo-liberalist resource extraction, it may be necessary to remove that hegemony by force. More importantly, ICL's victimhood culture hinders solidarity within local resistance movements and denies African women their rightful place in history as iconic revolutionaries and freedom fighters.

In exploring the link between neo-liberalism and the ICC, I have explored the Kenyan cases both to show an example of how neo-liberalism causes conflicts but also of how colonial attitudes abound in prosecuting these cases. I have also given these cases a wider historical context which is usually lacking when they are presented before tribunals. Putting these cases in a historical context is important in understanding the complexities of the causes of conflicts and hence the necessity for holistic resolutions/peace initiatives which, as I suggest in Chapter 6, should go beyond single individuals. I also use the Kenyan situation to introduce the idea of political iconography that I discuss further below in the Chapter 4.

Notes

1 Alpha Blondy, "*Le Cha-cha-cha du CFA*" *Vision* (Wagram Music 2011).
2 See amongst many, Sam Adelman and Abdul Paliwala (eds), *The Limits of Law and Development: Neoliberalism, Governance and Social Justice* (Routledge 2020); Yong-Shik Lee, *Law and Development: Theory and Practice* (Routledge 2020).
3 See Julio Faundez and Celine Tan (eds), *International Economic Law, Globalization and Developing Countries* (Edward Elgar Publishing 2012); Isabella D. Bunn, *The Right to Development and International Economic Law: Legal and Moral Dimensions* (Hart Publishing 2012); Colin Picker, Isabella D. Bunn and Douglas Arner (eds), *International Economic Law: The State and Future of the Discipline* (Hart Publishing 2008).
4 Lea Schneider, 'The International Criminal Court (ICC) – A Postcolonial Tool for Western States to Control Africa?' (2020) 1 (1) *Journal of International Criminal Law* (JICL) 90–109.
5 Mandiaye Niang, 'Africa and the Legitimacy of the ICC in Question' (2017) 17 *International Criminal Law Review* 615.

6 ICC-01/18-143 Decision on the Prosecution request pursuant to article 19(3) for a ruling on the Court's territorial jurisdiction in Palestine.
7 Walter Mignolo, 'Cosmopolitanism and the De-colonial Option' (2010) 29 *Studies in Philosophy and Education* 111–127.
8 Louis P. Pojman, 'Kant's Perpetual Peace and Cosmopolitanism' (2005) 36 (1) *Journal of Social Philosophy* 62–71, 62.
9 Ibid.
10 Antonio Franceschet, 'Four Cosmopolitan Projects: The International Criminal Court in Context' in Steven C. Roach (ed.), *Governance, Order, and the International Criminal Court: Between Realpolitik and a Cosmopolitan Court* (UOP 2009)180–204.
11 Pojman (note 8) 65.
12 James Herbert Paton, *The Categorical Imperative: A Study in Kant's Moral Philosophy* (Vol. 1023, University of Pennsylvania Press 1971) 135.
13 Jack Mahoney, *The Challenge of Human Rights: Origin, Development, and Significance* (Blackwell Publishing 2007) 179.
14 Charles Covell, *Kant and the Law of Peace* (Macmillan Press 1998) 49.
15 Ibid.
16 Ibid.
17 Ronald Tinnevelt and Thomas Mertens, 'The World State: A Forbidding Nightmare of Tyranny? Habermas on the Institutional Implications of Moral Cosmopolitanism' (2009) 10 (1) *German Law Journal* 63–80 at 63.
18 David Dyzenhaus, *The Unity of Public Law.* (Oxford, Hart Publishing 2004) 431.
19 Robert Fine, 'Kant's Theory of Cosmopolitanism and Hegel's Critique' (2003) 29 (6) *Philosophy & Social Criticism* 609–630.
20 For a defence of Hegel's approach rather than cosmopolitanism see Shlomo Avineri, *Hegel's Theory of the Modern State* (Cambridge University Press 1974) 181, 240.
21 Ibid.
22 See for example Richard Wolin, 'The Idea of Cosmopolitanism: From Kant to the Iraq War and Beyond' (2010) 3 (2) *Ethics & Global Politics* 143–153; Kjartan Koch Mikalsen, 'Kant and Habermas on International Law' (2013) 26 *Ratio Juris* 302; Luigi Caranti (2006) 'Perpetual War for Perpetual Peace? Reflections on the Realist Critique of Kant's Project' (2006) 5 (3) *Journal of Human Rights* 341–353.
23 Carl Schmitt, *The Concept of the Political: Expanded Edition* (University of Chicago Press 2008).
24 Ibid; See also Robert Fine, 'Crimes against Humanity: Hannah Arendt and the Nuremberg Debates' (2000) 3 (3) *European Journal of Social Theory* 293–311; Michael Salter, 'Neo-fascist Legal Theory on Trial: An Interpretation of Carl Schmitt's Defence at Nuremberg from the Perspective of Franz Neumann's Critical Theory of Law' (1999) 5 *Res Publica* 161–194.
25 Costas Douzinas, *The End of Human Rights: Critical Thought at the Turn of the Century* (Bloomsbury Publishing, 2000).
26 Emmanuel Chukwudi Eze, 'The Color of Reason: The Idea of 'Race' in Kant's Anthropology' in Jonathan O. Chimakonam and Edwin E. Etieyibo (eds), *Ka Osi Sọ Onye: African Philosophy in the Postmodern Era* (Vernon Press 2018) 85–122.
27 See for example Heather Roff, *Global Justice, Kant and the Responsibility to Protect: A Provisional Duty* (Routledge 2013); Lyndsey Stonebridge, 'Writing after Nuremberg: The Judicial Imagination in the Age of the Trauma Trial' in

Adam Piette and Mark Rawlinson (eds), *Edinburgh Companion to Twentieth-Century British and American War Literature* (Edinburgh University Press 2012) 101–108.

28 See for example Joseph W. Bendersky, *Carl Schmitt: Theorist for the Reich* (Princeton University Press 1983); Peter C. Caldwell, 'Controversies over Carl Schmitt: A Review of Recent Literature' (2005) 77 (2) *The Journal of Modern History* 357–387.

29 See also Errol A. Henderson, 'Hidden in Plain Sight: Racism in International Relations Theory' in Alexander Anievas Nivi Manchanda and Robbie Shilliam (eds), *Race and Racism in International Relations: Confronting the Global Colour Line* (Routledge 2014) 31–55.

30 Emmanuel Chukwudi Eze, 'The Color of Reason: The Idea of 'Race' in Kant's Anthropology' in Jonathan O. Chimakonam and Edwin E. Etieyibo (eds), *Ka Osi Sọ Onye: African Philosophy in the Postmodern Era* (Vernon Press 2018) 85–122.

31 Ibid., 98.

32 Ibid.

33 Ibid.

34 Ibid., 99.

35 Ibid.

36 Bernard R. Boxil (ed.), *Race and Racism* (Oxford University Press 2001).

37 Ibid., 449–471.

38 Immanuel Eze (note 30) 111.

39 Ibid., 113.

40 Ibid., 111.

41 David Harvey, *A Brief History of Neoliberalism* (Oxford University Press 2005).

42 Ibid., 2.

43 Ibid.

44 ICC, The States Parties to the Rome Statute. https://asp.icc-cpi.int/en_menus/asp/states accessed 6 March 2018.

45 Yuval Shany, *Assessing the Effectiveness of International Courts* (Oxford University Press 2014).

46 Critics of ICL face the risk of being seen as condoning atrocities as discussed by Christine Schwöbel (ed.), *Critical Approaches to International Criminal Law: An Introduction* (Routledge 2014).

47 Susanne D. Mueller, 'Kenya and the International Criminal Court (ICC): Politics, the Election and the Law (2014) 8 (1) *Journal of Eastern African Studies* 25–42.

48 Ibid.

49 Ibid.

50 See more generally Martti Koskenniemi, *The Politics of International Law* (Bloomsbury Publishing 2011); Christian Reus-Smit Thomas Biersteker and Steve Smith (eds), *The Politics of International la Vol. 96* (Cambridge University Press 2004).

51 Steven C. Roach, 'How Political Is the ICC? Pressing Challenges and the Need for Diplomatic Efficacy' (2013) 19 (4) *Global Governance: A Review of Multilateralism and International Organizations* 507–523.

52 I use rule of law here in the Foucauldian sense of law as a technology/tool of ruling/governing/oppressing which, depending on your perspective, is necessary for the smooth functioning of states. Others would similarly look at dictatorships as rule by law. On Moi's dictatorship see Gibson Kamau Kuria, 'Confronting Dictatorship in Kenya' (1991) 2(4) *Journal of Democracy* 115–126.

53 Andrew Moravcsik, 'The Origin of Human Rights Regimes: Democratic Delegation in Post War Europe' (2000) 54 (2) *International Organization* 217–252.

54 Beth A. Simmons and Allison Dammer, 'Credible Commitment and the International Criminal Court' (2010) 64 (2) *International Organization* 225–256.
55 Terrence L. Chapman and Stephen Chaudoin, 'Ratification Patterns and the International Criminal Court' (2013) 57 (2) *International Studies Quarterly* 400–409.
56 Sobral Marcos Felipe Falcão, Ribeiro Ana Regina Bezerra and Soares Gleibson Robert da Luz, 'Concepts and Forms of Greenwashing: A Systematic Review' (2020) 32 (1) *Environmental Sciences Europe* 1–12.
57 Contrary to popular narratives states often get legal counsel before operating torture regimes see Richard B. Bilder and Detlev F. Vagts, 'Speaking Law to Power: Lawyers and Torture' (2004) 98 (4) *The American Journal of International Law* 689–695.
58 See Phillips Coretta and Ben Bowling. 'Racism, Ethnicity, Crime and Criminal Justice' Crime, in Mary E. Vogel (ed.), *Inequality and the State* (Routledge 2020) 377–392.
59 Tom Ginsburg, 'The Clash of Commitments at the International Criminal Court' (2009) 9 (2) *Chicago Journal of International Law* 499–514.
60 Yvonne M. Dutton, 'Commitment to the International Criminal Court: Do States View Strong Enforcement Mechanisms as a Credible Threat?' One Earth Foundation Working Paper (not dated), http://www.oneearthfuture.org/siteadmin/images/files/file_43.pdf/ accessed 10 August 2010.
61 James Vreeland, 'Political Institutions and Human Rights: Why Dictatorships Enter into the United Nation's Convention Against Torture' (2008) 2 (62) *International Organization* 65–10.
62 Mueller (note 47).
63 Ryckman, Kirssa and Cline Ryckman, 'Ratification as Accommodation? Domestic Dissent and Human Rights Treaties (2016) 53 (4) *Journal of Peace Research* 582–596.
64 Christopher A. Sabatini, 'Whom Do International Donors Support in the Name of Civil Society?' (2002) 12 (1) *Development in Practice* 7–19.
65 Thomas Risse, Stephen C. Ropp and Kathryn Sikkink (eds), *The Power of Human Rights: International Norms and Domestic Change* (Cambridge University Press 1999).
66 Ibid., 5.
67 Ibid., 12.
68 See for example Dip Kapoor, 'Colonial Continuities, Neoliberal Hegemony and Adivasi (Original Dweller) Space: Human Rights as Paradox and Equivocation in Contexts of Dispossession in India' in Arnab Das and Subrata Sankar Bagchi (eds), *Human Rights and the Third World: Issues and Discourses* (Lexington Books 2012) 123–141.
69 Julio Faundez, 'Legal Reform in Developing and Transition Countries: Making Haste Slowly' (2000) 1 (1) *Law, Social Justice and Global Development*; Thomas Risse, Stephen C. Ropp and Kathryn Sikkink (eds), *The Power of Human Rights: International Norms and Domestic Change* (Cambridge University Press 1999).
70 Johan Galtung, *Theories of Peace. A Synthetic Approach to Peace Thinking* (International Peace Research Institute Oslo September 1967).
71 Amartya Sen, *Development as Freedom* (Oxford University Press 1999).
72 Stephen Davis, 'Richard Cobden: Ideas and Strategies in Organizing the Free-Trade Movement in Britain' (January 2015), http://oll.libertyfund.org/pages/lm-cobden accessed 10 March 2020.
73 Gustavo Esteva, 'Development' in Wolfgang Sachs (ed.) *The Development Dictionary. A Guide to Knowledge as Power* (2nd ed Zed Books 1992) 1–23.

74 Arturo Escobar, *Encountering Development: The Making and Unmaking of the Third World Vol. 1* (Princeton University Press 2011).
75 Frederick Cooper, 'Modernizing Bureaucrats, Backward Africans, and the Development Concept' in Frederick Cooper and Randall Packard (eds), *International Development and the Social Sciences: Essays on the History and Politics of Knowledge* (University of California Press 1997) 64–92.
76 David Simon, 'Separated by Common Ground? Bringing (Post) Development and (Post) Colonialism Together' (2006)172 (1) *Geographical Journal* 10–21.
77 Gustavo Esteva, 'Development' in Wolfgang Sachs (ed), *The Development Dictionary. A Guide to Knowledge as Power* (2nd ed Zed Books 1992) 1–23.
78 Frederick Cooper, 'Modernizing Bureaucrats, Backward Africans, and the Development Concept' in Frederick Cooper and Randall Packard (eds), *International Development and the Social Sciences: Essays on the History and Politics of Knowledge* (University of California Press 1997) 64.
79 Ibid.
80 Ibid., 65.
81 David Ekbladh, 'Harry S. Truman, Development Aid, and American Foreign Policy' in Raymond H. Geselbracht (ed), *Foreign Aid and the Legacy of Harry S. Truman* (Truman State University Press 2015) 61–72.
82 Andre Gunder Frank, *The Development of Underdevelopment* (New England Free Press 1966).
83 Frederick Lugard, *The Dual Mandate in British Tropical Africa* (W. Blackwood and Sons1922).
84 The origins of the term 'third world' are contested, with some arguing the name gained prominence during the Cold War as a term for nonaligned countries while others disagree. See Leslie Wolf-Phillips, 'Why Third World? Origin, Definition and Usage' (1987) 9 (4) *Third World Quarterly* 1311–1327 and also Joseph L. Love, '"Third World" a Response to Professor Worsley' (1980) 2 (2) *Third World Quarterly* 315–317.
85 Brian Clive Smith, *Understanding Third World Politics; Theories of Political Change and Development* (4th edn Palgrave Macmillan 2013).
86 David Kenneth Fieldhouse, *Economics and Empire 1830 to 1914* (Macmillan 1984).
87 Francois Partant, *La fin du développement: naissance d'une alternative?* (Francois Maspero Paris 1982).
88 Randall Baker, 'Protecting the Environment against the Poor' (1984) 14(2) *The Ecologist* 53–60.
89 Edward Goldsmith and Jerry Mander (eds), *The Case against the Global Economy: And for a Turn Towards Localization* (Routledge 2001).
90 Kates W. Robert, Thomas M. Parris and Anthony A. Leiserowitz, 'What Is Sustainable Development? Goals, Indicators, Values, and Practice' (2005) 47 (3) *Environment: Science and Policy for Sustainable Development* 8–21.
91 Gabriel Zucman, 'Global Wealth Inequality' (2019) 11 *Annual Review of Economics* 109–138.
92 Ibid.
93 Oxfam, Kenya: Extreme Inequality in Numbers, available at https://www.oxfam.org/en/kenya-extreme-inequality-numbers accessed 22 July 2021.
94 Ibid.
95 Kobena T. Hanson Korbla P. Puplampu and Timothy M. Shaw (eds), *From Millennium Development Goals to Sustainable Development Goals: Rethinking African Development* (Routledge 2017); Jeffrey D. Sachs, 'From Millennium Development Goals to Sustainable Development Goals' (2012) 379 (9832) *The Lancet* 2206–2211.

96 Anna Barford, 'Challenging Inequality in Kenya, Mexico and the UK' (2021) 42 (4) *Third World Quarterly* 679–698.
97 John Williamson, 'A Short History of the Washington Consensus' (2009) 15 *Law and Business Review of the Americas* 7.
98 Ibid.
99 Ibid.
100 Ibid.
101 Article 10 Maputo Protocol to the African Charter on Human and People's Rights on the Rights of Women to Peace; see also Fareda Banda, 'Blazing a Trail: The African Protocol on Women's Rights Comes into Force' (2006) 50 *Journal of African Law* 72–84.
102 Johan Galtung, *Theories of Peace A Synthetic Approach to Peace Thinking* (International Peace Research Institute Oslo September 1967).
103 Amartya Sen, *Development as Freedom* (Oxford University Press 1999).
104 Stephen Davis, 'Richard Cobden: Ideas and Strategies in Organizing the Free-Trade Movement in Britain' (January 2015), http://oll.libertyfund.org/pages/lm-cobden accessed 10 March 2020.
105 Chantal Thomas, 'Critical Race Theory and Postcolonial Development Theory: Observations on Methodology' (2000) 45 *Villanova Law Review* 1195–1220.
106 Antony Anghie, *Imperialism, Sovereignty, and the Making of International Law* (Cambridge University Press 2005) 245–272.
107 Ibid., 247.
108 J. Oloka-Onyango, 'Beyond the Rhetoric: Reinvigorating the Struggle for Economic and Social Rights in Africa' (1995) 26 *California Western International Law Journal* 1—71.
109 David Ransom and Margaret Bald, 'The Dictatorship of Debt' (1999) 46 (10) *World Press Review* 6, 7.
110 Anghie (note 106) 260.
111 Nira Wickremasinghe, 'From Human Rights to Good Governance: The Aid Regime in the 1990s' in Mortimer Sellers (ed.), *The New World Order: Sovereignty, Human Rights and Self-Determination of Peoples* (Oxford: Berg Publishers 1996) 305–326 at p. 306.
112 TRIPS Agreement (as amended on 23 January 2017), available at https://www.wto.org/english/docs_e/legal_e/27-trips_01_e.htm accessed 19 July 2022; See more generally Duncan Matthews, *Globalising Intellectual Property Rights: The TRIPS Agreement* (Routledge 2003).
113 Danielle Archibugi and Andrea Filippetti, 'The Globalisation of Intellectual Property Rights: Four Learned Lessons and Four Theses' (2010) 1 (2) *Global Policy* 137–149.
114 Christopher May and Susan Sell, 'Forgetting History Is Not an Option! Intellectual Property, Public Policy and Economic Development in Context' (2007) Dynamics of Institutions and Markets in Europe (DIMES) Working Paper No 28, available at http://www.dime-eu.org/working-papers accessed 2 July 2021.
115 Ikechi Mgbeoji, 'Colonial Origins of Intellectual Property Regimes in African States' in David Armstrong (ed.), *Routledge Handbook of International Law* (Routledge 2009) 342–356.
116 Christopher May and Susan Sell (note 114).
117 James Bacchus, 'An Unnecessary Proposal: A WTO Waiver of Intellectual Property Rights for COVID-19 Vaccines' (2020) 78 *Cato Institute, Free Trade Bulletin*; Michael A. Santoro, 'Human Rights and Human Needs: Diverse Moral Principles Justifying Third World Access to Affordable HIV/AIDS Drugs' (2005) 31 *North Carolina Journal of International Law and Commercial Regulation* 923.

118 The Doha Declaration on the TRIPS Agreement and Public Health was adopted by the WTO Ministerial Conference of 2001 in Doha on 14 November 2001.
119 Cristian Timmermann and Henk van den Belt, 'Intellectual Property and Global Health: From Corporate Social Responsibility to the Access to Knowledge Movement (2013) 34 (1) *Liverpool Law Review* 47–73.
120 Described by various authors as a form of communal ethics found among many groups in Africa. See Mogobe B. Ramose, 'The Philosophy of Ubuntu and Ubuntu as a Philosophy' in Pieter H. Coetzee and Abraham P. J. Roux (eds), *Philosophy from Africa: A Text with Readings* (Oxford University Press 2002) 230–237.
121 Carla Hesse, 'The Rise of Intellectual Property, 700 BC-AD 2000: An Idea in the Balance' (2002) 131 (2) *Daedalus* 26–45, 35.
122 For a general critique of the rule of law see amongst others Brian Z. Tamanaha, *Law as a Means to an End: Threat to the Rule of Law* (Cambridge University Press 2006); Graham Harrison, *The World Bank and Africa: The Construction of Governance States* (Routledge 2004).
123 Alvaro Santos and David M. Trubek (eds), *Introduction in The New Law and Economic Development: A Critical Appraisal* (Cambridge University Press 2006); Deval Desai, 'Power Rules: The World Bank, Rule of Law Reform, and the World' in Christopher May and Adam Winchester (eds), *Handbook on the Rule of Law* (Edward Elgar Publishing 2018).
124 See for example, Mohan Mathur Hari, 'Investor-Friendly Development Policies: Unsettling Consequences for the Tribal People of Orissa' (2009) 10 (4) *The Asia Pacific Journal of Anthropology* 318–328.
125 Ibid.
126 Julio Faundez, 'Legal Reform in Developing and Transition Countries: Making Haste Slowly' (2000) 1 (1) *Law, Social Justice and Global Development* 2000–2001.
127 As was the case for example in *Bhe and others v the Magistrate of Khayelitsha and others in 2005 (1) BCLR (Butterworths Constitutional Law Reports) 1 (CC).*
128 Alison J. Ayers, 'Imperial Liberties: Democratisation and Governance in the "new" Imperial Order' (2009) 57 (1) *Political Studies* 1–27.
129 Andrew J. Crozier, 'British Exceptionalism: Pride and Prejudice and Brexit' (2020) 17 *International Economics and Economic Policy* 635–658.
130 Joel F. England, 'The Response of the United States to the International Criminal Court: Rejection, Ratification or Something Else' (2001) 18 *Arizona Journal of International and Comparative Law* 941.
131 Julio Faúndez and Celine Tan (eds), *International Economic Law, Globalization and Developing Countries* (Edward Elgar Publishing 2010) 12.
132 See for example Joseph Kipkemboi Rono, 'The Impact of the Structural Adjustment Programmes on Kenyan Society' (2002) 17 (1) *Journal of Social Development in Africa* 81–98.
133 For a wider discussion on this topic, see Julio Faúndez and Celine Tan (eds), *International Economic Law, Globalization and Developing Countries* (Edward Elgar Publishing 2010).
134 Ralph Miliband, 'The Coup in Chile' (October 1973) 10 *The Socialist Register* 451–474.
135 Nicolas Cook, *Côte d'Ivoire Post-Gbagbo: Crisis Recovery* (Congressional Research Service 2011).
136 Ibid., 2.
137 Ibid., 46.
138 Gabrielle Lynch, 'Electing the "Alliance of the Accused": The Success of the Jubilee Alliance in Kenya's Rift Valley' (2014) 8 (1) *Journal of Eastern African*

Studies 93–114; See also Susanne D. Mueller, 'Kenya and the International Criminal Court (ICC): Politics, the Election and the Law' (2014) 8 (1) *Journal of Eastern African Studies* 25–42.

139 See in general Alan Boyle and Christine Chinkin, *The Making of International Law* (OUP 2007); Sibille Merz, '"Missionaries of the New Era" Neoliberalism and NGOs in Palestine' (2012) 54 (1) *Race & Class* 50–66.

140 Fanny Benedetti, Karine Bonneau and John Washburn, *Negotiating the International Criminal Court: New York to Rome, 1994–1998* (Leiden: Martinus Nijhoff 2013)153; see also Cherif Bassiouni, 'Negotiating the Treaty of Rome on the Establishment of an International Criminal Court' (1999) 32 *Cornell International Law Journal* 443; Chris Tenove, *Justice and Inclusion in Global Politics: Victim Representation and the International Criminal Court* (PhD diss. University of British Columbia 2015).

141 The victim-advocacy organization REDRESS is often credited with drafting the language for the victim participation provisions and lobbying behind the scenes for its inclusion in the statute. See in particular Marie Törnquist-Chesnier, 'NGOs and International Law' (2004) 3 (2) *Journal of Human Rights* 253–263.

142 Lohne Kjersti, 'Global Civil Society, the ICC, and Legitimacy in International Criminal Justice' in Hayashi Nobuo and Cecilia M. Bailliet (eds), *The Legitimacy of International Criminal Tribunals* (Vol. 2, Cambridge University Press 2017).

143 Alison Van Rooy (ed.), *Civil Society and the Aid Industry* (Routledge 2013).

144 John Williamson, 'A Short History of the Washington Consensus' (2009) 15 *Law and Business Review of the Americas* 7.

145 See for example Heidi Nichols Haddad, 'After the Norm Cascade: NGO Mission Expansion and the Coalition for the International Criminal Court' (2013) *Global Governance* 187–206.

146 See also William F. Fisher, 'Doing Good? The Politics and Antipolitics of NGO Practices' (1997) 26 (1) *Annual Review of Anthropology* 439–464.

147 Gustavo Esteva, 'Commoning in the New Society' (2014) 49 (1) *Community Development Journal* i144–i159.

148 Joost Augusteijn, *The Irish Revolution, 1913–1923* (Macmillan 2002).

149 Adekson J'Bayo, 'The Algerian and Mau Mau Revolts: A Comparative Study in Revolutionary Warfare' (1981) 3 (1) *Comparative Strategy* 69–92.

150 Che Guevara, *Reminiscences of the Cuban Revolutionary War* (Duke University Press 2019).

151 Sabelo Ndlovu-Gatsheni, 'The Nativist Revolution and Development Conundrums in Zimbabwe' (2006) 4 *ACCORD Occasional Paper* 1–40.

152 *Prosecutor v Thomas Lubanga Dyilo Judgment Pursuant to Article 74 of the Statute, Trial Chamber I ICC-01/04-01/06,2012 para 1358.*

153 For wider discussion on this topic see Frédéric Mégret, 'Is the International Criminal Court Focusing Too Much on Non-State Actors?' in Margaret M. deGuzman and Diane Marie Amann (eds), *Arcs of Global Justice: Essays in Honour of William A. Schabas* (Oxford University Press, 2017) 173.

154 *Prosecutor v Thomas Lubanga Dyilo Judgment Pursuant to Article 74 of the Statute, Trial ChamberI ICC-01/04-01/06,2012 para 1358.*

155 Ibid., para 9.

156 Ibid., para 23.

157 ICC, About the Court found on the ICC's website https://www.icc-cpi.int/cases accessed 14 June 2020.

158 See for example Nicholas Garrett, 'Taming Predatory Elites in the Democratic Republic of the Congo: Regulation of Property Rights to Adjust Incentives and Improve Economic Performance in the Mining Sector' in Carl Bruch, Carroll Muffett and Sandra S. Nichols (eds), *Governance, Natural Resources, and Post-conflict Peacebuilding* (Routledge 2016).

159 See for example, Stephen Kabel, 'Our Business Is People (Even If It Kills Them): The Contribution of Multinational Enterprises to the Conflict in the Democratic Republic of Congo' (2004) 12 *Tulane Journal of International and Comparative Law* 461.
160 Decision on the 'Prosecution request pursuant to Article 19(3) for a ruling on the Court's territorial jurisdiction in Palestine' ICC-01/18-143 5 February 2021.
161 Ibid.
162 Ibid.
163 I use resistance here in its simplest form i.e. opposed to/revolt against hegemony, but also in its perspectival/theoretical and romance form. See Mathew Sparke, 'Political Geography — Political Geographies of Globalization III: Resistance' (2008) 32 (3) *Progress in Human Geography* 423–440; Mona Lilja Mikael Baaz, Michael Schulz and Stellan Vinthagen, 'How Resistance Encourages Resistance: Theorizing the Nexus between Power' (2017) 10 (1) 'Organised Resistance' and 'Everyday Resistance,' *Journal of Political Power* 40–54.
164 Donald Macintyre, 'Civilian Casualties: Human Rights Groups Accuse Israelis of War Crimes,' The Independent on Sunday, 15 January 2009.
165 Briefing to the UN Security Council based on data from Palestinian Ministry of Health, by Under-Secretary-General Holmes, UN Doc. S/PV. 6077, 27 January 2009.
166 Israel Ministry of Foreign Affairs, The Operation in Gaza — Factual and Legal Aspects, July 2009, available at http://www.mfa.gov.il/MFA/Terrorism+Obstacle+to+Peace/Terrorism+and+Islamic+Fundamentalism-/Operation_in_Gaza-Factual_and_Legal_Aspects.htm accessed 3 July 2020.
167 Human Rights Council Resolution S-9/1 on the Grave Violations of Human Rights in the Occupied Palestinian Territory, Particularly due to the Recent Israeli Military Attacks Against the Occupied Gaza Strip, UN Doc. A/HRC/S-9/L.1, 12 January 2009.
168 Report of the United Nations Fact Finding Mission on the Gaza Conflict, UN Doc. A/HRC/12/48, 25 September 2009 (hereafter 'Goldstone Report').
169 Ibid., para 1886, 1891, 1921, 1950.
170 Ibid., para 46.
171 Ibid.
172 Ibid., para 60.
173 Ibid.
174 Ibid., para 109.
175 See for example Richard D. Rosen, 'Goldstone Reconsidered' (2011) 21 *Journal of Transnational Law & Policy* 35.
176 See UN General Assembly Resolution 73/158, the General Assembly reaffirmed the right of the Palestinian people to self-determination, including the right to their independent State of Palestine, and urged all States and the specialised agencies and organisations of the United Nations system to continue to support and assist the Palestinian people in the early realisation of their right to self-determination. The Assembly also called for the realisation of the Palestinian people's human rights, including the right to self-determination, in its Resolutions 73/19, 73/96 and 73/99; in Resolution 73/18, the General Assembly, having considered the report of the Committee on the Exercise of the Inalienable Rights of the Palestinian People (A/73/35), requested the Committee, inter alia, to continue to exert all efforts to promote the realisation of the inalienable rights of the Palestinian people, including their right to self-determination. The Assembly invited all Governments and organisations to extend their cooperation and support to the Committee in the performance of its tasks, recalling its repeated call for all States and the specialised agencies and organisations of the

United Nations system to continue to support and assist the Palestinian people in the early realisation of their right to self-determination, including the right to their independent State of Palestine. In Resolution 73/255, the General Assembly reaffirmed the right of the Palestinian people to sovereignty over their natural resources, including land, water and energy resources.

177 State Of Israel office of the Attorney General, The International Criminal Court's lack of jurisdiction over the so called "Situation In Palestine" 20 December, 2019, available at https://www.gov.il/en/departments/news/iccs-lack-of-jurisdiction-over-so-called-situation-in-palestine-20-dec-2019 accessed 3 July 2020.

178 *International Rights Advocates V. Apple, Microsoft, Dell, Tesla United States District Court For The District Of Columbia Case 1:19-Cv-03737 Document 1 Filed 12/15/19.*

179 Frederic Mégret, 'Not "Lambs to the Slaughter": A Program for Resistance to 'Genocidal Law,' in Rene Provost and Payam Akhavan (eds), *Confronting Genocide* (Springer 2011) 195.

180 Raiss Tinmaing and Azeezah Kanji, 'Resisting the Rohingya Genocide: From Pity to Solidarity, Inside and Beyond the ICJ' (2020) 17 *TWAILR Reflections* 1–9.

181 Ibid.

182 Ratna Kapur, *Erotic Justice: Law and the New Politics of Postcolonialism* (Taylor & Francis Group 2005).

183 See more generally, Ann Cora Presley, *Kikuyu Women, the Mau Mau Rebellion, and Social Change in Kenya* (Routledge 2019).

184 On the wider topic see Janell Hobson (ed.), *The Routledge Companion to Black Women's Cultural Histories* (Routledge 2021).

185 Umoren E. Uduakobong, 'The Symbolism of the Nigerian Women's War of 1929: An Anthropological Study of an Anticolonial Struggle' (1995) 16 (2) *African Study Monographs* 61–72.

186 Ibid.

187 Ibid.

188 Ibid.

189 Celia Nyamweru and Neil Carrier, 'Reinventing Africa's National Heroes: The Case of Mekatilili, a Kenyan Popular Heroine' (2016) 115 (461) *African Affairs* 599–620.

190 Tabitha Kanogo, 'Kikuyu Women and the Politics of Protest: Mau Mau' in Sharon Macdonald, Pat Holden and Shirley Ardener (eds), *Images of Women in Peace and War: Cross-Cultural and Historical Perspectives* (Palgrave 1987) 78–99.

191 Ibid.

192 Samson Kaunga Ndanyi, 'Cinema and Wage Labour in Colonial Kenya' (2019) 27 *Afrika Zamani* 119–136.

193 Felix K. Ekechi, 'Historical Women in the Fight for Liberation' in Valentine Udo James and James S. Etim (eds), *The Feminization of Development Processes in Africa: Current and Future Perspectives* (PRAEGER 1999) 95–113.

194 Cora Ann Presley, 'The Mau Mau Rebellion, Kikuyu Women, and Social Change' (1988) 22 (3) *Canadian Journal of African Studies/La Revue canadienne des études africaines* 502–527.

195 Tabitha Kanogo (note 190) 78–99.

196 Katherine Bruce-Lockhart, '"Unsound" Minds and Broken Bodies: The Detention of "Hardcore" Mau Mau Women at Kamiti and Gitamayu Detention Camps in Kenya, 1954–1960' (2014) 8 (4) *Journal of Eastern African Studies* 590–608.

197 Maria Nzomo, 'Kenyan Women in Politics and Public Decision Making' in Gwendolyn Mikell (ed.), *African Feminism: The Politics of Survival in Sub-Saharan Africa* (University of Pennsylvania Press 2010) 232–254.
198 Ibid.
199 Ibid.
200 Ibid.
201 Ibid.
202 Georges Sorel, *Reflections on Violence* (Cambridge University Press 1999).
203 Frantz Fanon, *The Wretched of the Earth* (trans. Constance Farrington, Penguin 1967).
204 David Berman and Christopher Michaelsen, 'Intervention in Libya: Another Nail in the Coffin for the Responsibility-to-Protect' (2012) 14 *International Community Law Review* 337.
205 Hannah Arendt, *On Violence* (Harcourt Brace 1969) 79.
206 Ibid., 52.
207 Hannah Arendt, *On Revolution* (Penguin 1990) 19.
208 Hannah Arendt, *On Violence* (Harcourt Brace 1969) 10, 54, 80; Patricia Owens, *Between War and Politics: International Relations and the Thought of Hannah Arendt* (OUP 2007) 57.
209 See Elizabeth Frazer and Kimberly Hutchings, 'Argument and Rhetoric in the Justification of Political Violence' (2007) 6 (2) *European Journal of Political Theory* 180–99; Elizabeth Frazer and Kimberly Hutchings, 'On Politics and Violence: Arendt Contra Fanon' (2008) 7 (1) *Contemporary Political Theory* 90–108.
210 Georges Sorel, *Reflections on Violence* (Jeremy Jennings (ed.) Cambridge University Press 1999) 85.
211 Ibid., 105–106.
212 Ibid.
213 Ibid.
214 Ibid.
215 See for example Riley Quinn, *An Analysis of Frantz Fanon's The Wretched of the Earth* (CRC Press 2017).
216 Frantz Fanon, *Black Faces, White Masks* (trans. Charles Lam Markmann, Grove 1967); Neil Roberts, 'Fanon, Sartre, Violence, and Freedom' (2004) 10 (2) *Sartre Studies International* 139.
217 Giorgio Agamben, *Homo Sacer: Sovereign Power and Bare Life* (Stanford University Press 1998) 31; Stephanie Polsky 'Down the K. Hole: Walter Benjamin's Destructive Land surveying of History' in Andrew Benjamin (ed.), *Walter Benjamin and History* (A&C Black 2005) 69–87.
218 Walter Benjamin, 'Critique of Violence' in Marcus Bullock and Michael W. Jennings (eds), *Walter Benjamin Selected Writings Volume 1 1913–1926* (Harvard University Press 1996) 248.
219 Ivor Chipkin, Mark Swilling *et al.*, *The Politics of State Capture* (NYU Press 2018).
220 Walter Benjamin (note 218) 252.
221 Ibid., 248.
222 Gorgio Agamben, *State of Exception* (University of Chicago Press 2005) 53.
223 Julius Malema's speech at Mandikizela Mandela's funeral, available at https://www.youtube.com accessed 28 June 2021.
224 Langston Hughes, Harlem in *The Collected Poems of Langston Hughes* (Vintage 2020).
225 See for example, Abou B. Bamba, *African Miracle, African Mirage: Transnational Politics and the Paradox of Modernization in Ivory Coast* (Ohio University Press 2016); Suaka Yaro, *An Investigation into the Causes and Ramifications of Political Conflict in Ivory Coast* (diss. Walter Sisulu University 2012).
226 James Fox, *White Mischief* (Random House 2012).

227 Karen Blixen, *Out of Africa* (Vol. 9, Penguin UK, 2001).
228 Kuki Gallmann, *I Dreamed of Africa* (Penguin UK 2007).
229 Joseph Conrad, *Heart of Darkness* (Palgrave Macmillan 1996).
230 Stephen Hopkins, *The Ghost and the Darkness* (Paramount Pictures 1996).
231 John le Carre, *The Constant Gardner* (Hodder and Stoughton 2001).
232 Ocampo's 50-Hour Kenyan Swoop, *The Nation* 7 November 2009.
233 Human Rights Watch (2008), Ballots to Bullets: Organized Political Violence and Kenya's Crisis of Governance. http://www.hrw.org/sites accessed 6 November 2017.
234 Ibid.
235 Connor Joseph Cavanagh, 'Land, Natural Resources and the State in Kenya's Second Republic' in Adebusuyi Adeniran and Lanre Ikuteyijo (eds), *Africa Now! Emerging Issues and Alternative Perspectives* (Palgrave Macmillan 2018) 119–147.
236 Ibid.
237 Roger Southall, 'The Ndungu Report: Land & Graft in Kenya' (2005) 32 (103) *Review of African Political Economy* 142.
238 Jacqueline M. Klopp, '"Ethnic Clashes" and Winning Elections: The Case of Kenya's Electoral Despotism' (2001) 35 (3) *Canadian Journal of African Studies/ La Revue canadienne des études africaines* 473–517.
239 Ibid.
240 See for example Leonardo Becchetti Pierluigi Conzo and Alessandro Romeo, 'Violence, Trust, and Trustworthiness: Evidence from a Nairobi Slum' (2014) 66 (1) *Oxford Economic Papers* 283–305.
241 See in particular Sophie T. Rosenberg, 'The International Criminal Court in Côte d'Ivoire: Impartiality at Stake?' (2017) 15 (3) *Journal of International Criminal Justice* 471–490; Susanne D. Mueller, 'Kenya and the International Criminal Court (ICC): Politics, the Election and the Law' (2014) 8 (1) *Journal of Eastern African Studies* 25–42.
242 Kiama Kaara, 'The Crisis in Kenya Today: Accident of a Fraudulent Election's Outcome or a Deep-Seated Structural Problem of the Country's Political Economy and History?' (2008) Centre for Civil Society. Paper: www.ukzn.ac.za/ccs accessed 8 August 2018.
243 Ibid.
244 Ibid.
245 Oginga Odinga, *Not Yet Uhuru* (Heinemann 1967) 253.
246 Peter Kagwanja, 'Courting Genocide: Populism, Ethno-nationalism and the Informalisation of Violence in Kenya's 2008 Post-election Crisis' (2009) 27 (3) *Journal of Contemporary African Studies* 365–387.
247 Simon Kimani Ndungu, 'Kenya: Class, Ethnicity, and the Construction of a Fragmented Post-colonial Society, 20 June 2008. http://mediareviewnet.com/2013/01/kenya-class-ethnicity-and-the-construction-of-a-fragmented-post-colonial-society/ accessed 15 March 2018.
248 Brock Bersaglio, 'Green Violence: Market-Driven Conservation and the Reforeignization of Space in Laikipia, Kenya' in Sharlene Mollett and Thembela Kepe (eds), *Land Rights, Biodiversity Conservation and Justice: Rethinking Parks and People* (Routledge 2018) 71–88.
249 The Waki Report (2008). http://www.knchr.org/Portals/0/Reports/Waki_Report.pdf accessed 26 December 2017.
250 *The Prosecutor v. Joseph Kony, Vincent Otti, Raska Lukwiya, Okot Odhiambo and Dominic Ongwen ICC-02/04-01/05*; Whether the local Acholi community was agreeable to Kony's referral is disputed by Christian Noll, 'The Betrayed: An Exploration of the Acholi Opinion of the International Criminal Court' (2009) 26 (1) *Journal of Third World Studies* 99–119.
251 *The Prosecutor v. Omar Hassan Ahmad Al Bashir ICC-02/05-01/09.*

252 Franziska Boehme, '"We Chose Africa": South Africa and the Regional Politics of Cooperation with the International Criminal Court (2017) 11 (1) *International Journal of Transitional Justice* 50–70.
253 Known as the Waki Commission.
254 The Waki Report (2008) (note 249).
255 Thomas Obel Hansen, 'Transitional Justice in Kenya-An Assessment of the Accountability Process in Light of Domestic Politics and Security Concerns' (2011) 42 (1) *California Western International Law Journal* 1–36.
256 Gissel Line Engbo, 'Justice Tides: How and When Levels of ICC Involvement Affect Peace Processes' (2015) 9 *International Journal of Transitional Justice* 428–448.
257 *The Prosecutor v. Francis Kirimi Muthaura, Uhuru Muigai Kenyatta and Mohammed Hussein Ali, ICC-01/09-02/11* and *The Prosecutor v. William Samoei Ruto, Henry Kiprono Kosgey and Joshua Arap Sang, ICC-01/09-01/11.* https://www.icc-cpi.int accessed 13 August 2016.
258 Decision on the Application by the Government of Kenya Challenging the Admissibility of the Case Pursuant to Article 19(2)(b) of the Statute. http://www.icc-cpi.int accessed 27/08/16.
259 Ibid.
260 Article 17 Rome Statute.
261 Owen Bowcott, 'ICC Drops Murder and Rape Charges against Kenyan President' *The Guardian,* 5 December 2014.
262 Decision on Prosecution's application for a further adjournment, 3 December 2014, CC-O 1/09-02/1 1-98 page 26.
263 Sewell Chan and Marlise Simons, 'South Africa to Withdraw from International Criminal Court' *The New York Times* 21 October 2016.
264 BBC world news, 1 February 2017.
265 See for example Dermot Groome, 'No Witness, No Case: An Assessment of the Conduct and Quality of ICC Investigations' (2004) 3(1) *Penn State Journal of Law & International Affairs* 1–29.
266 *The Prosecutor v. Uhuru Muigai Kenyatta*, Decision on Defence Application Pursuant to Article 64(4) and Related Requests, ICC-01/09-02/11, T.Ch. V, 26 April 2013, Concurring Opinion of Judge Christine Van den Wyngaert, paras 1, 4–5.
267 Ibid.
268 Christian M. De Vos, 'Investigating from Afar: The ICC's Evidence Problem' (2013) 26 *Leiden Journal of International Law* 1009.
269 Ibid.
270 This was particularly problematic in the *Lubanga* case. Verrijn Stuart Heikelina, 'The ICC in Trouble' (2008) 6 (3) *Journal of International Criminal Justice* 409–417; On the use of intermediaries more generally see Nicole De Silva, 'Intermediary Complexity in Regulatory Governance: The International Criminal Court's Use of NGOs in Regulating International Crimes' (2017) 670 (1) *The ANNALS of the American Academy of Political and Social Science* 170–188.
271 Ray Murphy, *The Irish Times* 6 June 2013.
272 *Prosecutor v Uhuru Muigai Kenyatta* Notice of withdrawal of the charges against Uhuru Muigai Kenyatta, ICC-01/09-02/11-983 (5 December 2014); ICC-OTP, Statement of the Prosecutor of the International Criminal Court Fatou Bensouda on the withdrawal of charges against Mr. Uhuru Muigai Kenyatta 5 December 2014.
273 James Verini, NYTimes.com accessed 22 June 2016; Dermot Groome, 'No Witness, No Case: An Assessment of the Conduct and Quality of ICC Investigations' (2004) 3(1) *Penn State Journal of Law & International Affairs* 14.
274 James Verini, ibid.

275 KNCHR (Kenya National Commission on Human Rights) (2008) The Cry of Blood. Report on Extrajudicial Execution and Disappearances.
276 *The Prosecutor v. Uhuru Muigai Kenyatta, Decision on Defence Application Pursuant to Article 64(4) and Related Requests ICC-01/09-02/11.*
277 James Verini (note 273).
278 Ibid.; see also KNCHR (Kenya National Commission on Human Rights) (2008) The Cry of Blood. Report on Extrajudicial Execution and Disappearances; on witness handling procedures at the ICC see, Sylvia Ngane Ntube, *The Position of Witnesses before the International Criminal Court* (Brill Nijhoff 2015) 234–334.
279 On prosecution's poor preparation see generally Dermot Groome, 'No Witness, No Case: An Assessment of the Conduct and Quality of ICC Investigations' (2004) 3(1) *Penn State Journal of Law & International Affairs* 1–29.
280 Kenya Citizen TV, ICC Hearings Uhuru Testifies. www.youtube.com accessed 15 June 2021.
281 James Verini, NYTimes.com accessed 22 June 2016.
282 Ibid.
283 Ibid.
284 *The Prosecutor v. Jean-Pierre Bemba Gombo ICC-01/05-01/08 Second Public Redacted Version of "Mr. Bemba's claim for compensation and damages 9-30.*
285 Uhuru Kenyatta quoted in Albert Isaac Olawale, *"Back to the Future: Rethinking Alternatives to External Intervention in African Conflicts." Indigenous Knowledge Systems and Development in Africa* (Palgrave Macmillan 2020) 171.
286 Albert Bandura, *Social Learning Theory* (Prentice Hall 1977); on this behaviour and experimentation of colonial officers in Africa see Christopher Prior, 'A Brotherhood of Britons? Public Schooling Esprit De Corps and Colonial Officials in Africa c. 1900–1939' (2013) 98 (330) *History* 174–190.
287 On decolonial thinking see José-Manuel Barreto, 'Decolonial Thinking and the Quest for Decolonising Human Rights' (2018) 46 (4–5) *Asian Journal of Social Science* 484–502.
288 Ngugi wa Thiong'o, *Decolonising the Mind: The Politics of Language in African Literature* (East African Publishers 1992).
289 Michel Foucault, *The Archaeology of Knowledge* (Harper and Row 1972).
290 Jacques Derrida, *Of Grammatology* (Johns Hopkins University Press 1974).
291 Christine Schwöbel (ed.), *Critical Approaches to International Criminal Law* (Routledge 2014).
292 Lionel Nichols, *The International Criminal Court and End of Impunity in Kenya* (Springer 2015).
293 Kamari Maxine Clarke, *Affective Justice: The International Criminal Court and the Pan-Africanist Pushback* (Duke University Press 2019).

4 Le Jour D'apres? Black iconography at the ICC

Indepance *chacha tozui e*
Indépendance cha cha le jour d'apres…
…Les promesses de lendemain, les promesses de l'aube
D'un état souverain où le sol se dérobe
Entre milices et rebelles, pillages et recels
Peuples que l'on déplace comme des cheptel…s
J'ai repris cette chanson fédératrice
Symbole de la crédulité de nos prémices
Entre indépendance et armistice
Mais pour que nos démocraties progressent
Faut qu'elle apprennent de leurs erreurs de jeunesse
Mon pays est un continent émergent
Bâti en moins de 50 ans…[1]

Introduction

In Chapters 2 and 3, I explored how the seemingly independent states are still subject to colonialism through international organs such as the ICC. In this chapter, I proceed to show how the appearance of accused black men at the ICC is the epitome of this colonialism. I explore this by showing how the emerging iconography involving the African accused at the ICC reflects the existing and inherited biases of a colonial justice system towards the black body. I interrogate this through the wider notion of justice being 'seen to be done' and through a post-colonial and critical race perspective, to address the phenomenon of the law as a vehicle through which the 'otherisation' of the black citizen is commodified and universalised.

To universalise western law, the criminal law industrial complex requires the 'hard drive' through which its coloniality is expressed and exercised. Here, I trace the archaeology of the claimed universalist 'norms' applied at the ICC to a specific Eurocentric legal architecture, including courthouse construction, courtroom design and use of language. What this engagement with legal architecture shows is the insidious exercise of power by a largely Eurocentric

DOI: 10.4324/9781003304173-4

legal structure on the black body – since the days of slavery and ongoing at the ICC. This continuous coloniality is exemplified by the imagery emanating from the ICC showing the over-representation of the black accused at the court which reproduces a poisonous cocktail that equates the African male with murder and plunder. The predominantly male accused reproduce patterns already documented in the UK and in the USA for example, where the black male is over-represented in the 'criminal' justice system.

My intentions in this chapter are to analyse the 'acting out' of the law at the ICC by interrogating the physical manifestations and the projection of law and power through architecture and personnel. The physical architecture and personnel around the 'law' are a doctrine in themselves but are also a material manifestation of the law as practiced. This interrogation, especially as it relates to the ICC/Africa discourse is critical because authors like Ann Sagan[2] and Martti Koskenniemi[3] are linking how the iconography at the centre of ICL not only explains specific social-cultural influences on legal action, but actively shapes those actions. In line with these arguments, I argue that having a largely Eurocentric legal architecture at the ICC distorts the claim to universality and perpetuates global colonialism because it means that the ICC relies on Eurocentric artefacts as a visual presentation of the necessity, scope, and function of ICL. In our discourse, colonial iconography becomes universal and accepted as the norm(s) through which international justice is served. The contradiction in this is plain for scholars to dissect, but literature reviewed as part of this work shows limited efforts by international lawyers to engage with colonial iconography at the ICC. Resistance towards the ICC from African states is not seen through this prism and is seen only through the prism of the accused trying to evade justice. This, the chapter argues, limits international legal scholarship, and narrows the lens through which law should be scrutinised. My contention is that a wider lens should be utilised in the understanding of the history of ICL to include the scrutiny of the forms, functions, and meanings of the artefacts upon which the legitimacy of international criminal law and of practices at the ICC is founded.

I begin this discourse in the section titled 'What is Iconography?' below by explaining the meaning of iconography in the context of the ICC/postcolonial discussion. In the section 'Le Jour D'apres. Political Iconography and the ICC,' I link the discourse on iconography with the discussions on decolonising presented in Chapter 2, particularly in relation to neo-colonialism and the 'lie of independence.' I explain the significance of the iconic freedom at midnight images as they pertain to the 'father of the nation' romance and freedom hero myths of figures like Kenyatta, Mandela, Nehru *et al.* The ICC was, for example, either blind to the potency of the Kenyatta name in Kenya's anti-colonial romance or knew and sought to weaponise it. It was however clear that Kenyatta was aware of the capital his name held in Africa and in the diaspora and used it to his advantage. He understood that in the wider black community, an even more potent image in a political sense is of a 'leader' being subjected to perceivably 'unfair' legal shenanigans, especially those taking place in a foreign land.

In Section "Iconography of the Black Accused" I discuss the over-representation of the black accused at the ICC and the imagery it produces. I argue that the images of black men before a Eurocentric court reproduce what is already occurring in the USA and UK courts and risks mirroring the American prison/legal industrial complex which is argued to be slavery in all but name.

In the section 'The Black Accused, Law and Language' I extend this discussion of the over-representation of the black accused at the ICC to the alienation of black epistemologies from law, including for example the lack of African languages as official legal languages at the ICC.

Before concluding, I argue in the section "Iconography of Colonial Court Architecture and the ICC" that all this alienation happens in a 'hostile' environment which is the Eurocentric court building. I argue that not only is the Eurocentric legal architecture oppressive by design, alienating the black accused further, it is designed to maintain the already existing racial and power hierarchies. This alienation is however supposed to be hidden by, for example, clothing the ICC court building in a corporate façade that signifies 'transparency' but which at the same time shows the hijacking of the law by marketisation forces. Law as an industry therefore becomes the template, with hints of a past marriage between law and slavery, with ominous implications for the African.

What is Iconography?

Courtroom iconography, including court architecture is a well-established scholarship area and I engage with literature on the wider topic in the section on 'Iconography of Colonial Court Architecture and the ICC.'[4] This section serves the limited but necessary purpose of explaining the meaning(s) of iconography but does not explore one type or another, as I do that in the following sections. For our discourse, iconography should be understood both as 'imagery' and as a method(ology); a way of doing/interpreting as well as a school of thought or a field of study.[5] In continuing the multi-disciplinary nature of my work, this definition is borrowed from art history which, after attributing certain works of art to particular artists, then goes on to ask, 'What does the work of art depict?' or, more precisely, 'What is the theme or subject of this work of art?'[6] This approach to art history has produced iconography which is a field within art history that is exclusively concerned with answering that question. Iconography therefore is "the branch of art history concerned with the themes in the visual arts and their deeper meanings or content."[7]

In what is pertinent to our discourse on the ICC, Van Straten indicates that the word 'themes' should be understood in a broad sense. Iconography considers a representation both as a whole and as a collection of details.[8] For this reason, the picture of Uhuru Kenyatta at the ICC, while perhaps having the meaning of an accused before a court of law, becomes for the purposes of this study the theme of an iconographic study. In extending Van Straten's definition to this image, in its "deeper meanings or content" this book sees other aspects of images of Kenyatta at the ICC than the photographer or casual observer may have noted. These deeper meanings are attributed to these images with references to visual and literary sources and allusions to cultural, social, and historical facts[9] which I discuss further in this chapter.

The first and most important of these objectives is to determine what is depicted in an artwork (image, design, building etc.) and to reveal and explain the deeper meanings intended by the artist/architect. A second, intermediary concern involves tracking down the direct and indirect sources – both literary and visual – used by the artist. A further area of iconography is "the investigation of certain pictorial themes, especially their development, traditions, and content through the ages."[10] In a work of art, one can distinguish three levels of meaning which simultaneously represent three stages or phases of iconographic research. The first level or phase is the exact enumeration of everything that can be seen in the work of art without defining the relationships between things. The second level of meaning is the 'theme' or 'subject' or the things that we see, brought into relation with one another. The third level is the deeper meaning or content of the work of art as intended by the artist.[11] In addition to the three iconographic levels of meaning, we may distinguish a fourth level or phase, which we may designate as the iconological interpretation. It is the task of iconology to look beyond queries about artist and subject to a third question: 'Why was it created?' or, more precisely, 'Why was it created just so?' With the help of the three iconographical phases and the iconological phase, we can define which tools are necessary for an iconographic – and, to a lesser extent, iconologic – investigation.[12]

In Chapter 1, I explained that I use my standpoint as a black man and black lawyer to explore the discourse at hand. I would refocus the reader to that perspective which is linked here with iconography to encompass a wider visual research school of methodologies. In that sense, my use of iconography should be seen as a way of 'seeing' or 'looking' at the ICC as discussed in more detail by Chalfen[13] who interrogates cultural influences on how we see and observe and on the meanings we attribute to that which we observe. In a wider context, "Iconography can best be described as a qualitative method of visual content analysis and interpretation, influenced by cultural traditions and guided by research interests originating both in the humanities and the social sciences."[14] Visuals are treated as historic sources relating to culture, politics, society, and life at a given time in the past. As historic material they also bear witness to visual forms of expression in the present and can thus illuminate both past and present communication processes.[15]

Therefore, from my standpoint, I explore the imagery emanating from the ICC, including images of the accused and of court personnel including judges and lawyers, and architectural presentations to argue that the representation of the black accused at the ICC reproduces colonial relationships and significantly, that the images are useful to both the accuser and the accused in a macabre power play that has no grass roots justice at its core. This chapter argues that Uhuru Kenyatta, for example, uses the iconography of his ICC appearances to further his political project.[16] It is my argument that this use of court appearances as a platform for power is not a new phenomenon and, as I show later, several 'anti-colonial' leaderships have been born out of such court appearances.[17] In relation to Kenyatta, I argue that the ICC was blind to the political capital that accrues to many black leaders seen to be 'fighting' against white domination. The ICC was further blind to the exposure that they gave Kenyatta in an election season.[18]

Hobbes, in his seminal work *Leviathan*, had already established the potency of shaping intellectual and popular knowledge through visual production and the political potency of material and mental images.[19] Of interest to my work is the unusual practice by the prosecutor in the Kenyatta case of giving a running commentary on the proceedings using popular media and live television coverage. This, I argue, was meant to project power but succeeded in the opposite. Broadcasting, as we see below, was a particularly useful tool for the British colonial government in ensuring the continuation of the empire or at least the visuals of empire after 'independence.' When the imagery of Kenyatta's appearance at the ICC is interpreted this way, two results emerge; one, the ICC as a representative of an all-powerful global 'state' failed in its attempt to project power and its failures were broadcast. Second, the local elite represented here by Kenyatta succeeded in broadcasting to their followers that they were also equal to the performance of the macabre power dance.

Political Iconography and the ICC

As an area of study, the imagery of the all-powerful ICC litigating situations from Africa has had limited if any academic attention. I have not found any scholarly work that interrogates the iconography of the ICL as it relates to African cases at the ICC. As part of the interrogation of the re-production of pre-existing colonial relationships between Africans and criminal law, I will discuss at this point the production of Iconographic moments by the ICC which were particularly powerful in the Kenyan cases.

For the prosecutor, the Kenyan cases were to set an example of how to prevent future political violence in Kenya (Africa? The World?).[20] The president appearing before the ICC live on camera was meant to be an iconic moment when the powerful finally faced justice. However, the prosecutor failed to understand that images mean different things to different audiences, as I explain in this section. The image of black leaders being prosecuted by a white legal system has extraordinarily strong resonance in Africa and the diaspora and has been a potent anti-colonial instrument well-harnessed by the 'independence' leadership in Africa. What is relevant to our discourse here is the complete blindness of a white legal system to the messages that those images sent to the continent. Black figures, including Mandela and Jomo Kenyatta, benefited greatly from their suffering under white justice systems, both becoming icons of anti-colonial movements.[21]

To explain the position that the Kenyatta name holds in the Kenyan's political romance, I will digress for a moment and detail Kenyatta's role in iconographic moments reproduced by the ICC through his son Uhuru. Before I do that though and for the purposes of setting firm grounds for the ICC appearances becoming 'iconic' moments, I posit that the ICC as a colonial court suffers, as most colonial institutions do, from self-induced amnesia regarding the court being a place where black anti-colonial 'heroes' are born.[22] Jomo Kenyatta is purposely mentioned here because his son Uhuru inherited his political capital to become the Kenyan president. To a generation of Kenyans, the Kenyatta name is almost sacred, an icon against colonialism.[23] As part of the famous Kapenguria six, Kenyatta was detained by the British government as part of a crackdown on the *Mau Mau* 'leadership.' Kenyatta, who lived in London during most of the liberation struggle, came out of this detention a hero and claimed the presidency.[24] Kenyatta, I should add, was part of a European educated elite that took over from colonial governments all over Africa and Asia in what myself and other post-colonial theorists now see as a well-coordinated robbery of African people's aspirations for true independence.[25] Kenyatta, like Mandela after him, adopted free market capitalism with zeal and did not redistribute the confiscated land to its original owners as hoped.[26] The irony in Kenyatta's ascension to power is that his betrayal of *Mau Mau* revolutionaries remains the darkest episode in the global black liberation movement to date because he continued the colonial government's detention of the *Mau Mau* and their movement remained a banned organisation under his and subsequent independent Kenyan governments until 2003.[27] On the other hand, with the help of the British state, Kenyatta was able to create an image of the liberator without whom 'independence' would have been elusive, if not unattainable.[28] This betrayal of the African independence movement is crucial in our post-colonial discourse for two main reasons. First, it meant that a mostly western leaning elite, including Kenyatta and Mandela, took over the 'new' African states and second, most crucially, it meant the continuation of the colonial state and colonial institutions, including the colonial economy and legal systems. The last is crucial in our discourse as it is my contention that this continuity led to the current ICC interventionism in Africa and the subsequent conflict between the African elite and global/human rights elite at the ICC.

In relation to our discourse on iconography, Kenyatta and other Kapenguria detainees became icons of independence while their trials became iconic moments in Kenya's political romance.[29] The Kenyatta appearances at the ICC were later to be compared to this iconic moment in Kenya's history.[30] The contradiction of this occasion being seen as an iconic liberating moment is not lost to a scholar, especially given the fact that travelling to the Hague meant Kenyatta had at least to accept the supremacy of ICL over and above his power as the president and therefore, by association over and above the sovereignty of his nation. However, his defiant appearance became a valuable political theatric. It is my contention that Kenyatta, as most southern leaders still do, trod the knife edge of continuously selling his people the illusion of independence while knowing that his Eurocentric but black-led government was a vassal state to the 'mother' colonial state.

This illusion of independence is, I argue, not a creation of Kenyatta's genius, but a colonial legacy created in the 'freedom at midnight' episodes of the 1960s when most countries in Asia and Africa gained their *Uhuru*[31] from Britain and France. In elaborate ceremonies the colonial states managed to create a situation where their defeat in some cases, especially in Kenya after years of armed struggle, was presented as a triumph. Crucial to our discourse on the continued coloniality at the ICC, the colonial state presented itself as both liberator and guarantor of the future ex-colonial state. The calculated presence of British royalty during these 'hand over' occasions gave the impression of continued power and victory rather than the defeat of colonialism.[32] The colonial state egged the willing local elites to make dreamy pronouncements of utopia.

> At the stroke of the midnight hour when the world sleeps … India will awake to life and freedom. A moment comes, which comes but rarely in history, when we step out from the old to the new, when an age ends, and when the soul of a nation, long suppressed, finds utterance.[33]

These intoxicating words inspired similar illusions of independence all over the 'commonwealth' and the romantic father of the nation myth was birthed by the colonial midwives in India, Malaysia, Kenya, Malawi, Ghana, and other newly formed states. My contention is that although the local elite may have had some illusions of freedom, they were always reminded to the contrary even in those early days. This was better exemplified in Botswana where, moments before 'freedom at midnight,' Princess Marina of Kent's chaperone became worried that she might have a bad hair day due to a gathering sandstorm and suggested that celebrations be suspended. "You cannot postpone independence!" retorted Seretse[34] who I think might have worried more about missing his moment of glory than about his people's true independence. Although history does not record the state of Princess Marina's hair after the incident, scholars, including David Cannadine, argue that the independence day iconography was part of the British scheme of managing the end of their empire by ensuring that the newly formed states recognised where actual power lay.[35] The presence of the British royals in these ceremonies was meant to portray exactly this point in what Cannadine says was a symbolic reestablishment of the hierarchical ranking simultaneously to the formal ending of imperialism.[36]

Earlier, I argued that Kenyatta used the ICC's choice to broadcast his appearances using mass media as an opportunity to further his political project. The ICC and Kenyatta were both borrowing from the 'freedom at midnight' episodes. This was because, while establishing the hierarchy of power, these iconographic moments also provided the colonial state with the opportunity to broadcast to their citizens at home that their racial supremacy remained intact.[37] The images broadcast by the British media during and after Indian independence and the careful management of official publicity meant that the public in both England and India (and all former colonies) was only presented with the 'British version' of the history of decolonisation. This was also useful in presenting these occasions as the fulfilment of the very ideals that led to the establishment of the empire i.e. to bring government to the ungoverned spaces.[38] Similarly, I argue that the ICC used these live broadcasts to portray itself as an all-powerful institution while on the other hand, Kenyatta's appearances at the Hague served to show the citizens back home that he was still all powerful and would return triumphant.

Linked to this idea of broadcasting, I further argue that the ICC also serves another iconic post-independence purpose. This is the aim to broadcast globally that the African cannot self-govern or at least cannot do so without chaos, just as the bloody and chaotic partition created by the British in India/Pakistan was used by sections of the British and American press to re-evaluate and raise doubts as to the capacity of the Indians to govern themselves.[39] The chaos, although planted by the British themselves, was used as an example of the fulfillment of colonial prophets like Churchill, who saw empire as important for India's stability and good governance. Consequently, but for vastly different reasons, the very act of 'independence' and the chaos that followed was used to justify imperial rule which led to pro and anti-independence camps not just in India but in most other ex-colonial states.[40]

It is this sphere, in which the ex-colonies are presented as unable to self-govern, that I argue the ICC occupies. The ICC in this respect becomes simultaneously a confirmation of this necessity of empire and a pedagogic institution – showing the African how to do government and law, and 'caning' them when 'naughtiness' appears in this pedagogical relationship. As an interventionist institution however, the ICC and other international bodies are not themselves an original idea because even while the African was becoming intoxicated with ideas of freedom in the 1960s s/he was being asked to thank his/her colonisers for the luck of being occupied and enslaved. For example, and this is relevant to our discourse on the ICC, at the celebrations of Congo's *Madaraka*, King Baudouin of Belgium gave a speech praising early Belgian colonisation of the Congo and the good work of King Léopold II, while claiming that Belgium had made many sacrifices for the Congo.[41] The Congolese needed to show some gratitude for Belgium's benevolence in trusting the Congolese with their own country's independence.[42] This luckily did not go unchallenged as Patrice Lumumba stood up to challenge the king:

> ...No Congolese worthy of the name will ever be able to forget that this independence has been won through a struggle, an urgent and idealistic struggle from day to day in which we did not spare our energy or our blood. We have experienced contempt, insults and blows endured morning and night; we knew law was never the same for the whites and blacks ... Who could forget the hangings and shootings in which perished so many?[43]

The king's words had not been simply a matter of bad colonial manners but a reflection of the real resentment the west felt of African self-governance as portrayed by the sham transfer of power shenanigans detailed here. This is because Belgium was already scheming, with the help of their local collaborators, to regain control of the vastly rich Congo and within a week of Lumumba's heroics, the shamed King's government had taken advantage of local divisions to militarily intervene in the country.[44] To date seven (26%) of all cases before the ICC emanate from the Congo although the Jean-Pierre Bemba case involved incidents occurring in a different country.[45] These cases revolve around armed conflicts in the mineral rich Eastern Congo, the same territory Belgium and other western powers wanted annexed from the Congo state to become Katanga.[46]

But if the liaison between Lumumba and the bad-mannered King was iconic, what have become similarly iconic in later times are the frequent visits by his countrymen to the Hague, as have those by Mr. Uhuru Kenyatta, a son of that other iconic African, Jomo Kenyatta. In the following section, I detail how Mr. Kenyatta's short-lived affair with the ICC produced a progeny of mistrust and accusations of colonialism.

Iconography of the Black Accused

If the image of Kenyatta at the ICC made Kenyans recall similar colonial mischief, to some of us in the diaspora, it represented yet another colonial legacy; an image of a black man in court accused of crimes he vehemently denies. I interrogate the images produced by the over-representation of the black accused at the ICC from a critical race theory perspective linking this to the already existing biases against black people in the criminal justice systems, for example in the USA and the UK. I argue that because France, USA and the UK were instrumental in drafting the Rome Statute: their colonial biases and the racism inherent in their own criminal justice systems were inherited by the ICC. Crucially as colonial states, they can still maintain their global power status using the ICC as a vehicle because, for example, the ICC is part of the UK's stated global agenda and support for international criminal justice is a core part of the UK's foreign policy.[47] Because he who pays the piper calls the tune, the UK maintains its control of the ICC through funding by contributing £8.9 million in 2017.[48] The UK's funding is largely in line with that of other key EU member states, who paid over 60% of the ICC's 2009 budget of €94.17m, leading some commentators to indicate that the EU is unconstitutionally dominating the ICC through financing.[49] This link to funding is important in that it shows the 'soft' power behind ICC operations and it is my contention that the ICC's involvement in situations such as Kenya and Ivory Coast are based on these behind-the-scenes machinations.

The influence of western powers at the ICC was recently seen in the ongoing power struggle between the ICC and the USA. Judges had stopped investigations around US activities in Afghanistan because, according to them, "investigations and prosecution was unlikely to be successful because the expectation is that those targeted, including the United States, Afghan authorities and the Taliban, would not cooperate."[50] This was despite the judges concluding that the prosecutor's "request establishes a reasonable basis to consider that crimes within the ICC jurisdiction have been committed in Afghanistan and that potential cases would be admissible before the court."[51] The prosecutor had indicated that there is evidence to suggest that from May 2003

> members of the US armed forces and the CIA have committed the war crimes of torture and cruel treatment, outrages upon personal dignity, and rape and other forms of sexual violence pursuant to a policy approved by the US authorities.[52]

In my view, the USA's stance displayed here contradicts its role in, for example, agitating for the ICC's intervention elsewhere. In the Kenyan cases for example, the USA was at the forefront of agitating for the accused to be brought to trial at the Hague and effectively campaigning for Kenyatta not to be elected as president in Kenya.[53] This fuelled the suggestion that foreign interests, and specifically the United States were tacitly supporting Mr. Odinga as their preferred candidate for Kenya's presidency[54] which when seen together with the Gbagbo case suggests the instrumentation of the ICC for political/regime change purposes.

Apart from their influences at the ICC, there are marked similarities between the USA and the UK criminal justice systems. Both have policies leading to the privatisation of the justice system and an increase in a privately run prison industrial complex.[55] This privatisation is crucial in that, as I explain severally in this book, there is an over representation of black men in this industrial complex, leading me and other commentators to make the link with slavery because the industry is making money out of black people's imprisonment. I extend the same argument in warning that ICL is already in the early days of mirroring this practice. More relevant to our post-colonial discourse is that these two countries occupy apex roles in global power play and their professed egalitarian justice systems are compromised by the over-criminalisation of the black body.[56] In this regard therefore, the ICC is not unique as a criminal justice system portraying the imagery of the all-powerful prosecutor/judge and the largely white lawyer fraternity prosecuting and/or defending a largely black group of accused.

This over-representation of the black accused becomes more toxic with the dissemination of imagery through mass media and the consequential forming of opinions of guilt or innocence, either in the courts or in the public mind. This is true in both the domestic contexts of the UK and USA and in the ICC. For example the bright custody outfits for a largely black prison population in the USA creates a subsequent public association of black men and crime as well as the presumption of guilt by a jury because of the imagery of cuffs and bright prison uniforms.[57] Commercial advertising has long utilised colour to form public opinions and eventually the public who become used to brightly clothed black men in criminal courts, will associate black men with crime in general.[58] This, I argue, has the long lasting effect of a general assumption that a claim against any black man must be justified and inhumane treatment at the hands of state agencies seen as fit and proper. Similarly, although the accused at the ICC are not in brightly coloured outfits, an association of black men/leadership with 'impunity' becomes etched in the public's mind. This public perception in my view is a powerful tool for the right to intervene/change of regime industry but also may lead to the public, particularly in the west, not closely interrogating the way these cases at the ICC are brought.

These public perceptions are important because research on sentencing in the UK and USA constantly shows that minorities, and particularly black people, are arrested more often than white people and are more likely to be sentenced to prison terms than white people.[59] There are various explanations for the differences between black people and white people in their experiences of the criminal justice system(s) with some suggesting that minorities engage differentially in deviant and criminal behaviour while others says that the criminal justice system (CJS) treats minorities differently.[60] What concerns me in the discourse about the ICC vs Africa is that when this local research is translated to an international level, it becomes apparent that CJS are seen as less legitimate by minorities as compared to white people, based on personal experiences of their own unjust treatment as well as the experiences of others in the same community.[61]

Therefore, I perceive the ICC as less just because all I observe is people looking like me on trial and no white men on trial at the Hague. Thus, my negative experiences of UK/USA domestic CJSs influence my perceptions of the ICC's legitimacy and black people often have more negative attitudes towards the CJS even when considering the same objective event as white people.[62] This does not mean that the court does not have black officials working in it, as do many colonial institutions. The legitimacy I challenge here is not so narrowly defined but entails 'epistemological' colonialism which, for example, is not addressed by prominent African women judges who detail their brilliant legal scholarship and careers at international tribunals in their seminal work.[63] One way of looking at these judges' work is that it promotes African voices in these high international tribunals/offices. Similarly, one can see the judges making the claim that, as African women, they are equal to the task – as equal as white men? They may also act as an inspiration to other elite African women who strive for international jobs. If I were to look at their work from that perspective, these African judges work to support my hypothesis that Africa does have the capacity to deal with international crimes in the continent as these prominent judges worked in Africa before moving to the Hague. But alas! I am not persuaded to see their work from any other but a decolonising perspective. And from this perspective, the good judges succeed only in claiming their agency as legal elites to participate in the highest levels of their profession but fail in my view to be of any decolonising inspiration. Their work ends up emphasising the need for and perpetuating colonial law if the law allows qualified and well-meaning individuals of African descent to serve on benches. The argument I make in this book is that a colonial system will have a similar effect on a black body whether the officer involved is black or white, female, or male. It is more pertinent to ask why black professionals work for racist/oppressive/colonial institutions and, like these prominent judges and others, promote these institutions amongst their populations?

There are two main reasons I could find why black professionals tend to support racist organisations. First, these organisations seek to employ token black people as one way of dealing with criticisms of racism/legitimacy.[64] Accepting a few 'safe' outsiders not only addresses legitimisation but simultaneously excludes most black women from the knowledge validation process.[65] This is because these few black women in positions of authority must work within the taken-for-granted assumptions of black female inferiority shared by the scholarly community and by the culture at large.[66] Yvette Abrahams also notes this phenomenon in academia when she says that she goes through a contradictory experience where the very fact of her economic exploitation as a black academic could put her in a situation where she is teaching racist and sexist texts and hence is complicit in her own and others' oppression.[67] While writing about the Cape Lady, she says that colonial capitalism demanded of her to either completely assimilate or be exposed to sexual ridicule as a Khoekhoe woman. Her exploitation was completed in a very particular, racialised and gendered way.[68]

It would appear from the recent UK Government's Commission on Racial Disparities Report[69] that some black/brown people have no issue with this tokenism or indeed its utility in legitimisation and would spew outright distortions of facts on colonialism, structural racism and slavery to appease master.[70] The African judges and other black elites like the ones in the discredited Commission prove only that there are powerful socio-political forces in society that select for 'success' those BME people who generally support the establishment and are unlikely to 'rock the boat' – generally regarded as 'token-blacks.'[71] Fernando Suman, while writing about his experiences working in the NHS, says that:

> …when an official body is set up to consider issues of race and culture, it is either these 'token blacks' who are invited to participate or people (a) carefully chosen for being 'safe' from the point of view of the establishment, which generally wants to suppress any views that may challenge powerful professional groups or government policy; and (b) who seem to follow personal rather than community agendas. …The way institutional racism operates has become masked by the divisions between groups and the ability of the national system to divide and rule, which dates from the days of 'divide and rule' in the Empire. White supremacy still rules although perhaps less obviously than it used to—and white in this instance includes some black and brown faces.[72]

And rocking the colonial boat is to be avoided at all costs it seems, as we saw recently in relation to the ICC. One of the last acts of Fatou Bensouda as a prosecutor was to close the preliminary examination of the war crimes committed by British soldiers in Iraq.[73] Bizarrely, she confirmed that there is a reasonable basis to believe that members of the British armed forces committed the war crimes of wilful killing, torture, inhuman/cruel treatment, outrages upon personal dignity, and rape and/or other forms of sexual violence.[74] However, despite no soldier/general or political leader being brought to justice in the UK for this,[75] the prosecutor could not find evidence that the UK investigative and prosecutorial bodies had engaged in shielding.[76] Shortly after, Madam Bensouda retired as the prosecutor. If the reader was yet to be convinced on my selectivity arguments, here was an opportunity for the ICC to dispel the views expressed in this book on selectivity but what we see is yet another example of Article 17 being interpreted to favour a powerful state. Compare and contrast this approach to the one taken in Kenya for example, where promises of local processes were seen as attempts to evade justice – hence the Kenyan cases.

Second, although there is no doubt that self-interest and group identification motivate human behaviour, system justification theory shows that for various reasons, "people have the motive to defend and justify the social status quo, even among those who are seemingly most disadvantaged by it."[77] One can for example see Bensouda's/the African judges' positions regarding ICL as motivated by self-interest as members of an elite class or that they have already anticipated and rationalised that the neo-liberal hegemony is here to stay and hence they need to protect their positions within it. This is a well-researched trend where people shift preferences toward future social and political arrangements that become dominant.[78]

It is not just defending the system that is harmful to the African. Research has also identified that the actual practice of the 'black officer' at times becomes over-zealous in the implementation of racist law. For example, a study done in Cincinnati tested whether increasing diversity by recruiting black officers in the police decreases biased police behaviour against black citizens.[79] Findings suggested, surprisingly, that black suspects were more likely to be arrested by a black officer than a white officer.[80] The explanation for this phenomenon was that black officers feel caught in a loyalty quagmire where they must pick a side and behave in a manner that makes their allegiance to the white male-dominated police force clear. They do this by (over-)enforcing the law against black people and proving (by numbers) that they do not favour their fellow black people while enforcing the law.[81]

Recognising that most of this research has been done only at a domestic level, I advance a theoretical linkage between these local racial disparities in criminal justice contact and legitimacy amongst black people and the emerging distrust of Africans towards the ICC because I argue that Africans do not have faith in their local 'colonial' CJS and these localised negative views of the criminal legal systems have an impact on how black citizens view the law.[82] This in turn starts to explain why it takes little if any incitement for African people to be sceptical about the ICC despite the previous enthusiasm, as discussed in Chapter 2. It is therefore relatable to a black citizen globally when an accused at the ICC questions the legitimacy of the ICC because they themselves have experienced their own CJS as biased and racist. The narrative that the ICC could be biased and racist has meaning for black citizens globally: the treatment they experience locally, intentional or otherwise, negatively impacts the legitimacy of the law.

Therefore, imagery is important not just because of visual over-representation of black faces as accused and the legitimacy questions that follows from it, but because this imagery has a direct link with the court(s)' sentencing practices. For example research has shown that in the USA, if a defendant is perceived to be stereotypically black, he is more likely to be sentenced to death, where that is an available sentencing option, than a white person.[83] The relevant research isolated various other factors and found that this was even more likely when the victim was white and the defendant black.[84] Apart from death penalties, harsh sentencing and increased imprisonment are seen as affecting black people disproportionately.[85] And therefore I submit that this over-representation of black accused at local levels is reproduced at the ICC which brings to the international level a vicious cycle that leads to support for harsh criminal-justice policies amongst a general public influenced by the imagery of blackness.

It would not be far-fetched from my perspective to hypothesise that the ICC is widely accepted in the west particularly because of this over-representation of the black accused. In two experiments in the USA for example, researchers showed that when the penal system is portrayed as only affecting black people, the population (white people) were more supportive of draconian penal policies than if the penal system was less black. Worryingly, the general population thought there was more crime being committed just because black people were disproportionately represented in penal system.[86] In a rather macabre twist, the legal industrial complex thrives by this leading of the population(s) to support discriminative polices which produce very clear and visible disproportionality through exposing the public to extreme racial disparities, in turn perpetuating a vicious cycle.[87]

Because the ICC has only convicted and sentenced African men, there is no data to compare how they would have sentenced white convicts. There could be a temptation however to compare sentencing at the ICC with the ICTY, but such comparisons do not make any sense in the context of this book because the contention here is that the ICC is supposed to be a global court while the ICTY was situation specific. However, research shows there is not much of a discrepancy in the sentences given by the ICTY and the ICC so far. For example, by February 2021, the ICC had sentenced three individuals to sentences ranging from 14 years (Lubanga), 12 years (Katanga) and 9 years (Al Mahdi). Other sentences in the Bemba *et al.* case were commuted for time spent in custody.[88] On the other hand, of 57 persons convicted by February 2007 at the ICTY, 20 (35%) received sentences of less than 10 years, 28 (49%) sentences of between 10 and 20 years and 9 (16%) sentences above 20 years with one life sentence.[89]

The overt racial disparity already taking shape at the ICC particularly in regard to the accused and the victims at the ICC, has insidious connotations for Africans because scholars are increasingly making the link between this criminal justice industrial complex and slavery. To make this predication real in the reader's mind, consider that the ICC jurisdiction is always expanding to include non-state actors, as already discussed in Chapter 3. This means that the ICC has a ready market in the many weak states and 'ungoverned' spaces in Africa to 'germinate' cases. To return to the core argument however, the contention is that despite slavery being abolished, the same legal instruments that abolished it created new forms of slavery. For example, the American constitution is increasingly being seen by activists and scholars to have simultaneously abolished and perpetuated slavery through the 13th Amendment because it allows individuals to be enslaved as a punishment for a crime.[90] What agitates activists is that this amendment suggests that slavery is an appropriate method of penal code 'rehabilitation' while all other forms of involuntary servitude are illegal.[91] What becomes even more concerning is the fact that because the particular crimes that needs to be punished with 'slavery' are undefined within the 13th

Amendment, individual states are left to decide what these crimes are (without federal guidelines) which means in practice that African Americans are criminalised on an industrial scale, leading to their renewed enslavement.[92]

The southern states utilised this loophole to great effect and this continues to date with the CJS and prisons becoming a way of actualising this renewed enslavement: even as legal slavery was ending, they developed a penal system that was able to legally return black populations to slavery conditions.[93] These conditions are not only commercial enterprises for the 'lawyer' led industries such as bond/bail and prison real estate, but there is an increasing use of prison populations in manufacturing.[94] The ICC legal industrial complex does not yet equal the USA in terms of the bodies in prison, but further research is necessary to find out the size of the consultancy, lawyer, NGO, fixer industry that is already well established around ICC operations in African states. At this point, I am hoping that the reader can recall my discourse in the previous chapter on how western states, while seemingly leaving African states to be free states, created a global system that in effect meant no change: it is my view that the similarities between these two historical moments affecting black people are not a coincidence.

I conclude this section by arguing that in the wider reproduction of knowledge discourse, the ICC and international lawyer fraternity feigned surprise at the rate at which the ICC has been rejected in Africa and that their reaction is founded on the same feigned blindness most local lawyers in the UK and the USA display regarding the disproportionate effect of CJSs on black accused: hence their continued uncritical participation in the industry. It is impossible from my own experiences working as a lawyer in the UK or in the USA and from the research mentioned above not to notice the disparities in the criminal justice systems, including the fact that black people are disproportionately over-represented as 'merchandise' of the criminal justice industrial complex, including prisons.[95] However, more central to our discourse is that the developing mistrust of the ICC in Africa should be linked to the research I explored earlier, showing that black people generally view the CJS as illegitimate and less just than white people due to their own personal experiences of ill treatment.[96] More concerning for the advocates of the ICC is the fact that it is not just the black people directly impacted by this ill treatment who feel the system is illegitimate, but the wider black community who view the CJS as illegitimate.[97] Therefore the eventual rejection of the ICC by Africans should not surprise a postcolonial scholar because there is evidence to show the connection between racial discrimination within the CJS and the perceived legitimacy of the law.[98] Because globalisation has affected every corner of the globe, it would be racist to assume that the African following trials at the Hague on his/her TV does not see themself represented by the accused/victim at the ICC.

The Black Accused, Law and Language

If the over-representation of the black accused breeds mistrust of the ICC, this cannot be fully understood without an exploration of the associated alienation of African legal traditions and languages there. This section addresses these issues in relation to what this means for a de-colonised legal system. In observing media coverage and video archives of the Kenyan cases[99] for example, I note that the presence of the black accused is set amidst an array of accompanying Eurocentric court rituals and the other particularly important component of this iconography of the ICC, language. The ICC I argue, has reproduced two main colonial characters of the relationship between Eurocentric law and the African citizen. One is that no African language is an official language at the ICC and the other, related to this, is the use of translators and interpreters. The initial point to make is that, apart from legal texts and instruments, including the Rome Statute that establishes the ICC, being in French and English, they are also written in highly technical legalistic language. This means they are essentially written in another language – that of the Law. Scholars, including Constable, describe the many ways in which law relates to, or is, language. Lawyers and judges work in and through language. "It is more than a tool or resource; it constitutes the shelter from which we know the world and act in it … Our claims of law happen through our words in the world."[100] To fully comprehend the coloniality of the ICC's exclusive use of European languages is to therefore first understand that law in itself is a distinctive language as well as a linguistic institution over and above its being a social institution manifested in non-linguistic ways.[101] Therefore one cannot explore whether law is an extension of the empire without addressing the language issues at the core of it because "laws are coded in language, and the processes of the law are mediated through language. The legal system puts into action a society's beliefs and values and it permeates many areas of life."[102]

While the effects of interpreting legal proceedings and texts has been researched and well documented, the effects of the law itself being a language requiring interpretation is a topic less researched and discussed in the context of the ICC. For this to be discussed in relation to decolonising the ICC is particularly crucial because authors indicate that speech patterns and deliveries could influence courts' opinions on the credibility or otherwise of testimonies.[103] In African cases at the ICC therefore, accents and proficiency in European languages become central in the defendants' cases as the way their testimony is presented affects its believability. While the accused's testimony may be jeopardised by poor command or lack of foreign languages, this also means that if law is seen as a language, the lawyer becomes a translator – in a sense the lawyer loses her/his role as solely representing his/her client and takes on a dual role of translator and lawyer simultaneously. Where there was already a gap between lawyer and client, this duality expands that gap. This is because the translator is faced with the same kind of gap as the lawyer, a gap marked by language.[104]

There are those, like James Boyd, who see no contradictions in a lawyer being an interpreter as they view the lawyer's role as a reviewer of texts, like a literary critic.[105] However my point is different in that the lawyer dealing with the black accused has to navigate triple language worlds and at times more; from legalistic language to French to English to local language for example. This interpretation of language after the interpretation of law influences legal proceedings in ways that can affect the outcome of those proceedings. This is particularly so in the outcome of trials where the reliability of evidence is assessed by jurors. It is now a well-documented fact that, as interpreters translate for example from English to Spanish and Spanish to English, they alter the assignment of agency of acts (who did an act), making such agency implicit where it was explicit and explicit where it was implicit.[106] They also alter the style of witness testimony, making it more or less 'powerful' and formal. The activity of interpreters also changes the organisation of the speaker's speech pattern which dilutes the meanings/ power of spoken words.[107]

This discourse around language in relation to decolonising the ICC is crucial because it touches the core of the decolonising argument that, in addition to loss of land, Africans did not regain the use of their languages in the post- colonial government.[108] This is crucial in relation to law and other cultural norms because, as Ngugi states,

> language is a carrier of a people's culture; culture is a carrier of a people's values; values are the basis of a people's self-definition - the basis of their consciousness. And when you destroy a people's language, you are destroying that very important aspect of their heritage … you are in fact destroying that which helps them to define themselves … that which embodies their collective memory as a people. It is precisely what imperialism in fact did.[109]

In Africa, colonial languages remain prominent in government and business and as the mode of instruction in education.[110] This use of colonial languages means that the majority of citizens are excluded from the 'governing' process, and it also means that the resulting reconstruction of memories has been undertaken in the colonisers' favour; using his/her language and her/ his mode of recording(s).[111] Essentially, the resulting government remained colonial in nature as experts, including Ngugi, identify the dominance of colonial languages in Africa both in government and literature as the continuation of colonialism.[112]

In international law, the continued use of colonial languages as universal is a concern to say the least. Most African countries still use colonial languages as their 'official' languages, which is replicated at the ICC. Therefore a link between the local colonial language's use and its mirroring at the ICC is important for our discussion, particularly as I raise the question of the ICC's legitimacy in this book. UNESCO, for example, reported that only 63 African languages (out of an estimated 1,000–2,000 spoken on the continent) are used in justice systems and only 26 countries allow African languages in legislation.[113] With only an estimated 10%–15% of the African populace fluent in official European languages,[114] the linguistic alienation in formal domains of law and justice is clear. This then translates to an uncomfortable fact that only an estimated 10%–15% of Africans would be able to read let alone access the Rome Statute. Understanding the legal language of the Statute would be an even larger conundrum. This impasse was captured better by Ngugi who described the scene in a typical African court, where the applicable law is written in a European language and the officials of the court conduct proceedings in a European language. If the accused can speak only an African language, he or she will require an interpreter.

> The defense, prosecution and the judge occupy a linguistic sphere totally removed from the person whose guilt or innocence is on the line … This was the way it was in the colonial era; this is the way it is in the postcolonial era.[115]

Iconography of Colonial Court Architecture and the ICC

The continuation of the colonial at the ICC exists not only through language but also in the idea of justice and world order as represented outwardly by the ICC's court building. Therefore in this section, I interrogate the ICC courthouse and courtroom architecture from that perspective. This is necessary because our environment is shaped by architecture which realises in design and physical form society's desires and needs and in so doing, architecture mirrors society by manifesting its values and needs.[116] In this regard, the ICC buildings are the physical manifestation of the stated 'global' society's needs and values and we may therefore use it to explore wider global ideology. The way we design and manage spaces sold as 'global' and universal in ownership and access is important in a post-colonial dissection of international bodies such at the ICC. This is because of the increasing acceptance in international law scholarship of the political nature of the law. If law is political, so is the space where this law happens, which is intimately tied to ideology and politics and not just an object existing in no context. The shaping and modelling of space has always been a political and ideological process that is inspired by historical and natural elements.[117] My contention here is underlined by the well-documented fact that one of the most long-lasting effects of colonialism has been the colonial architecture in previously occupied territories in Africa, Asia, and Latin America for example.[118]

Rasmussen argues that architecture should be easily comprehensible to all because it is made by ordinary people, for ordinary people.[119] I think this is true when architecture is organic and grassroots led, as it was/is in villages where housing is still locally designed and built. However, architecture – especially relating to municipal spaces – has been used over the years by the elite to shape and propagate ideologies. It is important to note that European metropolitan architecture was heavily exported to Africa and other colonies and the emerging urbanisations were copies of or reflected European architecture, but to legitimise their rule, colonisers occasionally incorporated selected native forms and aesthetics. This selected use of local elements, especially in the design of public buildings, was also meant to suppress or diminish local resistance to the occupation.[120] This political use of architecture is common in eurocentrism. Rosebloom, for example, notes that just as the architecture of socialist and fascist cities reflected the ideology of their societies, architecture in America also mirrors that state's unique values and ideals.[121]

The irony of the Netherlands hosting the ICC building at the Hague and becoming a centre for global justice, with its long history of slavery, colonialism and modern-day racism, has never been lost on me, a child of the still enslaved and colonised. Apart from Dutch settlers designing Apartheid for example, the Dutch were pioneers in the slave trade and were the first to 'export' slaves to Africa.[122] The ICC's building has always appeared to me as a series of interconnected glass boxes, one taller than the others. Did the architects realise that the shorter towers appear like shipping containers from a certain perspective? Was this a deliberate tribute to the sea-going, slave-trading globalisation? Should one interpret this to mean that the boxes contain/detain the court (justice)? The literature I have reviewed does not say what the boxes mean, but Africa should not worry about being left out as an inspiration for the design because some of its flora may be found in the ICC's well-kept gardens.[123]

The architects who designed the ICC's building at the Hague describe its aim as,

> …to communicate trust, hope and – most importantly – faith in justice and fairness. The building requires the courage to be an ambassador for the credibility and values of the ICC … It is important that a formal institution like the ICC does not constitute barriers for people. On the contrary, it expresses the very essence of democratic architecture.[124]

If the building is supposed to portray the claimed global inclusivity, it fails at the design stage because it is full of contradictions. Transparent yet highly secure, accessible yet you need a passport to visit.[125]

The building is isolated from its neighbours by a ring of security measures:

> After passing the large plaza and the security check, the route leads outside once again, to a walled space that leads up to the main entrance. Inside these walls, the building is surrounded by water, reminding one

> of a castle moat. The building itself is transparent and opaque at the same time. Its façade is covered with trapezoidal windows. The angles of the glass alternate to create a feeling of movement and reflection, but also designed to defeat sniper targeting.[126]

I think the reference to snipers is meant to add suspense and dramatic effect to the theatrics inside the building. However, from a liberating thought perspective, one cannot but contrast the ICC building with *Gacaca* courts. *Gacaca* by its very nature did portray a sense of freedom/organicism in my view, although this was obviously achieved intentionally.

In what is pertinent to our ICC discourse, Rosebloom notes that court architecture reveals a legal ideology in flux.[127] The ICC building at the Hague is a good example of Rosebloom's observation that

> while courtroom designs have remained largely unchanged, conveying a certain stability and continuity within our legal system, changes in courthouse exteriors to styles reminiscent of corporate architecture seem to indicate that something is changing in the way the public perceives law's role in contemporary society.[128]

While the ICC building design is claimed to represent transparency values,[129] a more convincing argument is that ICC rejection of the "old classical style may be interpreted as an expression of society's increased discontent with the law and its growing uncertainty regarding the system's ability to administer justice."[130] Disguising the internal functions of the law behind a corporate facade could be interpreted as an attempt to convey corporate order and to overcome uncertainty by embracing corporate values such as efficiency, order, and predictability. It proceeds on the basis that the internal functions of the building are anchored in something perceived to be secure, or at least more secure than the current perception of the legal system. The corporate structure symbolises what today's society considers or recognises to be stable and the need to house the internal application of the law in that stability. In this way, the exterior facade functions as corporate advertising that masks prevalent, negative views about the law's state of efficiency and legitimacy.[131]

Because the building has so far predominantly 'contained' African cases, the 'clothing' of the court in a shiny corporate façade is crucial for my post-colonial discourse because there is a historical marriage of the law and capital as I have already discussed in relation to the USA justice system, as well as a history between slavery and the law. This marriage of law and colonial capital, represented in my view by the iconic ICC building at the Hague, signifies capital becoming enmeshed in 'securing rule of law,' which is not a new phenomenon because this was the basis of empire building. For example, when the British East India Company went to India for trading purposes, it quickly became the effective government by gaining administrative and judicial powers including that of revenue collection. Traders became judges, founding the Privy Council as the highest court of appeal, while the English legal notion of precedent was introduced in the region.[132]

Dissecting the ICC architecture with this new lens, we see that capital investment in the buildings designs the law itself. This insidious colonial trick is repeated at the ICC's building design to advertise to the public a perception of the law as efficient, predictable, and stable, as represented by the corporate façade. The ICC's building unwittingly lays bare the politics of law and capital while at the same time revealing the attempts to hide this fact in plain sight by effortlessly creating a parasitic relationship, where the wounded reputation of the legal system aligns itself with the power, wealth, and largeness of the corporate structure and society's perception of it on the outside.[133] Once seen as the symbol of monumentality, power, and stability, classical architecture has given way to society's new perception of monumentality, power, and stability: the corporate structure.[134] I would say that the design and outlook of the ICC building subtly broadcast the fact that after slavery and the colonisation and domination of the globe through capitalism by corporations like the East India Company, current attempts to decolonise the global order or even public space is itself are a futile endeavour – capital is still in charge. And so, capital frustrates any attempts to escape from its 'capture,' presented here by the ICC glass boxes, and simultaneously presents itself once again as the liberator. This is in line with the practice commonly known as ethics washing, in which corporations are increasingly selling themselves as pro-human rights or pro-clean environment.[135]

It is however important to explore at this point how I view this physical architecture as linking to the over-representation of the black male in criminal justice systems and by extension the over-representation of the African accused at the ICC. My argument is that the ICC risks reproducing the neo-enslavement of black men through an increasingly commercialised justice system, as discussed earlier in relation to America and the 13th Amendment. I argue that the ICC is signalling its alignment with the private corporate sector by its architecture, in preparation for a future where the private sector becomes ever more active in provision of international criminal law services, leading to the (in)famous private bond/bail/prison industrial complex. I further posit that the ICC's corporate exterior facade is signalling a perception that justice is impossible without the business model. This vision of the law as aligning itself with the corporate sector is identified as consistent with the dominance of plea bargaining in the USA criminal justice system where over 95% of all cases are decided by plea bargaining.[136]

For my commercialisation point, it is notable that the ICC, like the ICTY, is procedurally a hybrid common and civil law court. In these two legal traditions, there is an increase in the practice of judges becoming resource managers rather than independent 'umpires' and their roles increasingly include budgetary considerations with a focus on hastening case conclusions.[137] Because of this, plea bargaining which started at the ICTY with *Erdemovid*,[138] has arrived at the ICC. This commercial practice of time management and resource allocation led to the judges' acceptance of plea bargaining at the ICTY and later at the ICC, which then led to the managerial judging system replacing the orthodox adversarial criminal trial model with an increase in plea bargains.[139] Plea bargaining was recently seen at the ICC in the *Mahdi* case discussed in Chapter 5. In accepting his guilty plea as a mitigating factor in sentencing, trial chamber judges indicated that his plea saved the court time and resources, the court was at pains to point out that there was overwhelming evidence of his guilt nonetheless.[140]

In plea bargaining at local level and at these ICL courts we see private individuals being encouraged by the courts to operate independently of the legal principles applied in the courtroom and to apply the market principle of bargaining e.g., how much is manslaughter worth.[141] My contention is that the ICC architecture reflects this private dealing by adopting the corporate style to symbolise people's perception of a mechanistic plea bargaining process that occurs between private individuals independent of the courtroom and public realm. The corporate façade symbolises the political wave of plea bargaining by physically connecting the courtroom functions with the iconographical symbol of the private sector, the corporate structure. Finally, this dissonance of disparate elements, internally and externally coupled with the masking of the interior, is suggestive of a post-modern style.[142] One of the cornerstones of post-modernist thought is the idea of pastiche.[143] Pastiche is the layering of sensible and non-sensible, related and non-related styles over one another. The layering of the new exterior courthouse corporate design over the legal functions within is the iconographical example of pastiche.[144] On the inside lies the traditional public realm of the courtroom where the constitutional principles continue to be applied. Wrapped around the courtroom is the fundamentally different private corporate design. I wonder, however, if the Hague building designers considered the stone throwing and mudslinging involved in ICL before housing this law in a glass box. In my view, the glass corporate design of the Hague building tends to portray fragility rather than the predictable, 'business as normal' stability envisaged.

Apart from the externals of the court building prophesying the commercialisation of international criminal law, the design and layout of the courtrooms themselves as power spaces has been well researched. Increasingly, researchers are interrogating with rigour, the interaction between law, place and space and how these are brought together as a governing tool, as was well documented by Foucault.[145] In that regard, when one looks at how court rooms are designed as detailed by Rosenbloom, Foucault's arguments on how space is fundamentally about the exercise of power comes to live especially how the separation is made between defendants, lawyers, judges, jurors and the public.[146] When one views courtrooms in this manner, they are not just a flat, immobilised surface but are alive with meanings and effects. In a criminal law setting such as the ICC, where oral testimony is crucial and the procedure is adversarial, the courtroom becomes a theatre where performance means everything. In this theatrical setting the credibility of a witness could be put in jeopardy by the poor architectural design of space, sight lines or acoustics.[147]

While the designers claim that the ICC building is a democratic space, in reality the Court at the Hague repeats an already established format where power relations are the core considerations,

> ...different parties will not coincidently run into each other. Staff are separated from audience; judges are separated from attorneys; defence separated from prosecution ... public galleries of the courtroom are open to visitors, but strict rules apply. Visitors are requested to be silent, pay attention, and to dress suitably. The gallery is separated from the courtroom by a thick glass.[148]

In this regard therefore, one cannot discuss the courtroom design, especially the ICC's court room design, without the necessary consideration of post-colonial power relations and the obvious tensions in the ICC's Court house and courtroom design in portraying both power and authority and judicial independence or impartiality in the same breath. Court rooms are designed in such ways that there are different roles for everyone in the courtroom to play and the space is organised in such a manner as to make clear where power lies.[149] This is done in seating arrangements, lighting, furniture arrangement, and court entry points.[150] With judge/lawyer court attire to suit, this power role playing completes the theatre inspired courtroom design.[151]

A visit to one of the ICC courtrooms shows that the classical sitting arrangements detailed above have not changed much, there is however a notable shift from the heavy wooden set-ups of the archetypical English courtroom to soft leather corporate style seats as well as to a heavy reliance on technology. So far, my research has not identified literature dealing with this shift in the ICC's courtroom furniture design. I would argue that while the socialist ideology called for a circular, minimal design to promote an equal and communal society[152] and fascist ideology called for an axial, repetitive, monumental design to promote order and rigidity in society,[153] the neo-liberalist ICC portrays the pre-eminence of capitalisation of the law as a commodity in its courtroom design. This corporate court design fails to relate to grassroots justice because it is far removed from the sites where these crimes occurred, and therefore I argue that the ICC is not appropriate as a court setting for these African situations. The *Gacaca* model would be a more appropriate set-up, allowing mass participation and giving no space for Eurocentric lawyers.[154] Often held outdoors, those courts allowed community participation and most importantly ensured that those who actually committed the atrocities were held accountable to their victims and the community.[155]

I will explore *Gacaca* as a viable alternative in fuller detail, later in Chapter 6, but it is important to mention it here in relation to courtroom design and architecture. In contrast to Eurocentric courts, *Gacaca* and other 'southern' heritage courts are better equipped to deal with collective atrocities because of their communal nature while, as we see above, Eurocentric courts are obsessed with power relations and their courtroom designs heighten the senses of inclusion and exclusion. This exclusion is truly relevant in the context of the ICC being staged at the Hague which is far-removed from where the African cases originate. The court being far away from Africa is however not accidental, as research shows that courthouse designers feel contempt and fear for the public that uses those courts.

Therefore, the ICC being in the Hague rather than Arusha, for example, where there have been international tribunals in the past,[156] shows the cosmopolitan mistrust of the unruly and potentially disruptive African and hence the need to shield the court from him or her. For example, Paul Rock showed that court designs also extend to zones outside the court rooms and limit public access.[157] His study showed that the exclusionist culture is fuelled by the fear of an unruly and disruptive public and this mistrust of the public extends to court staff's understanding of the court as their territory.[158] An attempt to visit any court hearing at the Hague, or indeed any local British court, confirms this 'ownership' of space that is demonstrated by court staff and the lawyer fraternity. This is because court houses are designed with expanded 'nonpublic' spaces for administration purposes and other reserved areas with no public access, displaying yet again the idea of territory and hierarchy.[159] For the African accused, victim or observer visiting the ICC at the Hague, these spaces emphasise the outsider-insider dichotomy I explored earlier on.[160]

In the *Gacaca* model, I argue that we see no 'lawyers only zones' or docks, no court room jingoism, no Victorian fashion sense, and no use of the French or English languages with unhealthy doses of Latin. There is no sense of exclusivity because exclusivity designs have real impact on the fairness of proceedings. Scholars like David Tait argue that court design, especially in the use of docks, exposes the oppressive foundations of the courtroom.[161] He further argues that if the accused is to be seen as a fellow citizen of the jury, then their sitting arrangements should be similar.[162] Rather than being on the margins, defendants should also be able to sit with their legal teams to give instructions, receive feedback and be consulted when necessary.[163]

As opposed to the *Gacaca* model, the Eurocentric ICC replicates a nineteenth century elitist barrister caste setting where the defence legal team sits, almost conspiratorially, alongside prosecutors and away from their defendants.[164] This Eurocentric courtroom does not promote positive lawyer-client dialogue and the sitting arrangements, especially the existence of docks, preclude the presumption of innocence while the intimacy of the defence and prosecution lawyers signals conspiracy rather than fair trial.[165] Although, for example, Kenyatta was not placed in a dock at the ICC, the placing of a defendant in the dock is inherently prejudicial and unfair to her or him.[166]

Crucially for the defendant at the ICC, court designs have direct impact on the accused's right to a fair hearing and the use of the courtroom, in particular sitting allocation, can impact due process. Although this principle is yet to be tested at the ICC, in *V v United Kingdom [1999]*,[167] the defendant (a minor) was successful in claiming that the cumulative effect of various aspects of the trial translated into the denial of a fair hearing and gave rise to a breach of his human rights.[168] Most significantly, the courtroom's physical layout was found to have interfered with his right to a fair hearing.[169] I therefore suggest it would be legally important to test this principle in relation to the physical situation of the court at the Hague in relation to African defendants and the court's insistence that the accused be present at non-crucial/procedural hearings at the ICC.

Conclusions

In this chapter, I began by detailing how images from the ICC are perceived by global audiences as well as audiences from the accused's own state, and how both the court and the accused have used such images. We have seen, for example, how the ICC, at least in the Kenyatta case, was naïve if not blind to political messaging and the power of courtroom appearances. I have also explored the interaction between the ICC's physical architecture and the idea of 'acting out justice' or justice being 'seen' to be done. The Eurocentric environment in which the African trials happen is a physical expression of the 'global' populace's relationship with the ideals of justice and in my view reflects the distortion of the term 'global.' The literature reviewed on the ICC and its relationship with the African cases ignores the power of the messaging involved in court architecture and space utilisation, including my argument that included in this messaging is the idea that international justice can only be served in a European city/space. The African as (still) the outsider and the European's role as the insider now has a material form. As we saw in Chapter 2, the cosmopolitan space is always selling a mirage to the African, and the law at the Hague is deliberately 'built' to be legitimately un-African. It logically follows that the African's capacity to call this judiciary to account is always debatable. What this chapter demonstrates therefore is that the space where justice is being seen to be done should be a contested space as it currently reduces the African citizen to a mere spectator at the ICC, the sphere where their justice is supposedly being delivered. The spatial and metaphysical distance between the African citizen and the ICC is exposed here because Africans become mere spectators of trials directly affecting them and there is little possibility of the African citizen participating in this arena.

In relation to this idea of participatory justice, the chapter deals with how architecture affects the conditions of 'judgecraft' or projection of power.

In recent times, the idea of transparency in the judicial arena has become the 'thing' to work towards and concerted efforts are made to design court houses around this view of transparent and participatory justice. For example, to promote an idea of transparency and break from the past, glass is extensively used in the design of the federal German court.[170] This seems to be what the ICC's building designers borrowed from because, as already noted, the ICC building is intended to portray transparency. In another 'new beginnings' design messaging, the Constitutional Court in South Africa is designed to project a conception of transformative constitutionalism.[171] Conversely however, housing ICL in this glass cage not only portrays fragility but also a sense of insecurity that comes with the knowledge that this form of law is exclusive. This is because ideas of inclusivity are not taken on board in the ICC court design as it is a purely Eurocentric design that ignores architectural influences from other corners of the world. To counter this Eurocentric law architecture, the chapter suggests looking at the example set already by *Gacaca* courts in Rwanda as an example of justice being served locally. The *Gacaca* model is suggested because, I argue, the presentation of the ICC as the place and site where all justice is served is a misapprehension formed by a deliberate effort inherited from past colonial courts to present the law as unique and only meted out by a select few. In that sense the Court is reduced to a cabal of a few elites and, therefore, it is the antithesis of a body able to resolve conflicts in the interests of a wider social justice.

In addition to physical architecture, I have dealt with the over-representation of black people in criminal justice systems. I explored how the use of colonial architecture, including language, at the ICC continues colonial practices of the past. The claim by the ICC to be a new way of acting out international justice is exposed here as a charade and the continuation of the past. The corporate outlook in architectural design of the ICC building and the courtrooms is linked to the argument that neo-liberalism has pervaded the legal sphere to the extent that corporations are seen as the guardians of the law and curators of stability for an increasingly edgy and untrusting global populace. Once again, the founders of colonialism are embraced as liberators, allowing them space to plunder the global south's resources without much notice. The over-representation of African accused at the ICC is well linked here with the discourse of the images of the black body in local CJS and with the iconography of the ever-present black criminal. This, in relation to our focus on the black body and criminal law, is crucial because inevitably, images and the representation of the African in legal imagery reduce the black body to a stereotype in the opposition of 'Good' and 'Evil'.

Notes

1 Baloji, *Le jour d'après* in Kinshasha Succursale (Crammed Discs 2010); in this remake, Baloji interprets the classic Grand Kalle's *independence cha cha cha* and laments broken promises. If the reader is still with me, you will recall at the

beginning of Chapter 3, Alpha Blondy sings of being tired of the *cha cha cha*, referencing Grand Kalle's independence song, but Alpha is alluding to the lack of it.

2 Ann Sagan, 'African Criminals/African Victims: The Institutionalised Production of Cultural Narratives in International Criminal Law' (2010) 39 (1) *Millennium* 8–9.

3 Martti Koskenniemi, 'Legal Cosmopolitanism: Tom Franck's Messianic World' (2003) 35 (2) *New York University Journal of International Law and Politics* 485.

4 See for example Judith Resnik and Dennis Edward Curtis, *Representing Justice: Invention, Controversy, and Rights in City-States and Democratic Courtrooms* (Yale University Press 2011).

5 Roelof Van Straten, *An Introduction to Iconography: Symbols, Allusions and Meaning in the Visual Arts* (Routledge 1994) 3.

6 Ibid.

7 Ibid, 6–10

8 Ibid.

9 Ibid.

10 Ibid., 4.

11 Ibid.

12 Ibid.

13 Richard Chalfen, 'Looking Two Ways: Mapping the Social Scientific Study of Visual Culture' in Eric Margolis and Luc Pauwels (eds), *The SAGE Handbook of Visual Research Methods* (SAGE 2011) 24–48.

14 Marion G. Müller, 'Iconography and Iconology as a Visual Method and Approach' in Eric Margolis and Luc Pauwels (eds), The SAGE Handbook of Visual Research Methods (SAGE 2011) 285.

15 Ibid., 286.

16 Susanne D. Mueller, 'Kenya and the International Criminal Court (ICC): Politics, the Election and the Law' (2014) 8 (1) *Journal of Eastern African Studies* 25–42.

17 Awol K. Allo, 'The Courtroom as a Site of Epistemic Resistance: Mandela at Rivonia' (2020) 16 (1) *Law Culture and the Humanities* 127–150.

18 See for example Gabrielle Lynch, 'The International Criminal Court and the making of a Kenyan President' (2015) 114 (772) *Current History* 183.

19 On Hobbes generally, see Glen Newey, *Routledge Philosophy Guidebook to Hobbes and Leviathan* (Routledge 2008).

20 James Verini, 'The Prosecutor and the President' *nytimes.com*, 22 June 2016 accessed 20 July 2020.

21 For an understanding of how these 'fathers' of the nation became icons, see for example the case of Nkrumah in Ghana as discussed in Harcourt Fuller, 'Father of the Nation: Ghanaian Nationalism, Internationalism and the Political Iconography of Kwame Nkrumah 1957– 2010' (2015) 16 (1) *African Studies Quarterly* 39–75.

22 As well as Jomo Kenyatta and the Kepenguria six see also the shaping of Mandela and others from the Rivonia trial discussed by Kenneth S. Broun, *Saving Nelson Mandela: The Rivonia Trial and the Fate of South Africa* (Oxford University Press 2012).

23 On how Uhuru Kenyatta inherited his father's legacy, see amongst others: Gabriel Oguda, 'Fifty Years on, Kenyatta Junior Faces Challenge of Fulfilling His Father's Promise of True Freedom# Kenya@ 50' (2013) *Africa at LSE*.

24 For a detailed discussion of the Kapenguria six trial, see Slater Montagu, *The Trial of Jomo Kenyatta* (Secker and Warburg 1956).

25 See for example Kenyatta's life in London discussed in Simon Gikandi, 'Pan-Africanism, and Cosmopolitanism: The Case of Jomo Kenyatta' (2000) 43 (1) *English Studies in Africa* 3–27 where Kenyatta is said to have presented as

a Victorian English gentleman. He was also said to be a man who fitted well in most situations in Ann Beck, 'Some Observations on Jomo Kenyatta in Britain: 1929–1930' (1966) 6 (22) *Cahiers d'Études Africaines* 308–329.

26 See for example Miatta Fahnbulleh, 'In Search of Economic Development in Kenya: Colonial Legacies & Post-Independence Realities' (2006) 33 (107) *Review of African Political Economy* 33–47.

27 Annie E. Coombes, 'Monumental Histories: Commemorating Mau Mau with the Statue of Dedan Kimathi' (2011) 70 (2) *African Studies* 202–223.

28 For Kenyatta's betrayal of the revolution, see Anaïs Angelo, 'Jomo Kenyatta and the Repression of the 'Last' Mau Mau Leaders 1961–1965' (2017) 11 (3) *Journal of Eastern African Studies* 442–459.

29 KENYA TO CHARGE SIX AS TERRORIST LEADERS. 1952. *New York Times (1923-Current file)*, 18 November 1952. https://search.proquest.com/docview/112343582?accountid=14182 accessed 4 October 2019.

30 Tee Ngugi, Comparing Suspects to Kapenguria Six Is Historical Sacrilege, *The East African*, Nairobi 24 April 2011.

31 *Uhuru* is a Swahili word meaning independence and as fate would have it, the Kenyan president's first name.

32 Robert Holland, Susan Williams and Terry Barringer (eds), *The Iconography of Independence: 'Freedoms at Midnight'* (Routledge 2013).

33 Quoted in Sarveppali Gopal, *Jawaharlal Nehru: A Biography* (Oxford University Press 2004) 178.

34 Susan Williams, *Colour Bar: The Triumph of Seretse Khama and His Nation* (Penguin 2006) 317.

35 David Cannadine, 'Ornamentalism-The British Empire as a Spectacular and Colourful Extension of the Social Order of the Home Country' (2001) 51 (5) *History Today* 12–19.

36 Ibid.

37 David Cannadine does not use the same words but suggests that the images were used to reassure the public that despite the colonial states becoming independent, it would be business as usual.

38 David Carradine (note 35).

39 Ibid.

40 Ibid.

41 Marouf Hasian Jr and Rulon Wood, 'Traumatic Realism and Sublime Decolonization: Remembering the Mass-Mediated Representations of King Baudouin's and Patrice Lumumba's Speeches on Congolese Independence Day, June 30, 1960' (2009) 6 (2) *Controversia* 15–44.

42 For the sacrifices the Congo was supposed to be thankful for, see for example Robert G. Weisbord, 'The King, the Cardinal and the Pope: Leopold II's Genocide in the Congo and the Vatican' (2003) 5 (1) *Journal of Genocide Research* 35–45. As a private property the king committed untold atrocities in what Weisbord refers to as genocide before the term was coined as we know it today.

43 Patrice Lumumba, *The Truth about a Monstrous Crime of the Colonialists* (Moscow Foreign Languages Publishing House 1961) 44–47.

44 Robert Holland, Susan Williams and Terry Barringer (eds), *The Iconography of Independence: 'Freedoms at Midnight'* (Routledge 2013).

45 *The Prosecutor v. Jean-Pierre Bemba Gombo ICC-01/05-01/08.*

46 Oliver Boehme, 'The Involvement of the Belgian Central Bank in the Katanga Secession 1960–1963' (2005) 33 *African Economic History* 1–29.

47 UK Support and Funding for the International Criminal Justice Statement made on 17 July 2018 in Parliament by the Secretary of State for Foreign and Commonwealth Affairs found at https://www.parliament.uk/business/publications/

written-questions-answers-statements/written-statement/Lords/2018-07-17/HLWS837/ accessed 13 October 2019.

48 Ibid.

49 African Business, Who Pays for the ICC? 1st October 2011 available at https://african.business accessed 27 September 2020.

50 Decision Pursuant to Article 15 of the Rome Statute on the Authorisation of an Investigation into the Situation in the Islamic Republic of Afghanistan ICC-02/17-33 12 April 2019.

51 Ibid.

52 Ibid.

53 Gabe Joselow, US Official Says Kenya's Elections Have 'Consequences' VOA, 7 February 2013. https://www.voanews.com accessed 14 October 2019.

54 Tim Murithi, 'Ensuring Peace and Reconciliation While Holding Leaders Accountable: The Politics of ICC Cases in Kenya and Sudan' (2005) XL (2) *Africa Development* 73–97.

55 Trevor Jones and Tim Newburn, 'Comparative Criminal Justice Policymaking in the United States and the United Kingdom: The Case of Private Prisons' (January 2005) 45 (1) *The British Journal of Criminology* 58–80.

56 For the biases in the criminal justice system in the UK see David Lammy, *An Independent Review into the Treatment of, and Outcomes for, Black, Asian and Minority Ethnic Individuals in the Criminal Justice System* (Lammy Review 2017).

57 The Prisoner's uniform has great significance and it is a research area: see for example Jennifer Craik, 'The Cultural Politics of the Uniform Fashion Theory' (2003) 7 (2) *The Journal of Dress, Body & Culture* 127–147; Jennifer Craik, *Uniforms Exposed: From Conformity to Transgression* (Berg Publishers 2005); Nathan Joseph and Nicholas Alex, 'The Uniform: A Sociological Perspective' (1972) 77 (4) *The American Journal of Sociology* 719–730.

58 For how colour affects our preferences see Mubeen M. Aslam, 'Are You Selling the Right Colour? A Cross-cultural Review of Colour as a Marketing Cue' (2006) 12 (1) *Journal of Marketing Communications* 15–30.

59 Michael Rocque, 'Racial Disparities in the Criminal Justice System and Perceptions of Legitimacy: A Theoretical Linkage' (2011) 1 (3) *Race and Justice* 292–315.

60 Ibid.

61 Ibid.

62 Ibid.

63 Dawuni Josephine Jarpa and Hon. Akua Kuenyehia (eds), *International Courts and the African Woman Judge: Unveiled Narratives* (Routledge 2017).

64 Hill Collins, *Black Feminist Thought* (Unwin Hyman 1990) 204.

65 Ibid.

66 Ibid.

67 Yvette Abrahams, 'Ambiguity is My Middle Name: A Research Diary' in Nomboniso Gasa (ed.), *Women in South African History: They Remove Boulders and Cross Rivers* (HSRC Press 2007) 421–452, 432.

68 Ibid.

69 Commission on Race and Ethnic Disparities, The report of the Commission on Race and Ethnic Disparities (31 March 2021), available at https://www.gov.uk/government/publications/the-report-of-the-commission-on-race-and-ethnic-disparities accessed 4 July 2021.

70 See a commentary on their finding by Paul Miller, '"System Conditions", System Failure, Structural Racism and Anti-Racism in the United Kingdom: Evidence from Education and Beyond' (2021) 11 (2) *Societies* 42.

71 Fernando Suman, 'Persistence of Racism through White Power' *Institutional Racism in Psychiatry and Clinical Psychology* (Palgrave Macmillan 2017) 135–152.
72 Ibid.
73 ICC The Office of the Prosecutor, Situation in Iraq/UK Final Report 9th December 2020, available at https://www.icc-cpi.int/Pages accessed 6 July 2021.
74 Ibid., para 2.
75 Ibid., para 6.
76 Ibid., para 12.
77 Gary Blasi and John T. Jost, 'System Justification Theory and Research: Implications for Law, Legal Advocacy, and Social Justice' (2006) 94 (4) *California Law Review* 1119–1168.
78 Ibid.
79 Robert A. Brown and James Frank, 'Race and Officer Decision Making: Examining Differences in Arrest Outcomes between Black and White Officers' (2006) 23 (1) *Justice Quarterly* 96–126.
80 Ibid.
81 Ibid.
82 For the universality of black mistrust of CJS see for example, Michael J. Mitchell and Charles H. Wood, 'Ironies of Citizenship: Skin Color, Police Brutality, and the Challenge to Democracy in Brazil' (March 1999) 77 (3) *Social Forces* 1001–1020.
83 Jennifer Eberhardt *et al.*, 'Looking Deathworthy: Perceived Stereotypicality of Black Defendants Predicts Capital-Sentencing Outcomes' (2006) 17 (5) *Psychological Science* 383–386.
84 Ibid.
85 Devah Pager, *Marked: Race, Crime, and Finding Work in an Era of Mass Incarceration* (University of Chicago Press 2007); see also David Lammy (note 57) as well as Barbara Hudson, 'Discrimination and Disparity: The Influence of Race on Sentencing' (1989) 16 (1) *Journal of Ethnic and Migration Studies* 23–34.
86 Rebecca Hetey and Jennifer L. Eberhardt, 'Racial Disparities in Incarceration Increase Acceptance of Punitive Policies' (2014) 25 (10) *Psychological Science* 1949–1954.
87 Ibid.
88 The ICC found at https://www.icc-cpi.int/Pages/cases accessed 19 February 2021.
89 Mark B. Harmon and Fergal Gaynor, 'Ordinary Sentences for Extraordinary Crimes' (2007) 5 (3) *Journal of International Criminal Justice* 683–712.
90 See Ava DuVernay, '13th' (Documentary) (Netflix 2016).
91 A. E. Raza, 'Legacies of the Racialization of Incarceration: From Convict-Lease to the Prison Industrial Complex' (2011) 11 *Journal of the Institute of Justice and International Studies* 159.
92 Ibid.
93 Angela Davis, *Are Prisons Obsolete?* (Seven Stories Press 2003) 29–31: see also Avery F. Gordon, 'Globalism and the Prison Industrial Complex: An Interview with Angela Davis' (1999) 40 (2–3) *Race & Class* 145–157; and Ava DuVernay, '13th' (Documentary) (Netflix 2016).
94 Ann Heather Thompson, 'The Prison Industrial Complex: A Growth Industry in a Shrinking Economy' (2012) 21 (3) *New Labor Forum SAGE Publications* 39–47.
95 Michael Rocque, 'Racial Disparities in the Criminal Justice System and Perceptions of Legitimacy: A Theoretical Linkage' (2011) 1 (3) *Race and Justice* 292–315.

96 Ibid.
97 Ibid.
98 Ibid.
99 Steven Kay QC Part 1 and 2 Examination-in-chief of Uhuru Kenyatta at the ICC on 29 September 2011 available at www.youtube.com accessed 14 October 2019.
100 Marianne Constable, 'Democratic Citizenship and Civil Political Conversation: What's Law Got to Do with It? (2012) 63 *Mercer Law Review* 877–889.
101 John Gibbons, 'Language and the Law' (1999) 19 *Annual Review of Applied Linguistics* 156–173.
102 Ibid., 156.
103 See more generally William M. O'Barr, *Linguistic Evidence: Language, Power, and Strategy in the Courtroom: Studies on Law and Social Control* (Academic Press 1982)
104 Clark D. Cunningham, 'A Tale of Two Clients: Thinking about Law as a Language' (1989) 87 *Michigan Law Review* 2459.
105 James Boyd White, 'Law as Language: Reading Law and Reading Literature' (1982) 60 *Texas Law Review* 415.
106 Susan Berk-Seligson, 'The Bilingual Courtroom: Court Interpreters in the Judicial Process' (1993) 20 (2) *American Ethnologist* 400–401.
107 Ibid.
108 See more generally Ngugi wa Thiong'o, 'Decolonising the Mind' *The Politics of Language in African Literature* (Heinemann 1981).
109 Eyoh Hansel Hdumbe, 'Language as Carrier of People's Culture: An Interview with Ngugi wa Thiongo' (1985) 14 (3) *Ufahamu: A Journal of African Studies* 157.
110 Ibid.
111 Rebecca Saunders, 'Lost in Translation: Expressions of Human Suffering, the Language of Human Rights and the South African Truth and Reconciliation Commission' (2008) 5 (9) *Revista Internacional de Direitos Humanos* 52–75.
112 Ngugi wa Thiongo (note 108).
113 UNESCO, *Why and How Africa Should Invest in African Languages and Multilingual Education: An Evidence- and Practice-Based Policy Advocacy Brief* (UNESCO Institute for Lifelong Learning 2010).
114 Ibid.
115 Ngugi wa Thiong'o, 'The Language of Justice in Africa,' Lecture of 16 September 2013, available at http://pmrcblog.files.wordpress.com/2013/09/prof-ngugis-speech.pdf accessed 20 July 2019.
116 Edward W. Soja, *Postmodern Geographies: The Reassertion of Space. Critical Social Theory* (Verso 1989) 78.
117 Henri Lefebvre and Michael Enders (trans.), 'Reflections on the Politics of Space' (1976) 8 (2) *Antipode* 30–37.
118 For a discussion on how colonial architecture has shaped spaces, see Carlos Nunes Silva, 'Colonial Architecture, and Urbanism in Africa. Intertwined and Contested Histories' (2013) 28 (1) *Planning Perspectives* 156–159.
119 Steen Eiler Rasmussen, *Experiencing Architecture* (Massachusetts Institute of Technology Press 1959) 9–12.
120 Carlos Nunes Silva, 'Colonial Architecture, and Urbanism in Africa. Intertwined and Contested Histories' (2013) 28 (1) *Planning Perspectives* 156–159.
121 Jonathan D. Rosenbloom, 'Social Ideology as Seen through Courtroom and Courthouse Architecture' (1998) 22 *Columbia-VLA Journal of Law & the Arts* 463.

122 David Anderson, Dr Carolyn Brown *et al.* (eds), *Slavery in Dutch South Africa* (Vol. 44, Cambridge University Press 1985).
123 Renske Vos and Sofia Stolk (2020) 'Law in Concrete: Institutional Architecture in Brussels and The Hague' (2020) 14 (1) *Law and Humanities* 57–58.
124 schmidt/hammer/lassen architects, The International Criminal Court: The Hague/The Netherlands Found at https://www.shl.dk/the-international-criminal-court/ accessed 11 June 2020.
125 Renske Vos and Sofia Stolk (note 123).
126 Ibid.
127 Jonathan D. Rosenbloom, 'Social Ideology as Seen through Courtroom and Courthouse Architecture' (1998) 22 (4) *Columbia-VLA Journal of Law & the Arts* 463–523
128 Ibid., 520.
129 Itself a borrowing from Germany, see Thorten Bürklin, *The Federal Constitutional Court of Germany: Architecture and Jurisdiction* (Basel 2004).
130 Jonathan Rosenbloom (note 127).
131 Ibid.
132 Munir Muhammad, 'The Judicial System of the East India Company: Precursor to the Present Pakistani Legal System' (2011) 13 *Annual Journal of International Islamic University Islamabad* 53–68.
133 Ibid.
134 Ibid.
135 See for example William S. Laufer, 'Social Accountability and Corporate Greenwashing' (2003) 43 *Journal of Business Ethics* 253.
136 Gerald B. Lefcourt, 'Responsibilities of a Criminal Defense Attorney' (1996) 30 *Loyola of Los Angeles Law Review* 63.
137 Maximo Langer, 'The Rise of Managerial Judging in International Criminal Law' (2005) 53 *American Journal of Comparative Law* 835.
138 *The Prosecutor v. Erdemovid, ICTY Trial Chamber, Case No. IT-96-22-T.*
139 Maximo Langer (note 137).
140 *The Prosecutor v. Ahmad Alfaq Al Mahdi ICC-01/12-01/1* Judgment and Sentence.
141 Robert L. Shapiro, 'For the Defense' (1996) 30 *Loyola of Los Angeles Law Review* 105, 106.
142 Jean -Francois Lyotard, *The Postmodern Condition: A Report on Knowledge* (trans. Geoff Bennington and Brian Massumi, University of Minnesota Press 1984).
143 Alan Hunt, 'The Big Fear: Law Confronts Postmodernism' (1990) 35 *McGill Law Journal* 507, 510.
144 Ibid.
145 Michel Foucault, *Discipline and Punishment: The Birth of the Prison* (Penguin 1977).
146 Jonathan D. Rosenbloom, 'Social Ideology as Seen through Courtroom and Courthouse Architecture' (1998) 22 *Columbia-VLA Journal of Law & the Arts* 479–496.
147 Katherine Taylor Fisher, *In the Theatre of Criminal Justice: The Palais de Justice in Second Empire Paris* (Princeton University Press 1993).
148 Renske Vos and Sofia Stolk, 'Law in Concrete: Institutional Architecture in Brussels and The Hague' (2020) 14 (1) *Law and Humanities* 57–58.
149 Jonathan D. Rosenbloom, 'Social Ideology as Seen through Courtroom and Courthouse Architecture' (1998) 22 *Columbia-VLA Journal of Law & the Arts* 463.
150 Ibid.

151 Ibid.
152 For a general discourse on this topic see Robert R. Taylor, *The Word in Stone: The Role of Architecture in the National Socialist Ideology* (University of California Press 1974).
153 Evgeny Dobrenko and Eric Naiman, *The Landscape of Stalinism: The Art and Ideology of Soviet Space* (University of Washington Press 2003).
154 Ramji-Nogales Jaya, 'Designing Bespoke Transitional Justice: A Pluralist Process Approach' (2010) 32 (1) *Michigan Journal of International Law* 1–72.
155 Philip Clark, *The Gacaca Courts, Post-Genocide Justice and Reconciliation in Rwanda: Justice without Lawyers* (Cambridge University Press 2010).
156 Olivier Dubois, 'Rwanda's National Criminal Courts and the International Tribunal' (1997) 37 (321) *International Review of the Red Cross (1961–1997)* 31.
157 Paul Rock, *The Social World of an English Crown Court: Witness and Professionals in the Crown Court Centre at Wood Green* (Clarendon Press 1993).
158 Ibid., 275.
159 Linda Mulcahy, 'Architects of Justice: The Politics of Courtroom Design' (2007) 16 (3) *Social & Legal Studies* 383–403.
160 This also includes the differences between localised understanding of justice and westerners' understanding of justice – and how it should be served. See in general Phil Clark, *Distant Justice: The Impact of the International Criminal Court on African Politics* (Cambridge University Press 2018).
161 David Tait, 'Glass Cages in the Dock: Presenting the Defendant to the Jury' (2011) 86 Chicago-Kent Law Review 46.
162 Ibid.
163 Ibid.
164 Ibid.
165 Ibid.
166 Ibid.
167 *V v United Kingdom [1999] ECHR 171.*
168 Ibid.
169 Ibid.
170 Thorten Bürklin, *The Federal Constitutional Court of Germany: Architecture and Jurisdiction* (Basel 2004).
171 Wessel Le Roux, 'Bridges, Clearings and Labyrinths: The Architectural Framing of Post-Apartheid Constitutionalism' (2004) 19 *SAPR* 629–645.

5 Monsieur Cuvier Investigates

Africa as Testing Site

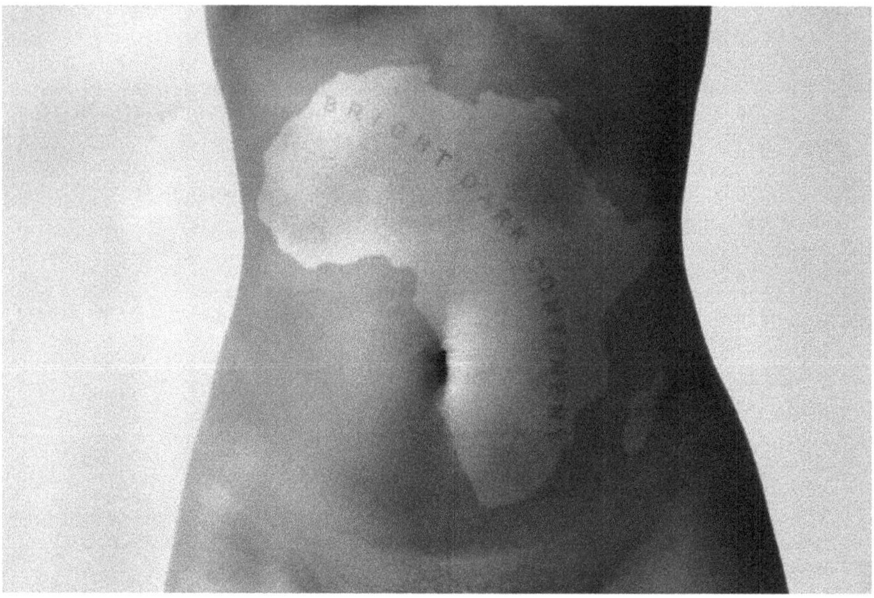

Source: Ingrid Mwangi, *Static Drift* (2001).[1]

> *Africa is the only continent you can love—, be sure to leave the strong impression that without your intervention and your important book, Africa is doomed … Describe, in detail, naked breasts (young, old, conservative, recently raped, big, small) or mutilated genitals, or enhanced genitals. Or any kind of genitals. And dead bodies. Or, better, naked dead bodies. And especially rotting naked dead bodies … Always end your book with Nelson Mandela saying something about rainbows or renaissances. Because you care.*[2]

DOI: 10.4324/9781003304173-5

Introduction

In the previous chapter, I explored the idea of the iconography produced at the ICC, the positioning of the accused black man and the associated meanings of those images and architecture. This chapter extends that argument but now I address the geographical site(s) which produce(s) those accused and most importantly, address yet another form of iconography at the core of ICL, the raped and helpless African woman, the marauding African man, the hungry child, the burnt villages, the saviour white people. The wider claim I make in this chapter is that the African's own body becomes not just a physical testing site, but a metaphysical site, where nonphysical ideas/norms/epistemologies are tested, reproduced, instrumentalised. Instead of concentrating on the imagery, I focus on the law that these images produce at the ICC and hence argue that the places those images come from are essentially a 'breeding' ground for ICL and the associated industry.

Through this, I address the question as to whether Africa is being used as a testing site for international criminal law. What I have discovered however, is that not only is that the case in relation to the Rome Statute, it is also the case that Africa is acting as a reproduction site for pre-existing international norms set by earlier international tribunals but presented as new in areas that include rape, cultural destruction, and victim participation. In the case of *Bemba* for example we see the testing of Article 28, while in the case of *Mahdi* we see the testing of Article 8. I use the term 'testing' deliberately because, for example, the decisions in both *Bemba* and *Mahdi* have variously been presented as 'ground-breaking' but are in effect regurgitation of laws already set in other international legal instruments and adjudicated by past tribunals such as the ICTR and ICTY. This reproduction is based, I argue, in the embedded colonial legal systems and structures that dominate local and international law both in Africa itself and in Europe.

I argue that, considering that the tribunals for Yugoslavia and Rwanda tried similar crimes, the ICC is actively distinguishing itself from that 'past' to justify its existence. Most crucially, these tribunals ruled on issues including rape and cultural destruction and were themselves using the already existing international criminal law as opposed to the Rome Statute. I also argue that the ICC is cognisant of past and current claims of imperialism in international law and hence it desperately claims uniqueness in its judgements rather than just indicating that it is following already set precedent.[3] This claim of particularism suggests a break with the past and signals a shift in paradigm from the old to the new which in my view is impossible for an international law body to claim given the history I detailed earlier of the links with slavery and colonialism. I would not be alone in linking the current ICL regime to slavery as authors like Emily Haslam have recently done the same.[4] What is relevant to my discussion here is Emily Haslam's depiction of an ICL founded by the events at the 'abolitionist' stages of the end of slavery and the subsequent ignored legacies of that process in birthing the human rights movement, which extends to how the ICC defines victims and criminals, particularly in the African context.[5] More poignant for my discourse in this book is that these slavery and colonial histories demarcated Africa as the perpetual site for 'awfulness'[6] which places the burden on the white man, and now more often the white woman, of perpetually endeavouring to resolve its problems. This white man/woman burden (African victim) is traced by Emily Haslam to that abolitionist era where the African is from the start seen as having no legal agency of his/her own to end/fight against his/her enslavement.[7] Importantly though, the chapter shows that these laws are an internationalisation of Eurocentric laws that disproportionately affect the black accused, and which have a tendency towards commercialisation of the law, with ominous connections to slavery. Commercialisation of the law is however not the only risk posed by ICL as there is a wider industry connected to the war/peace complex which has not just the criminal African but also the African victim at its core.

In five main sections I will explore specific areas of ICL where the ICC has used situations in Africa to operationalise the Rome Statute and to test and expand already existing international law. Before I do this however, it is important for me to explain briefly what I mean by testing and how Africa has in the past been a site for international testing. I do this in the section titled 'A History of Testing, (Re)production, Instrumentation' below. In the section 'Rape as War Crime,' I explore the ICC's decisions in *The Prosecutor v. Jean-Pierre Bemba Gombo*[8] in relation to rape as a war crime and explain how this decision, while it was the first time Article 28 was operationalised, was not as ground-breaking as presented because it was just a replication of already existing laws. I explore subsequently why the ICC sells its decisions as new, emerging, ground-breaking. Afterwards in 'Fuck/White Saviour Complex,' I explore victim participation. I explore how victims' participation relates to justice and fair trial as well as the concern that the ICC needs to perpetuate a victims' narrative for its survival because the African victim is/was necessary for its very foundation. In the section *'L'addition S'il Vous Plait?* Plea Bargains at the ICC,' I address the plea bargaining which arose in *The Prosecutor v. Ahmad Al Faqi Al Mahdi*[9] in further detail, connecting it with the wider discourse on its effects on the black accused. Before ending with 'Conclusions,' I discuss cultural destruction in the section titled 'Cultural Destruction' using the *Mahdi* decision which was the operationalisation of Article 8.

A History of Testing, (Re)production, Instrumentation

In the novel *The Constant Gardener*, Le Carre tells a story of an international conspiracy to test pharmaceutical products on unsuspecting African victims.[10] At the risk of reviewing the novel here, I briefly trace this fiction to real life instances of testing done on African bodies as a classic case of art imitating life, because in *Abdullahi v Pfizer*[11] a pharmaceutical clinical trial on an unsuspecting population in Kano, Nigeria by the drugs company Pfizer led to the deaths of 11 children while multiple others suffered brain damage, blindness, and deafness after being given the experimental drug Trovan. The conclusion from a panel of medical experts was that Pfizer had undertaken the clinical trials without the parents' consent and without authorisation by the Nigerian government, which led to the ensuing legal drama. Over several hearings in different courts[12] Pfizer continually argued that the cases should be heard in Nigeria rather than the USA and that they had complied with all the necessary regulations in Nigeria but they eventually reached an out of court settlement after the Court of Appeal held in January 2009 that the Alien Tort statute[13] allowed the suit against Pfizer to be brought to a court in the United States by the Nigerian victims and their families. It is notable for our ensuing discourse that only after the courts ruled that the MNE was liable under American law did they settle this matter.

In yet another pharmaceutical example, American dugs researchers used 17,000 unsuspecting Zimbabwean women to test the then unproven HIV medicine AZT without their proper and informed consent. This medication was supposed to limit mother-to-child transmission of HIV but the women given this trial drug were not told and did not comprehend the trial methods, whether the drug was effective, the side effects or in fact if they were in a placebo group. Women were forced to be on the trial and half of them were treated with the placebo although there were proven life-saving treatments available, which in turn led to an estimated 1,000 babies contracting HIV/AIDS.[14]

What we see through these cases is that when westerners (MNEs) commit crimes in Africa, they prefer to be tried in Africa because they realise, for the many reasons detailed in this book, that they will escape scrutiny. We also see in these cases African states becoming a site where it is increasingly difficult for local communities to achieve 'justice' because it appears that 'impunity' has to be eradicated for the African elite but not for western MNEs. A psychotic quality of international law becomes apparent through these 'testing cases' in which, on one hand, Africa is seen as competent by 'commercial law' while on the other it is deemed incompetent by 'criminal law' because, to avoid responsibility when asked to account for their actions in Africa, MNEs frequently argue that their 'mother' courts in USA/Europe are not the appropriate courts and that claims against them should only be brought in Africa in *forums non conveniens* arguments. This practice is particularly harmful to communities where these MNEs have exploited and catastrophically damaged the environment as is perpetually the case in the Niger Delta.

For example in a ruling to be criticised as legally unsound, the community affected by this environmental disaster were not allowed to challenge the Shell company in the UK for damage caused by their Nigerian subsidiary in *the Bodo Community and Others v The Shell Petroleum Development Company of Nigeria Ltd.*[15] The claimants wanted Royal Dutch Shell, which is the parent company and based in the UK, to be held liable for its operations in Nigeria but the UK court's ruling was that "there is simply no connection whatsoever between this jurisdiction and the claims brought by the claimants, who are Nigerian citizens, for breaches of statutory duty and/or in common law for acts and omissions in Nigeria, by a Nigerian company."[16]

In this case, we see the High Court applying complex tort law principles of nuisance and avoiding more relevant public international laws, on the environment for example.[17] More worryingly, the court clearly avoids applying well established law that would have allowed the claim to prevail in the UK. Already, the House of Lords in *Lubbe v Cape Pl*[18] had ruled that it is possible to show that a parent company owes a direct duty of care in tort to anybody injured by a subsidiary company in a group. The law was later well articulated in *Owusu v Jackson*[19] which said that if the defendant or one of the defendants is domiciled in the UK, consideration of the *forum non conveniens* principle is not allowed. It had also been applied in *Global Multimedia International Ltd v Ara Media Services,*[20] in *Attorney General of Zambia v Meer Care & Desai (A Firm),*[21] *UBS AG v HSH Nordbank*[22] and in *A v A (Children: Habitual Residence).*[23]

Therefore we see the lengths MNEs go to avoid facing justice in European countries for ills done in Africa. Contrasting the complementarity principle of the Rome Statute with these *forum non conveniens* cases brings up very worrying issues in the selectivity of international law. For example, it appears from a post-colonial scrutiny that in the UK High Court, the judge was willing to accept that African courts (Nigerian) are well-equipped to deal with the complexities of the issues raised by claimants in a situation that raised important international law questions. However, in criminal cases of an international nature, Africa is seen as inadequate and not able to deal with the complexities of those cases. Crucially, as we see in the Kenyan cases, the argument is that the state would influence witnesses, although in the commercial cases, the fact that there might be interference with the smooth running of the Shell case, if it was to be heard in Nigeria, was seen as tactically useful by Shell. Tragically in both the environmental cases and African cases at the ICC, we see victims trusting foreign justice systems more than their local justice systems. This is the pressing reason why books like this are needed to eliminate this mental slavery, a dilemma that would be resolved by actualising the African Court, as discussed later in Chapter 6.

What this short discussion on pharmaceutical testing and the environmental cases shows is that the west is not hesitant in using Africa as a testbed for new ideas, but also that when found out 'international law' acts to safeguard western MNEs from accountability. More crucially, they are not shy of using weak legal structures to ensure they escape 'justice.' Therefore I argue that, following the examples outlined above, the ICC was in good company when, in the early days of the Kenya vs ICC drama, Moreno Ocampo announced that Kenya will set an example to the world on how to manage past violence and how to create a peaceful recovery process in the future.[24]

I would argue that Ocampo's statement was intended to test the Rome Statute in the Kenyan situation, but also to 'instrumentalise' it to achieve (un)stated goals. The ICC was not the first to 'instrumentalise' technologies for modelling other countries' politics. This had been done before, as explored for example by Naomi Klein in her seminal work *The Shock Doctrine*,[25] and I apply this manner of thinking here to link the international criminal law complex to a wider neo-colonial project. In her argument, Klein traces the torture methods recently used in CIA dark sites to an idea developed by the psychiatrist Dr Ewan Cameron of using shock to re-programme human personalities with the aim of 'curing' people of Marxism and converting them to capitalism.[26] These methods were later to be employed openly under world's gaze at Guantanamo bay and included various forms of sensory deprivation, ranging from solitary confinement, light deprivation, and disorientation through disrupted feeding times. Before Guantanamo Bay however, these methods of torture were tested in Latin America.[27]

What creates a synergy between these ideas and my ICC testing theory is the fact that Klein envisaged an individualised/localised idea of torture manufactured in the USA that is then exported to Latin America and 'universalised' to include changing Latin American governments and economies so that they are more suited to the American ideal, which then allows America a foothold to exploit the region. There are always local agents to aid neo-colonialism, and according to Klein, local agents were trained in the USA in the methods of the Chicago school of hyper-capitalism so that they could later manage their economies in the prescribed manner, which meant removing Latin America's left leaning leaders, like Salvador Allende, from power and influence. The coups that followed in Argentina and Chile for example were the initial 'shock' that would confuse the population and hinder it from resisting. Extensive privatisation of the economies then followed with the second shock: torture. Anyone resisting this privatisation and free-market capitalism, including trade union leaders, priests, nuns, activists, artists, musicians, writers, workers, and peasants would be killed, tortured, or disappeared.[28]

It is not far-fetched therefore to apply Klein's theory in a situation like Kenya and Ivory Coast, two countries whose cases at the ICC were remarkably similar and whose situations arose from a crisis of transitioning from one local elite to the other. In each case, the elite lacking western support ended up at the Hague. In using similar tactics like the ones Klein described, I argue here that colonial states use political upheavals and reproduce colonialism through international institutions like the ICC to intervene and gain political and economic footholds in certain countries in Africa.

Rape as War Crime

> *Monsieur Cuvier investigates*
> *between my legs, poking, prodding,*
> *sure of his hypothesis.*
> *I half expect him to pull silk*
> *Scarves from inside me, paper poppies,*
> *then a rabbit! He complains*
> *at my scent and does not think*
> *I comprehend, but I speak*
> *English. I speak Dutch. I speak A little French as well, and*
> *languages Monsieur Cuvier*
> *will never know have names.*[29]

In this section, I explore the *Bemba* decision at the ICC relating to rape as a war crime. I argue that although heralded as a ground-breaking decision, *Bemba* was in fact a reproduction of the precedents already set by the ICTY. In that sense, it acted only as a reproductive vessel for 'war rape' jurisdictions but, pertinent to our subject, it was an occasion for the ICC to experiment with the Rome Statute. In addition, I posit that *Bemba* also showcases the reproduction of racist legal practices where the focus on the black victim and accused is informed by an imperialistic understanding of the world. It is however important to note that the literature I have reviewed has shown this area to be a much broader arena for research than this book can cover, and therefore only a limited history is offered here for the purposes of context.

To put the Bemba case in its full context, it is important to note that Bemba was not actually charged with war rape but under Article 28 of the Rome Statute[30] on the responsibility of commanders and other superiors which states that, in addition to other grounds of criminal responsibility under this Statute for crimes within the jurisdiction of the Court:

a. A military commander or person effectively acting as a military commander shall be criminally responsible for crimes within the jurisdiction of the Court committed by forces under his or her effective command and control, or effective authority and control as the case may be, as a result of his or her failure to exercise control properly over such forces, where:
    i. That military commander or person either knew or, owing to the circumstances at the time, should have known that the forces were committing or about to commit such crimes; and
    ii. That military commander or person failed to take all necessary and reasonable measures within his or her power to prevent or repress their commission or to submit the matter to the competent authorities for investigation and prosecution.

b With respect to superior and subordinate relationships not described in paragraph (a), a superior shall be criminally responsible for crimes within the jurisdiction of the Court committed by subordinates under his or her effective authority and control, as a result of his or her failure to exercise control properly over such subordinates, where:
    i The superior either knew, or consciously disregarded information which clearly indicated that the subordinates were committing or about to commit such crimes;
    ii The crimes concerned activities that were within the effective responsibility and control of the superior; and
    iii The superior failed to take all necessary and reasonable measures within his or her power to prevent or repress their commission or to submit the matter to the competent authorities for investigation and prosecution.[31]

In addition, it is also important for me to detail some of the key findings at the Trial Chamber stage and later at the Appeals Chamber stages to draw out the key issues that arose in the case. The Trial Chamber decided[32] that the duty to prevent encompasses the duty to stop crimes that are about to be committed or crimes that are being committed.[33] The decision distinguished itself from the decisions already made at the *ad hoc* tribunals in that the judges said the tribunals do not make reference to a duty to "repress" but use the terms "to prevent or to punish,"[34] although they also said that the notion of "repress" overlaps the duty of prevention to a certain degree, particularly in terms of the duty to prevent crimes in progress and crimes which involve ongoing elements being committed over an extended period.[35] The judges admitted that Bemba took "a few measures" in response to allegations of crimes committed by MLC troops in the CAR but they were limited "in mandate, execution, and/or results."[36] In that respect the measures were inadequate and their inadequacy was "aggravated" by indications that they were not "genuine."[37] This was because the measures were primarily motivated by Mr Bemba's desire to counter public allegations and rehabilitate the public image of the MLC.[38]

The chamber mentioned that amongst the measures Bemba could have taken were withdrawal of the MLC troops from the CAR in November 2002 but that it was not until March 2003 that the MLC troops were withdrawn on Bemba's order. Moreover, the motivations in withdrawing the troops were only political.[39] The central point in the decision however was that

> Bemba had ultimate disciplinary authority over the MLC contingent in the CAR, but failed to empower the full and adequate investigation and prosecution of allegations of crimes internally within the MLC and made no effort to refer the matter to the CAR authorities, or cooperate with international efforts to investigate the crimes.[40]

In what turned out to be the main failure of this decision, the judges failed to carefully consider the crucial issue that Bemba was not at the battlefield, which could have affected his ability to take the necessary and reasonable measures. However, they held that "despite his remote location, Mr Bemba had the authority and ability to take measures to prevent and repress the commission of crimes."[41]

This faulty causation was to be challenged at the Appeals Chamber which found Bemba not guilty, concluding that Bemba took all necessary and reasonable measures within his power to prevent or repress the commission of crimes by his subordinates during the 2002–2003 CAR Operation.[42] The Appeals Chamber decided by a majority that the Trial Chamber paid insufficient attention to the fact that the MLC troops were operating in a foreign country and the impact this had on Bemba's ability to take measures.[43] The Appeals Chamber also ruled that the Trial Chamber erred in treating Bemba's motivations as determinative of the adequacy of the measures[44] and that they had failed to establish that Bemba purposively limited the mandates of the commissions and inquiries.[45] The Appeals Chamber more importantly, assessing reasonableness, considered the operational realities on the ground at the time faced by the commander.[46] The Appeals Chamber held that it needs to be proved that a commander did not take specific and concrete measures that were available to him or her and which a reasonably diligent commander in comparable circumstances would have taken. In this regard the Appeals Chamber indicated that the Trial Chamber must identify the specific concrete measures a commander should have taken and it is not the responsibility of the accused to show that the measures he or she did take were sufficient.[47]

In addition the Appeals Chamber ruled that it is not a commander's duty to take each and every possible measure at his or her disposal because a commander may choose the least disruptive measure as long as it can reasonably be expected that this measure will prevent or repress the crimes.[48] The Appeals Chamber also noted that most of the criminal incidents occurred at the beginning of 2002–2003 but that little evidence was presented regarding specific criminal acts towards the end of the operation, which they viewed as crucial evidence.[49] The Appeals Chamber noted that the document containing the charges did not specifically identify the redeployment of troops as a necessary and reasonable measure that Bemba should have taken and therefore Bemba was not sufficiently notified of this factual allegation as a necessary and reasonable measure.[50]

The Appeals Chamber further ruled that the Trial Chamber lost sight of the fact that the measures taken by a commander cannot be faulted merely because of shortfalls in their execution.[51] It also held that it was an error to consider Mr Bemba's motivation as having a material impact on the entirety of its findings on necessary and reasonable measures because that perspective permeated the Trial Chamber's assessment of the measures that Mr Bemba had taken.[52] On the status of Bemba as a remote commander, the

Appeals Chamber ruled that the Trial Chamber failed to appreciate that, as such, he was not part of the investigations and was not responsible for the results generated[53] and the Trial Chamber had paid insufficient attention to the fact that MLC troops were operating in a foreign country with the attendant difficulties for Mr Bemba's ability as a remote commander to take measures.[54]

Taking the law as set in the statute and interpreted by the court above brings out two main themes; 1) there is an emerging tendency by the Trial Chamber at the ICC to present its judgements as unique; and 2) it works incredibly hard to distinguish cases before it or based on the Rome Statute from previous/existing international law on the same subject/issue. For example, judges were engaged in the painful semantic gymnastics of distinguishing 'repress' from 'prevent' and 'punish' when detailing what commanders must undertake. With this in mind, it is therefore important to put Bemba's case in the context of wider 'war rape' discourse because it is widely acknowledged that the sanctioned rape of civilians by military invaders has gone unpunished and unrecognised as a war crime for most of history. During World War Two, Japanese soldiers abducted over 10,000 Korean and Philippine women for use as sexual slaves.[55] The Japanese Army also raped Chinese women in Nanking in the course of the war.[56] During Kristallnacht the Nazis launched the attack against Jewish ghettoes that formally commenced the Holocaust, gang raping Jewish women as part of their efforts to destroy resistance.[57] The Russian Army committed many acts of rape against German women upon their entry into Berlin at the conclusion of World War II.[58] More recently, the Pakistani Army raped women in Bangladesh during the latter's war for independence in 1971.[59] The recognition of rape as a war crime has been advocated since the end of World War II and was given prominent consideration during the International Criminal Tribunals for both the Former Yugoslavia and Rwanda during the past decade. Rape was first introduced as a war crime in the Nuremberg War Crimes Trials at the conclusion of World War II, but it was not included among the final judgements handed down.[60] In contrast, in the Tokyo War Crimes Trials, also held at the conclusion of World War II, Japanese commanders were convicted of command responsibility for the rapes committed by their soldiers.[61]

Bemba was therefore not the 'first' rape conviction at an international tribunal as international tribunals have handed down convictions for rape in other past cases. The ICTY decided that rape constitutes a war crime in the *Prosecutor v. Kunarac, Kovac, and Vukovic* case and in the *Prosecutor v. Delalic & Delic* had identified the systematic rape of Bosnian Serb women at the Celebici detention camp as acts of torture.[62] Hazim Delic, the Bosnian Muslim deputy commander of the camp was convicted of breaching the Geneva Conventions and committing war crimes as acts of torture for his part in the raping of the Bosnian Serb women at the Celebici camp.[63] Zdravko Mucic was convicted of command responsibility for the rapes and sexual assaults that took place under his watch as the camp commander.[64] Neither was convicted specifically of rape, only torture and command responsibility. In *Prosecutor v. Akayesu,* the International War Crimes Tribunal for Rwanda found Jen-Paul Akayesu, a communal leader, guilty of genocide for encouraging the raping of Tutsi women.[65] It is important to note that ICTY ruled that by committing such acts, defendants violated Articles 3 and 5 of the ICTY Statute and Article 3 of the Geneva Conventions, but the Trial Chamber still needed to define what constitutes a rape under international law. The elements of rape are nowhere to be found in the Statute of the Tribunal, any existing treaties, or customary international law.[66] The Trial Chamber culled the elements of rape as a crime from the law of major legal systems of several nations including Germany, Sweden, and the United Kingdom.[67]

It is therefore appropriate to conclude that the Bemba decision was not as significant as *Prosecutor v. Kunarac, Kovac, & Vukovic* which marked the first occasion that an international tribunal has explicitly ruled that the systematic rape of women during an armed conflict constitutes a war crime. Prior to that decision, the issue of whether the organised and systematic rape of women by military forces constitutes a war crime and breach of the Geneva Conventions had been an open question. More significantly, the *Vukovic* decision had interpreted the provisions of Article 3 of the Geneva Conventions to include rape, meaning that the Rome Statute and hence the ICC was not critical in ensuring that these crimes are punished; other jurisdictions, local or regional, could in my view prosecute war rape because the principles enunciated in Article 3 now explicitly prohibit the raping of civilians during war. Therefore Article 3 meant that, henceforth, other international accords and treaties that provide for the protection of civilians and prisoners of war also include a prohibition against rape whether explicitly stated or not. Finally, and significantly, the definition of rape under customary international law that was adopted by the ICTY is gender neutral as opposed to earlier interpretations that protected only women.[68]

The only uniqueness of the *Bemba* case then, is that it is the first time Article 28 of the Rome Statute was operationalised by the ICC.[69] Article 28 deals with command responsibility which is the failure of a military commander and some civilian leaders to prevent or suppress subordinates from committing war crimes and the failure to punish subordinates after they have committed those crimes.[70] Bemba becomes peculiar in that, as I explain below, he was charged with crimes committed by members of his MLC who were 'on loan' to the then CAR president. To simplify, his charge was akin to the French president being charged for crimes committed by his solders in the same territory.[71] In that sense, although he was the political head of the movement, he was not in the CAR with the concerned unit and, as we have seen, the case becomes a test in our context in that sense and in the fact that there were multiple actors in that conflict who were accused of the same crimes, including French soldiers.

To understand Bemba's case in a post-colonial context is to first gain an insight into his role in Congo (DRC) politics at the time, but it is also to gain an understanding of the tragic history of the Congo which is far wider than I can explore in one section of a chapter.[72] My exploration of the Bemba case, however, has uncovered the continuous and insidious involvement of the colonial states, particularly France and Belgium, in the perpetual disruption of the Congo as I will explore further in this chapter and the political power machinations behind the high profile African Cases at the ICC.[73] This is because Bemba was for a brief period the vice president in the DRC following the peace accord in 2003 and would later be a formidable opponent for the then president Joseph Kabila in 2006-2007 elections after which he fled to exile after threats on his life.[74] His subsequent arrest and prosecution by the ICC was based on the allegations that his group, the MLC (Movement for the Liberation of Congo) committed numerous crimes between 25 October 2002 and 15 March 2003 in the CAR while responding to a call for support from Mr Ange Félix Patassé.[75]

Bemba is a perfect example of the selectivity with which the ICC approaches cases emanating from Africa by exclusively focusing on some high-profile individuals to the exclusion of grassroots perpetrators. In Kenya for example, there have been no local processes to enable peace-building/healing akin to *Gacaca* nor have any local operatives been charged with the murders which took place in 2007.[76] First, Bemba was not tried for his part in the war in his native DRC where he was a major player, but for the war in the CAR where he was a peripheral actor. As the leader of the MLC, he had led an armed rebellion and it was alleged that he was involved for four years with various crimes committed in the areas under his group's control, although crime was prevalent in the country generally.[77] It is important for our discourse that, if charging high profile individuals like him was meant to end 'impunity' that aim often failed in Eastern Congo where the conflict continued even after Bemba and others had been arrested; in fact, even the conflict he was arrested for in the CAR continues to date.[78]

Bemba was also a pioneer in that he was the first to be tried and acquitted of crimes initially charged under Article 28 because the Appeals Chamber acquitted him by majority, as seen above.[79] For the discourse in this book however, the initial puzzle is why the ICC investigation of Bemba was not for his involvement in the DRC conflict, even though the ICC was investigating both DRC and CAR conflicts. The selection of Bemba raises even more questions because, when one looks at the main actors in the CAR at the time of the war the MLC were involved in, the person who was said to have employed the MLC, Mr Patassé was never tried for any crime. It appears to me that Mr Patassé fitted the definition of command and control as detailed by Article 28. Mr Patassé died an 'innocent' man because he was never charged by any court, let alone the ICC, allegedly because there was no evidence to charge him.[80] Mr Patassé in fact returned from exile and ran for president in 2008 without being subjected to any prosecution.[81]

The second and most worrying factor was that it was not just Bemba's MLC that was involved in the conflict as even the ICC itself indicated that an armed conflict 'not' of an international character was happening, involving the armed group of Mr Bozizé on one hand and groups in alliance with Mr Patassé on the other, the latter including various mercenaries from Chad, Libya, and France.[82] Apart from the Bemba outfit therefore, other more insidious actors were also involved on Patassé's side and the ICC is guilty of conveniently not listing them as active and more lethal participants in this conflict. The most concerning aspect of this case from a post-colonial perspective is not just the ICC v Bemba dalliance, but that French and other European mercenaries were active in the same conflict, led by the notorious former French gendarme Paul Barril, a man straight out of your favourite Le Carré novel with a history of the commercialisation of death in Africa by leading private militias in various conflicts in African countries.[83]

This selectivity in prosecuting some actors as opposed to others becomes the ICC's hallmark as we have discussed elsewhere regarding the *Kenyatta* and *Gbagbo* cases. Specific to Bemba, authors like Felix Dahinda argue that this selectivity excluded local actors and did not deal with the real causes of the conflict, nor did it address the many atrocities committed in that conflict.[84] Worryingly though, Dahinda rightfully argued that the ICC succeeded only in stigmatising a whole community of the *Banyamulenge* as criminals as the ICC process saw the MLC as synonymous with the whole of the wider *Banyamulenge* ethnic group.[85] Apart from this selectivity in initiating the Bemba case, the ICC's engagement with rape as a war crime has also been criticised as gender imbalanced by some authors, including Hannah Baumeister[86] who traces the development of the jurisdiction from the tribunals discussed above and engages more importantly with the background to rape being included in the Rome Statute and the influences brought to bear on that by the actors who drafted the Rome Statute. Baumeister argues that despite seeming progressive, the ICC's provisions on sexualised violence excluded other issues in conflicts, such as forced marriages, and that in addition, the definition of rape by the ICC may seem awkward and regressive.[87] She argues that subjective normative structures of the drafters influenced this narrow understanding of war sexualised crimes.[88] What I notice is that even authors like Baumeister do not acknowledge the main gap in this foundational stage which is the absence of legal drafters from, for example, Eastern Congo or other African regions where the meanings of words and language around sexuality are far different from a western notion of sexuality/marriage/consent/lack of. This lack of representation at the authorship stages has the consequence that women may be using language/words detailing their lived experiences which are not captured by a Eurocentric meaning of 'rape' under the law.

This background is well covered by such authors as Felix Dahinda,[89] but I interrogate the ICC's ruling on the *Bemba* case to make the argument that while *Bemba* was lauded as ground-breaking, it was in my view a continuation and application of already existing jurisprudence as already explored above. It is my view that the commentators' need to view *Bemba* as a ground-breaking decision is misplaced, not least because the crimes alleged were punishable not only by many domestic jurisdictions but by other international legal instruments as already explored. Authors like Nicola Henry[90] tend to fall in this category of looking at rape as war crime as a new frontier in international law. Although Nicola Henry notes that wartime rape is not unique to modern day conflicts and indicates that it has been existent throughout human history, I disagree with her that it has received sporadic attention throughout history and that Rape remains 'unspeakable,' particularly within the law. This is because, as we see in Bemba, ICTY and the Rwanda Tribunal, increasingly rape is being prosecuted. The literature I have reviewed shows that prosecution and scrutiny of rape during wars has been a consistent presence since the Nazi war. The sporadic attention Nicola Henry suggests comes from the fact that large scale wars have also been sporadic. What has not happened is ending the actual crimes or the wars that generate them.

Where I strongly agree with Nicola Henry is in the argument that rape features less prominently in the remembering of conflicts once they end and more often there are heated political debates around this remembrance.[91] Perhaps Nicola Henry needs to acknowledge there is no hiding from the politics of wars but her argument touches on the importance of commemorating history which is at the core of my discourse in relation to the postcolonial nature of international law. Although I would argue that Nicola Henry's view of remembrance shows a Eurocentric view of memories, particularly in advocating 'publicity' as opposed to privacy of memories, her writing touches on a theme common in southern societies of collectiveness in remembering. I therefore posit that just because events have not been publicly commemorated in a Eurocentric forum or Eurocentric literature that does not mean they are not remembered. Nicola Henry and other authors in this area fall into the trap of perpetuating the notion that there is only one way of remembering.

Remembrance in the manner suggested by these Eurocentric scholars suggests a neat historical order of events where a benevolent Eurocentric legal order restores the woman's integrity and autonomy through prosecuting rape in African wars. In this imperialist view of the world, "conflicts emerge from the darkest realms of the psyche of the other, who must be protected and healed by Western instrumental rationality and care."[92] Ratna Kapur argues that this form of approach and the gendered "victimization rhetoric" in international law leaves no space to imagine a subject that is empowered.[93] As a grandchild of a woman *Mau Mau* revolutionary, I tend to agree with Kapur because it is my view that the perpetuation of the African woman as victim stops us celebrating our mothers who have been intimately involved in liberation struggles, from the *Mau Mau*, to the Panthers. It is also in my view a form of deliberate 'fragmentation,' a divide and rule tactic by the neo-liberal hegemony, for what would be more potent than a united front against this 'epistemic occupation' led by African mothers?

In the context of 'international crimes' however, this Eurocentric approach reproduces racist practices of investigating and punishing rape as a war crime, as practised in post-World War II Europe. This is because when rape as a crime of war is discussed, less is said about the rapes committed by the Americans and the Allies during World War II and the subsequent targeting of black soldiers for prosecution.[94] Robert Lilly explores this in relation to prosecutions in England, France and Germany and it is pertinent to my discourse on the race bias in prosecuting crimes that he details the significance of race in prosecuting wartime rape, particularly in England.[95] It is startling to learn that the only soldiers to be executed for rapes taking place in England were black even though rape was not a capital offence in England.[96] Robert Lilly explored the anti-miscegenation laws still existing in the USA until 1967, how they informed the prosecution's biases and how this racism has manifested in the manner in which rape trials were conducted.[97] The Visiting Forces Act of 1942[98] permitted the American military to use capital punishment in England as a disciplinary tool to control the perceived danger of African-American troops socialising with British women, and the potential explosive violence between white and African-American troops.[99]

Robert Lilly details how the more 'honest' American racism confronted and improved the English type of racism by ensuring racial anxieties in English communities could be stoked by the presence of all black companies, thereby creating a stronger impression of being racially overwhelmed by their presence, and then reinforcing the fear through racist proclamations that rape was becoming too prevalent among black troops. Race, according to Lilly, was not less significant in France and Germany but the significance of rape was diluted and complicated by taking place in the middle of highly active conflict zones. Again, those sentenced to death for rape in France were almost all black soldiers.[100] In Germany, Lilly details disproportionate sentencing of black accused as well as disproportionate use of death sentences for this group although the case studies presented in relation to Germany frequently feature white assailants.[101] I would like the reader to remember my discourse on the imagery of the black accused and make the connection between that discourse, Robert Lilly's research, and the Bemba case at the ICC. The link between those military cases and my discourse is important, particularly if one considers that this was the Nuremberg era, when modern ICL was birthed. The significance of the 'first' modern era international rape accused being mostly black men is not lost on me and on those interested in institutional memories where institutions store and reuse/refurbish old practices.[102] In addition to the influences of western countries at the ICC's foundational stages, this is one of the reasons why I argue that the ICC is reproducing local/racist criminal justice practices in the manner referred to by Robert Lilly. Feminist legal scholar Doris Buss draws parallels between the fact that the vast majority of international criminal indictments fall disproportionately on black men and the racialised nature of the North American penal system.[103]

I argue that there are two levels of difficulties with this Eurocentric approach towards communal crimes in Africa. The first is a philosophical problem where we see the demarcation of Africa as 'the site,' where these 'types' of crimes continue to occur and Europe/America as the site where law and order prevails and needs to be 'donated' to the crime ridden site. In this light then, we need to look at the Bemba case and rape as war crime in the context of the discussion of the boundaries drawn by the cosmopolitan ICC in what I would refer to as the wider metaphysical imperialist discourse. In this discourse, the western political imaginary has a deeply entrenched but simple logic of "civilised" (European) and "barbarian" (other).[104] This simplistic understanding of the universe extends to other differences such as masculinity and femininity and leads to the existing international conflicts classifications of state sponsored violence (western invasions/right to intervene) as '"good" while other violence not sponsored by the west is 'bad' violence which has to always be racialized, tribal or barbarian 'other'."[105] Martti Koskenniemi sees this simplistic differentiation of 'civilisation' versus 'barbarism,' as the core foundation of international law where the 'barbarian' societies are like children who allow their unrestrained passions to rule their behaviour of wantonly indulging in non-moderated vice.[106] This manner of demarcating societies allows the creation of the imaginary borders between 'civilisation' and the other side's monstrosities, dangers, and temptations.[107] In an argument that sums up this philosophy Ann Sagan[108] indicates that "in order to corroborate the court's cosmopolitan and liberal identity, the ICC utilises discourses of gender, race and culture through the representation of the African subject as both criminal and victim."[109] The 'universal' rule of law is a form of contemporary civilising tool that those who support the ICC utilise to showcase how the horrors of barbarism may be stopped, or minimised using this international justice system.[110] The victim at the ICC becomes Agamben's *homo sacer*; a unit of measurement of the benefits of this cosmopolitanism and its agents of dominance like the Rome Statute. [111]

The core principle of criminal law is shattered by this canonisation of the demarcation between the criminal and the victim in the Rome Statute text because criminal law is founded on having the capacity to 'prove' the accused innocent (found not guilty) and for allowing ambiguity between these two roles, hence the 'innocent till proven guilty' mantra. Ann Sagan argues that this victim vs criminal dichotomy works as a marker of exclusion and inclusion in the international order – the victim as the insider and the perpetrator as the outsider – in a manner similar to the way states defines citizenship.[112] This manner of looking at ICL supports my discourse in that, although the cosmopolitan idea of victimhood and criminality are subjectivities that theoretically extend to conflicts happening outside Africa, the exclusive indictment of Africans at the ICC has made African 'criminals' and 'victims' the key markers of the boundaries of international 'community' in relation to contemporary international criminal law.[113] Therefore, as others have also noted, this supposedly new and emerging international order still views Africa in its relation to the civilised cosmopolitan as the barbaric other-Africa.[114]

In an argument which chimes with the debate on iconography that I engaged with in Chapter 4, Ann Sagan suggests that to define itself, the supposed liberal/universal criminal law depends on the African subject, especially at the ICC.[115] The African criminal becomes a permanent signifier of impunity, a narrative boosted and rooted in repeated images of the perpetrators of violence in African conflicts. The narrative of the African criminal finally facing justice becomes the court's sole mission in its first decade.[116] As I detailed in Chapter 4 on iconography, the demarcations of insider and outsider are readily provided the aesthetics necessary to complete the picture of this supposed impunity in the global public's mind, including the racialised and gendered image of the African victim and criminal. The African in this argument is trapped by the straitjacket of the law because the ICC views the African simultaneously as the victim who desperately needs saving by the cosmopolitan law, and at the same time, as the criminal who, because of his impunity, necessitates cosmopolitan law. This contradiction is the ICC's *raison d'être* without which it is not able to expand and reinforce its jurisdiction or effectiveness.

Therefore, the black body is used by the cosmopolitan law to corroborate its necessary narrative of legitimacy and illegitimacy, justice, and progress.[117] The normalisation of the imagination of both the criminal and the victim as historically Africans strengthens the already existing demarcations of civilisation and barbarity. This binary situation is existentially critical for the ICC because a criminal Africa is portrayed as the undesirable status quo, while lawful Africa, which the ICC might create by its interventions, promises a clear contrast and excites a hopeful vision of a radically different future. Through perpetuating the "dichotomies of criminal–victim, insider–outsider and civilisation–barbarism, the ICC views itself as a necessary balance to the abuses of modern statehood."[118] While we see here the ICC imagining itself as a parallel sovereign, my post-colonial perspective would view its use of impunity rhetoric as reproducing the precursor to imperialism, founded on the need to extend the rule of law to regions plagued by internal disorders, that was accompanied by what Naeem Inayatullah and David Blaney describe as the association of non-European peoples "with a pre-social state that became paradigmatic of a state of disorder and anarchy."[119] In the contemporary period, the presentation of Africa as a site of disorder, underdevelopment and chaotic, ethnically based violence reduces our ability to understand any conflict other than through the prism of ethnicity and race.[120] This in turn makes those conflicts seem natural and non-political and removes the role of politics in resolving those conflicts. This manner of understanding African conflicts makes them a fertile ground for the simplistic rhetoric of 'impunity' and makes Africa a perfect site to 'germinate' cases for the ICC's jurisdiction. In addition to impunity rhetoric, the rule of law is another useful soundbite which underlines the liberal narrative of international law's inevitability, emergence, and critique, and also strengthens the insider–outsider dichotomy utilised in relation to the African citizen. The rule of law is the 'soundtrack' which accompanies liberalism's view of international criminal law and is supposed to denote international criminal laws' already universal applicability.[121] As Koskenniemi argues, "this cosmopolitan narrative presents law as 'inevitable,' already universal and irresistibly under way."[122] For the cosmopolitan, "the structures of 'sovereignty, identity, and inequality have already lost but hang around like zombies, not knowing they [have] died."[123] The coloniser is always aware of the lie of the 'independent state' and the ICC as a colonial structure is able to conveniently use 'universality of the rule of law' as a technology for further undermining the already weakened African states that cannot always guarantee adequate governance in some of their territories due to their colonial/slavery/neoliberal legacies. The ICC is conveniently able to attribute this lack of governance to 'impunity' and not to colonial legacies for example. It is able to use these situations to demarcate the boundaries between lawful society and its outsiders.[124] This predicament makes law's universal applicability the cure for all ailments and relevant to every situation, and at every moment.[125]

As Koskenniemi says, "international criminal law presents itself as 'firmly sociological' seeming to reflect 'what is already out there' rather than the projection of a mere moral utopia."[126] For example, the Kenyan situation at the Hague was meant to end 'impunity' (presumably of the political elite) but Moreno Ocampo presented the Kenyan cases as an example of how future conflicts would be litigated. In this way, international law downplays its own capacity to make or produce conditions in society and instead presents itself as a product of that society and hence the ICC is sold as a by-product of the rule of law, and not as a producer of that rule of law.[127] In the same manner, the idea of impunity hints at a time and space where the rule of law prevailed, thereby hiding the way in which the focus on 'rule of law' and 'impunity' is used to germinate conditions for the domination of a 'universality' narrative.[128] The ICC hopes (against hope) that propagating the idea of the inevitability of the 'rule of law' will make it non-political and protect it from criticism. Through this, the ICC walks the ever-tighter rope of presenting the international community simultaneously as multicultural and pluralistic while at the same time also unequivocally a single entity. For example, the ICC/Africa conflict shows that African states see themselves as different or being treated so from other member states. This fantasy tends to present the world as made of 'equal' relationships between states instead of an existing hierarchy; the ICC hopes this will allow it to continue to sell itself as the benevolent guardian of this mosaic by protecting the African victim, which in turn shields the ICC against the critique of imperialism.[129] This mosaic, as I explored in Chapter 4, allows the essential aesthetics of victimhood which are grounded to specific images and identities instrumentalised by the human rights/NGO industrial complex to expand ICL jurisdiction. The industrial complex instrumentalises the gendered representation of victimhood in what Carla Rose Shapiro identifies as

> ...culturally available and assimilable signs of the ubiquitous dying African baby, the close-up portraits of character-laden African faces, the dusty refugee or internally displaced persons (IDP) camp teaming with women and children, and the rich colours of African tapestry worn by Darfurian women.[130]

Having demarcated Africa as the place ridden with crime and inhabited by the savage criminal, the second difficulty I find with this Eurocentric approach is its individualist nature compared to what I argue for in this book – a structural understanding of these crimes, including their colonial sources. My line of argument that a holistic/communal approach is necessary is supported by the work of feminist writers like Tonia St. Germain and Susan Dewey[131] who argue that the prosecution-driven ICC cannot provide a solution to communal violence where there is a total social breakdown because of its focus on the individual.[132] In most cases, it is the community in general that is culpable and therefore individual prosecutions are not suited to conflict resolution.[133] That, as I argue later on, is better addressed through local justice systems like *Gacaca*. The current war rape regime at the ICC can be traced to Euro-American feminist legal framers who, I argue, first failed to engage with the structural exclusions in their own societies. Those exclusions might help frame the international legal discourse in wider capitalist exclusions because such patterns extend to the global arena and could explain the causes of the wars that the liberal west pretends to punish. I would add that because these Eurocentric framers are beneficiaries of colonial privileges and global inequalities they exonerate themselves from involvement in the cause of these conflicts by germinating and perpetuating the 'single perpetrator narrative' in which particular individuals rather than broader social systems (in which the framers play a central role) perpetrate all forms of exclusion, including barbaric racism and sexism.[134] Their manner of addressing justice therefore ignores two main issues: first, their role in fomenting global inequalities and divisions and wars through interventionist policies, and second the willful blindness to the intersections of race, culture, and sexuality in discourses such as rape as a war crime.[135] From a southern perspective however, these approaches are seen to exclude solutions emanating from the sites where these crimes occur and in the process, as I have argued elsewhere, act as a disempowering factor enabling the infantilising of local solutions or become harmful to some women while benefiting others.[136] This is because, by always promoting their Eurocentric solutions as the dominant norm(s), they exclude southern perspectives and disregard work done by grassroots feminists in finding localised solutions.[137]

The African's body is useful not just to legitimise universalism; researching the African is big business. Conflict economies are often seen only in relation to the natural resources which fuel them. However, it is time we start talking not just about conflict diamonds or cobalt, but also about conflict 'knowledge.' As I have found during my research, conflict situations in Africa have not just produced the ICC/legal industry, but also a related war/peace research complex. In Chapter 3, I explored how the 'development' empire has concentrated on southern countries being forced to standardise their laws and have in place mechanisms to protect intellectual property rights. I will explore this further here in relation to how IPR underpins a knowledge industry, particularly with the African woman as its subject/product. I argued in Chapter 3 that the protection of IPR means knowledge generated using communal resources is privatised, and worse still, the benefit of such knowledge is not shared with the communities generating that IP as in the case of HIV medications and as is currently being repeated with Covid vaccines. The UK's leading Russell Group of universities is particularly proud of its commercialisation of research.[138] Russell Group universities are keen to showcase how research undertaken in UK universities has led to many successful IP licences and spin-off companies.[139] They also say that successful commercialisation requires sustained long-term investment in research, often over many years or even decades, and they are proud that these business results are easier to quantity than other 'quality of life' outcomes.[140]

Most importantly though, they say that the UK's universities' academic research underpins the success and competitiveness of many UK businesses.[141] This is because businesses have easy access to research expertise and also benefit directly by access to publicly funded IP.[142] Co-funding research with university partners also enables companies to access leading research talent and to lever public funding, to accelerate the development of an area of research, and to pursue more research than the company would be able to afford by itself.[143] Furthermore, 19 out of 20 Russell Group institutions use a commercialisation company or have a department within their institution to manage consultancies and commercial interactions. For example, Oxford University Consulting has a client base that includes Astra Zeneca, Microsoft, the National Audit Office and the UN Development Programme. Many Russell Group academics have formed their own consultancy companies to externalise their research. A survey of over 8,000 Russell Group academics found that 13.1% had formed or run a consultancy company based on their research.[144]

And therefore, universities where this research is based are themselves big business. In the UK for example, universities, together with their international students and visitors, generated £95 billion of gross output in the economy in 2014–2015.[145] Universities generated a £52.9 billion or 2.9% gross value-added contribution to the UK GDP in 2014–2015 and contributed £14.1 billion/2.7% of total tax receipts received by HMRC in the same year.[146] Significantly, from a decolonising perspective, students from outside of the EU were responsible for 80% of this total impact. Through all their spending, and that of their visitors, they generated £20.6 billion of gross output, £11 billion in gross value-added, almost 200,000 jobs (almost 170,000 full-time equivalent jobs), and £2.7 billion of tax receipts.[147] This is significant for two reasons. First, these students, a significant number from African states, are transferring their families'/countries' wealth to the west, as we explored in Chapter 2, but also they are transferring an even more valuable commodity; they are collecting data on their people (for example those studying war rape in the DRC) which is then stored/owned by the west through the universities. Second these students will become the elite of the future; agents of the west because their relationship with their people will be shaped by this Eurocentric 'researching' of their people.

Western universities are however part of the wider war/NGO industrial complex, as detailed by Dennis Dijkzeul.[148] He describes an ecosystem in which NGOs, local operatives, donor agencies and warlords collude to perpetuate an ecosystem that has at its core war in the Eastern Congo.[149] A cursory look through your preferred search engine (I used Google Scholar) will provide hundreds of research materials and data on sexual violence in the Eastern DRC, the fact that this material exists means populations and their suffering have produced this knowledge and that a thriving research/academic industry has been born out of it. However, what we do with this data is the more pertinent point in relation to my instrumentalisation/ICL industrial complex. This and other associated ecosystems thrive for reasons that are better detailed by Laura Heaton who reported on the *Luvungi* debacle in the DRC.[150] In that incident, an initial six rape cases reported by women to a local medical practitioner, some of which had occurred in domestic settings, became "mass rape" through an inter-play of factors including misreporting, exaggerations by the community and amplified by NGOs.[151] Laura Heaton notes that although the initial misreporting was identified, the mass rape narrative remained, mostly because the foreign gaze was focused on the rapes and that translated into more funding targeted to combating rape.[152] The sad phenomenon was that local women felt that if they claimed to have been raped, they were more likely to receive support from services than if they presented with other complaints.[153] An industry had thus mushroomed with most multi-donor funds between 2010 and 2011 going disproportionately to sexual violence programmes, compared to nearly all other sectors.[154] The sexual violence budget was nearly double the size of the budget for all security sector reform and just under half the size of the entire peace building trust fund.[155] Funding for internally displaced people, estimated at 1.4 million people in the eastern DRC at the time, was less than half of the funding for sexual violence.[156]

But this industrial complex is part of a wider web of war industry, as detailed by Gargi Bhattacharyya who argues that westerners' obsession with sex and the sexuality of occupied/colonised communities could be linked to the use of feminism and associated rhetoric being incorporated, for example, in the UK's and America's colonial foreign policies.[157] This has included the justification of wars where intervention is seen in the light of promoting women's rights, which was very useful in demarcating 'them' vs 'us;' those who do not respect women's right and 'us' who do leading to the much caricatured Bush/Blair dalliance.[158] Despite the overall public opposition to the Iraq war for example, enforcement of women's rights through war continues to be regarded as a laudable goal.[159]

And therefore, for this industry, the African woman is reduced to just an object/item/unit, a number useful for its business model. My argument against a Eurocentric approach to resolving sexualised crimes in the African context is that it is a continuation of the dehumanisation of the African woman exemplified by the caging and displaying of our ancestors in days past. That is better exemplified by the dehumanisation of the Cape Town African lady[160] in which the African woman's body continuously becomes a site for study and

> ...a mystery to the white European gaze, which consequently caged it and turned it into a mere object of curiosity and knowledge: the excessiveness of her genitalia and buttocks were shown as a proof of the wild sexuality characterizing black women.[161]

I find similarities in the western feminist fixation[162] with sexualised crimes in war situations in Africa with this caging and studying, the prodding, as if no other crimes, including the murder of women, occur during wars. I argue that this obsession requires the African woman to be in a constant state of overexposure, showing the perpetual contradictions inherent in the white saviour syndrome. The African woman in these rape cases (Eurocentric law or even state sponsored *Gacaca*) is physically present yet she is the 'spectacle' as we shall see in my discussion regarding *Gacaca* courts which entailed the reliving of rape ordeals by the survivors with very intimate details having to be disclosed in an open court to 'prove' legal definitions of rape. Similar to the Cape Town lady, this interrogation means that rape survivors are

> hardly accepted as a human being; they exist mostly as an image, an icon, something to be looked at, but at the same time, she represented a non-image, the negation of her image, as the only parts of her body that were regarded as worthy of attention is her genitalia.[163]

In the same vein I argue that the Eurocentric gaze directed at the African woman's body or the pretence of safeguarding her integrity/dignity are not only nefarious but continue a colonial tendency to over-emphasise the African's sexuality. I submit that in order to have their modern-day Cape lady, the contemporary 'saviour' must create the right conditions in which material for study is readily available through perpetual wars.

This leads to two of the main criticisms that I have explored above. First is the hierarchical approach to crime with rape becoming the apex, the worst crime that could occur in war, and second is the denial of local/affected women's sexual and political agency. In a country of over 90 million inhabitants,[164] I can safely assume that Congo DRC has a good portion of healthy safe relationships/families where sexualised crimes are absent. I can also assume that a good number of those people have healthy sexual relationships; it is hardly the rape capital of the world.[165] I have explored this categorisation as 'rape capital' above, noting that it should be seen as a colonial/racist demarcation by the European (civilised/barbaric), but more importantly it has produced the industry I expose here and which others have explored in relation to militarisation/securitisation of rape in war, naming it *Sexurity*.[166] There is evidence that local people in *Bukavu* detest the imposition of foreign interventions and the refusal of international agencies to listen and respond to their experiences, needs and proposals.[167] Local people resist foreign interventions as they view them as not addressing the structural causes of the rapes, including the plurality of violence/needs.[168] One victim complained that she was worried about a variety of concerns, including death of loved ones and loss of property but international observers only wanted to speak to her about rape.[169] To other survivors, returning to their land and providing for their families again was more important than being recognised as sexualised crime victims.[170] But local people were also alive to the instrumentalisation that I speak about here as they complain that international agencies are more concerned about funding and, most importantly, they complained that those who came to help had no expertise in offering the psycho-social support needed.[171] But overall, there is a feeling that local voices/experts are ignored and rape is seen as the only issue to be addressed on a long list of other local concerns.[172]

I am aware that my dehumanisation argument is a powerful one and makes some uncomfortable. But that is the point of this whole book and indeed the point of decolonising discourse(s). I would however not be the first and hopefully not the last to critique western feminism in African settings as this has been done variously by many African women. Obioma Nnaemeka, for example, argued that the western approach to issues like female circumcision dehumanises the African woman.[173] Yvette Abrahams also says that the detached, non-racialised white feminism ends up sowing divisions in the black community.[174] White feminism's manner of approaching sexualised crimes sees black men as sexist and violent and also deduces from this assumption that the emanations of that sexism will destroy the black community, which is reminiscent of the sexual politics of lynching practiced in the days still not gone by the USA/UK where black men were/are seen always as a rape threat to white women.[175] Objecting to the white saviour complex does not however translate into us not agitating for peace or justice for our people.

A critique of western feminism is not the focus of my discourse and an attempt to read or associate my ideas with any form of complicity with crimes against women would be nefarious, racist. The tendency by the hegemony to attack critiques as ignoring or advocating for atrocities has been noted by scholars like Christine Schwobel.[176] She warns that there are some who want this approach to ICL to be stopped because of the alleged complicity.[177] However she also calls for self-reflection because there is also a tendency for those of us engaging in critique to view ourselves as outside the 'ecosystem' we are critiquing.[178] And the 'ecosystem' is the focus of my critique in this area because Christine Schwobel also warns of the instrumentalising of the victims or those 'we' claim to speak for.[179] Instrumentalism has at its core the idea that modern capitalists are able to formulate public policies which represent their long-term class interests and to secure the adoption, implementation, and enforcement of those policies through state institutions.[180] Therefore power, and who possesses it are crucial in this approach as they determine who controls resources, how these resources are allocated, and with what intention.[181]

It is important to note that the fact that rape and other forms of sexual abuse are happening in war is not disputed in any literature I have reviewed, neither am I disputing it.[182] My critique is the selectivity that is applied by the ICC and related industry in addressing it. I explained in Chapter 4 for example that the ICC investigated British soldiers' actions in Iraq and found that they committed rape and other sexualised crimes and yet decided not to initiate proceedings against anyone. In addition, a question for future research is whether there is a global trend towards more sexual and other forms of violence against women generally. For example, in the UK, where there has been no war for a while (at least not of the DRC format) there were an estimated 800,000 sexual assault cases in the year ending March 2018.[183] A key statistic however is that out of 2,405 alleged sexual offences before magistrates in 2017, 60.8% were committed by white people, 7.4% by black people, 7.4% and by Asian people.[184] I would recommend that *Médecins Sans Frontières* urgently send aid workers to London and the home counties to investigate this phenomenon, for what makes a rape in *Ituri* more universal than a rape in Islington?

One of the most powerful standpoints I have ever come across on this topic is from Yvette Abrahams.[185] As a KhoeKhoe woman academic, she was perhaps able to capture the anger that I tried to utilise in this book better than I could. It is in this manner that I critique the emerging industry around black bodies, specifically black women's bodies in conflict situations. Granted, I am not a black woman. I am however a son, a grandson, a cousin, brother to many African women. I should remind the reader to have the discourse on revolution in Chapter 3 in mind while engaging with the arguments I make here. African women like Yvette Abrahams can speak on their own behalf. However, as Yvette Abrahams herself notes, we as black men have historical experiences which should enable us to understand what our sisters are going through because we have suffered similar violent deformations.[186]

Yvette Abrahams wrote in anger to reclaim the narrative of the Cape 'Untie' as she calls her from appropriation by the white narrative.[187] She says that this reclaiming, her engagement with the issue, cannot be just an intellectual/academic exercise.[188]

> ...It is personal. I am these people ... this is not about their history. It about my history, my people, and the fight not just to take our land, make us slaves, but to determine our very identity through racial and gendered power.[189]

And the telling of these historical events by us is important from my perspective as they should at least contribute to explaining the birth of the violence we see in the African state today as 'we' understand it. This is because we cannot always have white people define the problem for us, and then quickly prescribe the solution. First, we reclaim some dignity for ourselves and our mothers, but more importantly, we could point to the solution. It is now commonly held by therapeutic professions like social work, for example, that perpetrators of abuse have themselves suffered abuse in the past.[190]

It would not therefore be far-fetched for me to hypothesise that part of the root cause(s) of abuse we witness today in places like Eastern Congo may be related/inherited from the trauma of atrocities perpetrated by slavers, the Belgian colonisers and their local agents.[191] It is important to have these explorations because, as we have already seen, the colonial state machinery was inherited intact by the 'independent' state. The independent state also not only inherited abusive, coercive, and authoritarian institutions such as the police forces, but also colonial jails, including colonial officers' attitudes to the local populations.[192] In Kenya for example, the colonial prison complex that detained freedom fighters is still in use.[193] The Kenyan police force remains as brutal towards the people as it was during white rule.[194] The atrocities committed by the British in Kenya which remain unaddressed include torture, disappearances, rapes, and mass killings.[195] Is it a wonder then that the post 'independent' elite who inherited that state mechanism reproduce these practices? Therefore, without even addressing the trauma caused by slavery, colonialism and modern capitalism, 'peace' becomes just an illusion.

Peace becomes an illusion because the current approach is precisely designed to make it so. What I have identified is the ever-expanding knowledge production industry centred on the suffering of African victims. This industry has failed not only to end violence against the women it claims to represent but has meant the focus on ending the war is marginalised, as Laura Heaton suggests above. At the ICC, the focus on prosecuting the individual for communal crimes including rape means that often the actual perpetrators are never challenged. In addition, I argue that this manner of 'justice' perpetuates the neo-colonial/neo-liberal understanding of the world, including the treatment of African women who become a useful tool in the (re)production of the iconography of victimhood. As we see with Nicola Henry's argument on memories discussed above, this means the wrong, or at best selective, memories are highlighted. For example, as I have indicated, African women like my grandmother are not recorded as liberation heroes but as victims. It also cements the demarcation of Africa as the site where these truly awful characters are to be found, perpetuating a vicious cycle of international 'interventionist' engagement with Africa. What I am advocating is that local initiatives by local women should be strengthened and practitioners should move beyond collecting data to progressively end the violence and the circumstances that allow this violence. Practitioners in this field may be able to borrow from social work safeguarding models like contextual safeguarding which looks at abuse in a more holistic and structural context, acknowledges the practitioner's biases and does not deny the survivor their agency.[196] But I guess the ICL/white saviour complex is not keen on therapeutic/holistic approaches to peace because such an approach will require past colonial ills to be acknowledged and accounted for, and reparations made. It would also mean that, instead of perpetuating a peace industry, we can finally stop the wars.

Fuck/White Saviour Complex

> *Her name is Jane or Amber/She will have the best intentions/She will have the petal of this reason for a tongue/She will have been five/The glow of the National Geographic will have bathed her face golden/She will have paused on the dark child's swollen belly/thin limbs/ribs/the flies/She will have slipped off her big sister's Louboutins/skipped the playroom/through her mother's walk-in wardrobe/to the pool/to ask if the child could attend supper/Her mother's laugh will shimmer her diamonds/She will explain/ the world is the world/Some work hard/like your father/forging oil contracts/Some just don't/But we are still to help the poor in Africa/She would have wanted ever since/ Her utmost sincerity will cut you to silence/She will bloom anew*[197]

As discussed in the sections above in relation to rape, we see a form of activist led law at the ICC as the court takes a pedagogical role to protect the African from self-destruction. This pedagogic perspective extends to victim participation in trials at the ICC although victim participation in criminal trials is not a new phenomenon because, as discussed below, victims have on occasion taken the initiative to initiate criminal cases. It is however the case that victim participation in actual trials is more prevalent in civil law traditions than in common law.[198] It is therefore important for me to briefly detail the role of victims in a common law jurisdiction. The orthodox in common law practice is to have, at least in theory, an adversarial arrangement in criminal proceedings where the prosecution and the defence take oppositional positions. This is done before a judge and a jury. The judge acts largely as a referee who guides the jury though their function of fact-finding. In this setting, the victim is usually a witness on the prosecution's side.[199] In the USA and, more recently the UK, victims are able to provide 'impact statements' although unlike at the ICC, these are not presented during trials but at the sentencing phase and they are supposed to offer the victim's perspective that could (not must) contribute to determining an appropriate sentence.[200]

By contrast, victims and judges tend to play a different and core role in the civil law system where one or more investigating judges generally supervise the compilation of a dossier to which the accused must respond at trial. As opposed to common law arrangements, the judge in the civil law tradition is actively inquisitorial and controls the trial's direction by questioning witnesses. As opposed to common law, victims are able to initiate proceedings and could seek compensation through becoming civil petitioners in the criminal prosecution.[201] This is where the ICC borrows heavily from civil jurisdiction because at the ICC victims gain similar trial rights, including the right to make claims for compensation, and may fully participate in the whole of the trial, including interrogating witnesses and being legally represented.[202] The ICC follows France, Cambodia, ICTY, and *Gacaca* in Rwanda which had victim participation in trials of war crimes suspects. In France, victims participated as *parties civiles* between 1991 and 1998 in trials of alleged Nazi war criminals. The practice has also been a feature of Cambodia's trial of the former Khmer Rouge leadership.[203]

As we see elsewhere in this chapter, these two legal traditions were brought together in the negotiating and drafting phase of the Rome Statute and, as discussed earlier on, western NGOs played a significant role in the inclusion of victims' participation at the ICC.[204] The differences detailed above in relation to civil and common law orthodoxies came to the fore during the Rome Statute drafting stage because a victim-oriented draft presented by France and New Zealand was strongly opposed by delegations from common law countries like Australia, the UK, and the USA who preferred the traditional position of the victim as a prosecutor's witness.[205] Despite the worries of many concerning the legal and political complications of such a system, victim participation won the day after the French delegation gained support from several influential victim-oriented NGOs[206] and a coalition of African and South American states, leading to Article 68 of the Statute.[207] Common law countries, including the USA and the UK, worried that this provision would alter the prosecution's focus[208] but eventually and due to extensive lobbying from various NGOs,[209] the Statute also provided for victims' compensation in Article 75.[210] From a post-colonial perspective, we can see from the above that the debate was only whether the ICC should adopt a common law or civil law tradition and not, for example, *Buenvivir* or *Ubuntu*. Literature shows that despite southern states being represented in the drafting stages, no 'southern' epistemologies were considered as part of these discussions on victim participation nor for example did African languages feature anywhere in the emerging Statute.[211] As I will explore in the next chapter, there were African centric examples such as the *Gacaca* model already established by the Rwanda tribunal.[212] I will discuss the *Gacaca* further in Chapter 6, and how it could form a part of a reformed global legal system that is pluralist in conception.

The main proponents of victim participation argue that it is wrong for victims to be relegated to a single role as witnesses in international criminal law (and domestic criminal law) given, as we have explored, that they can already claim compensation in many civil law jurisdictions and have substantive rights to life and liberty.[213] In this light, several authors see victims' role as central to international justice[214] and others see it as important in the pursuit of ICL's effectiveness and legitimacy.[215] This school of thought traces victim participation to the UN declaration of Basic Principles of Justice for Victims of Crimes and Abuse of Power, adopted by the UN General Assembly on November 29, 1985 which sets out basic principles of justice, including the right of victims to have access to the judicial process and to receive prompt redress for the harm they have suffered.[216] Victim participation at the ICC builds on this declaration and was strengthened by experiences from the ICTY and ICTR in relation to victims' experiences and the growth in influence of victims' rights movements both domestically and internationally.[217] The main motivation was the thinking that if victims are not allowed to participate fully, the legal outcomes of these tribunals may not be accepted by the affected communities,[218] though it was also recognised that a fine balance needed to be maintained because, owing to the seriousness of the allegations, the right of the accused to a fair trial must also be protected.[219] Second, there was the reasoning that the ICC needed to discharge its legal duty[220] under Article 68(3) of the Rome Statute to allow opportunities for victims to express their rights.[221] This article provides victims with procedural rights to represent their personal interests and claim reparations at the ICC as compared to the ICTY and ICTR because, unlike those tribunals, the Rome Statute had paved the way to the establishment of a victims' trust fund.[222] I would however argue that it is questionable whether victim participation leads to the achievement of justice as claimed by proponents.[223] Given the collapse of high profile cases such as those of Gbagbo and Kenyatta, it is even questionable whether the prosecution's concern with 'ending impunity'[224] is serious and extends beyond mere rhetoric. It is even more doubtful that the prosecution is concerned with the welfare and recovery of individual victims, as claimed by some.[225]

While victim participation is not a new trend in criminal law, Africa becomes yet again the testing ground for victim participation at the ICC because the *Lubanga* Case was the first important decision in the matter of victim participation at trial stage.[226] It was a trend-setting case in that it was the first trial held before the ICC and also the first in which victims actively participated in the proceedings as independent actors.[227] Yet another African case, *Katanga and Ngudjolo* was the first important ruling regarding victim participation at pre-trial stage.[228] Victim participation as envisaged by the Rome Statute and already in practice at the ICC faces a philosophical challenge which in my view has not been addressed by the literature reviewed so far on this topic. Although the scope of this book does not allow for discussions of wider penal philosophy, it is important to note that not all scholars look at victim participation from the tinted perspective of a victims' rights activist. Aya Gruber for example sees the philosophical groundings of victim focused criminal trials as founded on our emotional attachment to the 'innocent victim' as opposed to the abusive or careless victim.[229] In criminal law, it follows from this perspective that, save for very limited circumstances, society is largely reluctant to attribute blame or focus on potential role(s) the victim may have played in the totality of the alleged crime.

> The women sent palm leaves to other women in the neighbouring villages ... the traditional way of inviting people to an emergency meeting. They marched to the DO's office and forced him to dismiss the warrant chief. On December 13th, their demonstration turned violent. A panicked colonial medical officer accidentally hit some of the women with his car. The warring women smashed his car. Early on December 14th, the women's drum summoned a meeting. It was a war Drum. One of the women who beat the Drum was the chief's wife ... On the fateful December 14th, the women in their war outfit, their faces painted with charcoal and white clay, heads decorated with fern, and waists covered with short wrapper and fern, chanted their war songs. Brandishing their weapons of pestles, cassava sticks, young palm leaves and short sticks, they danced towards the Native court, the perceived centre and symbol of colonialism and economic exploitation. There, they burnt down the colonial government buildings, the Native court, staff quarters and the colonial commercial buildings of the Nigerian Products Company Limited. Filling the air with victory songs, the women danced as many more joined them...[230]

In addition to the victim having criminal responsibilities themselves, we have already seen when discussing rape as war crime, that the focus on gendered victimisation is viewed by authors like Ratna Kapur[231] as taking away agency from the victims, although, like all other critiques, she is not advocating that crimes not be prosecuted. In addition, we saw in Chapter 3 that this victimhood denies African women who have had core roles in revolutions such as that of the *Mau Mau* in Kenya their historical prominence. Those who advocate for the Rohingya genocide victims for example, argue against the orthodox in international law that "portrays genocide victims as passive, helpless targets of atrocity."[232] The Rohingya activists argue that they are victims of the ICL's need to categorise/frame groups such as refugee vs terrorist ignoring the fact that the Rohingya have been resisting oppression on their own with minimal international support and they "are not passive objects for Western pity and salvation, but a people whose ongoing struggles to survive in the face of genocide should compel international solidarity."[233]

What I have observed and experienced through participating in discussion forums and through engaging with literature in this field is the ever-present danger identified by Christine Schwobel and discussed earlier in the Rape as War Crime section that there has generally been the standard/hegemonic/western manner of engaging with the arguments around reaffirming African women's agency. This hegemony is increasingly being challenged by TWAIL and other critiques, including my own, and challenging Eurocentrism as 'the' only perspective means running the risk of being accused of condoning atrocities. I have not come across any academic literature by critics which advocates for atrocities and many in society (this author included) would find blaming women for violence against them or for rape indefensible.[234] The argument here is that women, including my grandmother, were not only agents of their own freedom(s) but were fighting the same white hegemony that now purports to support their freedoms. The idea that my grandmother and other African women freedom fighters need(ed) an 'international' legal system with the abundance of 'humanity' to bestow this humanity back to them should be laughable. I say this because the current ICL regime envisages a victim with no agency and a Eurocentric law that donates this agency now and then. Although writing about criminal justice in the USA, Gruber's views are highly applicable while studying the ICC as she argues that this ideal/powerless victim imaging is largely a product of the politically powerful victims' rights movement and is closely intertwined with negative defendant characterisations[235] and tough-on-crime politics. These politics result in black males being disproportionately over-represented in the criminal justice systems in both the USA and the UK. This powerless ideal victim also leads to less focus on sexual assaults on men, for example, as men have traditionally only been portrayed as strong, never as vulnerable.[236] Because these two nations and other western countries, including France, were instrumental in the shaping of the Rome Statute as already explored, Gruber's views, when applied in our discourse mean that the outwardly proclaimed intention of the ICC to 'end impunity' could be driven by this characterisation of the accused and hence by a retaliatory view of justice rather than by the stated moral aspects. By placing the victim at the core of the trials and sentencing, the ICC promotes 'justice' as vengeance because the victim is present during the trial to (re)live the trauma of the incident(s), which provokes outrage.[237]

This victimhood narrative in jurisdictions like the USA is seen simultaneously as a cause and effect of increasing tough-on-crime sentiments through which the victim participation procedures regularly result directly or indirectly in harsher sentences and less protection for the accused which leads to the uncomfortable conclusion that victims' rights under the constitution outweigh those of defendants.[238] This Eurocentric vengeance is transferred from local jurisdictions to the ICC through victim-centred NGOs with unmitigated influence at the ICC, as discussed elsewhere in this book. It is my view that these powerful NGOs are the ICC's equivalent of local, usually right/far right, political groupings in the west propagating tough-on-crime politics which instrumentalise the victim(s) for political ends. This in turn results in the inversion of criminal law practice where a previously state/prosecutor led sphere shifts drastically toward private citizens.[239] This in my view should be the main critique of victim participation at the ICC, that is, the defendant is faced with a duality of charges as presented by the prosecutor in person and the prosecutor via the victim's legal team. This situation came up in the *Lubanga* case where twice during the trial, the victims' lawyers succeeded in changing or adding charges against the accused.[240] In addition, the victims' legal team successfully petitioned the court to change the characterisation of the conflict from an internal to an international conflict even though the prosecutor had not indicated this in the original charges.[241] This would not be allowable in the UK for example as charges are the sole responsibility of the prosecution.[242]

The Kenyan cases and the *Gbagbo* case highlighted another major difficulty with the ICC's victim centric approach. They showed the problem of the unreliable victim because not all victims are 'harmed and humble.' Some victims are "indeed trustworthy, truthful, blameless, and ultimately innocent. Others, however, are bad actors themselves, have memory failures, falsely identify, provoke, and even lie. Some victims are in fact, and indeed encouraged by society to be, vengeful."[243] Yet quite clearly, the complexity and diversity of victims' characteristics is not emphasised by the victims' rights movement or those advocating tough-on-crime policies.[244] Placing the victim at the centre of trials, as practiced by the ICC, ignores the fact that it may not be in the victim's best interests to participate in trials and forgive the perpetrator because some victims "advocate mercy and forgiveness as part of the process of closure."[245] As we explore in Chapter 6, the forgiveness advocated here is that in which the already convicted offender seeks forgiveness openly and honestly and not state sponsored forgiveness, as was seen at the TRC. The forgiveness that is led by the victims' own agency reaffirms their humanity in that they retain "uncontested authorship essential to responsibility and resolution. Forgiveness, rather than vengeance may, therefore, be the act that eventually frees the victim from the event, the means by which the victim may put the experience behind them."[246]

An issue that not so far been addressed adequately by researchers is this problem of the bad character witness, for example where that witness lies about being a victim, or when they tell lies in their evidence; this is something that comes up regularly in the cases at the ICC. It should be noted that victims are usually called as witnesses at trial, but that not all witnesses are victims. The Kenyan cases for example brought up a significant deficit in redressing wrong-doings by victims or witnesses. This is because the

ICC can be viewed as adopting this one-sided characterisation of victims as faultless and does not provide for increased scrutiny of wrongful victim behaviour.[247] According to the OTP the Kenyan cases collapsed after the Kenyan state refused to cooperate in gathering further evidence and after various OTP witnesses recanted their evidence or failed to appear.[248] In addition, the OTP used known militia in gathering evidence against the accused and although the prosecutor admitted that the militia leader was instrumental in the violence and had admitted his role in the violence, he was not charged as he was willing to give evidence against Kenyatta.[249] This 'prosecutors' deal' with a crucial witness highlights a wider problem in relation to both witnesses' behaviour and evidence handling and especially the OTP's practice of compensating witnesses financially which came under criticism during both the *Kenyatta* and *Gbagbo* cases with Kenyatta's attorney claiming in court that some witnesses tried to extort him in exchange for favourable evidence.[250]

The other difficulty linked to this is that because of this victim centric tradition, there are no mechanisms at the ICC to deal with victims who may have contributed to their injuries. There are however existing criminal law doctrines in local jurisdictions that assess liability to victims,[251] negating defendants' *mens rea* rather than lessening liability due to the wrongful behaviour of the victim.[252] Self-defence, provocation, defence of others, and defence of property, for example, lessen defendant liability or exculpate defendants based on wrongful victim behaviour in very specific sets of circumstances. There are no defences, however, that exculpate or mitigate punishment more generally based on victim behaviours in a variety of criminal situations.[253] The result is that the criminal law arbitrarily covers certain victim liability situations but not others. For example, there is a litany of cases where convictions of murder have been reduced to manslaughter after evidence of chronic abuse by the victim had showed women acting out of desperation. For example, in *R v Ahluwalia (Kiranjit)*[254] the defendant successfully appealed on the grounds of diminished responsibility after evidence was presented revealing that she was assessed as suffering from endogenous depression due to chronic domestic violence.[255] In *R v Butler (Diana Helen),* the appeal court was not only willing to look at evidence of abuse by the deceased victim, but also at the defendant's past experiences of abuse from her ex-husband and ruled that it was satisfied that at the time the defendant killed the victim, she was suffering from mental illness brought on by a prolonged history of being subjected to sexual and physical abuse and humiliation from her ex-husband, and later from the victim.[256]

Given the problematic nature of victim participation as detailed above, why then does the Rome Statute/ICC see victim participation at its core? The reason is that whether victim participation is viewed as positive or not depends on one's perspective of the intended consequences of a criminal trial or conviction. This area of discourse is far more extensive than the scope of this book and is covered by the wider penal theory which is a specific subset of moral philosophy exploring the theoretical bases for criminal sanctions.[257] For the purpose of framing the ICC's approach in African cases, it is important to note that there are broadly two categories of penal theory: "deontological" and "consequentialist." A deontological doctrine, also known as an "agent-relative" doctrine, is a theory in which "the moral principles governing human action are exclusively agent-relative".[258] This means that morality derives from a source independent of empirical outcomes.[259] A consequentialist doctrine, "also known as a teleological doctrine in its purest and simplest form is a moral doctrine which says that the morally right act in any given situation is the one that will produce the best overall outcome."[260]

The most influential deontological penal theory is retributivism which is most often associated with the work of Immanuel Kant.[261] Kant thought that punishment should not be administered to enhance another good either for "the criminal himself or the society but must in all cases be imposed only because the individual on whom it is inflicted has committed a crime."[262] On the other hand, the ICC could be described as a fusion scheme with a bias towards consequentialist theories of punishment, justifying punishment on the ground that it produces some desired situation in society. Russell Christopher describes a shared characteristic of consequentialist penal theories as the goal of crime prevention. Both crime and punishment are evils, but punishment is only a qualified evil. The evil of punishment may be outweighed by the good consequences that it generates. That is, punishment is a necessary evil that may be justified by its diminution of the incidence of crime.[263] The desired state of affairs can consist of many different things, for example deterring crime or saving money.[264] In this context, the ICC aims at ending global impunity by applying a highly elitist western judicial system while few of the crimes it seeks to hinder happen in the west.

Due to its aim of ending impunity and 'setting an example' the ICC, like all other proponents of consequentialist penal ideas, depends on the empirical success of the criminal law in achieving the desired situation.[265] Has this happened? I argue that it has not. For example, for all the various cases at the ICC emanating from Eastern Congo, if the goal was to end war in the Eastern Congo and the sexual violence we explored earlier, that aim has consistently failed. Similarly, the recent political chaos witnessed in Kenya after the 2018 presidential elections makes the same point. This is because this form of futuristic cause-effect analyses shows the impotence of consequentialism as future examples evidence their failure to meet stated objectives. This makes consequentialism a slave to future results and only truly valid retrospectively,[266] which in turn makes its purported prospective justificatory force at best speculation[267] and at worst mere rhetoric. However, we see proponents of punishment for the sake of punishment, like Jeremy Bentham, arguing that where punishment has not achieved deterrence that fact does not negate the need for punishment because, for him, it simply means that deterrence is not a proper justification for that specific system of punishment.[268] The second and perhaps more persuasive criticism is that consequentialism counsels the use of unjust, unfair, or immoral means to achieve good ends, so long as there is a net balance of utility.[269] The biases by the ICC against African States already discussed seem to fall into this category because part of the ICC preamble indicates that,

> …the most serious crimes of concern to the international community as a whole must not go unpunished in order to put an end to impunity for the perpetrators of these crimes and thus to contribute to the prevention of such crimes.[270]

Although seemingly problematic in a post-colonial/testing context, the OTP announcement that Kenya will set an example to the world on how to manage past violence and how to create a peaceful recovery process in the future falls within this criticism.[271]

Therefore, as we see with the preamble to the Rome Statute, the ICC adopts this utilitarian theory, with deterrence at its core rather than rehabilitation of offenders. Through the *Mahdi* case the ICC also tested another consequentialist goal of redistribution. Redistribution in this context means not only economic redistribution of funds from the criminal to the victim,[272] but also emotional redistribution of pain from the victim to the criminal, often referred to as "closure."[273] The ideology embracing the redistribution of pain is evident in many aspects of criminal law and is especially manifest in the death penalty context where failure to reach a verdict leading to a death sentence is viewed as devaluing the victim's life and extending their family's pain. This leads to prosecutors advocating for death sentences to reaffirm the victim's worth and the assumption is that victims' statements ensure that juries pass death sentences to service their pain.[274] In addition, redistribution ideology is reflected in restorative justice theory. Restorative justice promotes the idea that the basis for punishment should be restoring the victim.[275] The victim ought to be made whole through the operation of positive law. While victim restitution and restoration is a general goal of restorative justice theory, the restorative justice ideology does not necessarily prescribe the exact method of achieving that goal.[276] Proponents of victim participation see the ICC as the arena of healing through vengeance and punishment of the defendant which is intended to provide the victim with "closure." However, as we have seen above, some experts contend that forgiveness is the best method of closure.[277] It is also my view that this 'transference of pain' is better suited to domestic courts because of the proximity between the accused and the victims rather than to the ICC because of its focus on elites for communal crimes. This means the intended transference from the victim to the perpetrator does not happen as, often, the perpetrator is not the one charged. Indeed, the victim is often not at court. This is one of the reasons why I advocate *Gacaca* as the best suited model for these African situations.

The impact on the accused's right to a fair trial and presumption of innocence is in my view the most potent argument against victim participation. The accused has already been assigned guilt by the identification of 'victims' of an alleged crime before he/she is convicted as the perpetrator. To produce a victim in relation to the particular defendant, the components of a crime in legal terms must have occurred.[278] The victim may have experienced a crime, but not necessarily because of that defendant. The right to be presumed innocent in international criminal law was well established before the ICC came into being through the statutes of both the ICTY[279] and ICTR.[280] Article 66 of the Rome Statute also made presumption of innocence central to the ICC's engagement with the accused.[281] In addition, the application and interpretation of law pursuant to the Court "must be consistent with internationally recognized human rights."[282] In addition to the Statute and Rules of Procedure and Evidence, IHRL is considered as the most important source of law.[283] The ICC itself has indicated that the accused's human rights must also be protected, as the dissenting opinion in the Gbabgo case indicated, when it comes to a fair trial. Judge Herrera Carbuccia said that internationally recognised human rights must be adhered to at the ICC[284] especially when it comes to presumption of innocence.[285] Therefore,

> article 66 setting out the presumption of innocence, as any other provision of the Statute, must be interpreted and applied consistently with internationally recognized human rights, as required by article 21(3) of the Statute. The right to be presumed innocent until proved guilty is enshrined in many international human rights instruments. Consequently, the respective case-law of the judicial and other authorities dealing with alleged violations of international treaties can be an important source for the interpretation of the scope of article 66 of the Statute.[286]

In my view, firmly identifying the victim directly related to a particular individual precludes the accused from being innocent in that victim's mind to start with, as it does also in the court of public opinion where the person is being accused of the most serious of crimes. This is particularly so for public figures who cannot erase those public memories even when acquitted.

In legal doctrine, the presumption of innocence is considered 'one of the cornerstones of modern criminal procedure,'[287] which has the power to "legitimize the conviction and punishment."[288] It aims at establishing and complying with the rule of law as the basis for a criminal sanction. According to Safferling, at the trial stage the presumption of innocence has three different aspects; (i) burden of proof, (ii) proof of guilt, and (iii) conduct of officials[289] which all derive from IHRL.[290] These three aspects need to coexist in order to cover the purpose of the principle in its entirety, something that is called the broader formula.[291] It is the full recognition of the presumption of innocence which has the highest standards when it comes to protection of fundamental rights.[292] The discourse on the evidential realm of this presumption of innocence is in my view more important and is one that I find the active involvement of victims encroaches on, as already detailed, because of the overturning of the orthodox one versus one approach and its replacement by what is a two versus one formula for hearings. And as we see in the *Lubanga* case discussed above, the prosecutor and the victims' legal team could connive to deny the defence access to exculpatory material.[293]

However, the burden of proof at the ICC still rests with the OTP and the standard of proof seems to be beyond reasonable doubt but in reality the burden/standard(s) applied at the ICC is in doubt when one scrutinises more closely the trial stages at the ICC. The burden seems to shift because in the *Lubanga* case we see the victims' legal team agreeing with the prosecution that defence should not access exculpatory material[294] and in the Kenyan cases, we saw the OTP asking the accused to provide the OTP with the incriminating evidence necessary to convict them.[295] We do not see victims being involved with procedural issues in the UK criminal law setting for example and although they appear as prosecution witnesses, their statements are treated with the same level of scrutiny as those of any other witnesses and victims would not have any influence on evidence disclosures to the defence.[296]

The proof of guilt, when it comes to the ICC, needs to fulfil the standard of 'beyond reasonable doubt'[297] to refute the presumption of innocence. This means that the OTP must convince the Court of the guilt of the accused based on such standard. However, I argue that the participation of victims at all stages of the trial means that it is the OTP plus the victim's lawyers who are proving the case. It is a major concern though that this 'gold' standard is only applicable at the trial phase and that there are several standards of proof depending on the phase of the proceedings. For instance, for the OTP to start an investigation, the Rome Statute requires under Article 15 (3) that the Prosecutor concludes there is a 'reasonable basis to proceed.' Contrary to the UN *ad hoc* tribunals, the decision of the OTP is subject to judicial scrutiny, as he or she must seek the authorisation of the Pre-trial Chamber in order to proceed with the investigation which is supposed to ensure oversight.[298] Following their conclusions, one can with confidence say that in the *Kenyatta*, *Gbagbo* and *Bemba* cases, the Pre-trial Chamber failed in this duty but also failed in fulfilling its obligations under Article 58 where it should have been satisfied that there are reasonable grounds to believe that crimes under the court's jurisdiction have been committed.[299] The chamber needs to be satisfied that "there are reasonable grounds to believe that the person committed the crime alleged."[300] The difficulty in these two provisions is that there is no need to be convinced beyond reasonable doubt, but a new evidential threshold of 'reasonable grounds to believe'. One could see therefore how the involvement of the victims' lawyers at this point tilts the balance to favour the OTP for the reasons I explored earlier in relation to the *Lubanga* case for example.

In the same three cases we see the Pre-trial Chamber not adhering to Article 61 (7) which requires the chamber to consider whether evidential thresholds for each crime charged are met. This is the basis for the chamber to confirm or decline the charges against the suspect, a moment in which the standard of substantial grounds to believe prevails. This can be described as a turning point from the pre-trial to trial stage which aims at avoiding trials based on unfounded charges.[301] These different standards of proof mean in my view that because the thresholds are lower in the initial stages, victim participation may strengthen an otherwise weak case on the OTP's side. The ICC becomes unique in any criminal law system in that the presumption of innocence is measured with different scales at each stage and only applies beyond reasonable doubt at the trial stage despite several pre-trial opportunities to do so, although the pre-trial hearing in the *Lubanga*[302] case suggested that pre-trial stages are for the benefit of the accused, which in my view is an oxymoron as no defendant volunteers for any trial as a 'test' of hitherto unknown benefits for their human rights.

Victim participation also affects the application of the burden of proof as established under Article 66 (2) which places the burden on the prosecutor to prove the defendant guilty.[303] As already argued above, the victim having access to evidential material at the earliest stages has the capacity to enhance the OTP's case as it enables them to provide their own additional evidence. There are safeguards under the right not to be compelled to incriminate oneself, or to confess guilt under Article 55[304] and under 'no case to answer'[305] as recently exemplified by the Gbagbo judgement of acquittal because the prosecutor had not met the burden of proof in relation to the charge sheet.[306]

The third aspect of complying with the rule of law which I argue the OTP failed to comply with in the Kenyan cases is the conduct of officials. Whether the reported ill-conduct by the prosecutor during the *Kenyatta* cases constituted an interference with the accused's right to a fair trial should, for example, be the subject of future research.[307] I say future research because the OTP indicated in 2017 that it would investigate those allegations against the then prosecutor, Moreno Ocampo, but there has been no update on them since.[308] However, I posit that, if proven, the allegations against the former prosecutor would fall within the conduct of officials which affects fair hearings because in relation to the ICC, 'conduct of officials' embraces judges, the OTP and the Registry.[309] Therefore, members of the Court "must under all circumstances refrain from utterances which would presume the guilt of the suspect."[310] The conduct of officials shall comply with presumed innocence until this is refuted by a judgement of guilt beyond reasonable doubt. The allegations against the former prosecutor are serious because they contradict the Statute's requirements that the prosecutor is of

> …high moral character and neither the Prosecutor nor a Deputy Prosecutor shall engage in any activity which is likely to interfere with his

> or her prosecutorial functions or to affect confidence in his or her independence. They shall not engage in any other occupation of a professional nature.[311]

The allegation also raises concerns of criminal acts because the reports state that

> a Court press officer received secret payments from a New York banker to 'push' a certain case at the Office of the Prosecutor, and another ICC official shared with third parties information obtained from a Libyan prosecutor as part of that country's cooperation with the ICC.[312]

To conclude this discussion on victims, the final criticism I would pose is that the selected victims may not actually represent the real people who suffered atrocities because these crimes involved mass victimisation.[313] The fact that crimes brought to the ICC are events involving mass victimisation implies that, most often, victims do not know whether or not the suspect indeed committed the crimes. This occurs because victims were probably victimised by someone other than the individuals who are brought to trial, as they are mainly heads of criminal organisations, leaders of terrorist groups or heads of states – people who allegedly gave the orders, not those who executed the acts. This translates to the awkward position that the 'victim' presented by the ICC may often not be 'the' victim and it is the case that the accused elite is not the actual perpetrator. Therefore the intended pain transference or 'closure' for the victim, if that was the intention, remains just an illusion.

L'addition S'il Vous Plait? Plea Bargains at the ICC

While discussing court architecture in Chapter 4, I argued that clothing the ICC building in a corporate facade signals the prominence of the dirty liaison between law and commerce with connotations of colonialism and slavery. I also warned that this heralds commercial practices at the core of ICL, exemplified by the plea bargains already prominent in local common law CJS. In this section, I explore *The Prosecutor v. Ahmad Al Faqi Al Mahdi*[314] (hereafter *Mahdi*) where I argue that the ICC reproduces western criminal justice systems which are well documented, as seen elsewhere in this book, as disproportionately affecting the black accused. I refer in particular to plea bargains, which the Rome Statute calls plea agreements in Article 65(5).

In *Mahdi*, it appears that the judges were cognisant of the history of such bargains and the precedent they were reproducing by accepting Mr Mahdi's admission of guilt because they made the effort to explain the history of how this discredited mechanism entered the Rome Statute and how the compromise was made between civil and common law jurisdictions where such plea bargains are common.[315] The judges however did not persuade the prosecution against encouraging Mr Mahdi to admit guilt early on and to cooperate with the prosecution which then influenced his lenient sentencing.[316] The current plea-bargaining regime in the international arena can be traced to the ICTY,[317] although in its early days, the ICTY and its president Antonio Cassese were against the practice because he was of the view that the ICTY was not a local court but one that is charged with the duty of trying the accused persons of the most serious of all crimes, including genocide, torture, murder, sexual assault, wanton destruction, persecution and other inhumane acts and that no one should be immune from prosecution for such.[318] It appears Cassese's views were not formed out of conviction because he rapidly changed them in the course of the tribunal as the caseloads became unmanageable.[319] The ICTY subsequently changed course and in the *Todorovic* case, the prosecutors entered into a plea bargain where the accused faced reduced sentencing for his cooperation.[320] This acceptance of plea bargain led to changes in the ICTY's rules and eventually the ICTY attached Rule 62(vi) to its procedures governing plea bargaining.[321]

Plea bargains became the order of the day at the ICTY after *Todorovic* because before entering their pleas, most of the accused bargained with the prosecutors and by 2009 some 20 defendants had entered a plea bargain of guilty before the ICTY.[322] We see this practice of plea bargaining starting at the ICTY and subsequently being copied by the ICTR which, although initially reluctant to have plea bargains, changed its rules to include Rule 62(B) which governed plea bargaining.[323] This was seen in the *Prosecutor v Ruggiu* case where the trial asserted that guilty pleas would be met with sentencing discounts: "[I]t is good policy in criminal matters that some form of consideration be shown towards those who have confessed their guilt, in order to encourage other suspects and perpetrators of crimes to come forward."[324]

Plea bargaining is therefore not unique to *Mahdi* but raises significant concerns in my view in relation to their place in criminal justice systems in relation to the black accused and especially in the decolonising context. Considering that I argue the ICC is predominantly trying black accused, it is important that I address why *Mahdi* sets a typically colonial precedent. The main benefit the judges saw in Mahdi 'confessing' is that his early guilty plea saved the court's resources and therefore it is appropriate to address this point and other arguments against plea bargains at the beginning. What I have discovered is that plea bargaining as a research area is far broader than I can cover in this one section and therefore I will give a brief overview for context only.

Considering the arguments we explored regarding victim participation, the ICC's rhetoric on impunity seems hollow when one considers plea bargains. And so, the reduction of victims' 'power' is my main argument against plea bargains. This seems to be what Cassese had in mind – although he rapidly changed his view – and also Michael Scharf who argued that ICL by its very nature prohibits plea bargains as the "crimes within these international tribunals' jurisdiction are too reprehensible to be bargained over."[325]

In addition, plea bargaining is open to criticism for two other broad weaknesses. First, it is viewed as detrimental to justice because plea bargains sometimes involve the prosecution dropping part of the charges in return for a guilty plea and therefore, the accused are not tried in relation to all of the allegations made against them.[326] This is related to the criticism that because of the nature of plea bargains some accounts of events will be omitted from future historical records if a full trial is not held.[327] This means future memorising of events will be incomplete, although in my view it is debatable whether the evidence provided in trials is a correct narrative of the event(s).[328]

Second, and this is particular to the ICC, plea bargaining is seen to affect credibility.[329] This is more of a public relations problem in my view as we have already seen in the Kenyan cases that justice was denied not by plea bargains but by the prosecutor's ineptitude, compounded by the determination of the elites involved that the cases should collapse.[330] A more potent critique applies when plea bargains are seen in the context of complementarity. In its simplest form, complementarity translates into the idea that the ICC does not have jurisdiction in situations unless the unwillingness or inability of national authorities is proven.[331] According to Rauxloh therefore, if plea bargains become prevalent, the ICC is failing to discharge the duty it owes to victims, having claimed that it alone could bring these individuals to trial.[332]

However, some scholars see benefits in plea bargains. One of the main benefits claimed is that plea bargaining at international tribunals serves victims' interests. Schneider for example sees plea bargaining as important because it promotes victims' recovery from atrocities, at times committed by their own governments.[333] Others say that the perpetrators' acknowledgement of atrocities allows reconciliation.[334] Another perceived benefit is that these bargains spare the witnesses' logistical difficulties in travelling to foreign lands, which may put them and their families at risk and, crucially, it helps to avoid the trauma of testifying.[335] This argument, as we see in my discussions on victim participation as well as those in the chapter on architecture goes to the core of the colonial nature of ICL. It is the very nature of the far away foreign courts that is problematic and costly with no local connection to the locations where atrocities are said to have happened. Hence, the suggestion that plea bargains are in the victim's interests seems far-fetched, if not misleading.

Another group of scholars sees the cost/financial benefits of plea bargains. Kovarovic for example argues that plea bargaining at international tribunals has varied benefits, the main one being cutting costs in terms of both money and time.[336] In addition, Scharf indicates that trials at the ICTY and the ICTR generally took over one full year to complete, and cost upwards of $50 million.[337] This estimate does not include the time spent gathering evidence and preparing for trial, nor does it include the time spent on sentencing appeals.[338] In comparison, the ICC's budget in 2010 was approximately $137,327,000 with the majority of this money earmarked for trial-related costs.[339] Thus, trial-related costs in 2010 consumed roughly 95% of the ICC's yearly budget. That same year, however, the ICC presided over just three active trials: those of Thomas Lubanga Dyilo, Germain Katanga and Mathieu Ngudjolo appearing in a joint trial, and Jean-Pierre Bemba Gombo and two of these trials had extended beyond one full year. Those who see plea bargaining as positive therefore see it as a way in which the ICC could use other alternatives to trial, including Alternative Dispute Resolution (ADR),[340] instead of trials that would otherwise become incredibly lengthy and costly. This cost analysis goes to the core of my argument in this book, that the African is just a unit of trade-off. It is relevant to my slavery analogy that the international community is able to calculate how much money is saved by not charging an alleged perpetrator; this, in my view, is the same as allocating a monetary price to the life lost through the perpetrator's alleged actions. This also relates to the argument I made earlier on instrumentalisation, which means that from the grassroots there is a cost analysis/business model developing around the African body which the ecosystem is able to keep tab(s) on throughout this macabre supply chain. The question of the ICC's legitimacy considering plea bargains is a potential area of future research. One could ask the question of whether, since the victim is active in the whole of a case's lifecycle(s) at the ICC, would it not be much more convenient for the victim to approach the perpetrator for payments/compensation directly and cut out the middleman (the ICC)? This way they can save themselves time and get a bargain? I picture victim-chasing legal firms in the future advertising in Eastern Congo. The ICC, possibilities are endless!

Others like Rauxloh would like to see some savings through these bargains so that the industrial complex can be expanded and the lawyer fraternity can get a bigger share of the cake. Those savings could be used to extend the ICC to reach more situations and instigate new investigations and trials. The surplus finances should be utilised for investigations and lawyers' fees. Analogous to charity/green washing,[341] this ICL industrial complex needs to be seen to be doing some good and therefore Rauxloh says that some of the savings can be used to fund reparations to victims.[342] I see risks in the thinking expounded by these scholars, including Rauxhol, who seem to advocate a legal industrial complex that sets resources budgets designed to perpetuate a cycle of atrocities and tribunals. Rauxhol, I argue, supports the ICC in its reproduction of local criminal law jurisdictions' plea bargaining that disproportionately affects black accused. These plea bargains see private individuals being encouraged by the courts to operate independently of the constitutional principles applied in the courtroom and apply the market principles of bargaining e.g., how much is manslaughter worth?[343] This capitalisation of the law targets black accused, leading to over representation of the black accused in prisons and the black body becoming a significant consumer of 'law products' including privatised bails and prison facilities in a 'soft' reproduction of slavery practices.[344]

To conclude this section, I broadly agree with Cassese's earlier view, that there should be crimes beyond plea bargains especially if they had already met the legal thresholds set for example on Genocide, but t I see plea bargains as a form of an acknowledgement by the ICC that these trials were show trials whose functionality ended with the inception of trials at the ICC. The real reasons for these trials are not therefore the search for justice but the perpetuation of iconographies upon which power relations amongst the elites are based and the confirmation of racial hierarchies as described variously in the previous chapters. In line with the idea of *tribunalisation* I explored in Chapter 2, these plea bargains suggest the ongoing commercialisation of ICL and the horrific thought that the ICC at least contemplates the possibility of 'pricing' or allocating financial, time, resources value to 'genocide' for example. This becomes a more daunting prospect because it creates the possibility of the ICC 'pricing' African bodies in practices reminiscent of slavery where once again the African body is a unit of bargain, paraded in an auction far away from home.

Cultural Destruction

Apart from plea bargains, *Mahdi*[345] gave the ICC its opportunity to test Article 8 of the Rome Statute on cultural destruction which was not new in ICL but reflected the already existing international law on destruction of cultural property during war. For clarity it is important that I detail the relevant Article 8 provisions here; Article 8(2)(a)(iv) prohibits extensive destruction and appropriation of property not justified by military necessity and carried out unlawfully and wantonly.[346] Article 8(2)(b)(ii) prohibits intentionally directing attacks against civilian objects. Article 8(2)(b)(ix) prohibits intentionally directing attacks against buildings dedicated to religion, education, art, science or charitable purposes, historic monuments, hospitals, and places where the sick and wounded are collected. Article 8(2)(b)(xiii) prohibits destroying or seizing the enemy's property, unless such destruction or seizure be imperatively demanded by the necessities of war, and pillaging a town or place, even when taken by assault is prohibited by Article 8(2)(b)(xvi). Article 8(2)(e) details other violations related to the laws and customs applicable in armed conflicts not of an international character.[347]

Mr Mahdi was found guilty of intentionally directing attacks against religious and historic buildings in Timbuktu, Mali, in June and July 2012 and sentenced to nine years' imprisonment as well as a Reparations Order of 2.7 million euros.[348] The reparations order also became a first in relation to cultural destruction at the ICC and is particularly poignant in relation to post-colonial discourse as discussed later in this section. In my view however, the importance of the *Mahdi* case in relation to the ICC is that it brought good news after the fiasco of the Kenyan cases, although other scholars argue that *Mahdi* was successful mostly because he confessed and also due to the fact that most of the evidence was captured on video and readily available in public.[349] There are also those like William Schabas who suggest that the conviction was not legally sound because Mahdi's actions did not meet the threshold of an 'attack' as detailed in Article 8 of the Rome Statute.[350] Schabas, I would argue is being pedantic in his argument as he is, like the court itself, playing a game of semantics. The real issue with Mahdi is not whether or not he attacked the cultural sites: the issue is why he was not tried for civilian deaths and why he was not tried in Mali. Schabas's argument on interpretation does not aid a post-colonial discourse and could be interpreted as supporting the strictness of 'rule of law' interpretations that discriminate against black men as detailed elsewhere in this book. Schabas however does argue that in cases of ambiguity, the definition (of 'attack' in this case) shall be interpreted in favour of the person being investigated, prosecuted, or convicted according to Article 22(2) of the Rome Statute.[351] The ICC, he argues, differs from other international tribunals in that it is prescriptive in terms of interpretation of the Statute and does not allow for liberal and teleological approaches to judicial interpretation.[352]

However, as with all other cases emanating from Africa at the ICC, the real significance of *Mahdi* lies in the extension, through judicial interpretation, of what is not acceptable during combat. The protection of cultural property becomes henceforth central to the laws of war. It is therefore important to discuss the history of law on cultural destruction here in order to understand *Mahdi* in the context of this chronology because the ICC is not a pioneer in this field: this way of looking at war started during the Renaissance period[353] leading to the initial multilateral prohibition of cultural property destruction in the late-nineteenth century.[354] Finally, buildings dedicated to religion, art, science, or charitable purposes and "historic monuments" were protected by what is the predecessor to Article 8, the Hague Convention on the Laws and Customs of Wars on Land of 1907.[355]

Endeavours to prosecute the perpetrators of cultural destruction after World War I failed and showed that states were ignoring the laws put in place in 1907.[356] However, the post-World War II trials at Nuremberg set out to correct these mistakes and Article 6(b) of the Nuremberg Charter allowed for the prosecution of those who engaged in "plunder of public or private property, wanton destruction of cities, towns or villages, or devastation not justified by military necessity."[357] This Charter and the Nuremberg trials are seen as pioneers of the concrete enforcement of cultural destruction laws.[358] It is however important for our post-colonial discourse to note that that while some Nazis were prosecuted for these crimes, the allies were not held accountable for wanton destruction of cities, including the firebombing of Dresden where over 1,300 heavy bombers from the RAF and the USAAF dropped nearly 4,000 tonnes of explosives on Dresden's civilian centre in just over two days in February 1945.[359]

After the Nuremberg trials, the 1954 Hague Convention followed, putting the protection of cultural sites at the centre of laws regulating conflicts, with Article 28 of the Convention providing that signatories to this convention should make local laws to prosecute cultural destruction.[360] It is important therefore for our discourse on the ICC to note that, already, this convention allowed 'universal' application and did not require a 'specialised' court. Although the 1954 Convention indicated that individuals could be held accountable,[361] it did not as far as prescribing specific offences emanating from its provisions[362] and member states had discretion on implementation.[363]

Protection of cultural property was again emphasised after the Geneva Convention by the 1977 Additional Protocols to the same conventions.[364] It was not however until the *Jokic* Case that these protocols were applied and emphasised when the ICTY Trial Chamber said that they prohibited "any acts of hostility directed against the historic monuments, works of art or places of worship which constitute the cultural or spiritual heritage of peoples."[365] Thc ICTY Tribunal also adopted the International Committee of the Red Cross (ICRC) commentary to Protocol I, which afforded cultural sites additional protection over and above the protection offered to civilian sites.[366]

Until the *Jokic* casc, and dcspite the protections already provided in the 1954 Convention and the 1977 Protocols, cultural destruction continues to date even after the *Mahdi* decision. Which is probably proof of my point that the law is in most cases not 'the' most appropriate solution for social order breakdown and more holistic solutions are needed to address sources of conflicts. As long as there is war, destruction of cultural items will occur but the Gulf War I in 1991 showed that it is possible to attempt at least to 'buffer' cultural sites because in that war, the aggressors, the United States, created 'no fire' zones in a rather unsuccessful attempt to avoid the destruction of cultural property: this had the consequence of allowing looters to act unhindered.[367] It is therefore safe to say that Article 8 of the Rome Statute and the subsequent *Mahdi* case followed already established law and therefore there was no novelty in the case as regards setting any international precedents. This is because of the chronology I have detailed above and also, in particular, because Article 3(d) of the Statute establishing the ICTY dealt specifically with the same crimes already prohibited by Article 8.[368]

Apart from Article 8 and the *Mahdi* case being replications, the 1954 Convention had already been implemented and shown to work in local jurisdictions post-conflict. For example, in prosecuting crimes committed by the Khmer Rouge regime, Article 7 of the Cambodian Law establishing the Extraordinary Chambers allowed the prosecution of cultural destruction pursuant to the 1954 Convention.[369] However, it is notable that, until *Mahdi*, cultural destruction in African wars had not been treated with the seriousness it deserves, as exemplified by the differences in Article 3(d) of the ICTY and Article 3 of the Statute establishing the Rwandan Tribunal which only mentions plunder but does not specifically list cultural, religious and other sites, as does the ICTY provision.[370] The statute establishing the Special Court for Sierra Leone is observed to have the same weakness.[371] The idea that African culture is worthless and cannot be universal, or that there is no culture to protect is, I think, what lies behind such disparities between the protection of sites by the ICTY and in Cambodia on the one hand and in the Rwanda and Sierra Leone Statutes on the other.[372] This lack of 'universal' status means that no UNESCO register existed in Rwanda, Sierra Leone, or Congo to ensure that, as happened in former Yugoslavia, evidence was readily available of the items destroyed, such as the Old Town of Dubrovnik where many buildings had been marked as protected buildings.[373]

The existence of a cultural items register/list in Dubrovnik therefore allowed the easy identification of particular sites as well as of the specific military commanders who ordered the bombings, because it was evidentially possible to locate which commander was responsible for that specific region near the sites.[374] This was similarly possible in the Cambodian situation because specific systematic attacks against places of worship including Buddhist pagodas, mosques of the Cham people, and churches could be identified.[375] In a theme I will revisit later, in Cambodia, we see the identification of 'non-tangible' cultural items in need of protection because it was noted that the Khmer Rouge targeted minorities, intellectuals, Buddhist monks and art performers.[376] Therefore, even in punishing cultural destruction, we see the colonial thinking in treating UNESCO registered sites more favourably as compared to undocumented sites. Although this could be interpreted as due to UNESCO protection providing a ready evidential base, that protection is limited in scope and leads to ICL treating some cultural sites as more 'universal' than others because, for example, the cultural atrocities committed in Rwanda had less international importance.[377] As I discuss in Chapter 6, this materialistic Eurocentric understanding/view of the universe leads to identification of cultural sites as only physical/material sites as opposed to 'spiritual' culture like the human to human traditions and folklore which were for example destroyed in the Rwanda genocide. The same may be said, as I have detailed above, of Cambodia, where a near erasure of traditional Cambodian performing arts – a unique, intangible, cultural heritage – was almost accomplished by the Khmer Rouge following the killings of Buddhist monks as well as around 90% of oral performers in the course of the Cambodian genocide.[378]

In the previous sections, I discussed how the ICC furiously presents its rulings as ground-breaking in a desperate attempt to detach itself from the already exposed coloniality of ICL. We see the same trend in the *Mahdi* Judgement, where the judges take great pains to show how their decision should be distinguished from others in the past.[379] They display an exemplary use of semantics to explain why their decision should be distinguished from earlier decisions by the ICC itself and the ICTY. For example they said that *The Prosecutor v. Bosco Ntaganda*,[380] or *The Prosecutor v. Germain Katanga and Mathieu Ngudjolo Chui*[381] related only to attacks against persons and not attacks against 'cultural objects.' They also went to great lengths to distinguish Article 8(2)(e)(iv) of the Rome Statute from the jurisprudence of the ICTY because they argued that, in contrast, the ICTY statute was different because its applicable law does not govern 'attacks' against cultural objects but rather punishes their 'destruction or wilful damage.'[382] By doing so the ICC was ensuring that *Mahdi* is seen in a different light to ICTY's decision in *the Prosecutor v. Pavle Strugar,*[383] which had already indicated that damage or destruction of the cultural property was a war crime. Through these legalistic gymnastics, the judges achieved the precedent setting status they sought for *Mahdi,* but unfortunately, they did so by fragmenting and confusing already existing good law on cultural destruction. I argue that addressing fragmentation is crucial in the post-colonial discourse because in the same decision, they separated attacks on the person from attacks on culture, which is highly problematic from a southern perspective because most southern epistemologies do not separate the individual from their culture – the culture is in the human as can be seen in the killing of monks and cultural performers in Cambodia discussed above.[384] I will discuss this notion of all-encompassing culture in Chapter 6 where I outline southern norms, including *Ubuntu* and *Buenvivir* amongst others, as my proposed alternatives to the Eurocentric hegemony at the ICC.

The court's failure to coherently explain why *Mahdi* was precedent-setting leads me to posit that the court is aware that it is reproducing already existing laws and is continuously engaged in frantic efforts to cement its relevance, especially following the collapse of high-profile cases and emerging post-colonial criticisms. The theme of the perpetually emerging/ground-breaking law has also been noted by other scholars, including Koskenniemi who argues that the ICC hopes to avoid a critique that it is imperialist through these regular non-concrete promises of an ever receding futuristic utopia that 'disappears as it is approached.'[385] I should add therefore that law in Koskenniemi's analogy becomes the 'opium of the masses' to which the global south is addicted with no hope of recovery. My addiction analogy is probably a more suitable one because the ICC avoids scrutiny as a cultural producer through this presentation of an idealistic inevitability, constant 'newness' and the supposed critical nature of the law it propagates. I argue that condemning the impunity of a largely African political class is an aggressively political stance, but through the promises of newness and adopting a cosmopolitan discourse, the ICC perpetuates the fallacy that it is non- political. Because there cannot be a criminal without a victim, no space is allowed for interrogation of the process of constructing these two binary subjects in the presentation of ICL as constantly emerging and evolving. This process of constructing victim versus criminal by cosmopolitan society erodes/replaces African states' sovereignty.[386]

In a post-colonial discourse however, the *Mahdi* decision, although seemingly trend-setting, is of little significance in relation to colonial cultural destruction and in association with international law. The more important decisions are cases in local jurisdictions seeking the return of rooted cultural artefacts, such as the *Italian Nostra* case.[387] In that case *Tribunale Amministrativo Regionale* (the Regional Administrative Tribunal TAR) upheld a government decree to return the 'Venus of Cyrene' to Libya. This decision is important in that it predates the *Mahdi* case and, importantly, held that Italy was obliged to return the Venus because, amongst other reasons, an obligation to do so was derived from the customary rule that required restitution of the cultural heritage of occupied states.[388]

The Italian tribunal helpfully traced such an obligation back to the peace treaties concluded after the end of the First World War, and before that to the Regulations annexed to the Hague Conventions of 1899 and 1907,[389] and later to the Hague Convention of 1954[390] and to the Vienna Convention of 1983.[391] Significantly, the TAR held that such an obligation was already contained in Article 10 of the Italian Constitution which automatically incorporated customary international law into the Italian legal system, thereby giving these customary laws a constitutional status that means they prevail over other conflicting domestic laws.[392] It is notable that none of the judges in the *Mahdi* case mentioned the TAR decision because that decision implies that local jurisdictions are more than capable of applying already existing international law enforcing accountability for cultural destruction happening outside their jurisdictions. The TAR decision is also important because it helps to trace looted objects and offers the hope of returning them to their homes. More importantly, it may reduce the trading in looted objects.[393] In a post-colonial context, *Mahdi* complements the TAR decision as far as payment of reparations is concerned because Mr Mahdi was ordered to pay reparations to the Timbuktu community.[394] It is however notable that major museums, including the British Museum, continue to hold looted cultural items and refuse to return them to their rightful owners.[395]

There are however authors who argue that pursuing cultural destruction though ICL means losing focus about what it is critical to pursue.[396] A critique that I find persuasive comes from Lostal, who argues that the ICC's emphasis on cultural destruction in the *Mahdi* case took precedence over the protection of populations as crimes against populations occurred at the same time, including murder, rape, and the torture of civilians.[397] However, I diverge from Lostal's critique of attaching significance to 'intangible' heritage as she argues that the ICC uses an anthropological approach to international law in that the Trial Chamber put undue emphasis on the "symbolic and emotional value for the inhabitants of Timbuktu in assessing the gravity of the crime committed and that, given its world heritage listing, the attack also affected people throughout Mali and the international community."[398] Lostal should be forgiven for her Eurocentric position as she wrongly views culture as largely materialistic. She therefore wrongly argues that concentrating on this aspect of culture, as was the case in *Mahdi*, is not productive in the sense that it is a historically inaccurate way of looking at culture and may hinder the protection of 'tangible' cultural heritage in the future.[399] The only other argument I find persuasive is that Lostal argues that focusing on the local importance of these cultural sites as meeting the threshold of international crimes may have the unwanted effect of not actually protecting those sites. For example, Lostal questions whether it would constitute a war crime if local populations held a plebiscite that allowed the destruction of historical statues or places of worship? In a similar argument, would it be a defence of such crimes if there was a proof that local populations had no attachment to the cultural sites in question?[400]

In conclusion, we see the ICC in *Mahdi* using a situation of war in an African country to test the Rome Statute on its people without protecting those people. In this sense the ICC takes a predictable pedagogic and colonial stance of 'protecting' the African, including his/her culture but misses the point of protecting the Timbuktu populations from the still on-going conflict. In a wider 'ending impunity' drive, the ICC conveniently ignores similar atrocities in Syria and Libya occurring at the same time. This selectivity means that the 'justice' that the ICC practices is at best selective and at worst arbitrary. *Mahdi* shows the ICC's on-going impetus to aggressively ensure that its continuation is guaranteed: if it fails to convict other high profile accused, it will always have *Mahdi* to point to as a success, thereby extending its widely challenged legitimacy in global governance.

Conclusions

In this chapter we see that, so far, most cases at the ICC are from Africa, which means that both the victims and the accused have been African and mostly black Africans. Here we see the reproduction of colonial and racist undertones in the demarcation of Africa as the place where victims and perpetrators of international crimes are found, as discussed by Marti Koskenniemi and other authors. In *Bemba* we see this demarcation of civilisation/barbarism in war rape prosecution and the uncomfortable links it has with previous war rape trials after World War II where the racial biases were exposed. We also see the perpetuation of the victim without agency and the infantilisation of local initiatives for finding solutions that fit their local circumstances, which is tied in with the NGO ICL/IEL industrial complex that binds these 'sites' in a perpetual need for international interventionist agencies like the ICC.

In *Mahdi*, I explored the testing of Article 8 on cultural destruction and found not only testing but also the reproduction of old laws. In relation to post-colonial significance, I argue that *Mahdi* fades when compared to local decisions on the return of looted cultural items, such as the Italian *Nostra* case where the court ordered the return of the 'Venus of Cyrene' to Libya. *Mahdi* however brought up important issues for discourse including reparations and plea bargains. Plea bargains are seen in this chapter as detrimental to the black accused as they have extensively been used, for example in the

USA, to commercialise law in a soft reproduction of slavery. I also critique plea bargains for not affording the victim an opportunity to be heard and because they may herald the age of pricing 'genocides' or the black body in a return of slavery practices.

Mutatis Mutandis, as it was in the slavery days, the product for this neo-liberal industry is the African body. This is because the African victim is core to the ICC's very existence. The victim being central to criminal proceedings at the ICC overturns the orthodox understanding of criminal law proceedings where the prosecution provides evidence and the defendant counters the evidence. In the ICC context, I argue that the balance is tilted to the prosecution's advantage as the victim is involved in the collecting of evidence, in distilling the evidence, and in trial procedures which tilts the balance against the defence and has an impact on fair hearing. Victim participation faces the added problems of whether a victim is ever without fault and also of the ICC's replication of a colonial view of the African victim with no agency of their own, which cements the colonial saviour-victim dichotomy. The perpetuation of the African woman as a victim is exposed here as a scheme to deny our sisters their rightful iconic place in liberation history but also acts to fragment their necessary solidarity with their brothers. The ICC's concentration on one individual, usually the leadership, leads to the situation where at the end, the victim does not receive justice as the actual perpetrators of violence are still free. What however confirms Africa as 'the site' is that the precedent being set by the ICC using African situations is not being replicated elsewhere, including in places where atrocities are commonly reported to occur, for example in Palestinian territories or in Myanmar. This replication feeds not just lawyers' love of the law but also the perpetuation of a white saviour industry with the African as its currency.

Notes

1 Ingrid Mwangi, Static Drift (2001). This is a two part piece consisting of the Africa map used here, contrasted with a map of Germany etched on the artist's body with the words; Burn out Country. More on the artists work at https://mwangihutter.art.
2 Binyavanga Wainaina, 'How to Write About Africa' (2005) *Granta* 92–95.
3 Preston King, *Thinking Past a Problem: Essays on the History of Ideas* (Routledge 2013) 84.
4 Emily Haslam, *The Slave Trade, Abolition, and the Long History of International Criminal Law: The Recaptive and the Victim* (Routledge 2019).
5 Emily Haslam, 'International Criminal Law and Legal Memories of Abolition: Intervention, Mixed Commission Courts and Emancipation' (2016) 18 *Journal of the History of International Law* 420.
6 I use this word to include wider negative stereotypes about Africa and include the emotional detachment shown by many westerners when discussing issues concerning Africa.
7 Emily Haslam (note 4).

8 *Judgment on the appeal of Mr Jean-Pierre Bemba Gombo against Trial Chamber III's "Judgment pursuant to Article 74 of the Statute" ICC-01/05-01/08-3636-Red. 08 June 2018 | Appeals Chamber | Decision.*
9 *The Prosecutor v. Ahmad Al Faqi Al Mahdi ICC-01/12-01/15.*
10 John Le Carré, *The Constant Gardener: A Novel* (Scribner 2004); see also Helen Tilley, *Africa as a Living Laboratory: Empire, Development, and the Problem of Scientific Knowledge, 1870–1950* (University of Chicago Press 2011).
11 *Rabi Abdullahi v Pfizer, Inc. United States Court of Appeals for the Second Circuit Docket Nos: 05-4863-cv (L), 05-6768-cv (CON).*
12 The initial case at the Southern District court of New York had found that Nigerian courts are an adequate alternative for the dispute. *Abdullahi v. Pfizer, Inc, 2002 U.S. Dist. LEXIS 17436 at *1 (S.D.N.Y. September 17, 2002) (Abdullahi I).* Claimants appealed to the United States Appeals Court for the second Circuit which sent the case for consideration to the District Court; *Abdullahi v. Pfizer, Inc., 77 Fed. Appx. 48, 2003 U.S. App. LEXIS 20704 (2d Cir. N.Y., October 8, 2003) (Abdullahi II).* The District Court again found that Nigeria provided an adequate alternative forum. *Abdullahi v. Pfizer, Inc., 2005 U.S. Dist. LEXIS 16126 (S.D.N.Y., August 9, 2005) (Abdullahi III).* Another claimant brought a claim before a Connecticut District Judge with the same outcomes as the Abdullahi cases – *Ajudu Ismaila Adamu v. Pfizer, Inc., 399 F. Supp. 2d 495, 503 (N.Y.S.D. 2005).*
13 One of the oldest federal laws in the USA, the Alien Tort Statute (codified in 1948 as 28 U.S.C. § 1350 gives federal courts jurisdiction over lawsuits filed by foreign nationals for torts committed in violation of international law. See more generally, *Curtis A Bradley, International Law in the U.S. Legal System* (2nd Ed. Oxford University Press 2015).
14 Harriet A. Washington, 'Why Africa Fears Western Medicine' *The New York Times*, 31 July 2007.
15 *The Bodo Community and Others v The Shell Petroleum Development Company of Nigeria Ltd [2014] EWHC 1973.*
16 Ibid.
17 For this discussion see Elena Merino Blanco and Ben Pontin, 'Litigating Extraterritorial Nuisances under English Common Law and UK Statute' (2017) 6 (2) *Transnational Environmental Law* 285–308.
18 *Lubbe v Cape Pl [2000] UKHL 41.*
19 *Owusu v Jackson (Case C-281/02) [2005] QB 80.*
20 *Global Multimedia International Ltd v Ara Media Services [2006] EWHC 3612.*
21 *Attorney General of Zambia v Meer Care & Desai (A Firm) [2006] 1 CLC 436.*
22 *UBS AG v HSH Nordbank [2009] 2 Lloyds Rep 272.*
23 *A v A (Children: Habitual Residence) [2014] AC 1.*
24 Gabrielle Lynch, *Performances of Justice: The Politics of Truth, Justice and Reconciliation in Kenya* (Cambridge University Press 2018) 58.
25 Naomi Klein, *The Shock Doctrine: The Rise of Disaster Capitalism* (Allen Lane 2007).
26 Ibid.
27 Ibid.
28 Ibid.
29 Elizabeth Alexander, *The Venus Hottentot* (University Press of Virginia 1990) 3–6.
30 Rome Statute of the International Criminal Court (last amended 2010) 17 July 1998.
31 Ibid.

32 *Bemba, ICC, ICC-01/05-01/08 424. Decision Pursuant to Article 61(7)(a) and (b) of the Rome Statute, PTCH II, 3. 7. 2009, §438.* Hereinafter referred to as Bemba, Decision Pursuant to Article 61(7)(a) and (b) of the Rome Statute.
33 Ibid., para 202.
34 Ibid., para 206.
35 Ibid., paras 205–206.
36 Ibid., paras 719–720.
37 Ibid., para 727.
38 Ibid., para 728.
39 Ibid., para 730.
40 Ibid., para 733.
41 Ibid., para738.
42 *Bemba, ICC, ICC-01/05-01/08 A, ACH, 8. 7. 2018, § 171. Hereinafter referred to as Bemba Appeals Chamber Judgment.*
43 Ibid.
44 Ibid., para 178.
45 Ibid., para 181.
46 Ibid., para 170.
47 Ibid.
48 Ibid.
49 Ibid., para 184.
50 Ibid., para 187.
51 Ibid., para 180.
52 Ibid., para 191.
53 Ibid., para 192.
54 Ibid., para 171.
55 Yuki Tanaka, *Japan's Comfort Women: Sexual Slavery and Prostitution during World War II and the US Occupation* (Routledge 2002); Shana Swiss and Joan E. Giller, 'Rape as a War Crime: A Medical Perspective' (1993) 270 (5) *Journal of the American Medical Association* 612.
56 Maria B. Olujic, 'Women, Rape, and War: The Continued Trauma of Refugees and Displaced Persons in Croatia' (1995) 13 (1) *Anthropology of East Europe Review* 62–67.
57 Ibid.
58 Ibid.
59 Ibid.
60 Shana Swiss and Joan E. Giller, Rape as a War Crime: A Medical Perspective (1993) 270 (5) *Journal of the American Medical Association* 612.
61 John R. Pritchard Sonia M. Zaide and Donald Cameron Watt, *The Tokyo War Crimes Trial Vol 18* (Garland Pub 1981); see also the shaming of the Japanese establishment and in the international legal systems by various actors in The International Women's Tribunal in Tokyo 2000 in Christine M. Chinkin, 'Women's International Tribunal on Japanese Military Sexual Slavery' (2001) 95 (2) *The American Journal of International Law* 335–341.
62 *Prosecutor v. Delalic and Delic Judgement IT-96-21 Feb16 1998.*
63 Ibid., para 644.
64 Ibid., para 775.
65 *Prosecutor v. Jean*-Paul Akayesu ICTR-96-4 Sep 2nd1998 Judgement para 195.
66 *Prosecutor v. Kunarac, Kovac, and Vukovic IT-96-23 Feb 22 2001 para 437.*
67 Ibid.
68 Geneva Convention relative to the Protection of Civilian Persons in Time of War 12th August 1949 art3 75 U N T S 287.

69 I will not engage with a critique of Article 28. For that see Joshua L. Root, 'Some Other Men's Rea - the Nature of Command Responsibility in the Rome Statute' (2013–2014) 23 *Journal of Transnational Law & Policy* 119.
70 *Prosecutor v. Kordic & Cerkez, Case No. IT-95-14/2-T, Judgment, 447 (Int'l Crim. Trib. for the Former Yugoslavia Feb. 26, 2001); Prosecutor v. Bagilishema, Case No. ICTR 95-1A-A, Judgment (Reasons), 35 (July 3 2002).*
71 See for example, Angelique Chrisafis and Sandra Laville, 'No Charges Sought over Abuse Claims against French Troops in the CAR' *The Guardian*, 5 January 2017.
72 For such an exploration, see Thomas Turner, *The Congo Wars: Conflict, Myth and Reality* (Zed Books 2007).
73 See in general Kamari Maxine Clarke and Sarah-Jane Koulen, 'The Legal Politics of the Article 16 Decision: The International Criminal Court, the UN Security Council and Ontologies of a Contemporary Compromise' (2014) 7 (3) *African Journal of Legal Studies* 297–319; Courtney Hillebrecht and Scott Straus, 'Who Pursues the Perpetrators: State Cooperation with the ICC' (2017) 39 *Human Rights Quarterly* 162.
74 For the political settlements of the time in the DRC see Filip Reyntjens, 'Briefing: Democratic Republic of Congo: Political Transition and Beyond' (2007) 106 (423) *African Affairs* 307–317.
75 *Prosecutor v. Jean-Pierre Bemba Decision Pursuant to Article 61(7)(a) and (b) of the Rome Statute on the Charges of the Prosecutor against Jean-Pierre Bemba Gombo ICC-01/05-01/08-424 (15 June 2009) para 212.*
76 Stephen Brown and Chandra Lekha Sriram, 'The Big Fish Won't Fry Themselves: Criminal Accountability for Post-Election Violence in Kenya' (2012) 111 (443) *African Affairs* 244–260.
77 For a wider exploration of the conflict, see Gerard Prunier, *Africa's World War: Congo, the Rwandan Genocide and the Making of a Continental Catastrophe* (Oxford University Press 2008); Rene Lemarchand, *The Dynamics of Violence in Central Africa* (University of Pennsylvania Press 2009).
78 Ibid.
79 *Judgment on the appeal of Mr Jean-Pierre Bemba Gombo against Trial Chamber III's "Judgment pursuant to Article 74 of the Statute" ICC-01/05-01/08-3636.*
80 Katy Glassborow, 'Locals Want Patasse to Face Justice: But ICC Prosecutors Say They Lack Evidence of His Individual Criminal Responsibility for Crimes' (18 May 2009) Institute for War and Peace Reporting found at http://iwpr.net/report-news/locals-want-patasse-face-justice accessed 12 March 2020.
81 Marianne Meunier, Centrafrique: Le dernier voyage de Patasse (13 April 2011) *Jeune Afrique*. Found at http://centrafrique-presse.over-blog.com/article-lu-pour-vous-dans-j-a-centrafrique-le-dernier-voyage-de-patasse-71632978.html accessed 20/07/20
82 *Prosecutor v. Jean-Pierre Bemba, Decision Pursuant to Article 61(7)(a) and (b) of the Rome Statute on the Charges of the Prosecutor against Jean-Pierre Bemba Gombo, ICC-01/05-01/08-424 (15 June 2009), para 212.*
83 See International Federation for Human Rights (FIDH), *Fin de la transition politique sur fond d'impunité: Quelle réponse apportera la Cour pénale internationale?* (2005); Central African Republic, Annual Human Rights Reports Submitted to Congress by the US Department of State Vol. 28 (2003).
84 Felix Mukwiza Ndahinda, 'The Bemba-Banyamulenge Case before the ICC: From Individual to Collective Criminal Responsibility' (November 2013) 7 (3) *International Journal of Transitional Justice* 476–496.
85 Ibid.

86 Hannah Baumeister, *Sexualised Crimes, Armed Conflict and the Law: The International Criminal Court and the Definitions of Rape and Forced Marriage* (Routledge 2018).
87 Hannah Baumeister, 'Unravelling the Process of Defining War Rape and Forced Marriage in Times of Armed Conflict Under the Statute of the International Criminal Court: Actors and Structures' (ProQuest Dissertations Publishing 2015).
88 Ibid.
89 Felix Mukwiza Ndahinda (note 84).
90 Nicola Henry, *War and Rape: Law, Memory and Justice* (Routledge 2012).
91 Ibid.
92 Caroline Hughes and Vanessa Pupavac, 'Framing Post-Conflict Societies: International Pathologisation of Cambodia and the post-Yugoslav States (2005) 26 (6) *Third World Quarterly* 873–889.
93 Ratna Kapur, 'The Tragedy of Victimization Rhetoric: Resurrecting the "native" Subject in International/post-Colonial Feminist Legal Politics' (2003) 15 *Harvard Human Rights Journal* 11–36.
94 Robert J. Lilly, *Taken by Force: Rape and American GIs in Europe during World War II* (Palgrave Macmillan 2007).
95 Ibid.
96 In relation to England in particular, see Robert J. Lilly and Michael J. Thomson, 'Executing US Soldiers in England, World War II: Command Influence and Sexual Racism' (1997) 37 (2) *The British Journal of Criminology* 262–288.
97 Ibid.
98 See more generally Daniel G Williams, *Black Skin, Blue Books; African Americans and Wales 1845–1945: Writing Wales in English* (University of Wales Press 2012).
99 Robert J. Lilly and Michael J Thomson (note 96).
100 Robert J. Lilly (note 94) 153–183.
101 Ibid.
102 See for example Jack Corbett, Dennis C. Grube Heather Lovell and Rodney Scott, 'Singular Memory or Institutional Memories? Toward a Dynamic Approach' (2018) 31 (3) *Governance* 555–573.
103 Doris Buss, 'Performing Legal Order: Some Feminist Thoughts on International Criminal Law' (2011) 11 *International Criminal Law Review* 409–423.
104 Kimberly Hutchings, 'Cognitive Short Cuts,' in *Rethinking the Man Question: Sex, Gender and Violence* in Jane L. Plupart and Marysia Zalewski (eds), *International Relations* (Zed Books 2008) 33.
105 Ibid.
106 Martti Koskenniemi, *The Gentle Civilizer of Nations: The Rise and Fall of International Law 1870–1960* (Cambridge University Press 2001) 76.
107 Naeem Inayatullah and David Blaney, *International Relations and the Problem of Difference* (Routledge 2004) 51.
108 Ann Sagan, 'African Criminals/African Victims: The Institutionalised Production of Cultural Narratives in International Criminal Law' (August 2010) 39 (1) *Millennium* 8–13.
109 Ibid 9, 20.
110 Ibid.
111 Ibid.
112 Ibid.
113 Ibid.
114 Ibid.
115 Ibid.
116 Ibid.

117 Ibid.
118 Ibid.
119 Naeem Inayatullah and David Blaney, *International Relations, and the Problem of Difference* (Routledge 2004) 88.
120 Ibid.
121 Martti Koskenniemi, *From Apology to Utopia: The Structure of International Legal Argument* (Cambridge University Press 2005) 5.
122 Martti Koskenniemi, 'Legal Cosmopolitanism: Tom Franck's Messianic World' (2003) 35 (2) *New York University Journal of International Law and Politics* 485.
123 Ibid.
124 Ann Sagan, 'African Criminals/African Victims: The Institutionalised Production of Cultural Narratives in International Criminal Law' (2010) 39 (1) *Millennium* 8–9.
125 Ibid.
126 Ibid.
127 Ann Sagan, 'African Criminals/African Victims: The Institutionalised Production of Cultural Narratives in International Criminal Law' (2010) 39 (1) *Millennium* 8–9.
128 Ibid.
129 Ibid.
130 Carla Rose Shapiro, 'Visual Advocates: Depicting Darfur' in Amanda F. Grzyb (ed.), *The World and Darfur: International Response to Crimes against Humanity in Western Sudan* (McGill-Queen's University Press 2009) 223.
131 Tonia St. Germain and Susan Dewey, 'Justice on Whose Terms? A Critique of International Criminal Justice Responses to Conflict-Related Sexual Violence' (March–April 2013) 37 *Women's Studies International Forum* 36–45.
132 Ibid.
133 Ibid., 37.
134 Alan David Freeman, 'Legitimizing Racial Discrimination through Anti-Discrimination Law: A Critical Review of Supreme Court Doctrine' in Kimberlé Crenshaw (ed.), *Critical Race Theory: The Key Writings that Formed the Movement* (The New Press 1996) 29–45.
135 Beth Richie, *Arrested Justice: Black Women, Violence, and America's Prison Nation* (New York University Press 2012).
136 Sonia Lawrence, 'Feminism, Consequences, Accountability: Commentary on the 2004 Betcherman Lecture— Feminism, Law, and Public Policy: Family Feuds and Taxing Times' (2004) 42 (4) *Osgoode Hall Law Journal* 583–601.
137 Michèle Alexandre, 'The New Faces of Feminism: Feminism-in-Action and Organic Feminists in a post-Feminist Era' in Martha Albertson Fineman (ed.), *Transcending the Boundaries of Law: Generations of Feminism and Legal Theory* (Routledge 2010) 97–110.
138 Russell Group, "The Economic Impact of Research Conducted in Russell Group Universities" (2010).
139 Ibid.
140 Ibid.
141 Ibid.
142 Ibid.
143 Ibid., 8.
144 Ibid., 17.
145 UK Universities, *The Economic Impact of UK Universities, 2014-2015* (Oxford Economics 2017), available at: https://www.universitiesuk.ac.uk accessed 1 July 2021.
146 Ibid.

147 Ibid.
148 Dennis Dijkzeul, 'Heart of Paradox: War, Rape and NGOs in the DR Congo' in William E. DeMars and Dennis Dijkzeul (eds), *The NGO Challenge for International Relations Theory* (Routledge 2015) 262–286.
149 Ibid.
150 Laura Heaton, 'The Risks of Instrumentalizing the Narrative on Sexual Violence in the DRC: Neglected Needs and Unintended Consequences' (2014) 96 *International Review of the Red Cross* 625.
151 Ibid.
152 Ibid.
153 Ibid.
154 Ibid.
155 Ibid.
156 Ibid.
157 Gargi Bhattacharyya, *Dangerous Brown Men: Exploiting Sex, Violence and Feminism in the 'War on Terror'* (Zed Books 2013) 18–45.
158 Ibid.
159 Ibid.
160 Called by many Baartman, which I refuse to do as it further alienates her from her identity as we do not yet know her African name.
161 Ann Mary Doane, *The Desire to Desire* (Macmillan Press 1987) 212.
162 Nicola Henry, 'The Fixation on Wartime Rape: Feminist Critique and International Criminal Law' (2014) 23 (1) *Social & Legal Studies* 93–111.
163 Rephrasing Ann Mary Doane (note 161) 19.
164 The World Bank, World Development Indicators, https://datatopics.worldbank.org/world-development-indicators accessed 24 July 2021.
165 Chloé Lewis, 'The Making and Re-making of the 'Rape Capital of the World': On Colonial Durabilities and the Politics of Sexual Violence Statistics in DRC' (2022) 14 (1) *Critical African Studies* 57–72.
166 Charlotte Mertens and Maree Pardy, ''Sexurity' and Its Effects in Eastern Democratic Republic of Congo' (2017) 38 (4) *Third World Quarterly* 956–979.
167 Ibid., 968.
168 Ibid.
169 Ibid., 969.
170 Ibid.
171 Ibid., 970.
172 Ibid.
173 Obioma Nnaemeka, 'If Female Circumcision Did Not Exist, Western Feminism Would Invent It' in Susan Perry and Celeste Marguerite Schenck (eds), *Eye to Eye: Women Practising Development Across Cultures* (Zed Books 2001) 171–189; see amongst many, Oyèrónkẹ́ Oyěwùmí, *The Invention of Women: Making an African Sense of Western Gender Discourses* (University of Minnesota Press 1997); Mohanty Talpade Chandra, 'Under Western Eyes: Feminist Scholarship and Colonial Discourses' (1988) 30 (1) *Feminist Review* 61–88; Mohany Talpade Chandra, '"Under Western Eyes" Revisited: Feminist Solidarity through Anticapitalist Struggles' (2003) 28 (2) *Signs: Journal of Women in Culture and Society* 499–535.
174 Yvette Abrahams, 'Ambiguity Is My Middle Name: A Research Diary' in Nomboniso Gasa (ed.), *Women in South African History: They Remove Boulders and Cross Rivers* (HSRC Press 2007) 421–452, 424.
175 Ibid.
176 Christine Schwöbel (ed.), *Critical Approaches to International Criminal Law: An Introduction* (Routledge 2014) 8.

177 Ibid.
178 Ibid.
179 Ibid.
180 Clyde W. Barrow, *Critical Theories of the State: Marxist, Neomarxist, Postmarxist* (University of Wisconsin Press 1993) 13.
181 Ibid.
182 For statistics see, for example, Amber Peterman, Tia Palermo and Caryn Bredenkamp, 'Estimates and Determinants of Sexual Violence Against Women in the Democratic Republic of Congo' (2011) 101 (6) *American Journal of Public Health* 1060–1067; Kirsten Johnson *et al.*, 'Association of Sexual Violence and Human Rights Violations with Physical and Mental Health in Territories of the Eastern Democratic Republic of the Congo' (2010) 304 (5) *The Journal of the American Medical Association* 553–561.
183 Office of National Statistics, Sexual offending: victimisation and the path through the criminal justice system: An overview of sexual offending in England and Wales, using a range of National Statistics and official statistics from across the crime and criminal justice system (ONS December 2018), available at: https://www.ons.gov.uk accessed 5 June 2020.
184 Ibid.
185 Yvette Abrahams, 'Ambiguity Is My Middle Name: A Research Diary' in Nomboniso Gasa (ed.), *Women in South African History: They Remove Boulders and Cross Rivers* (HSRC Press 2007) 421–452.
186 Ibid., 424.
187 Ibid.
188 Ibid.
189 Ibid., 425.
190 See for example Arnon Bentovim, 'Family Systemic Approach to Work with Young Sex Offenders' (1998) 19 (1) *The Irish Journal of Psychology* 119–135; more generally Jon L. Winek, *Systemic Family Therapy: From Theory to Practice* (Sage 2009).
191 See Adam Hochschild, *King Leopold's Ghost: A Story of Greed, Terror, and Heroism in Colonial Africa* (Houghton Mifflin Harcourt 1999); Mary Annette Pember, *Intergenerational Trauma: Understanding Natives' Inherited Pain* (Indian Country Today Media Network 2016); inheritance of trauma is an emerging area of study and is increasingly used to explore intergenerational social/psychological issues. See for example Amy Lehrner and Rachel Yehuda, 'Cultural Trauma, and Epigenetic Inheritance' (2018) 30 (5) *Development and Psychopathology* 763–1777; David Cattell-Gordon, 'The Appalachian Inheritance: A Culturally Transmitted Traumatic Stress Syndrome?' (1990) 1 (1) *Journal of Progressive Human Services* 41–57.
192 Florence Bernault, 'The Shadow of Rule: Colonial Power and Modern Punishment in Africa' in Frank Dikötter and Ian Brown (eds), *Cultures of Confinement: A History of the Prison in Africa, Asia, and Latin America* (Cornell University Press 2018) 55–94.
193 Edward Nyaura Jasper and Margaret Njeri Ngugi, 'A Critical Overview of the Kenyan Prisons System: Understanding the Challenges of Correctional Practice' (2014) 12 (1) *International Journal of Innovation and Scientific Research* 6–12.
194 See for example Okia Opolot, 'The Role of the Police in the post-Election Violence in Kenya 2007/2008' (2011) 28 (2) *Journal of Third World Studies* 259–275.
195 Caroline Elkins, *Britain's Gulag: The Brutal End of Empire in Kenya* (Random House 2005).

196 See for example Carlene Firmin, *Contextual Safeguarding and Child Protection: Rewriting the Rules* (Routledge 2020).

197 Inua Ellams, 'Fuck/White Saviour Complex' in *The Actual* (Penned in the Margins 2020) 34.

198 Vivian Grosswald Curran, 'Globalization, Legal Transnationalization and Crimes Against Humanity: The Lipietz Case' (2008) 56 (2) *American Journal of Comparative Law* 376.

199 Ibid.

200 Ibid.

201 Ibid.

202 Ibid.

203 Eric Stover, Mychelle Balthazard and Alexa K. Koenig, 'Confronting Duch: Civil Party Participation in Case 001 at the Extraordinary Chambers in the Courts of Cambodia' (2011) 93 *International Review of the Red Cross* 503; Mahdev Mohan, 'The Paradox of Victim-Centrism: Victim Participation at the Khmer Rouge Tribunal' (2009) 9 (5) *International Criminal Law Review* 733–775; see also Susana SáCouto, 'Victim Participation at the International Criminal Court and the Extraordinary Chambers in the Courts of Cambodia: A Feminist Project?' (2012) 18 *Michigan Journal of Gender and Law* 297–359; and Thorsten Bonacker, 'Wolfgang Form, and Dominik Pfeiffer, Transitional Justice and Victim Participation in Cambodia: A World Polity Perspective' (2011) 25 *Global Society* 113–134.

204 Sam Garkawe, 'Victims and the International Criminal Court: Three Major Issues' (2003) 3 *International Criminal Law Review* 345–348.

205 Fanny Benedetti, Karine Bonneau and John Washburn, *Negotiating the International Criminal Court: New York to Rome 1994–1998* (Martinus Nijhoff 2013) 153; see also Cherif Bassiouni, 'Negotiating the Treaty of Rome on the Establishment of an International Criminal Court' (1999) 32 *Cornell International Law Journal* 443; and Chris Tenove, *Justice and Inclusion in Global Politics: Victim Representation and the International Criminal Court* (PhD Dissertation University of British Columbia 2015).

206 The victim-advocacy organisation REDRESS is often credited with drafting the language for the victim participation provisions and lobbying behind the scenes for its inclusion in the statute.

207 For discussion, see Sergey Vasiliev, 'Article 68(3) and Personal Interests of Victims in Emerging Practice of the ICC' in Carsten Stahn and Göran Sluiter (eds), *The Emerging Practice of the International Criminal Court* (Brill 2009) 638–658.

208 Christine Van den Wyngaert, 'Victims before International Criminal Courts: Some Views and Concerns of an ICC Trial Judge' (2011) 44 *Case Western Reserve Journal of International Law* 475.

209 Fanny Benedetti Karine Bonneau and John Washburn, *Negotiating the International Criminal Court: New York to Rome 1994–1998* (Martinus Nijhoff 2013) 153.

210 Rome Statute Art 75.

211 See for example Roy S. Lee (ed.), *The International Criminal Court: The Making of the Rome Statute: Issues, Negotiations and Results* (Martinus Nijhoff Publishers 1999); William A. Schabas, *The International Criminal Court: A Commentary on the Rome Statute* (Oxford University Press 2017).

212 See for example Phil Clark, 'Hybridity, Holism, and Traditional Justice: The Case of the *Gacaca* Courts in post-Genocide Rwanda (2007) 39 (4) *The George Washington International Law Review* 765–837.

213 Jonathan Doak, *Victims' Rights, Human Rights and Criminal Justice: Reconceiving the Role of Third Parties* (Hart 2008).

214 Valentina Spiga, 'No Redress without Justice: Victims and International Criminal Law' (2012) 10 (5) *Journal of International Criminal Justice* 1377–1394; Carolyn Hoyle and Leila Ullrich, 'New Court, New Justice? The Evolution of 'Justice for Victims' at Domestic Courts and at the International Criminal Court' (2014) 12 (4) *Journal of International Criminal Justice* 681–703; see also Claire Garbett, 'From Passive Objects to Active Agents: A Comparative Study of Conceptions of Victim Identities at the ICTY and ICC' (2015) 15 (1) *Journal of Human Rights* 40–59.

215 REDRESS, Representing Victims before the ICC: Recommendations on the Legal Representative System (REDRESS April 2015); ICC Assembly of States Parties, Report of the Bureau on Victims and Affected Communities and the Trust Fund for Victims and Reparations, ICC-ASP/11/32 (23 October 2012); Peter Dixon and Chris Tenove, 'International Criminal Justice as a Transnational Field: Rules, Authority and Victims' (2013) 7 (3) *International Journal of Transitional Justice* 408.

216 See United Nations, A/Res/40/34 (1985). The declaration defines victims of crime as

> persons who, individually or collectively, have suffered harm, including physical and mental injury, emotional suffering, and economic loss or substantial impairment of their fundamental rights, through acts or omissions that are in violation of criminal laws operative within Member States, including those laws proscribing criminal abuse of power.

It also states that victims' procedural rights must "be exercised in a manner which is not prejudicial to or inconsistent with the rights of the accused and a fair and impartial trial."

217 Charles P. Trumbull, 'The Victims of Victim Participation in International Criminal Proceedings' (2007) 29 *Michigan Journal of International Law* 777.

218 Ibid.

219 On rights of the accused see Rome Statute Art 67.

220 See ICC Assembly of States Parties, Official Records of the Assembly of States Parties to the Rome Statute of the International Criminal Court, Part IIA: Rules of Procedure and Evidence, Rule 85, ICC-ASP/1/3 and Corr.1 (3–10 September 2002). This rule defines victims as "natural persons who have suffered harm as a result of the commission of any crime within the jurisdiction of the Court." See also William A. Schabas, *An Introduction to the International Criminal Court* (4th edn, Cambridge University Press 2011); Cherif M. Bassiouni, *Introduction to International Criminal Law* (Martinus Nijhoff 2012).

221 Markus T. Funk, *Victims' Rights and Advocacy at the International Criminal Court* (Oxford University Press 2015); Susana SáCouto and Katherine Cleary, Victim Participation Before the International Criminal Court (November 2007) War Crimes Research Office American University Washington College of Law; Susana SáCouto and Katherine Cleary, 'Victims' Participation in the Investigations of the International Criminal Court' (2008) 17 *Transnational Law and Contemporary Problems* 73.

222 Peter G. Fischer, 'The Victims' Trust Fund of the International Criminal Court - Formation of a Functional Reparations Scheme' (2003) 17 *Emory International Law Review* 187; Rome Statute Art 68.

223 See ICC Assembly of States Parties, Report of the Court on the Strategy in Relation to Victims, ICC-ASP/11/40 (5 November 2012).

224 Jo-Anne Wemmers, 'Victims' Rights and the International Criminal Court: Perceptions within the Court Regarding the Victims' Right to Participate' (2010) 23 (3) *Leiden Journal of International Law* 629–643.

225 Luke Moffet, 'Elaborating Justice for Victims at the International Criminal Court Beyond Rhetoric and the Hague' (2015) 13 (2) *Journal of International Criminal Justice* 281–311; Emily Haslam, 'Victim Participation at the International Criminal Court: A Triumph of Hope Over Experience?' in Dominic McGoldrick Peter Rowe and Eric Donnelly (eds), *The Permanent International Criminal Court: Legal and Policy Issues* (Hart 2004) 315–334; See also Raquel Aldana, 'A Victim-Centred Reflection on Truth Commissions and Prosecutions as a Response to Mass Atrocities' (2006) 5 (1) *Journal of Human Rights* 107–126; Claire Garbett, 'The Truth and the Trial: Victim Participation, Restorative Justice, and the International Criminal Court' (2013) 16 (2) *Contemporary Justice Review* 193–213; Elisa Hoven and Saskia Scheibel, 'Justice for Victims' in Trials of Mass Crimes Symbolism or Substance?' (2015) 21 (2) *International Review of Victimology* 161–185.

226 *Situation in the Democratic Republic of the Congo in the Case of Prosecutor v. Thomas Lubanga Dyilo (Decision on Victims' Participation) Trial Chamber I ICC-01/04-01/06-1119 (18 January 2008);* see American University Washington College of Law, *Victim Participation at the Case Stage of Proceedings* (War Crimes Research Office 2009) 15–24.

227 Lucia Catani, 'Victims at the International Criminal Court: Some Lessons Learned from the Lubanga Case' (2012) 10 (4) *Journal of International Criminal Justice* 905–907.

228 *Situation in the Democratic Republic of the Congo in the Case of Prosecutor v. Germain Katanga and Mathieu Ngudjolo Chui (Decision on the Set of Procedural Rights Attached to Procedural Status of Victim at the Pre-Trial Stage of the Case) Pre-Trial Chamber I ICC-01/04-01/07 (13 May 2008).*

229 Aya Gruber, 'Righting Victim Wrongs: Responding to Philosophical Criticisms of the Nonspecific Victim Liability Defense' (2004) 52 *Buffalo Law Review* 433.

230 Umoren E. Uduakobong, 'The Symbolism of the Nigerian Women's War of 1929: An Anthropological Study of an Anticolonial Struggle' (1995) 16 (2) *African Study Monographs* 61–72 at 65.

231 Ratna Kapur, 'The Tragedy of Victimization Rhetoric: Resurrecting the "native" Subject in International/post-Colonial Feminist Legal Politics' (2003) 15 *Harvard Human Rights Journal* 11–36.

232 Frederic Mégret, 'Not 'Lambs to the Slaughter': A Program for Resistance to "Genocidal Law"' in Rene Provost and Payam Akhavan (eds), *Confronting Genocide* (Springer 2011) 195.

233 Raiss Tinmaung and Azeezah Kanji, 'Resisting the Rohingya Genocide: From Pity to Solidarity, Inside and Beyond the ICJ' (2020) 17 *TWAILR Reflections* found at https://twailr.com/resisting-the-rohingya-genocide-from-pity-to-solidarity-inside-and-beyond-the-icj/accessed 17/09/20

234 Hanna Cheryl, 'No Right to Choose: Mandated Victim Participation in Domestic Violence Prosecutions' (1996) 109 *Harvard Law Review* 1849, 1882.

235 For potential reasons why society views victims positively and tends to distance itself from alleged perpetrators, see Martha Minow, 'Surviving Victim Talk' (1992) 40 *UCLA Law Review* 1411–1434.

236 Gillian C. Mezay and Michael B. King, *Male Victims of Sexual Assault* (Oxford University Press 1992).

237 Lynne N. Henderson, 'The Wrongs of Victim's Rights' (1985) 37 *Stanford Law Review* 937–994.

238 Lynne Henderson, 'Co-Opting Compassion: The Federal Victim's Rights Amendment' (1997) 10 *St. Thomas Law Review* 579.

239 Aya Gruber, 'Victim Wrongs: The Case for a General Criminal Defence Based on Wrongful Victim Behaviour in an Era of Victims' Rights' (2004) 76 *Temple Law Review* 645–649.

240 *Prosecutor v. Lubanga Dyilo, Case No. ICC-01/04-01/06, Public Document with Ex Parte, Confidential and Public Annexes Submission of the Document Containing the Charges pursuant to Article 61(3)(a) and of the List of Evidence pursuant to Rule 121(3) (Aug. 28, 2006)*; Scott T. Johnson, 'Neither Victims nor Executioners: The Dilemma of Victim Participation and the Defendant's Right to a Fair Trial at the International Criminal Court' (2010) 16 *ILSA Journal of International and Comparative Law* 489.

241 Ibid.

242 Paul Roberts and Adrian Zuckerman, *Criminal Evidence* (Oxford University Press 2010) 331.

243 Lynne Henderson (note 238) 579.

244 Martha Minow, 'Surviving Victim Talk' (1992) 40 *UCLA Law Review* 1411–1434.

245 Lynne N. Henderson (note 237) 937–994.

246 Lynne Henderson (note 238) 579.

247 See Aya Gruber (note 239) 660.

248 Owen Bowcott, 'ICC Drops Murder and Rape Charges against Kenyan President' *The Guardian*, 5 December 2014.

249 Ibid.

250 Ibid.

251 The USA doctrines of provocation, self-defence, defence of others, and defence of property are all based, at least in part, on the fact that the victim did something wrongful or provoking. Victim blaming also enters the criminal case on an *ad hoc* basis as decisions not to prosecute, offers of favourable plea agreements, jury nullification, or more formally at sentencing. See, e.g., 18 U.S.C.A. § 5K2.10 (West 1996 Federal Sentencing Guidelines) providing for downward departure where a victim provokes a defendant's criminal behaviour.

252 For example, the provocation doctrine is often framed as negating the defendant's intent for the crime rather than assessing culpability for the defendant's intentional act considering the victim's wrongful behaviour. See Aya Gruber (note 239) at 672–677.

253 Ibid.

254 *R. v. Kiranjit Ahluwalia, 96 Cr App R. 133 (1993).*

255 *R. v Ahluwalia (Kiranjit) [1992] 4 All ER 889.*

256 *R. v Butler (Diana Helen) [1999] Crim LR 835.*

257 Penal theory is a far wider topic than could be covered in this section or indeed this book. For an in-depth discussion see Barbara Hudson, *Understanding Justice 2/E: An introduction to Ideas, Perspectives and Controversies in Modern Penal Theory* (McGraw-Hill Education 2003).

258 Samuel Scheffler (ed.), *Consequentialism and Its Critics* (Oxford University Press 1988) 45.

259 Paul H. Robinson, 'The Virtues of Restorative Processes, the Vices of "Restorative Justice"' (2003) *Utah Law Review* 375–380.

260 Russell L. Christopher, 'Deterring Retributivism: The Injustice of "Just" Punishment' (2001) 96 *Northwestern University Law Review* 843, 856.

261 My explorations here are do not concern cosmopolitanism/universalism, which is what my discussion earlier on Kant was about. Here I discuss crime and punishment (penal code) rather than global citizenship. I acknowledge that there are disputes amongst theorists as to whether Kant was a consequentialist or

not. For a debate on this, including Mill's Utilitarianism, see David Weinstein, 'Between Kantianism and Consequentialism in T. H. Green's Moral Philosophy' (1993) 41 (4) *Political Studies* 618–635.

262 Immanuel Kant, '*The Philosophy of Law* (trans. W. Hastie 1887) Reprinted in Sanford H. Kadish and Stephen J. Schulhofer (eds), *Criminal Law and Its Processes: Cases and Materials* (7th edn, Aspen Publishers 2001) 102.

263 Russell Cristopher (note 260).

264 Paul Schoeman, 'Easing the Fear of Too Much Justice: A Compromise Proposal to Revise the Racial Justice Act' (1995) 30 *Harvard Civil Rights–Civil Liberties Law Review* 543, 547.

265 Russell Christopher (note 260).

266 Ibid.

267 Richard A. Epstein, 'The Tort/Crime Distinction: A Generation Later' (1996) 76 *Boston University Law Review* 1, 3.

268 Jeremy Bentham, 'An Introduction to the Principles of Morals and Legislation' in Michael H. Tonry (ed.), *Why Punish? How Much? A Reader on Punishment* (Oxford University Press 2011) 51.

269 See for example Alan E. Fuchs, 'Autonomy, Slavery, and Mill's Critique of Paternalism' (2001) 4 (3) *Ethical Theory and Moral Practice* 231–251.

270 Preamble, Rome Statute of the International Criminal Court.

271 Gabrielle Lynch, *Performances of Justice: The Politics of Truth, Justice and Reconciliation in Kenya* (Cambridge University Press 2018) 58.

272 *The Prosecutor v. Ahmad Al Faqi Al Mahdi ICC-01/12-01/15.*

273 Susan Bandes, 'When Victims Seek Closure: Forgiveness, Vengeance and the Role of Government' (1999) 27 *Fordham Urban Law Journal* 1599.

274 Ibid.

275 See generally Kathy Elton and Michelle M. Roybal, 'Restoration, A Component of Justice' (2003) *Utah Law Review* 43.

276 Charles P. Trumbull, 'The Victims of Victim Participation in International Criminal Proceedings' (2008) 29 *Michigan Journal of International Law* 777.

277 See for example Henderson (note 237).

278 On *actus reus* and *mens rea* and other stories see Michael Allen, *Textbook on Criminal Law* (Oxford University Press 2013) 18, 58, 121.

279 UN Security Council, Statute of the International Criminal Tribunal for the Former Yugoslavia (as amended by Security Council Resolutions 1166 (1998), 1329 (2000), 1411 (2002), 1431 (2002), 1481 (2003), 1597 (2005), 1660 (2006), 1837 (2008) and 1877 (2009)), 25 May 1993, art. 21 (3).

280 UN Security Council, Statute of the International Criminal Tribunal for Rwanda (as amended by Security Council Resolutions 1165 (1998), 1329 (2000) 1411 (2002) and 1431 (2002)), 8 November 1994, art. 20 (3).

281 Article 66 Rome Statute of the International Criminal Court (last amended 2010) 17 July 1998.

282 Ibid. Art 21 (3).

283 Carsten Stahn and Göran Sluiter (eds), *The Emerging Practice of the International Criminal Court* (Brill Nijhoff 2009) 300.

284 *The Prosecutor v. Laurent Gbagbo and Charles Blé Goudé (Dissenting Opinion to the Chamber's Oral Decision of 15 January 2019) Trial Chamber I ICC-02/11-01/15 (15 January 2019) para 13–14.*

285 Ibid., para 37 when referring to presumption of innocence in the *case of Laurent Gbagbo and Charles Blé Goudé,* Judge Herrera Carbuccia mentioned IHRL, namely Article 11 of the Universal Declaration of Human Rights, Article 14(2) of the International Covenant on Civil and Political Rights, Article 7(1)(b) of

the African Charter on Human and People's Rights, Article 8(2) of the American Convention on Human Rights, and Article 6(2) of the European Convention on Human Rights.

286 *Situation in the Democratic Republic of the Congo in the Case of the Prosecutor v Callixte Mbarushimana (Decision of the Defence Request for an Order to preserve the impartiality of the Proceedings) PTCI ICC-01/04-01/10 (31 January 2011) para 9.*

287 Antonio Cassese (ed.), *The Oxford Companion to International Criminal Justice* (Oxford University Press 2009) 457.

288 Christoph Safferling, *International Criminal Procedure* (Oxford University Press 2012) 59, 379.

289 Ibid., 404.

290 Ibid., 403.

291 Salvatore Zappalà, *Human Rights in International Criminal Procedure* (Oxford University Press 2003) 83–84; Andrew Ashworth, 'Four Threats to the Presumption of Innocence' (2006) 10 (4) *The International Journal of Evidence & Proof* 241–247.

292 Salvatore Zappalà, (note 291), 83–84.

293 Scott T. Johnson, 'Neither Victims nor Executioners: The Dilemma of Victim Participation and the Defendant's Right to a Fair Trial at the International Criminal Court' (2010) 16 *ILSA Journal of International and Comparative Law* 489.

294 Ibid.

295 *International Criminal Court, Trial Chamber V(b), The Prosecutor v. Uhuru Muigai Kenyatta, February 5, 2014, 32.*

296 See more generally Paul Roberts and Adrian Zuckerman, *Criminal Evidence* (Oxford University Press 2010) Tyrone Kirchengast, *Victims and the Criminal Trial* (Springer 2016).

297 The Rome Statute Art 66 (3).

298 Antonio Cassese (ed.), *The Oxford Companion to International Criminal Justice* (Oxford University Press 2009) 457.

299 The Rome Statute Art 58 (1) (a).

300 Ibid. Art 58 (7).

301 See more generally Antonio Cassese (note 298).

302 *Prosecutor v Thomas Lubanga Dyilo (Redacted Version with Annex I Decision on the confirmation of charges) PTCI ICC-01/04-01/06 (29 January 2007) para 37.*

303 The Rome Statute Art 66 (2).

304 Yvonne McDermott, *Fairness in International Criminal Trials* (Oxford University Press 2016) 44–48.

305 Ibid., 46.

306 *Situation in the Republic of Côte d'Ivoire in the case of the Prosecutor v. Laurent Gbagbo and Charles Blé Goudé (Transcripts of Chamber's Oral Decision of 15 January 2019) Trial Chamber I ICC02/11-01/15-T-232-ENG ET WT 15-01-2019 1-7 SZ T (15 January 2019) para 3.*

307 Sven Becker Marian Blasberg and Dietmar Pieper, *The Ocampo Affair: A former ICC Chief's Dubious Links* (Spiegel International 5 October 2017).

308 ICC Statement on recent media allegations 5 October 2017, available at https://www.icc-cpi.int accessed 7 June 2020.

309 Christoph Safferling, *International Criminal Procedure* (Oxford University Press 2012) 59, 379.

310 Ibid., 409.

311 Art 42 Rome Statute; see also Art 45 on solemn undertakings by officials.

312 Sven Becker (note 307).
313 Marc S. Groenhuijsen *et al.*, 'Genocide, Crimes against Humanity and War Crimes: A Victimological Perspective on International Criminal Justice' in Rianne Monique Letschert *et al.* (eds), *Victimological Approaches to International Crimes: Africa* (Intersentia 2011) 9, 13; Antony Pemberton *et al.*, 'Coherence in International Criminal Justice: A Victimological Perspective' (2015) 15 (2) *International Criminal Law Review* 339–356.
314 *The Prosecutor v. Ahmad Al Faqi Al Mahdi ICC-01/12-01/15.*
315 See paras 21–29 of the judgement.
316 See para 109 of the judgement.
317 Michael P. Scharf, 'Trading Justice for Efficiency: Plea-Bargaining and International Tribunals' (2004) 2 *Journal of International Criminal Justice* 1070–1071.
318 Ibid.
319 Regina E. Rauxloh, 'Negotiated History: The Historical Record in International Criminal Law and Plea Bargaining' (2010) 10 *International Criminal Law Review* 739–740.
320 *Prosecutor v. Simic, Case No. IT-95-9-PT, Second Amended Indictment, ll 29-30, 34, 38, & 4047 (Int'l Crim. Trib. for the Former Yugoslavia Mar 25 1999.*
321 Rules of Procedure and Evidence U.N ICTY U.N. Doc. IT/32/Rev 45 Rule 62 bis (8 December 2010).
322 Janine Natalya Clark, 'Plea Bargaining at the ICTY Guilty Pleas and Reconciliation' (2009) 20 *European Journal of International Law* 415.
323 Rules of Procedure and Evidence, U.N. ICTR, U.N. Doc. ITR/3/Rev. 1, Rule 62(B) (14 March 2008).
324 *Prosecutor v. Ruggiu Case No ICTR-9732-DP Plea Agreement Between Georges Ruggiu and the Office of the Prosecutor 1 226 (12th May 2000).*
325 Michael P. Scharf (note 317).
326 Regina Rauxloh, 'Plea Bargaining - A Necessary Tool for the International Criminal Court Procedure' (2011) 94 (4) *Judicature* 178–185.
327 Nancy A. Combs, 'Copping a Plea to Genocide: The Plea Bargaining of International Crimes' (2002) 151 (1) *University of Pennsylvania Law Review* 1–157.
328 See in general Joseph D. Grano, *Confessions, Truth, and the Law* (University of Michigan Press 1996).
329 Damaska Mirjan, 'Negotiated Justice in International Criminal Courts' (2004) 2 (4) *Journal of International Criminal Justice* 1018–1039.
330 Ibid.
331 Michael J. Struett, *The Politics of Constructing the International Criminal Court: NGOs, Discourse, and Agency* (Springer 2008) 174.
332 Regina Rauxloh (note 326) 180.
333 Andrea Kupfer Schneider, 'Bargaining in the Shadow of International Law: What the Normalization of Adjudication in International Governance Regimes Means for Dispute Resolution' (2009) 41 *New York University Journal of International Law and Politics* 789–790.
334 Janine Natalya Clark (note 322).
335 Regina Rauxloh (note 326) 12.
336 Kate Kovarovic, 'Pleading for Justice: The Availability of Plea Bargaining as a Method of Alternative Resolution at the International Criminal Court' (2011) 2011 (2) *Journal of Dispute Resolution* 283.
337 Michael P. Scharf (note 317).
338 Ibid.
339 Kate Kovarovic (note 336).

340 Ibid.
341 On green washing see Frances Bowen, *After Greenwashing: Symbolic Corporate Environmentalism and Society* (Cambridge University Press 2014).
342 Regina E. Rauxloh, 'Plea Bargaining in International Criminal Justice: Can the International Criminal Court Afford to Avoid Trials?' (2011) 1 (2) *The Journal of Criminal Justice Research* 1–20.
343 Robert L. Shapiro, 'For the Defense' (1996) 30 *Loyola of Los Angeles Law Review* 105, 106.
344 Ava DuVernay, 13th (Documentary) (*Kandoo Films* 2016).
345 *The Prosecutor v. Ahmad Al Faqi Al Mahdi ICC-01/12-01/15.*
346 Article 8(2)(a)(vi) refers to grave breaches of the 1949 Geneva Conventions which were exemplified by destructions such as that of the Old Town of Dubrovnik according to the United Nations Commission of Experts Established Pursuant to Security Council Resolution 789, Destruction of Cultural Property (Annex 11), U.N. Doc. S/1994/674/Add. 2 (Vol. V) (1994).
347 Rome Statute Art 8. The Article contains a conflict at (2)(e) in that it does not protect cultural items in case of internal disturbances and tensions, such as riots, isolated and sporadic acts of violence or other acts of a similar nature.
348 *The Prosecutor v. Ahmad Al Faqi Al Mahdi ICC-01/12-01/1.*
349 For the wider discussions on the use of technology in evidence at the ICC, see Lindsay Freeman, 'Digital Evidence and War Crimes Prosecutions: The Impact of Digital Technologies on International Criminal Investigations and Trials' (2018) 41 *Fordham International Law Journal* 283.
350 William Schabas, 'Al Mahdi Has Been Convicted of a Crime He Did Not Commit' (2017) 49 *Case Western Reserve Journal of International Law* 75.
351 Rome Statute of the International Criminal Court (2002) 2187 UNTS 90 Art. 22(2).
352 William Schabas, 'Al Mahdi Has Been Convicted of a Crime He Did Not Commit' (2017) 49 Case Western Reserve Journal of International Law 75.
353 Toman Jiri, *Cultural Property in War: Improvement in protection: Commentary on the 1999 Second Protocol to the Hague Convention of 1954 for the Protection of Cultural Property in the Event of Armed Conflict* (UNESCO Publishing 2009) 4–10.
354 Project of an International Declaration Concerning the Laws and Customs of War (Declaration of Brussels) adopted by the conference of Brussels 27th Aug 1874 4 Martens Noveua Recueil (ser. 2) 219 Article 18(g).
355 Convention Respecting the Laws and Customs of War on Land art. 27, 1907, 36 Stat. 2277 (a907), T.S. No. 539, 3 Martenese Noveua Recueil (ser. 3) 461.
356 Matthew Lippman, 'Nuremberg: Forty-Five Years Later' (1991) 7 *Connecticut Journal of International Law* 1.
357 Agreement for the Prosecution and Punishment of the Major War Criminals of the European Axis, August 18, 1945; 59 Stat. 1544, 82 U.N.T.S. 279, E.A.S. No. 472 (August 18, 1945).
358 Bassiouni M. Cherif and James A. R. Nafziger, *Protection of Cultural Property, International Criminal Law I* (2nd edn, Bassiouni M. Cherif (ed.) 1999) 949–954.
359 For the legacy of the destruction of Dresden see Tony Joel, *The Dresden Firebombing: Memory and the Politics of Commemorating Destruction* (IB Tauris & Co 2013).
360 1954 Convention Art 28.
361 *Prosecutor v. Strugar, Judgment, ICTY Trial Chamber, at para. 223, Case No. IT-0 1 -42-T.*

362 David Keane, 'The Failure to Protect Cultural Property in Wartime' (2004) 14 (1) *DePaul-LCA Journal of Art & Entertainment Law* 15; see also Jean-Marie Henckaerts, 'New Rules for the Protection of Cultural Property in Armed Conflict' (1999) 81 *International Review of the Red Cross* 593.

363 Dieter Fleck *et al.*, *The Handbook of Humanitarian Law in Armed Conflicts* (Oxford University Press 1995) 403; Tom Haeck and Alice Priddy, *The Oxford Handbook of International Law in Armed Conflict* (Oxford University Press 2014).

364 Protocol Additional to the Geneva Conventions of August 12, 1949 and Relating to the Protection of Victims of International Armed Conflicts art. 53, 1125 U.N.T.S. 17512; Protocol Additional to the Geneva Conventions of August 12, 1949 and Relating to the Protection of Victims of Non-International Armed Conflicts art. 16, 1125 U.N.T.S. 609.

365 *Prosecutor v. Jokic, Sentencing Judgment, ICTY Trial Chamber, para. 50, Case IT-01-42/1-S.*

366 Ibid.

367 Bassiouni and Nafziger (note 358); Marion Forsyth, 'Casualties of War: The Destruction of Iraq's Cultural Heritage as a Result of U.S. Action During and After the 1991 Gulf War' (2004) 14 *DePaul-LCA Journal of Art & Entertainment Law* 73.

368 Statute of the International Tribunal for the Protection of Persons Responsible for Serious Violations of International Humanitarian Law Committed in the Territory of the Former Yugoslavia since 1991, S.C. Res., U.N. SCOR, 48th Sess., 3217th mtg, at 1-2, U.N. Doc. S/RES/827 (1993), reprinted in 33 I.L.M 1159 [The ICTY Statute]. Further indirect protection for cultural property was provided by Articles 3(c) of the ICTY Statute, which criminalises attacks on enemy property, and articles 2(d), 3(b), and 3(e) of the ICTY Statute, which criminalise destruction and plunder of enemy property.

369 Law on the Establishment of Extraordinary Chambers in the Courts of Cambodia for the Prosecution of Crimes Committed During the Period of Democratic Kampuchea, Reach Kram No. NS/RKM/0801/12, available at http://www.cambodia.gov.kh/krt/ english/index.htm accessed 12 April 2020.

370 Statute of the International Tribunal for the Protection of Persons Responsible for Genocide and other Serious Violations of International Humanitarian Law Committed in the Territory of the Rwanda and Rwandan Citizens Responsible for Genocide and other such Violations Committed in the Territory of Neighbouring States, between 1 January 1994 and 31 December 1994, S.C. Res. 955, U.N. SCOR, 49th Sess., 3453 rd. mtg, U.N. Doc. S/RES/955 (1994), reprinted in 33 I.L.M 1598 [The ICTR Statute].

371 Article 3(f) of the Statute of the Special Court for Sierra Leone, Annex to the Agreement between the United Nations and the Government of Sierra Leone on the Establishment of the Special Court for Sierra Leone, signed on 16 January 2002. Article 5 of the Statute also refers to general destruction of property (such as houses and public buildings) under Sierra Leonean law, yet without specifically mentioning destruction of cultural property.

372 Francesco Francioni and Federico Lenzerini, 'The Destruction of the Buddhas of Bamiyan and International Law' (2003)13 *European Journal of International Law* 619.

373 *The Prosecutor v. Strugar, Judgment, ICTY Trial Chamber at para 318-320, 461, Case IT-01-42.*

374 Hirad Abtahi, 'The Protection of Cultural Property in Times of Armed Conflict: The Practice of the International Criminal Tribunal for the Former Yugoslavia' (2001) 14 *Harvard Human Rights Journal* 1.

375 See Steven R. Ratner and Jason S. Abrams, *Accountability for Human Rights Atrocities in International Law-Beyond The Nuremberg Legacy* (2nd edn, Oxford University Press 2001) 294.
376 David Keane, 'The Failure to Protect Cultural Property in Wartime' (2004) 14 *DePaul-LCA Journal of Art & Entertainment Law* 1; on Cambodian Oral Performers, see http://www.cambodianmasters.org accessed 12 April 2020.
377 Francesco Francioni and Federico Lenzerini (note372).
378 David Keane, 'The Failure to Protect Cultural Property in Wartime' (2004) 14 *DePaul-LCA Journal of Art & Entertainment Law* 1, 15.
379 See particularly paras 15–16 of the judgment.
380 *The Prosecutor v. Bosco Ntaganda, Decision Pursuant to Article 61(7)(a) and (b) of the Rome Statute on the Charges of the Prosecutor Against Bosco Ntaganda, 9 June 2014, ICC-01/04-02/06-309.*
381 *The Prosecutor v. Germain Katanga and Mathieu Ngudjolo Chui, Decision on the confirmation of charges, 30 September 2008, ICC-01/04-01/07-717.*
382 Article 3(d) of the ICTY Statute criminalised 'seizure or destruction or wilful damage done to institutions dedicated to religion, charity and education, the arts and sciences, historic monuments and works of art and science.'
383 *Prosecutor v. Pavle Strugar, Judgement, 31 January 2005, IT-01-42-T para 308.*
384 See particularly regarding Cambodian Oral Performers, http://www.cambodianmasters.org accessed 12 April 2020.
385 Martti Koskenniemi, 'Legal Cosmopolitanism: Tom Franck's Messianic World' (2003) 35 (2) *New York University Journal of International Law and Politics* 485.
386 Ann Sagan, 'African Criminals/African Victims: The Institutionalised Production of Cultural Narratives in International Criminal Law' (2010) 39 (1) *Millennium* 13.
387 Tribunale Amministrativo Regionale del Lazio (Sez. II-quarter), 28 February 2007, No. 3518, Associazione nazionale Italia Nostra Onlus c. Ministero per i beni e le attività culturali *et al.*, reproduced in Guida al diritto-Il Sole 24 Ore, 2007, No. 21 paras 91–99. For a comment see Alessandro Chechi, 'The Return of Cultural Objects Removed in Times of Colonial Domination and International Law: The Case of the Venus of Cyrene' (2008) 18 (1) *The Italian Yearbook of International Law Online* 159–181.
388 Ibid.
389 Regulations annexed to Hague Convention (II) with respect to the Laws and Customs of War on Land, 29 July 1899 (entered into force 4 September 1900), AJIL, 1907, p. 66 (Article 56); and Regulations annexed to Hague Convention (IV) respecting the Laws and Customs of War on Land, 18 October 1907 (entered into force 26 January 1910), AJIL, 1908, p. 165 (Article 46).
390 Convention for the Protection of Cultural Property in the Event of Armed Conflict, 14 May 1954 (entered into force 7 August 1956), 249 UNTS 240.
391 Vienna Convention on Succession of States in respect of State Property, Archives and Debts (Article 15), 8 April 1983, ILM, 1983, Vol. 22, p. 306 ff. (not yet in force).
392 TAR (note 387).
393 See for example the discussions on looted Iraq artefact by Courtney Campbell, 'Arts and Arms: An Examination of the Looting of the National Museum of Iraq' (2009) 32 *Boston College International and Comparative Law Review* 423.
394 *The Prosecutor v. Ahmad Al Faqi Al Mahdi ICC-01/12-01/1.*
395 For a detailed discussion on the effects of colonialism on cultural destruction and looting, see Tim Barringer and Tom Flynn, *Colonialism, and the Object: Empire, Material Culture and the Museum* (Routledge 2012); for a discussion specific to reparations, see Neil G.W. Curtis, 'Universal Museums, Museum

Objects and Repatriation: The Tangled Stories of Things' (2006) 21 (2) *Museum Management and Curatorship* 117–127.

396 See for instance Oumar Ba, 'Contested Meanings: Timbuktu and the Prosecution of Destruction of Cultural Heritage as War Crimes' (2020) *African Studies Review* 1–20.

397 Marina Lostal, 'The Misplaced Emphasis on the Intangible Dimension of Cultural Heritage in the Al Mahdi Case at the ICC' (2017) 1 (2) *Inter Gentes - The McGill Journal of International Law & Legal Pluralism* 45–58.

398 Ibid.

399 Ibid.

400 Ibid.

6 *Umuntu Ngumuntu Ngabantu!* Decolonised ICL?

Introduction

Throughout this book, I have used my standpoint as a black African lawyer working in the colonial state to show the need for and the possibilities of an alternative to Eurocentric international law. I take this stand further in this chapter to show that alternatives do exist. In this sense I am in good company because decolonial theorists like Anibal Quijano have long argued that if one is to truly decolonise, then one must understand the inherent limitations of 'western' norms. This thinking has at its core the fact that knowledge and its reproduction are a colonial power game matrix.[1] Thus this Eurocentric epistemology needs to be dismembered and other rationalities given space to achieve any semblance of universalism in any sphere, let alone law.

It is my intention, therefore, to diverge from the habit of scholars, identified earlier while discussing TWAIL for example, to simultaneously view ICL both as colonial and also as the solution to problems caused by colonialism. Apart from Kamari Maxine Clarke,[2] none of the other scholars reviewed thus far deals conclusively with the idea of a viable alternative to the hegemony of the ICC as the apex arbiter in African conflicts. This chapter shows that these alternatives do exist and that there are authors writing about them. Alternatives have in fact been applied in selected instances, as was the case in Rwanda. The reason I proceed to suggest solutions is chiefly that I have adopted a methodology and a standpoint that critiques the current ICL regime as a reproduction of the colonial. To counter this hegemony, I rise to Fanon's challenge that intellectuals and others must join the anticolonial movement to play a crucial role in creating a truly independent alternative by looking to the past for inspiration in charting a new path towards a just world order.[3]

I argue in this chapter that there is need for plurality in law in contrast to the presentation of international law as universal. This means looking elsewhere, not to Europe/America, for inspiration and replacing Eurocentric law where necessary, especially in the global south. In search of this plurality and given the already established coloniality of the current

DOI: 10.4324/9781003304173-6

international regime with its destructive neo-liberalist approach, I suggest in the section titled 'ICL and Pluralism' below that the new 'grounding' norm(s) in international law should be southern alternatives such as *Ubuntu.* However, I warn in the section 'Ubuntu and the *Interlegality* Possibilities' of the risks inherent in this approach including 'orientalism,' and of the possibility of being hijacked by the neo-liberal local elite and their colonial masters. I show how this occurred in the section 'Forgetting Justice: The South African TRC Experiment, but also give an example of where it has worked in the example of the *Gacaca* courts in Rwanda where 'southern law' was well equipped to deal with crimes of an international nature in the section 'Remembering Justice: Gacaca Model. Before concluding this chapter, I bring the Ubuntu concept to its logical conclusion in the section the Pan African Criminal Court? *Petit à Petit...L'oiseau Fait Son Nid!* Here, I suggest that Ubuntu, should be the grundnorm that informs the emerging African Court which should in my view, replace the ICC in dealing with international law in Africa. This could be a starting point for Africa becoming self-sustaining/regulating in conflict management/resolution. In summary my argument is that that ICL needs to incorporate southern epistemologies in any case, but since Africa already has these norms in *Ubuntu/Gacaca*, ICC is not a solution for Africa and it should be replaced as a starting point by the planned Pan-African Court because the planned ACHRJ itself needs to embrace African epistemologies.

ICL and Pluralism

As we see expounded by Ngugi wa Thiongo,[4] Aníbal Quijano,[5] Walter Mignolo,[6] Frantz Fanon,[7] and Audre Lorde[8] amongst others, one cannot decolonise using the colonisers tools. My argument in this section is that since we have realised that the ICL/ICC is epistemologically imperialist and is not meant to liberate, it is imperative that its hegemony is challenged. The need for alternatives should be seen as a search for peace because we have enough evidence to show that the approach taken by the ICC so far has not achieved peace, for example in Eastern Congo despite most of the cases before the ICC coming from that region. I argue that this is because the ICC and other neo-liberal ideas are not themselves geared towards or rooted in peace as understood by the 'spaces' they colonise, such as Africa, because they are based on an Eurocentric epistemology that has no idea of peace without war.[9] In the simplest terms, a colonial understanding of peace presupposes war as default and I argue that southern epistemologies assume peace as a default.[10] This is because, as Maldonado-Torres further argues, the Eurocentric "master morality" is the foundation of racial policies, imperial projects and wars of invasion.[11] According to Moldonado-Torres, Eurocentrism is founded on "polemos or an eternal conflict that produces privileges upon which humanity, knowledge, and social relations are conceived and therefore war is tied up with European Modernity."[12] In this sense therefore there is a need for plurality in international criminal law because it may lead to the end of wars; as we shall see in the discussion on Ubuntu below, it translates less into subjugation and more towards the 'commons.'

Apart from Fanon who looked at revolutionary activism to decolonise, others like Andrea Bianchi have recently engaged with legal pluralism as a means to diversify international legal thinking.[13] Although it is important to say that Fanon was agitating for the eradication of, for example, settler colonialism and towards the real decolonisation of the resulting states, later scholars such as myself apply the same logic towards 'epistemological' decolonisation of the emerging world order. This need to decolonise the 'world order' as I have discussed in the earlier chapters has come about due to the realisation that the old order has in effect been reproduced in the current international legal relations. The first step towards this pluralism would be to start accepting other ways of thinking as expounded in this book and look at pragmatism as discussed by Siegfried Schieder amongst others[14] as a starting point of a path towards disrupting the hegemony of Eurocentric international law. This need for pluralism is important considering the TWAIL literature discussed above and also because, as Ingo Venzke argues, it is interpretative practice, rather than the recognised sources, that has become the main source of international law so that semantics in the international legal field become crucial as individuals who have semantic authority shape the law.[15] This raises the question of where international bodies such as the ICC gain authority for international territorial administration and how they gain public authority.[16] This argument, taken to its fruition, means that attempts must be made to have the 'south' provide both theoretical and jurisdictional alternatives to the current regime.

My book as a whole and this chapter in particular argue for co-existence of Eurocentric/'universalist' norms with southern epistemologies so that they both gain an equal footing in ICL. This could start with serious consideration of the *interlegality* theory as discussed by de Sousa Santos.[17] De Sousa Santos argues that legal pluralism is opposed to juridical monism, the latter signifying that there can be only one law or one juridical system produced by the state.[18] First, he argues that there always exists multiple legislative actors, both public and private and at many levels – local, national, or international – and therefore the idea of a uniform law is redundant. Instead, legal theory must acknowledge this multiplicity or *communis opinio;* instead of a singular legal base, contemporary societies are governed by an interconnected multiplicity of actors and norms.[19] What this means in simple terms is that in southern communities, particularly since colonialism, there have always existed several layers of 'law making.' There is organic law for example, which is not 'state made' and is applied within the family, the larger extended family (clan), and the immediate community, and there are even spiritual laws which govern people's relationships with each other. I apply de Sousa Santos' arguments in my suggestions of alternatives to the prevailing orthodoxy because he says that law is perpetually being made and hence there is no 'complete' law. What matters are the power dynamics of who rules on legalities of actions, or 'the politics of definition of law.'[20] It is this sphere of who decides, that this book interrogates because de Sousa Santos suggests that understanding the networks of actors and spaces where these politics occur is crucial in charting alternative paths.[21] I join an growing minority taking a stand and placing ourselves at the centre of the map-making, shining a light[22] onto southern norms and allowing them to define international law.

Pluralism as an alternative brings the TWAIL ideas I explored earlier to a reasonable conclusion in that it requires scholars to shine a light on southern epistemologies as viable alternatives to the Eurocentric/neo-liberal orthodoxy. I continue to do this later in this chapter in relation to *Ubuntu*. In addition, my advocacy of pluralism is a form of legal activism enshrined in this approach following de Sousa Santos and others who argue that there is a need for bottom-up legal reform from the global south.[23] A 'subaltern cosmopolitan legality' emerges to counter the hegemonic status of northern norms promoted by neo-liberalism. The 'south' in this approach is not a geographical space but an alliance of those on the receiving end of the ills brought about by global capitalism and therefore it exists everywhere as "the community of the victims."[24] This approach engages with the politics around law and wants to engage and shape those politics because "there is need to extend critical theory towards what is possible rather than just what exists."[25] However, as this book and the variety of literature it is based on show, the transnational community of suffering is not passive: the nefarious hegemony of the neo-liberal legal elite is evidently coming under strong scrutiny and their oppressive technologies are being challenged, as I do in this book.

My 'shining a light' on southern perspectives is therefore founded on the idea of de Sousa Santos that western norms cannot be universally valid, even if they pretend to be so.[26] De Sousa Santos believes that at their best these norms can only relate to the realities of western society if at all, and cannot pretend to account for realities in the global south. Therefore, southern epistemologies are better suited to deal with the realities of the global south and will lead to real transformation of the global power dynamics, creating a more equal world order.[27]

My interpretation of this argument by de Sousa Santos in relation to my discourse on the ICC, is that de Sousa Santos does not challenge the need for the existence of universalist ideas like *jus cogens* but challenges the idea that they can only be founded, sourced, or identified in the west/north. This is because others have identified a weakness in ideas like *jus cogens* in that it would appear that all human rights practitioners do is trace the norm to a particular statute for example the Rome Statute, add rhetoric to it, then proceed to identify the next norm.[28] De Sousa Santos, in his *interlegality* theory, argues, like Panikkar,[29] that universal norms can also be found and identified elsewhere, not solely in these western sources. As I detail later while discussing *Ubuntu*, southern continents like Africa, Asia and Latin America have unique histories and their ancient humanist principles of human dignity predate the *jus cogens* debate. Related to the source problem, my reading of de Sousa Santos is that the concept of 'international community' should be viewed with suspicion because, as I explored in earlier chapters, this cosmopolitanism excludes some, leading to 'civilising' projects such as the ICC. This brings up the problem of the 'expert knowers' who become the authors and the 'authority' behind international legal instruments, including the Rome Statute, and human rights. For example, there is over-reliance on Eurocentric *opinio juris* in developing *jus cogens* which excludes a whole group of experts in Asia, Africa, and Latin America. This over-reliance on *opinio juris* appears even more cynical when we remember our earlier explorations of who belongs to the Kantian cosmopolitan and the fact that some communities (European/Christian) are seen as civilised and others not.[30]

Therefore, Africa as a source of reform would not only resolve the impasse between the ICC and African states but fit in well with *interlegality* theory, and with the arguments of others, including Donnelly who warns against hierarchical positioning of norms with cosmopolitanism at the top because this presupposes other lower moral communities.[31] This need to devalue other communities or their normative foundations leads to instances where African states are simultaneously seen to be sovereign enough to be signatories to a treaty setting up the ICC and in the same breath as inadequate to try 'international crimes.' *Interlegality* would resolve this conundrum as it would allow Africa to develop its own capacities to address local crimes, even those seen as 'international.'

It follows therefore that this book helps enlarge the 'frame' of international criminal law authorship to include the often-ignored southern perspectives which imagine peace not always as the absence of armed conflict/war but the totality of the human experiences including for example a balanced *pacha mama* as we shall see later in this chapter. Such overarching perspectives are outside the realm of the Eurocentric law because as Luis Eslava's observes, the 'enframing' of International law often focuses on exceptional events and mainly ignores what this lens assesses as mundane.[32] Hence law can be seen as "mechanisms through which the world is viewed, apprehended and constructed according to parameters that are superimposed upon surrounding realities. In so doing they organise the world and our political responses to it."[33] Enframing can thus be a way of determining a certain world view and of emphasising certain events while being blind to others. Indeed, it can even become a technique of governance.[34] I take the view that in the Kenyan context for example, there was an over-emphasis on land being a cause of conflicts amongst the 'natives' alongside a complete ignoring of neo-liberal injustices, including those of settlers continuing to own vast tracks of land and vast areas being reserved for wildlife to benefit the mostly foreign owned tourism industry. The Kenyan situation could as easily be that of Ivory Coast or Congo where ICL conveniently locates the source of conflict with local 'warlords' rather than with the violence visited on the African continent by neo-liberal economics promoted by the World Bank and IMF and happily implemented with the help of/by international law.[35] It is convenient to blame land politics and ethnicity for violence while ignoring the actual causes even though scholars like Gurr have long linked political violence with economic inequalities.[36]

In conclusion therefore, the need for pluralism in international criminal law is a step towards decolonising and the end of 'governing' others using international law and institutions which was well articulated by Nkrumah, as discussed earlier. Nkrumah particularly warned of the proximity between Wall Street, the CIA, the colonial state, and international organisations and he exposed the fact that MNEs are necessarily not interested only in economic exploitation but have political control in mind as well. Nkrumah was indicating what Eslava and others have come to accept: international law has the ability to claim that standardised norms apply in the world at large. Neo-liberalism is then able to hide under this cloak of 'universalism' to fatally infect communities at all levels where mundane everyday interactions become vehicles of this deceit.[37]

Ubuntu and the *Interlegality* Possibilities

In this section, I discuss how uniquely southern norms can provide a more palatable ICL by realising this suggested *interlegality* from the normative level up to practice and procedures. I begin by proposing that the African norm of *Ubuntu* (in concert with other equal norms) should be part of 'the core' of global international interactions, including the law. *Ubuntu* is described by various authors as a form of communal ethics found among many groups in Africa.[38] The term is better exemplified by the Zulu proverb "*umuntu ngumuntu ngabantu*," meaning "a person is a person through people."[39] *Ubuntu* as it is widely understood came to be associated with the transition of South Africa from Apartheid but, as I discuss later, this romanticised usage is problematic in many ways, including the fact that in my view it was used to strangle the revolution and maintain the status quo.[40] In its very simplest form, *Ubuntu* requires one to strive for the whole of society.[41] Drucilla Cornell describes it as an

> activist ethic of virtue in which what it means to be a human being is ethically performed on a day-to-day basis, in a context in which how we

> are supposed to live together is constantly evoked and at the same time called into question.[42]

Because of the prevalence of colonial hegemony, such norms do not appear in international legal documents and although Africa had governed itself for centuries before colonialism through these organic norms, it is just more recently, with the end of Apartheid, that *Ubuntu* has gained prominence.[43] My aim here is to show that these African norms can become 'legal' norms as understood from a western perspective. The way *Ubuntu* gained current legal prominence was by being included in the interim constitution and in the South African Promotion of National Unity and Reconciliation Act of 1995 that governed the Truth and Reconciliation Commission (TRC).[44] Since then, authors who include Drucilla Cornell have argued that *Ubuntu* or the acceptance of human dignity became the *grundnorm* of the South African constitution.[45] That it is western authors and philosophers like Cornell who brought the norm to scholarly prominence is itself problematic in a post-colonial discourse, but I view her explorations of *Ubuntu* as a legal norm helpful for the purpose of the arguments I make here.

At the core of *Ubuntu* is the concerted strive for human dignity, and not toxic individualism and extraction, so it is the very opposite of neo-liberalism because of *Ubuntu's* inherent focus on 'we' and the 'commons' as we see in its definition. In addition, *Ubuntu* rejects the neat separation between law and ethics, which is a potent shield against the corruption inherent in neo-liberalism.[46] The fight for racial equality and social justice is therefore made possible by introducing dignity jurisprudence and therefore allowing the 'justiciability' of *Ubuntu* as a constitutional principle.[47] In this regard, Cornell explored South African case law post 1994 and observed that *Ubuntu* appears in various Constitutional and High Court's judgements as an "*interlegality*"[48] of the type discussed by de Sousa Santos.[49]

To counter that *Ubuntu* could not be applicable on a large scale, and that it was a vague norm, Cornell describes South Africa's current dispensation as a "*substantive revolution*" specifically because it is informed by *Ubuntu* in its aim to reconcile revolution and law.[50] Hans Kelsen[51] uses substantive revolution to refer to a revolution that does not involve a complete overthrow of a legal order along with its institutions but rather involves something more limited; it stresses the idea that "no existing law on the books could be enforced unless they were consistent with the rights that undergird and give significance to the meaning of the transformation from the older order to the new order."[52] I think this could be interpreted to mean that Ubuntu should co-exist with the prevailing Eurocentric constitutionalism, but my interpretation here is that Cornell is suggesting that, in this sense, no colonial law should be enforced if it goes against the principle of *Ubuntu* which predated colonial law. Therefore, *Ubuntu* is a possibly transformative foundational norm with the potential of a 'commons' oriented transformation in confronting capitalism.[53] It is related to the substantive revolution in that it implies a form of belonging together that is not based on social contract and not on national homogeneity. This then forms part of the substantive revolution which takes us beyond current thinking about the basis of national legal systems in which law is primarily rooted in the state.[54] Related to this is the idea of *Ubuntu* becoming justiciable.[55] What has the potential for global resonance is the idea that *Ubuntu* justiciability moves beyond the courts, and the people are freed to create their own way of being human together that has a potential to undermine conditions of neo-liberal capitalism.[56]

In my view, the revolutionary potential Cornell suggests lie in this capacity in *Ubuntu* for people to form their own defined humanness because therein we find the potential to form alliances with other ideas from the south like *BuenVivir*[57] as well as keeping humane western norms. This potential to form global alliances is strengthened by Cornell's argument that,

> …despite obvious differences; there is an alliance of a Kantian notion of dignity with the intellectual heritage of African humanism that is seen as rooted in the close connection between freedom and morality and the status of humanity as a moral ideal[58]

This potential of expanding *Ubuntu* globally and beyond the confines of state defined humanness, brings us closer to achieving global justice, if not revolution, because it allows ideas like *Ubuntu* to link with other philosophies like *BuenVivir* to go beyond 'man.' This means going beyond conventional understanding of capitalist defined relationships to include political spirituality as spirituality remains an invaluable reservoir of power and energy for the dispossessed.[59] Spirituality has informed revolutionary struggles from black women feminists to revolutions in Iran.[60] Spirituality is important to southern thinkers who have seen their revolutions falter. However, it is important to note that the faltering of these revolutions in places like South Africa, Zimbabwe, Venezuela or Brazil, as seen most recently, is due to a failure to face the full traumatic effects of revolutionary armed struggle, for example deaths of loved ones, displacements, detentions and the betrayal of the struggle's ideals by the ruling elite. In addition, it is difficult to maintain fidelity to a thoroughgoing liberation of all forms of human life that have been so distorted by racism, colonialism, phallocentricism, and advanced neo-liberal capitalism.[61]

In search of this moral legal order, Cornell agitates for change and radical rethinking of the status quo to confront the chaos brought about by neo-liberalism in order to realise human freedom.[62] Cornell argues that the feeling that capitalist domination has dealt a death blow to the ideal of freedom should in itself provide the impetus to imagine radical ideas for beginning again because we cannot just accept the status quo and continue to relate to each other as merely *homo economicus*.[63] My interpretation of Cornell is that she calls for discourses like this one, which critiques the hegemony and protests the occupation of subordinated spaces, demanding to be included in the public sphere, to be heard on equal footing. In doing this, we would aspire to realise a moral law.[64] I suggest that Cornell's ideas support my argument to change ICC's Kantian approach to justice and move towards the more reconciliatory Derridean ethic of hospitality[65] to achieve plurality of legal ideas, court processes, and intended outcomes.[66] Cornell argues against assimilation but for true openness to the other as, according to Derrida, "Justice always addresses itself to singularity, to the singularity of the other, despite or even because it pretends to universality."[67] Cornell suggests, as I do in this work, that if we embrace *interlegality*, *Ubuntu* and other southern norms cease to be 'exotic' ideas and we start engaging with our fellow human beings in the south with respect as they are impacted more by global inequalities and in that way we may find real solutions to global inequalities.[68]

In the section on law and language, I discussed the alienation that colonial law still visits on the global south. I indicated how the African is nothing but a spectator in colonial law/courts designed in a colonial manner and practised in foreign languages. In this respect Cornell's ideas support my call for the use of African languages in all situations relating to Africa in any international tribunal, especially where this affects the general population, as in cases that come before the ICC. Cornell also saw the importance of language in *Ubuntu*/law and argues that language not only helps us to give meaning to the world as we experience it, but also in expounding the future.[69]In this sense, use of Swahili/Gikuyu/Kalenjin language(s) in the Kenyan cases at the ICC would have made the cases more relatable to the local populations and would have captured the nuances particular to these communities. This would then have enhanced 'universal' jurisdiction because, in turn, it would mean that European lawyers working on African cases, ICC staff, judges, and drafters would have to learn these languages and in doing so, would incorporate the soul of *Ubuntu* in the ICL. This would introduce a different kind of hospitality to the west and ask the west to welcome differences which change their idea of 'human' to include others, "After all, this other is truly like ourselves."[70]

For this accepting of the other to happen, critical theory itself needs to be decolonised. This means including black phenomenology like *Ubuntu* in the mainstream/'universal' and finally putting an end to the notion that black people are sub-human. This must and will only happen with reparations by the beneficiaries of colonialism, slavery, and Apartheid to its victims. I therefore read in Cornell that the need for southern perspectives in fighting neo-liberalism equals a freedom from the neo-colonialism that the Washington consensus promotes.[71] Because we cannot trust capitalism to reform itself,[72] I argue that we need to decolonise education systems, including legal education globally, to decolonise minds in the manner Ngugi wa Thiongo suggested. According to George Sefa this decolonisation should mean including indigenous knowledge in Southern and Western academia because this will help rupture and challenge the political economy of knowledge production that accords certain privileges and legitimacy to certain forms of knowing while invalidating indigenous knowledges. This includes reclaiming indigenous cultures, languages, values, and worldviews and re-positioning them as an integral part of the education system.[73]

I suggest however that the reason why *Ubuntu* and other southern perspectives do not gain prominence in international law is due to their focus on commons.[74] We have already seen in earlier discussions that the major cause of conflict in all the situations before the ICC stems from post-colonial resource allocations which concentrate wealth in too few hands. To address this, we must not shy away from the potent possibilities of *Ubuntu* for overhauling racist capitalism as an economic norm on a large scale in conjunction with other southern norms. I see *Ubuntu* as a way of reorganising our economies from kleptomaniac neo-liberalism towards an economy of "enough." This would move us to solidarity and not extractive competition and to respect for *pacha mama* rather than ecocide.

To do this we need to link various "southern" perspectives with humanist European ideas. I am not alone in suggesting that international law should have an *interlegality* approach because the idea of 'universalist' norms versus the local has occupied legal scholars for a while. Abdullah An-Nai'm for example looked at the relationship between *Sharia* and human rights and argued that there was a need to involve other cultures in developing human rights. He argued this because most African and Asian countries did not participate in drafting the UDHR. As victims of colonisation, they were not members of the UN. When they participated, they did so based on an established framework and philosophical assumptions that had been adopted in their absence. An-Na'im suggests for example that that *Qur'an* could be read to emphasise the dignity and equality of human beings rather than to limit their freedoms, because the *Qur'an* speaks of the honour and dignity of humankind without distinction as to race, colour, gender, or religion.[75] This idea of humanity is important here because we find it referred to frequently in relation to *Ubuntu* and other southern philosophies.[76] It is a thread that seems to bind philosophies from Africa, Latin America, India, and Asia as well as European humanist movements. These epistemologies have the capacity to transform global relations to counter neo-liberalism and its project of making us *homo economicus.*

For ideas like *Ubuntu* to gain global prominence, they will need to act in concert with others from the wider southern regions including, but not exclusively, Latin America. In this section, I will briefly show the potential of such a union by detailing *BuenVivir*[77] a Latin American norm that in my view is similar to Ubuntu and that holds out the promise of intercontinental links with *Ubuntu.* According to Cerdán, *BuenVivir* is the Spanish translation for the *Aymara* indigenous concept *sumaqamaña* and the *Quechua* indigenous concept *sumac kawsay*; both are indigenous populations from the Andean region of South America.[78] Cerdán agrees with Esteva and Prakash about the need to act locally, but in solidarity with others globally, to counter the neo-liberalism which is threatening local spaces.[79]

Earlier, in Chapter 3, I explored how 'developing' has meant the imposition of foreign economic and legal norms as a continuation of the colonial. In contrast *Ubuntu* and *BuenVivir* are similar in that they offer indigenous philosophy as an alternative to this colonialism. This indigenous knowledge is important because it shares one important core characteristic: it has no vocabulary for the Eurocentric idea of poverty because the simplistic western idea of the "progressive transit from underdevelopment to development, cannot be found in indigenous conceptualisations of life."[80] In this respect, both *Ubuntu* and *BuenVivir* differ from western neo-liberalism in that they focus on human collective well-being, including spiritual wellbeing, and ensuring the protection of *pacha mama* is central to this balance. *BuenVivir* is not an attempt to modify the current paradigms, but it is in and by itself another paradigm which implies an exercise of decolonising power, knowledge and being: a transformation of the historical relations of domination that have imposed the western perspective as the one and only way of life.[81] This decolonising power in *BuenVivir* connects with the decolonisation theory by Fanon[82] discussed earlier as well as the ideas of others like Upendra Baxi who sees the 'development' as a northern imposed ideology that ignores the role of colonialism in the status of ex-colonised.[83]

As we see above when exploring Drucilla Cornell's ideas on *Ubuntu*, the obstacle faced by advocates of these southern norms is the counter-argument that they cannot be 'justiciable.' However, as we have already seen in relation to *Ubuntu* in South Africa, in 2008 and 2009, both Ecuador and Bolivia recognised *BuenVivir* in their constitutions and emphasised the nature of their states as pluri-cultural states.[84] In search of global alliances therefore, *BuenVivir* is a form of legal plurality, as discussed by de Sousa Santos, which links it uniquely to *Ubuntu* as a legal concept in South Africa and shows the capacity of these philosophies to have a global legal reach. I also see the focus on commons as important in addressing neo-liberalism's obsessions with private ownership of resources as promoted by IEL. Importantly, because of this openness to other epistemologies, we can see the potential of *Ubuntu* to form alliances with *BuenVivir* and other such norms from other regions, including Asia and the Middle East, and becoming revolutionary and leading a renaissance that is based on the deep historical roots of 'commons.'

My argument for these cross-cultural borrowings builds on the work of de Sousa Santos.[85] The link between these southern epistemologies is in the recognition that no one world view should dominate and hence colonise others: rather, I seek the co-dependence of a multiplicity of norms and therefore, these alliances should not just be between Latin America and Africa. My research shows that similar norms to *Ubuntu* are found in Asia as well.[86] Although neo-liberalism has suppressed and pushed these norms to the periphery, we see that in India for example the central purpose of the *Upanishads*[87] the concluding part of *Vedic* literature, was the uplifting of human life from the level of mere biological existence to a status of self-conscious spiritual being and in *Gita*, we see that humanism embraces all mankind.[88]

There are also traces of *Ubuntu*-like ideas in Buddhism where Buddha's only concern was humanity and its sufferings and the universality of this form of perspective is also evident from the fact that it is open for all human beings, irrespective of caste, creed, and sex.[89] Buddhism becomes revolutionary in the sense that it teaches that humanity cannot attain its highest goal until and unless human society as a whole enjoys freedom in both the secular and spiritual spheres of life.[90] The possibility of this global alliance expands further as we also find that China's *Confucianism*, also known as *Ruism*, shares much with *Ubuntu* in that it is described, amongst other things, as a way of life and a humanistic way of governing.[91]

Forgetting Justice: the South African TRC Experiment

Although I acknowledge and credit Cornell and other Europeans for shining a light on *Ubuntu*, from a post-colonial standpoint, it is important for African scholars like me to explore these ideas further. There are risks if African authors do not lead this discourse. My African standpoint for example allows me to draw on personal, family and community experiences as well as language and nuance to fully appreciate the potential of *Ubuntu*. This type of standpoint while exploring *Ubuntu* is important because often, and because of the prominence of South Africa's experiences with what I term transition from a pre-1990s colonial state to a modern colonial state, *Ubuntu* is largely seen as a peculiar regional Southern African norm rather than an Africa-wide norm or a global norm with different names and forms in Asia, or the Americas, as I discussed above.

The risk is that the western formulation of *Ubuntu* frames it as an exotic idea and in cases like South Africa, it was then used by neo-liberalists and Christian churches to hijack the revolution.[92] This is because when I look at the TRC in the context of decolonisation, I argue that rather than bringing about transformative justice, the status quo was maintained precisely because the neo-liberals used the Christian churches to equate *Ubuntu* solely with 'forgiveness' in which the divisions and strife of the past, "can now be addressed on the basis that there is a need for understanding but not for vengeance, a need for reparation but not for retaliation, a need for Ubuntu but not for victimization."[93] For this reason and others, I do not therefore view TRCs as African solutions to conflicts, neither do I view them as a solution at all because in South Africa for example, the TRC was used to defeat holistic justice. For the purposes of background, the TRC as a topic has been covered extensively, including the question of transformative justice, by authors like Van Marle.[94] Others, such as Meiring,[95] write that there was tension in the TRC because some felt that, as a legal process, it should not take a religious format.[96] In my view, a christian TRC was problematic because Afrocentric philosophers including Fanon,[97] Ramose,[98] and Ngugi[99] are sceptical as to the utility, if any, of the Judeo/Christian understanding of forgiveness in a decolonisation process.

The TRC and the Southern African experience show why we should be alert to coloniser manipulation of these southern epistemologies to enable them to remain in power in a new guise. During the TRC we, for example, saw the prominence of the Anglican church in aggressively promoting forgiveness though their main mouthpiece, Desmond Tutu. Tutu should have been sent by the church to the TRC to confess and ask for forgiveness for its cardinal sin of slave ownership and colonialism because only recently, in 2006, did his church acknowledged its role in the human trade.[100] In addition, the church's relationship with colonialism should have excluded it from leading the 'decolonisation' because the church was, and still is in many ways, the "religious arm" of colonial states – for example the Queen is both head of state and of the Anglican church.[101] Steve Biko noted that Africans were conquered using a highly exclusive religion and by some strange logic the conquerors argued that theirs was more scientific and ours mere superstition.[102]

The TRC in this sense acted as a smoke screen to simultaneously denounce Apartheid while reinforcing the coloniser's epistemology that founded Apartheid. This meant the 'independent' nation's acceptance of the continuation of colonialism on a metaphysical level, and signaled acceptance that Africans had no epistemologies to equal Christianity in guiding the nation through the crucial milestone of decolonisation. My contention is that if there was a consensus that the TRC had to take a religious form, it should have been that of agreed African traditional religion(s). My reasoning here is that this would have signaled decolonisation and reclaiming of African history because, during the early days of colonialism, there was no acceptance that African history existed[103] and consequently, "the one without history cannot have religion."[104]

This hijacking of *Ubuntu* has had lasting consequences as it meant that those accused of Apartheid crimes went free while freedom icons like Winnie Mandela were vilified because Tutu and his church not only represented a faith but a political ideology, a pro-capitalist, and Eurocentric centred approach to the law. Taken together with the lack of participation by the black consciousness movement and the Communist Party during this transition period, a Christian led process was not going to lead to any revolution because the church itself put in place the preconditions of capitalism[105] and participated in the worst form of capitalism, slave ownership.[106] On the other hand, the Communist Party was opposed to the maintenance of the status quo because its policy was redistribution of wealth and resources, including encouraging co-operative use of land, and it objected to privatisation.[107] The extension of religion to African epistemology in linking 'forgiveness' to *Ubuntu* was to extinguish the revolutionary fire because authors have subsequently noted that *Ubuntu* in the TRC revolved around tending to the psychological needs of victims and "put a spoke in the wheel of materially emancipating those who suffered, becoming a pretext for not tending to reparation."[108]

This anti-revolutionary epistemology meant that 'Christian forgiveness' was translated legally to an amnesty for criminal acts by Apartheid state officials and was set in law in the *AZAPO*[109] decision. In this case, the court in my view undermined the right of citizens to seek redress for the sake of 'peace' as it meant crimes committed by the Apartheid state were largely unaccounted for and state officials including the head of state went unpunished.[110] For the sake of our ICC discourse, one cannot but compare this treatment of de Klerk and other Apartheid state officials with the contemporary treatment of African elites at the ICC. Authors including Van Marle indicate that *AZAPO* was wrong in that the law is not usually best suited to deal with social injustices or recording and interrogating memories of historical events.[111] Others like Cornell view *AZAPO* positively because they trace the 'justiciability' of *Ubuntu* in that decision.[112] Cornell however promotes an idea of *Ubuntu* that I find difficult to accept. In fact, the selective tracing of forgiveness in *Ubuntu* stopped the African from seeking retribution and degraded African epistemology to a mythical-religious form which Magobe Ramose identifies as racist.[113] I agree with Ramose in this view and extend it to also mean a form of African Orientalism. The westerner selectively promoted *Ubuntu* to mean what benefits him/her/them. This took the form of forgiveness, which allowed the westerner to maintain their superior position in the economy. I borrow this phrase from Ali Mazrui who coined the term 'Black Orientalism' following Edward Said's lead. Mazrui noted that we are "witnessing the birth of a new Black paradigm which combines cultural condescension with paternalistic possessiveness and ulterior selectivity."[114] Fanon also warned against such selectivity as he argued that colonisers were "committed to destroying the people's originality by presenting cultural practices as religious, magical, fanatical behaviour."[115] This is what I think Said had in mind, i.e. that Orientalism encompasses more than geographical colonialism: it is also an epistemology that seeks to define us vs them in relation to how the European views self in relation to the other.[116]

> *...It is rather a distribution of geopolitical awareness into aesthetic, scholarly, economic, sociological, historical, and philological texts; it is an elaboration not only of a basic geographical distinction (the world is made up of two unequal halves, Orient and Occident) but also of a whole series of "interests" which, by such means as scholarly discovery, philological reconstruction, psychological analysis, landscape and sociological description, it not only creates but also maintains; it is, rather than expresses, a certain will or intention to understand, in some cases to control, manipulate...*[117]

However, my main critique of *AZAPO* is that it has directly led to the current injustices in South Africa in that it saw 'forgiveness' as the only way towards 'peace.' In taking this approach, *AZAPO* in my view went against existing international instruments[118] that had made crimes committed under Apartheid, such as torture and inhumane treatment, *jus cogens*[119] and acted contrary to the notion of *erga omnes* established in Barcelona,[120] supporting the idea that *jus cogens* includes an obligation that is binding on all states. The *AZAPO* judgement also brushed this *erga omnes* argument aside because it ruled that achieving peace was paramount in this instance and deemed it best left to the state concerned to decide what measures achieve reconciliation and reconstruction rather than applying a criminal law approach.[121] Although I would have advocated the criminal law route, it is noteworthy to again contrast this with the contemporary approaches at the ICC where criminal law rather than localised solutions is seen as the answer. However, *AZAPO* gets support from a prominent ICC/ICL scholar, Antonio Cassese, who surprisingly agrees with exceptions to the obligation to prosecute to achieve peace.[122] However, it is my view that since 'achieving peace' had not been established as a *jus cogens* equivalent to prohibition of Apartheid, the state had obligations towards the victims and the African community to punish Apartheid crimes. The African becomes a victim of 'history' and of her/his own history as African because his/her epistemologies, like *Ubuntu*, are selectively applied – wrongly – to achieve forgiveness as the predetermined outcome. *Ubuntu*'s humanising character was over-emphasised which left the reciprocal interaction between victim and perpetrator unaddressed. As a result *Ubuntu* is represented not as a mutual responsibility but as uncritically related to forgiveness.[123] According to Tutu, *Ubuntu* entails a general striving for social harmony and forgiveness as a very effective way of restoring social equilibrium.[124] Yet in my view Tutu conveniently ignored the real causes of the lack of social equilibrium, including the legacy of economic and cultural genocide created by colonialism. He also seemed to equate victims of Apartheid with the perpetrators, suggesting that forgiveness is a form of self-help therapy. Tutu promoted another injustice by infantilising African epistemology in presenting forgiveness as the only natural consequence of *Ubuntu* and thus victims are forced to forego claims for retribution, reparations, or vengeance.[125]

A poignant incident in the history of the TRC in South Africa is relevant to my argument that until all colonial crimes are accounted for, peace in most colonised spaces will remain a phantom. At the TRC, President de Klerk made lengthy submissions to the TRC that were intended to justify Apartheid rather than apologise for it.

> ...Deplorable as it now may seem, until the middle of the century hardly anyone in the European-dominated world considered that the indigenous peoples of the far-flung colonial empires were ready to rule themselves ... During the Anglo-Boer War Afrikaner nationalism had been widely admired throughout Europe and in the United States. However, in the climate of non-racialism, anti-colonialism and universalism that dominated global thinking in the wake of the Second World War, the concept of nationalism in general was in disrepute. As far as

> international opinion was concerned, the right to self-determination in Africa was associated only with black Africans ... The issues that we debated deep into the night centred on the question of how we could come to grips with this changing world on the one hand, and yet retain our right to our own national self-determination on the other? How would we avoid the chaos that was sweeping much of the rest of Africa ...? How could we defend ourselves against expansionist international communism and terrorism and yet make all South Africans free? The solution that we then came up with was "separate development.[126]

There is no acknowledgment by de Klerk of Apartheid being a crime against African people and he rubbed salt on the wound by reminding people of the long struggles by the Afrikaner for African land because for him, the need to resist British colonialists,

> ...led the Voortrekkers to leave the settled valleys of the Cape in the 1830s and to establish their own republics in the hinterland - in the Transvaal and the Orange Free State. It was their determination to rule themselves that involved them in several internal wars and subsequently led them, in two bitter wars, to resist the expansion of the British Empire. However, it should be emphasised that in none of these wars were they the aggressors. These people - my forebears - understood oppression. During their freedom struggle their homes were burned, their country was devastated...[127]

When the TRC was compiling its report, de Klerk fought to ensure that he was not criticised for his role in the government and when the TRC gave him notice that it would make findings to his detriment, as required by the relevant law, de Klerk filed for an injunction order[128] directing that the Commission be stopped from publishing negative findings about him.[129] Eventually the TRC removed criticisms of him from the final report.[130]

In comparison, the TRC was ruthless in its attitude toward a liberation icon, Winnie Madikezela Mandela.[131] Madikizela Mandela was, in my view, ahead of her contemporaries in understanding the nuances and symbolism of forgiveness as presented. She provided the only credible protest when she denied allegations against her, and in the process forcefully negated and disrupted the ultimate goal of having iconic figures like herself affirm the reconciliatory narrative.[132] Tutu, the ever keen agitator, implored her to apologise which she reluctantly did but she was nonetheless vilified in the report.[133] Her vilification showed that the TRC itself was unwilling to forgive her for its slights at her hands and was willing to punish Madikizela, contrary to their stated ideals of reconciliation. What followed was public humiliation of perhaps Africa's finest freedom fighter and, in contrast, few if any historians noted the significance of the TRC's removal of de Klerk's criticism from the final report.[134] Madikizela suffered the quite common assassination – although in her case only of character – suffered by many in Africa who argue against the post-colonial hegemony while those who collaborate rise to the top.

Related to this de Klerk and Madikizela Mandela paradox is the fact that victims of the Apartheid system were persuaded to forgive faceless phantoms.[135] This is better exemplified by the experiences of the Cradock four, widows who indicated that they were being asked to forgive but did not know whom to forgive.[136] Tellingly, Tutu was silent on their questioning of the very foundation of the TRC but was quick to applaud the daughter of one of the widows who was agreeable to the forgiveness scheme.[137] It appears that there was a clear attempt to ignore the lack of willingness to have this overarching forgiveness by many people, exemplified by these widows. The TRC fought against the philosophical challenge of 'forgiveness' represented by Madikizela Mandela in order to present the project as a success both in the hearing and its aftermath.[138] This, I argue, is because forgiveness was being used to build new 'refurbished' memories of the Apartheid era as we see with deletion of de Klerk's criticisms. Earlier, I suggested that Madikizela Mandela was ahead of her time in recognising the historical error that was forgiveness and the speed at which Africans were being asked to forgive. It was not until much later that authors like Van Marle identified the issue of time in relation to memories.[139] Van Marle suggests, rightly, "that to have correct memories recorded, it requires slowness and attentiveness to particularity. Law, on the other hand is not able to engage with memories and suffering due to a quest for speed, generalisations and formal injunctions."[140] This is an argument one could also make in relation to the African Cases at the ICC. Van Marle, for example, fittingly compares the *AZAPO* judgement and the TRC with its role in reconstructing and repairing South African society to the recording of a plane disaster by a black box.[141] This analogy of the black box is poignant in the sense that colonialism has never been recognised as an epistemological or cultural genocide against African people and milestones like *AZAPO*, TRC and 'freedom at midnight'/ *Madaraka* occasions were a chance to set this right, but yet again the black box was not found.

Apart from forgiveness impacting on memories, there was also a difficulty with the idea of 'truth.' The connotation was that by following a Christian notion of repentance those who appeared before the TRC committee were telling the truth. De Klerk, for example, reveals the difficulty with this view as it is noted by scholars that, "the search for the truth of the past is not a search for the true facts about the past, but the search for political responsibility which is almost impossible in the wake of a radically unjust past."[142] It is my view that when de Klerk used avoidance, shifting of responsibilities and justification of Apartheid, he was aware that he was evading future consequences as exemplified by his attempts to have negative findings removed from the final report. Apart from the fact that there were various versions of the events,[143] the TRC was itself conflicted between being a legal or a religious process which led to failure to 're-cast' the past and establish a common 'we.'[144] In fact, there was no 'we' because the rush to forgive meant that the process also 'forgot' half of the victims: women.[145] Apartheid's crimes against women, including rape, were ignored.[146] In addition, women were not seen as actors in any violence (if any) apart from Winnie Mandela or others who were activists in their own right. "They were not even asked what happened to them except as it happened to their families."[147]

The re-imagining of the 'we' after colonialism becomes problematic when these transitions are looked at again through a post-colonial lens. In the South African case as with many African states, we see privileged local elites who collaborated with the colonial state either directly or through propagating their epistemologies, like Tutu, taking charge and directing the process towards a predetermined neo-liberal path that excluded the majority. This is to say that the majority are simultaneously excluded from the process of setting the future and from the future itself in a moment of euphoric dreams of freedom as I discussed earlier regarding 'freedom at midnight' shenanigans in Chapter 4.

This reshaping of the 'we' faces further criticisms from African philosophers like Ramose who argue that it would not have been possible to reconcile the conquerors and the colonised without acknowledging the simple fact that a portion of the population were colonisers.[148] Ultimately, the TRC failed as a decolonising process because a "post-apartheid national identity and culture should have been constructed by looking to the past and reclaiming the native's history from the immobility to which it is condemned by the colonial system."[149] I therefore view the lack of decolonisation that resulted from forgiveness as 'the' major injustice because the African did not regain ancestral land, dignity, traditional forms of government, law, or religions. In addition, the TRC ensured that recorded memories are not in an African form. The recordings were not only in the coloniser's language and technology, but the results were also favourable only to the coloniser and a few post-colonial elites. Lack of decolonisation due to forgiveness meant that there was no reverting to African norms as '*grundnorms*' from the TRC onwards because although the Constitution of South Africa recognises traditional authorities, colonial constitutionalism limits the scope of traditional authorities.[150] This means that the (new) Eurocentric constitution always has precedence over customary law with the many conflicts that follow exemplified by *Bhe and others*.[151]

Ramose identifies the lack of 'justice' in the name of the Commission itself as signifying the lack of commitment to justice. I agree with Ramose that justice was abolished specifically in relation to the substantive form of sovereign title to territory; land as 'the' issue of liberation struggle was forgotten and this was tantamount to the continuation of enslavement by consent.[152] The reader is reminded here of the discourse in chapter four where land was seen as the cause of conflict in Kenya. This I should add is meant to be a warning to others in countries like South Africa or Namibia who may want their ancestral lands returned. Apart from loss of land, Africa(ns) did not regain the use of their languages in the post-colonial government. Colonial languages remain prominent in government and business and as a mode of instruction in education. This process was cemented by the TRC's use of English language which meant that the majority of citizens were excluded from the process.[153] It also meant that the resulting reconstruction of memories was done in the coloniser's favour; using her/his language and his/her mode(s) of recording.[154] Essentially, the resulting government remained colonial in nature as experts such as Ngugi have described the dominance of colonial languages in Africa, both in government and literature, as the continuation of colonialism.[155] The change of official language in government and education to local African languages would have had a major decolonising effect because, "language is reality"[156] and the solution starts with Africans decolonising their minds after the use of the colonisers' language, especially in government, had denied them control of their destiny.[157]

To conclude this section on TRCs, we see that equating victims with perpetrators by forgiveness hindered reparations because constructing reparation and *Ubuntu* as the opposite of victimisation compelled 'victims' to give up claims for reparation, whereas 'perpetrators' gained protection.[158] This can be linked to the fact that there are those for whom forgetting makes economic sense, especially the companies that profited from Apartheid.[159] I agree with Barnard that this silence regarding the role of big business during Apartheid and during the settlement was deliberate and was as a result of pressure by the international community for the ANC to renounce leftist/Marxist economic policies.[160] Instead of reshaping the economy, South Africa adopted neo-liberalism, which is seen by many as neo-colonialism. In other words, Apartheid was clothed in new gowns of liberalisation and privatisation and its economic advantages are now obtainable through more palatable and effective methods.[161] South Africa joined the rest of the supposedly independent states that are supposed to alleviate the poverty inherited from colonialism through the magic of market forces. As many in the south have found out, to remove colonial legacies through capitalism is an impossible task because neo-liberalism is not 'neutral' and, especially in South Africa, there was no reset or 'freedom at midnight' because economic power, property, and opportunities remained with the few.[162]

Remembering Justice: Gacaca Model

There is no better example of how African states could address post-violence settlements and 'justice' than Rwanda. I argued earlier that the main limitation of the Eurocentric ICL is the sole focus on individuals while the majority of 'grassroots' offenders are not held to account. I have also argued that at the ICC, the Kenyan cases essentially ended up being a power struggle between different elites with the Kenyan elite upstaging their fellow elites and the victims ending up with no 'justice.' As I explored in the discussion of plea bargains, part of the reason why the ICC and local courts are not able to address the communal nature of these crimes is resources. For example, in Rwanda, there was no capacity to charge over 120,000 genocide suspects in a justice system already weakened by the war.[163] The only way to address this was to revert to local dispute resolution councils or *Gacaca* courts[164] although this required enacting new laws to formalise the process.[165] The advantage of *Gacaca* was the mere fact that every community had a *Gacaca* council even before the genocide, so in 2005 there were about 11,000 throughout the country.[166] I will not detail the workings of the *Gacaca* courts or their historical background here for lack of space, but I will explore *Gacaca* as an example of an Africa-centric 'international crimes' court system.[167]

This form of local councils (courts) existed in most African communities before colonialism and existed and still exist parallel to colonial justice systems. For example, Chapter 12 of the South African Constitution states that the institution, status and roles of traditional leadership, according to customary law, are recognised.[168] It should be noted that traditional authorities are/were a form of government in the wider sense while *Gacaca* is a court within that context. Before the Rwanda genocide, *Gacaca*, like many similar councils of elders in Africa, dealt with land disputes and other domestic matters.[169] The main purpose of *Gacaca* was restoration of social cohesion rather than punishment and hence the focus was to bring about transparency about the genocide, speed up the trials and bring about reconciliation.[170] In the previous chapter, I discussed the limitations of the Eurocentric court architecture and one of the glaring defects of the colonial courts is that they are designed to try individuals but *Gacaca*, as an organic court, was able to adapt and deal with close to two million suspects.[171] Importantly, these trials were open for the community to participate in and focused not on the elite, as the ICC does, but on local operatives who committed the actual crimes. Venues were also local to the people directly impacted by these crimes as the trials took place in schools and outdoors.[172] This 'communal' nature of *Gacaca* was necessary because, as I discussed under the principle of *Ubuntu*, one is responsible for/to the community at large and therefore crimes committed publicly needed to be addressed in the open.[173] We already see the difference here in terms of the meaning of 'justice' being seen to be done, as practiced at the ICC, and justice as practiced by *Gacaca*. Through community participation in *Gacaca*, the court becomes a therapeutic space too because the open forum allows people to interrogate the accused directly, offering them the opportunity to come to terms with the loss of their loved ones.[174]

The thought of an Africa-centric judicial system addressing what was uniquely local, faced opposition from the Eurocentric hegemony, including many lawyers and human rights organisations, because they viewed *Gacaca* as incapable of addressing genocide.[175] In a post-colonial context, these Eurocentric sceptics displayed the biases already discussed in earlier chapters – that this Rwandan traditional court would trivialise genocide and that the 'lay' aspect of *Gacaca* threatened to undermine the due process rights of suspects.[176] This criticism fails to countenance any other way of practising the law than in a colonial court building staffed with lawyers trained in western ways, which goes to the core of my argument; a Eurocentric view cannot imagine that there were local legal systems before colonialism. In this regard, those versed in the knowledge of this *Gacaca* law cannot be 'lawyers' or 'judges' in a Eurocentric context. More insulting was the notion that those directly affected by the genocide did not have the ability to interrogate what occurred to their community.[177] Further critiques of the *Gacaca* courts showed the limits of Eurocentric engagement with these traditional legal systems, especially the limits of the Eurocentric meaning of 'justice' because part of the critique was that *Gacaca* would have been miles apart from the ICC, for example in the issue of compensation for victims and in gathering evidence to prove genocide because, for example, most witnesses had been killed.[178] This showed the limits of applying Eurocentric legal theories to understand traditions that go beyond the 'forensic.' Evidence in *Gacaca* was oral, communal detailing of events as people experienced them, as opposed to the neatly collected and filed forensic evidence in Eurocentric tribunals. Yet despite these naysayers, *Gacaca* proved to be the best suited forum to address genocide in the Rwandan context[179] which in my view provides a template for situations elsewhere in the global south.

It is imperative at this juncture to contrast the iconography and architecture of the colonial court discussed earlier in Chapter 4 at the ICC with the *Gacaca* courts. None of the ICC's power play schemes and court designs featured in *Gacaca* because the accused testified before the local community who chose the bench – *inyangamugayo* or "honest persons."[180] Unlike the ICC, where only lawyers could question witnesses, in *Gacaca* community members were permitted to do so.[181] One of the most significant contributions made by *Gacaca* and not acknowledged in any of the literature reviewed is its contribution to the understanding of the limits of the Eurocentric 'consequential' or utilitarian penal theory when it comes to mass participants in wartime crimes. Due to the communal nature of the crimes a Eurocentric penal code would have meant the state committing genocide itself in retaliation because, out of a population of seven million, two million would have faced the death penalty according to the then existing laws.[182] In this way *Gacaca* also deviates from colonial penal theory in that the Rwandan people explored punishments that took into account "the need for justice but also the need to reconcile and rebuild the country."[183] In other words I see *Gacaca* as a southern perspective that goes beyond 'justice' and imagines communities after trials have ended.

Gacaca courts however faced difficulties, such as the fact that due to their public nature, the hearings may have negatively impacted rape victim-survivors. Because witnesses, including rape survivors gave their testimonies before their neighbours, friends, relatives and the *inyangamugayo*, they were denied confidentiality[184] which extended their trauma.[185] It is probable that these fears and social pressures led to reluctance by rape victim-survivors to give their evidence at *Gacaca* courts, thereby denying them an opportunity for 'justice.'[186] The other important critique is that *Gacaca* may have overlooked the communal stigma associated with rape and the subsequent rejection that followed survivors.[187] The other concern for survivors was their immediate safety because the accused and their families were local to the victims, and given the grave consequences of a rape accusation, the threat of reprisals existed.[188]

Despite these challenges, numerous survivors testified before *Gacaca*[189] and were offered local therapeutic support by *Gacaca* to deal with anxieties, especially around the issues of stigma.[190] This aspect of local therapeutic support simultaneously happening with rape trials is also a practice Eurocentric courts could learn from because survivors were offered counselling in order to understand that they were not responsible for the crimes against them.[191] These support mechanisms made some rape survivors give *Gacaca* credit for giving them a platform to come to terms with their experiences[192] with many noting that it "unburdened their hearts" leading to both personal and social healing.[193]

Gacaca courts were not unique however in presenting survivors with these challenges because research shows that, due to stigma, public testimony does not always restore the dignity of the person or enhance their healing.[194] Re-living the genocide was detailed as a particularly traumatic experience for those who testified about their rape.[195] It would therefore be fair to say that participants' experiences before the *Gacaca* courts were mixed, as were the outcomes for survivors. It is also fair to note that *Gacaca* as practiced in Rwanda post-genocide was not the pre-colonial organic community court and therefore suffered from being state sponsored and elite engineered. Like all post-genocide courts tend to be, their outcomes (whether or not they worked) become more romanticised than their state origins.[196]

The outcomes for *Gacaca* courts should however be measured on the basis of their overall impact on the wider community because acceptance of guilt and subsequent apologies by mass perpetrators contributed in reducing communal tensions.[197] Although these confessions also brought with them difficulties of whether survivors would see them as genuine and offer the requested forgiveness or to the contrary not accept. There were cases where survivors forgave offenders who apologised sincerely.[198] For example, De Brouwer and Ruvebana interviewed a survivor who reported that when the confessions were genuine, it set survivors' hearts free as they knew when a perpetrator's apology was sincere.[199]

On the other side, there were some who experienced the confessions negatively, with some survivors reporting further victimisation because of the lack of confidentiality already discussed and because some survivors had not previously disclosed their experiences to avoid family and community stigma. Because of these confessions, their ordeals became public without their consent.[200] Painfully, there were instances where confessions were used by perpetrators as an opportunity to humiliate and cause more trauma,[201] perhaps as their last defiant stand against the victims.[202] In addition, there were instances where the full extent of the crime was deliberately concealed because even the perpetrators feared being labelled as rapists[203] which led to some survivors saying they could not forgive those who made only partial confessions.[204]

The other major lesson international tribunals such as the ICC could take from *Gacaca* is that Rwandan society showed willingness to learn from the difficulties outlined above and amended their domestic laws governing *Gacaca* operations to provide, for example, better confidentiality. First, Article 38 of the *Gacaca* law provided for closed hearings in cases where sexual violence was the issue.[205] Second, victims had the right to request that a judge be disqualified from hearing their case if they knew the judge prior to *Gacaca*. The ability to disqualify a judge appeared almost automatic and did not require the victim to demonstrate that the judge actually had a bias or conflict of interest.[206] In addition, rather than appear in person, women could write a letter containing their allegations: this was given to the district coordinator who then presented it to the court[207]

Although the *Gacaca* law says that it was based around confession, guilty plea, repentance, and apologies,[208] before concluding this discussion on *Gacaca* it is important to distinguish the confessional nature of the court from the Eurocentric plea bargains I discussed earlier, for example in relation to *Mahdi*. This is because, as seen in the discussions on *Ubuntu*, the *Gacaca* court was built around a uniquely southern idea of justice that is not 'transactional' but is a holistic idea of communal justice where one is not confessing to a few groups of judges and lawyers in a neat statement. This process goes deeper than a Eurocentric legal theory could fathom: this was not a simple guilty plea but a deeply complex 'spiritual' undertaking unique to southern epistemologies, as discussed in relation to *Ubuntu/BuenVivir* – in these southern perspectives, justice goes beyond the material realms.

The Pan-African Criminal Court? Petit À Petit … L'oiseau Fait Son NID!

Oh yeah!
Il n'est jamais trop tard,
Mes copains ont des voitures,
Il y en a d'autres a l'aventure,
Mes copains ils sont partis,
Oh mais moi je suis la,
Pour servir mon pays,
Je suis la
Petit a petit, l'oiseau fait son nid…[209]

As discussed above regarding *Ubuntu*, my approach seeks an international alliance of ideas from the south that provides a parallel/alternative universalist norm to the Eurocentric hegemony at the ICL. Since the slavery days however, there has been a movement which draws its inspiration from Africans' unique historical identity and collective experiences of enslavement and colonisation towards their emancipation.[210] The mainstay of this movement centres around Pan-Africanism which has been an ideology amongst Africans both in the continent and in the diaspora from the late nineteenth century to current times, its rallying point the idea of Africans working towards a self-reliant Africa.[211] This idea as envisaged by some thinkers is problematic from a decolonising perspective in relation to accepting the modern state as a unit of governance but nonetheless, Kamari Clarke suggests that the aim of Pan-Africanism is to garner unity of purpose towards the establishment of independent African states and forge unity amongst the black diaspora.[212] The core foundations of Pan-Africanism were the elevation of the uniqueness of the African people and the avoidance of uncritical absorption of western ideas, as expounded by Edward W. Blyden.[213]

> *…The African must advance by methods of his own. He must possess a power distinct from that of the European. It has been proved that he knows how to take advantage of European culture and that he can be benefited by it. Their proof was perhaps necessary, but it is not sufficient. We must show that we are able to go alone, to carve out our own way. We must not be satisfied that, in this nation, European influence shapes our polity, makes our laws, rules in our tribunals and impregnates our social atmosphere*[214]

As I discussed earlier, Kwame Nkrumah and others adopted this stance and envisaged a united Africa approach to counter neo-colonialism. The establishment of the OAU in 1963 seemed to at least draw its inspiration from this need for Africa to have a united voice on the global stage. I will not recount Pan-Africanism as an ideology here owing to lack of space, except to note that the current initiatives for African-centric solutions are inspired by glorious Pan-Africanist principles expounded by Pan-African icons like "Mwalimu" Julius Nyerere, Kenneth Kaunda, Steve Biko, Thomas Sankara, Samora Machel, Agostinho Neto, and Amílcar Cabra. Kamari Clarke suggests that by looking to the past to inspire the present and future we set "the moral conditions by which contemporary Africa can join the West in development partnerships."[215] I argue that these moral conditions include establishing local regimes through which to resolve conflicts and adjudicate human rights concerns and mean that African mechanisms must address more than 'political' rights, engaging with the underlying causes of conflicts.

The impression given by the 'ending impunity' mantra at the core of the Rome Statute suggests that human rights protection is a pioneering ideology, appearing in Africa with the emergence of the Rome Statute. However there have been mechanisms to protect and enforce human rights in the continent since the founding of the African states, although different commentators dispute their effectiveness.[216] I will not engage in this wider topic because it would need more attention than this section can offer. I detail just a brief synopsis to put my sketch of an African solution into a historical perspective as well as to show that the notion of African-based human rights protection is not a new phenomenon in post-colonial discourse. It is important to note that the very foundations of the African state were achieved in many instances by local revolutionary acts and that Britain and France fought aggressively against those who were advocating for freedom, equality, justice and dignity – ideals that later became the core objectives of the newly formed OAU.[217] In addition, the importance of human rights promotion and protection is central to the OAU charter; Article II (1)(b) required member states to work in unison and with intensity to achieve a better life for the peoples of Africa and (c) required them to defend their sovereignty, territorial integrity and independence; (d) to eradicate all forms of colonialism from Africa; and (e) to promote international cooperation, having due regard to the Charter of the United Nations and the Universal Declaration of Human Rights.[218] The OAU has now been replaced by the African Union (AU) but those founding values have remained the same.[219]

Therefore, we see the OAU being noticeably clear that its foundations lie with the enhancement of African people's rights. The OAU also created specific human rights instruments, including the African Charter on Human and Peoples Rights in 1981[220] which created the African Commission on Human and Peoples' Rights, the OAU Convention Governing the Specific Aspects of Refugee Problems in Africa of 1969,[221] and the African Charter on the Rights and Welfare of the Child of 1990.[222] The African Commission monitors compliance by state parties with the African Charter, *inter alia* in terms of their Rules of Procedure[223] and in terms of the Reporting Guidelines for State Reports.[224]

The establishment of the African Court on Human and Peoples' Rights by a protocol adopted on 10 June 1998 and entered into force on 25 January 2004 is the starting point towards the judicial self-reliance I advocate. The court rules on human right violations by member states and complements the protective mandate of the African Commission on Human and Peoples' Rights (African Commission).[225] This Court is operational but the other intended AU supreme judicial body, the Court of Justice of the African Union is yet to become operational. The current aim – in keeping with fulfilment of my wish for an African court dealing with ICL – is to merge these two courts into one through the Malabo Protocol on the Statute of the African Court of Justice and Human Rights[226] adopted on 1 July 2008.

The protocol will come into force 30 days after its ratification by 15 member states but as of April 2019, no member state had ratified, and only 12 had signed the protocol.[227] This court will cover all the crimes litigated at the ICC and goes further than the Rome Statute as I detail below and so it is not clear why some countries have not signed or ratified it yet. I speculate that it is because the protocol goes beyond what some leaders find comfortable, especially the idea of abolishing 'non-democratic' changes of government, which I take to mean 'no military coups.' The objective of the protocol is to merge the African Human Rights Court and the African Court of Justice into a single court and to extend the jurisdiction of this court to cover crimes under international law and transnational crimes.[228]

Due to lack of space, I will not detail the historical events and negotiations leading to Malabo but an eminent scholar in this field, Kamari Clarke, goes into detail in her recent work, including about the effects of political machinations around the Sudan and Kenyan situations and also Pan-Africanist endeavours to find African solutions to African problems.[229] It is important for our discourse on the ICC to state how this court impacts on the idea of African solutions as well as on the obvious implication for domesticating international crimes to an African Court which I support for the reasons articulated throughout this book. The Malabo Protocol is ground-breaking as an international legal instrument in that, for the first time, over and above the international crimes covered by the Rome Statute, a Pan-African treaty criminalises acts such as unconstitutional change of governments, hiring mercenaries, toxic waste dumping, and illicit exploitation of resources.[230]

It is particularly important from a post-colonial perspective that the protocol does not deny that these crimes are happening in Africa but goes a step further to indicate that it addresses the 'causes' of these crimes which, as I stated earlier, included illicit exploitation of resources. The International Criminal Section of the ACJHR covers similar crimes to the ICC. It is important for my *interlegality* proposal to note that the Malabo Protocol does not stop or hinder the ICC from operating and initiating investigations in states that have ratified both the Malabo Protocol and the Rome Statute.[231] In simpler terms, the state's obligations under the Rome Statute are not extinguished by the Malabo Protocol. It is therefore my view that once African states ratify the Malabo Protocol, and the court is operational that will create a more robust relationship of complementarity between the member states and the ICC because the ACHJR has inbuilt complementarity with national courts and regional economic communities.

Pauline Martini[232] predicts challenges in this complementarity as the courts compete for jurisdiction but I read mischief in such protestations as regional courts exist on other continents, for example the Inter-American Court of Human Rights. Amnesty International however argues that the difficulties would become more practical if the courts were to simultaneously be active in one situation.[233] It is problematic to concur with Amnesty that practical difficulties would arise 'only' if both courts decided to initiate the 'same case' or indict the same defendant at the same time because, as we have seen in the discourses around the Kenyan cases, practical issues, especially around availability of evidence, arose at the ICC even without a 'competing' court. Evidential difficulties will arise as they did in the Kenyan and Ivory Coast cases, not because of competing judicial needs but due to the respective courts' competencies. However, in the same report Amnesty indicated correctly that there is a weakness in the Malabo Protocol that competing obligations are not specifically dealt with by the ACHJR but I would argue that this is more of a campaigning stance than a legal one because if such problems arise, they would be resolved by other treaty laws, including the Rome Statute, through such provisions in Articles 90, 97 and 98.

Article 90 governs the way the ICC and state parties should resolve conflicting obligations when a state receives a request for surrender from the ICC and a request for extradition from another state, both concerning the same person.[234] According to Article 90(1), after receiving two parallel requests of different origins, a requested state shall notify the ICC and the requesting state of the situation. During a determination process, the guiding principle is that priority shall be given to the obligations under the Statute although a few limitations apply.[235] On the other side, Article 97 requires that, to resolve the matter, a state shall consult with the Court without delay where a state party receives a request concerning which it identifies problems which may impede or prevent the execution of the request.[236]

However, it is Article 98 which I think is more relevant to resolving any potential conflicts between obligations to the ICC and the ACJHR. This is because Article 98 was designed specifically for such situations to resolve the dilemma arising from a conflict between a state's international obligations.[237] Article 98 places international treaty obligations in a position superior to requests or orders from the Court for surrender or delivery of a suspect.[238] Crucially, Article 98 allows states to independently negotiate international treaties concerning jurisdiction over certain criminal suspects, and Article 98(2) prevents the Court from requesting the surrender of a suspect when such surrender would conflict with other international agreements.[239] Therefore, taken together, the three provisions show the inbuilt capacity for the ICC to work with the emerging ACJHR, at least in the early days of the African Court while the ICC winds up its operations in Africa.

I would argue that it does not make legal logic to say that if ICC invokes these Articles in a case of conflicting demands, a resolution will not follow, particularly given the ACJHR's clearly stated international law obligations. I read colonial mischief and undertones in Amnesty's stance because it is not clear why the burden should be on the African Court to resolve such a conflict even though the Rome Statute affords the ICC a mechanism to co-operate with 'regional organisations' and in this respect, it could seek cooperation from the ACJHR. The ACJHR is itself permitted to seek such co-operation by Article 46L(3) of the Amended ACJHR Statute.

The proposed ACJHR is criticised by others, including Amnesty international[240] as over-ambitious and created to shield the elite from prosecutions by providing immunity to sitting heads of governments.[241] I am not sure why Africans cannot be over-ambitious, but these criticisms should be seen as based on a mistaken assumption that ACJHR will be an isolationist court that takes no account of wider international law as the Malabo Protocol has clearly provided for. However, when looked at in the context of the wider ICL jurisdiction, these criticisms show their mischievous trait because, as already seen in the Sudan and Kenyan situations, the Rome Statute allows for these heads of government to be tried. My main argument against the ACHJR is that it shows a lack of courage and imagination in addressing African issues in its conception; it copies Eurocentric court structures and nowhere in the Protocol is the suggestion of African courts such as *Gacaca*. Therefore, while in a post-colonial sense the ACHJR is a major step in the right direction, the lack of acknowledgement of African epistemologies or local peace initiatives in any of its provisions is troubling and in this sense the court will act as yet another forum for reproducing colonial legal theories. Equally colonial is its use of foreign languages as official languages, including English, French, Arabic and Portuguese, which again shows the paradox of the African elite attempting the process of liberating the African using Eurocentric epistemologies clothed as Pan-Africanism. This is a sentiment expressed in different ways by Kamari Clarke who argues that this form of Pan-Africanism is made complex by the fact that the perspective used cannot be said to be 'purely' African because amongst other factors, the drafters were influenced by the same European legal systems and their own Eurocentric education.[242]

We see however that it is possible to successful try international crimes in African states even without the ACHJR being operational because of the already existing international law on *jus cogens* as demonstrated by the *Habré* case.[243] This case shows that despite the many political difficulties encountered, it was still possible to bring a high-profile trial to conclusion in an African setting and, crucially for our discussion on ACHJR, with the AU's authority. However, it should be noted that, as with *Pinochet*[244] and other prominent cases at the ICC, the *Habré* case was a colonial enterprise come full circle and should therefore be celebrated with a pinch of salt. As with all the high-profile cases discussed in this book, colonial shenanigans form the beginning and the end of these individuals' ascent and descent to/from power and their subsequent fate with 'justice.' As with Pinochet, the west was directly implicated in the abuses *Habré* committed while in power in Chad because his infamous security police (the DDS) were financed by foreign powers including the US and France.[245] While this case highlighted that local solutions with a universal outlook are possible, it is also significant in showcasing the clash of elitist notions of justice because, eventually, a verdict was reached in a typically 'French Court' in the African sun. In yet another clash of the elite drama, *Habré* refused to even acknowledge the court's authority but was nonetheless convicted on 30 May 2016 of crimes against humanity and was sentenced to life in prison in April 2017 by the Appeals Chamber.[246] No money has so far been recovered from him to pay for a $136 million trust fund created to pay remunerations to the victims of his crimes.[247]

In conclusion, this section shows that there exists the willingness to have real African-based solutions to African conflicts and the *Habré* case shows that it is possible to try high profile cases in Africa itself. Kamari Clarke sees this kind of Pan-Africanism as a way towards effective justice and towards Africa's renewed future. I agree with Kamari Clarke that this 'renewed' Pan-Africanism goes beyond the mere idea of African unity and

> …embodies the fight against feelings of racial subordination, assigned historically to the black body … This process of psychic self- making is part of the geosocial landscape in which internal feelings about Africa and its people merge with various exteriorities in the coproduction of African geographies of justice. But affects, as more than internal feelings brought into being by externalities, reflect structures of emotion imbricated along a zone that intersects with the past, the present, and aspirations for the future.[248]

Conclusions

In this chapter, I draw the conclusion that it is time for Africa to do away with the ICC as a peace producing project because the peace as envisaged by a Eurocentric epistemology may be 'the cause' of conflicts.[249] In addition to causing wars, peace as envisaged by the ICC leads to the continued 'epistemological' colonisation of Africa and therefore there is a need for an 'African-born' solution to African conflicts. An Africa 'owned' process that is based in Africa is necessary in order to avoid future reproduction of coloniality as practiced by the ICC.

This African epistemology or foundational norm is explored by showing the untapped possibilities of Africa specific legal norms underpinned by *Ubuntu* and practiced in the form of *Gacaca* courts. I have also explored and demonstrated the normative and constitutional character of *Ubuntu*, with its inherent potential for cross-continental liaisons with other southern perspectives from Latin America and Asia towards universal non-colonising legal norm(s). However, this chapter, while discussing the use of *Ubuntu* at the TRC has also warned that there are risks that these southern perspectives could be exoticised and hijacked by the neo-liberal agenda to stymie the revolution in favour of an Afrocentric future. This is because, as we saw with the TRC, the selective application of Ubuntu to mean just forgiveness when it was convenient to do so distracted the African revolutionary from seeking retribution and degraded African epistemology to a mythical-harmless form in order to work against the revolution and hence maintain colonial structures.

To reach this promise, Africa must domesticate ICL in a way that is particular to the continent through the establishment of an African Court as envisaged by the ACJHR in the AU's plan for an African Court. Although this court is yet to become operational, the Malabo Protocol provides for establishing ground-breaking international law norms with far reaching implications. This is because it provides for crimes that would capture destruction of the environment, unethical access to African resources, and armed changes of government amongst others. The obvious critique is that the Protocol provides for heads of state immunity but as argued, this is a red herring as the African Court will not delete previous international law that governs this area of ICL, including the Rome Statute. We also see in this light that it has always been possible for Africa to use the existing ICL regime to enforce human rights, as was the case with Habré.

My main critique of the ACJHR is that despite the normative and substantive possibilities of *Ubuntu* discussed above, the ACJHR does not make any reference to African norms. Nor does it envisage use of *Gacaca* style courts which would greatly enhance peace building and bring international justice to local people. This shows the elitist nature of law generally and the lack of decolonisation at the heart of the Eurocentric African lawyer. Nevertheless, the ACJHR is a starting point and a real opportunity to create a truly Pan-African court that tries all international crimes emanating from Africa and which can lend expertise to other regions in future. Since the ICC's main body of work is concentrated in Africa it must then be a logical conclusion that once the ACJHR is operational, the ICC should wind up its activities as they relate to Africa, but as it has accumulated legal technologies using African bodies, it could transfer this knowhow to African Lawyers on the continent in order to help make ACJHR functional.

Notes

1 Anibal Quijano, 'Coloniality of Power and Eurocentrism in Latin America' (2000) 15 (2) *International Sociology* 21.

2 Kamari Maxine Clarke, *Affective Justice: The International Criminal Court and the Pan-Africanist Pushback* (Duke University Press 2019) 180.

3 Frantz Fanon, *The Wretched of the Earth* (trans. Constance Farrington, Penguin 2001) 40–255.

4 Ngugi wa Thiong'o, *Decolonising the Mind: The Politics of Language in African Literature* (East African Publishers 1992).
5 Quijano Aníbal, 'Coloniality and Modernity/Rationality' (2007) 21 (2–3) *Cultural Studies* 168–178.
6 Walter D. Mignolo, 'Geopolitics of Sensing and Knowing: On (De)coloniality, Border Thinking and Epistemic Disobedience' (2011) 14 (3) *Postcolonial Studies* 273–283.
7 Frantz Fanon, *Toward the African Revolution: Political Essays* (Grove Press 1988).
8 Audre Lorde, The Master's Tools Will Never Dismantle the Master's House (Penguin Books 2017).
9 Nelson Maldonado-Torres, *Against War: Views from the Underside of Modernity* (Duke University Press Books 2008) 4.
10 Ibid.
11 Ibid.
12 Ibid.
13 Andrea Bianchi, *International Law Theories; An Inquiry into Different Ways of Thinking* (Oxford University Press 2016).
14 Siegfried Schieder in Harry Bauer & Elisabetta Brighi (Eds.), Pragmatism in International Relations (1st ed. Routledge 2008) 124.
15 Ingo Venzke, *How Interpretation Makes International Law; On Semantic Change and Normative Twist* (Oxford University Press 2012).
16 Armin Von Bogdandy and Ingo Venzke, *In Whose Name? A Public Law Theory of International Adjudication* (Oxford University Press 2014).
17 Boaventura de Sousa Santos, *Toward a New Legal Common Sense; Law, Globalization, and Emancipation* (Butterworths 2002).
18 Ibid., 437.
19 Boaventura de Sousa Santos, *Toward a New Common Sense: Law, Science and Politics in the Paradigmatic Transition After the Law* (Routledge 1995) 114–115.
20 Ibid.
21 Ibid.
22 Term borrowed from Martin Scorsese, Mick Jagger, Keith Richards, and Charlie Watts, *Shine a Light* (Twentieth Century Fox Home Entertainment 2008).
23 Boaventura de Sousa Santos and Cesar A. Rodriguez-Garavito (eds), *Law and Globalisation from Below; Towards a Cosmopolitan Legality* (Cambridge University Press 2005).
24 Ibid., 14.
25 Ibid.
26 Ibid.
27 Ibid.
28 William E. Conklin, 'The Peremptory Norms of the International Community' (2012) 12 (3) *European Journal of International Law* 837–861.
29 Raimundo Panikkar, 'Is the Notion of Human Rights a Western Concept?' (1982) 30 (120) *Diogenes* 75–102.
30 William E. Conklin, 'The Peremptory Norms of the International Community' (2012) 12 (3) *European Journal of International Law* 846.
31 Jack Donnelly, *Universal Human Rights in Theory and Practice* (2nd edn, Cornell University Press 2003).
32 Luis Eslava, 'Istanbul Vignettes: Observing the Everyday Operation of International Law' (2004) 2 *London Review of International Law* 3.
33 Ibid., 3–4.
34 Ibid.

35 See Julio Faundez, 'Legal Reform in Developing and Transition Countries: Making Haste Slowly' (2000) 1 (1) *Law, Social Justice and Global Development* 2000–2001.
36 See generally, Ted Robert Gurr, *Why Men Rebel* (Routledge 2015).
37 Luis Eslava (note 32).
38 Mogobe B. Ramose, The Philosophy of Ubuntu and Ubuntu as a Philosophy' in Pieter H. Coetzee and Abraham P. J. Roux (eds), *Philosophy from Africa: A Text with Readings* (Oxford University Press 2002) 230–237.
39 For an exploration of the usage of the term *Ubuntu* see Christian B. N. Gade, 'The Historical Development of the Written Discourses on Ubuntu' (2011) 30 (3) *South African Journal of Philosophy* 303–329.
40 Ramose B. Magobe, 'Reconciliation and Reconfiliation in South Africa' (2012) 5 *Journal on African Philosophy* 24.
41 Drucilla Cornell, *Law and Revolution in South Africa. Ubuntu, Dignity and the Struggle for Constitutional Transformation* (Fordham University Press 2014) 40.
42 Ibid.
43 Christian B. N. Gade, 'The Historical Development of the Written Discourses on Ubuntu' (2011) 30 (3) *South African Journal of Philosophy* 303–329.
44 Wessel Le Roux and Karin Van Marle (eds), *Law, Memory and the Legacy of Apartheid: Ten Years After AZAPO v President of South Africa* (The Pretoria University Law Press 2007).
45 Drucilla Cornell, *Law and Revolution in South Africa. Ubuntu, Dignity and the Struggle for Constitutional Transformation* (Fordham University Press 2014).
46 Ibid.
47 Ibid., 16.
48 Ibid.
49 Boaventura de Sousa Santos, *Toward a New Legal Common Sense; Law, Globalization, and Emancipation* (Butterworths 2002).
50 Drucilla Cornell, *Law and Revolution in South Africa. Ubuntu, Dignity and the Struggle for Constitutional Transformation* (Fordham University Press 2014) 10.
51 Hans Kelsen, *Pure Theory of Law* (University of California Press 1967).
52 Drucilla Cornell (note 50) 11.
53 Ibid., 44.
54 Ibid., 13.
55 Ibid.
56 Ibid., 1–18.
57 Paulina Cerdán, 'Post-Development and BuenVivir: An Approach to Development from Latin-America' (2013) 10 *International Letters of Social and Humanistic Sciences* 15–24.
58 Drucilla Cornell, *Law and Revolution in South Africa. Ubuntu, Dignity and the Struggle for Constitutional Transformation* (Fordham University Press 2014) 157–166.
59 Drucilla Cornell and Stephen D. Seely, *The Spirit of Revolution. Beyond the Dead Ends of Man* (Polity Press 2016) 49.
60 Ibid.
61 Ibid., 162.
62 Drucilla Cornell, *Moral Images of Freedom: A Future for Critical Theory* (Rowman & Littlefield 2007).
63 Ibid., 6.
64 Ibid., 24.
65 In his musings, Derrida made a distinction between unconditional hospitality, which he considered impossible, and hospitality which in his view was always conditional. Derrida saw hospitality as inviting and welcoming the 'stranger'/

other – which comes with some limitations/conditions. See amongst many, Dan Bulley, 'Ethics, Power and Space: International Hospitality beyond Derrida' (2015) 5 (2–3) *Hospitality & Society* 185–201.

66 Jacques Derrida, 'Force of Law: The Mystical Foundation of Authority' in Drucilla Cornell, Michel Rosenfeld and David Carlson (eds), *Deconstruction and the Possibility of Justice* (Routledge 1992) 3.

67 Jacques Derrida, 'Force of Law: The "Mystical Foundation of Authority"' trans. Mary Quaintance (1990) 11 (5/6) *Cardozo Law Review* 921–1045.

68 Drucilla Cornell and Stephen D. Seely (note 59).

69 Drucilla Cornell, *Moral Images of Freedom: A Future for Critical Theory* (Rowman & Littlefield 2007) 63–102.

70 Ibid., 69.

71 See more generally, Julio Faúndez and Celine Tan (eds) *International Economic Law, Globalization and Developing Countries* (Edward Elgar Publishing 2010); Thomas Piketty, *Capital in the Twenty-First Century* (Cambridge University Press 2014).

72 Drucilla Cornell (note 69) 102–147.

73 George D. J. Sefa, 'Rethinking the Role of Indigenous Knowledges in the Academy' (2000) 4 (2) *International Journal of Inclusive Education* 111–132.

74 Boaventura de Sousa Santos, 'Public Sphere and Epistemologies of the South' (2012) XXXVII (1) *Africa Development* 43–67; Paulina Cerdán, 'Post-Development and BuenVivir: An Approach to Development from Latin-America' (2013) 10 *International Letters of Social and Humanistic Sciences* 15–24.

75 See more generally Abdullahi An-Na'im, *Islam and Human Rights: Selected Essays of Abdullahi An-Na'im* (Mashood A. Bederin (ed.) Routledge 2017).

76 See Raimundo Panikkar, 'Is the Notion of Human Rights a Western Concept?' (1982) 30 (120) *Diogenes* 75–102.

77 Alberto Acosta (himself quoting Leonardo Boff), says that *BuenVivir* points to an ethic of that which is enough for the whole community, not just for the individual. It implies and integrates a holistic vision of the human being, immersed in the great earthly community that includes, besides humans, the air, water, soil, mountains, trees, and animals; it is to be in profound community with Pachamama with the energies of the Universe, and with God. Alberto Acosta, 'The Buen Vivir: An Opportunity to Imagine Another World' in Heinrich Böll Foundation (ed.), *Inside a Champion: An Analysis of the Brazilian Development Model* (Heinrich Böll Foundation 2012) 192–210.

78 Paulina Cerdán, 'Post-Development and BuenVivir: An Approach to Development from Latin-America' (2013) 10 *International Letters of Social and Humanistic Sciences* 15–24.

79 Gustavo Esteva and Madhu Suri Prakash, *Grassroots Post-Modernism: Remaking the Soil of Cultures* (Zed Books 1998) 282.

80 Paulina Cerdán (note 78).

81 Ibid.

82 Frantz Fanon, *The Wretched of the Earth* (trans. Constance Farrington, Penguin 2001).

83 Upendra Baxi, *Human Rights in a Post Human World; Critical Essays* (Oxford University Press 2009).

84 Ibid.

85 Boaventura de Sousa Santos, 'Toward a Multicultural Conception of Human Rights' (2002) 39 *Moral Imperialism: A Critical Anthology* 45.

86 Raimundo Panikkar, 'Is the Notion of Human Rights a Western Concept?' (1982) 30 (120) *Diogenes* 75–102.

87 For a discussion on this see, Easwaran Eknath, *The Upanishads: (Classics of Indian Spirituality)* (Vol. 2, Nilgiri Press 2007).

88 Easwaran Eknath, *The Bhagavad Gita: (Classics of Indian Spirituality)* (Vol. 1, Nilgiri Press 2007).
99 John P. Keenan, 'Review of Buddhist Theology: Critical Reflections by Contemporary Buddhist Scholars' (2002) 22 *Buddhist-Christian Studies* 230–234.
90 Ibid.
91 Yao Hsin-chung and Xinzhong Yao, *An Introduction to Confucianism* (Cambridge University Press 2000) 38–47.
92 Mogobe B. Ramose, 'Ubuntu: Affirming a Right and Seeking Remedies in South Africa' in Leonhard Praeg and Siphokazi Magadla (eds), *Ubuntu: Curating the Archive* (University of KwaZulu-Natal Press 2014) 121.
93 Truth and Reconciliation Commission, 'Truth and Reconciliation Commission of South Africa' (1998) *Final Report* (Vol. 1–5).
94 Wessel Le Roux and Karin Van Marle, *Post-Apartheid Fragments: Law, Politics, and Critique* (University of South Africa Press 2007); see also Deborah Posel, 'History as Confession: The Case of the South African Truth and Reconciliation Commission' (2008) 20 (1) *Public Culture* 119–141.
95 Pieter G. J. Meiring, 'Pastors or Lawyers? The Role of Religion in the South African Truth and Reconciliation Commission Process' (2002) 58 (1) *HTS: Theological Studies* 328–339.
96 Ibid.
97 Frantz Fanon, 'Algeria Unveiled' in Prasenjit Duara (ed.), *Decolonization: Perspectives from Now and Then* (Routledge 2004) 42.
98 Magobe B. Ramose, 'Reconciliation and Reconfiliation in South Africa' (2012) 5 *Journal on African Philosophy* 24.
99 Ngugi wa Thiong'o, *Decolonising the Mind. The Politics of Language in African Literature* (Heinemann 1981).
100 For a wider exploration of the church and slavery see, Reddie G. Anthony (ed.), *Black Theology, Slavery and Contemporary Christianity: 200 Years and No Apology* (Routledge 2016).
101 See generally Robert Morris (ed.), *Church and State in 21st Century Britain: The Future of Church Establishment* (Springer 2009).
102 Steve Biko, *I Write What I Like* (Heinemann 1978) 41.
103 John Donnelly Fage (ed.), *Africa Discovers Her Past* (Oxford University Press 1970) 1.
104 Denis Phillippe, 'The Rise of Traditional African Religion in Post-Apartheid South Africa' (2006) 34 (2/3) *Missionalia* 310–323.
105 Collins Randall, *Weberian Sociological Theory* (Cambridge University Press 1986).
106 James Walvin, 'Slavery, the Slave Trade and the Churches' (2008) 12 (2) *Quaker Studies* 3; Catherine Hall *et al.*, *Legacies of British Slave-Ownership: Colonial Slavery and the Formation of Victorian Britain* (Cambridge University Press 2014).
107 Simon Adams, 'What's Left?: The South African Communist Party After Apartheid' (1997) 24 (72) *Review of African Political Economy* 237–248.
108 Hanneke Stuit, *"Ubuntu, the Truth and Reconciliation Commission, and South African National Identity." Representation Matters* (Brill Rodopi 2010) 83–102.
109 *Azanian People's Organization ('AZAPO') and ors v President of South Africa and ors, Direct access to the Constitutional Court, CCT 17/96, ILDC 648 (ZA 1996).*
110 Cesare Pinelli, 'Legal Treatment of Past Political Violence and Comparative Constitutionalism' (2011) 2 *Comparative Law Review* 1.
111 Wessel Le Roux and Karin Van Marle (eds), *Law, Memory and the Legacy of Apartheid: Ten Years after AZAPO v President of South Africa* (The Pretoria University Law Press 2007).

112 Drucilla Cornell, *Law and Revolution in South Africa. Ubuntu, Dignity and the Struggle for Constitutional Transformation* (Fordham University Press New York 2014).

113 Magobe B. Ramose, 'Reconciliation and Reconfiliation in South Africa' (2012) 1 (5) *Journal on African Philosophy* 24.

114 Ali A. Mazrui, BLACK ORIENTALISM? Further Reflections on "Wonders of the African World" by Henry Louis Gates Jr (11 November 1999). http://www.h-net.org/~africa/sources/mazruigates2.htm accessed 3 August 2019.

115 Frantz Fanon, 'Algeria Unveiled' in Prasenjit Duara (ed.), *Decolonization: Perspectives from Now and Then* (Routledge 2004) 43–46.

116 Edward Said, *Orientalism: Western Concepts of the Orient* (Penguin 1978).

117 Ibid., 17.

118 Non-discrimination clause contained in Article 2 of the Universal Declaration of Human Rights, the International Convention for the Elimination of All Forms of Racial Discrimination which had been in force since 1969 and the Apartheid convention of 1976.

119 Vienna Convention on the Law of Treaties, 1969; norms considered peremptory in the sense that they are mandatory, do not admit derogation and can be modified only by general international norms of equivalent authority.

120 *Barcelona Traction, Light and Power Co. Ltd. (Belg. v. Spain), 1970 I.C.J. 3, 32 (Feb. 5).*

121 *AZAPO* para 30–31.

122 See Antonio Cassese, *International Criminal Law* (Oxford University Press 2003) 315–316.

123 Hanneke Stuit, *"Ubuntu, the Truth and Reconciliation Commission, and South African National Identity." Representation Matters* (Brill Rodopi 2010) 83–102.

124 Ibid.

125 Ibid.

126 Submission to the truth and reconciliation commission by Mr F. D. de Klerk, leader of the national party found at http://sabctrc.saha.org.za/documents/submit.htm accessed 1 July 2020.

127 Ibid.

128 *FW de Klerk and Another v The Chairperson of the Truth and Reconciliation Commission and the President of the Republic of South Africa: Case No. 14930/98 (Cape of Good Hope Provincial Division).*

129 TRC, Final Report Volume 6, p58 Para 22–30, available at; http://sabctrc.saha.org.za/reports/volume6/section1/chapter4/subsection3.htm accessed 1 July 2020.

130 BBC News 28/10/98, 'De Klerk Accusations cut from Report,' available at http://news.bbc.co.uk/1/hi/world/africa/202367.stm accessed 30 July 2016.

131 TRC, Final Report Volume 5 Subsection 23, Findings regarding Mrs Winnie Madikizela-Mandela and the Mandela Football Club, available at http://sabctrc.saha.org.za/reportpage accessed 1 July 2020.

132 Hanneke Stuit (note 123).

133 Antjie Krog, *Country of My Skull: Guilt, Sorrow, and the Limits of Forgiveness in the New South Africa* (Three River Press 2000) 391.

134 A more detailed critique is that of Mahmood Mamdani, 'Amnesty or Impunity? A Preliminary Critique of the Report of the Truth and Reconciliation Commission of South Africa (TRC)' (2002) 32 (3/4) *Diacritics* 32–59 who says that not only did the TRC not allow for the compensation of the wronged, it put the colonised and the coloniser in the same category, did not allow for the punishment of crimes against humanity and, notably, it did not acknowledge the dissent of one of the commissioners concerning the fact that Apartheid was not legally put on trial by the commission.

135 Ibid.

136 Cody Corliss, 'Truth Commissions, and the Limits of Restorative Justice: Lessons Learned in South Africa's Cradock Four Case' (2013) 21 *Michigan State University College of Law. International Law Review* 273.
137 Frances Reid and Deborah Hoffmann (Dirs), *Long Night's Journey into Day. A Documentary* (Seventh Art Releasing 2000).
138 Hanneke Stuit (note 123).
139 Wessel Le Roux Wessel and Karin Van Marle (eds), *Law, Memory, and the Legacy of Apartheid: Ten Years after AZAPO v President of South Africa* (The Pretoria University Law Press 2007).
140 Ibid., 24.
141 Ibid., 24.
142 Ibid., 3–9.
143 bid., 16.
144 Ibid., 17.
145 Rashida Manjoo, *Gender Injustice and the South African Truth and Reconciliation Commission* (Routledge 2012).
146 Ibid.
147 Ibid.
148 Magobe B. Ramose, 'Reconciliation and Reconfiliation in South Africa' (2012) 1 (5) *Journal on African Philosophy* 24.
149 Ibid.
150 Manfred O. Hinz, 'Traditional Governance and African Customary Law: Comparative Observations from a Namibian Perspective' (2008) 20 (2) *Human Rights and the Rule of Law in Namibia* 59–87.
151 *Bhe and others v the Magistrate of Khayelitsha and others in 2005 (1) BCLR (Butterworths Constitutional Law Reports) 1 (CC).*
152 Ramose (note 148).
153 Rebecca Saunders, 'Lost in Translation: Expressions of Human Suffering, the Language of Human Rights, and the South African Truth and Reconciliation Commission' (2008) 5 (9) *Revista Internacional de Direitos Humanos* 52–75.
154 Ibid.
155 Ngugi wa Thiong'o, *Decolonising the Mind. The Politics of Language in African Literature* (Heinemann 1981).
156 Steve de Shazer, *Words Were Originally Magic* (W.W. Norton & Company 1994) 9.
157 Ngugi wa Thiong'o (note 155).
158 Hanneke Stuit (note 123).
159 Jaco Barnard, 'Reading and Writing Archives: The TRC, Big Business and Reparations in Post-Apartheid South Africa' in Le Roux and Van Marle (eds) (note 139) 93–106.
160 Ibid., 104.
161 Edward Goldsmith and Jerry Mander (eds), *The Case Against the Global Economy and for a Turn Towards Localisation* (Earthscan 2001).
162 Solomon Johannes Terreblanche, *A History of Inequality in South Africa 1652 to 2002* (University of Natal Press 2002) 419.
163 National Service of Gacaca Jurisdictions (NSGJ), *Gacaca Courts in Rwanda* (2012) 14–15.
164 Ibid., 24.
165 Organic Law No. 08/96 of 30 August 1996, on the Organization of Prosecutions for Offences Constituting the Crime of Genocide and Crimes against Humanity Committed since October 1, 1990 was then complemented by organic Law N0 40/2000 of 26 January 2001 setting up *Gacaca* jurisdictions.

166 NSGJ (note 163) 50.
167 For a detailed exploration see Charity Wibabara, *Gacaca Courts versus the International Criminal Tribunal for Rwanda and National Courts: Lessons to Learn from the Rwandan Justice Approaches to Genocide* (Nomos 2014).
168 Constitution of the Republic of South Africa 1996.
169 Phil Clark, 'The Rules (and Politics) of Engagement: The Gacaca Courts and Post-Genocide Justice, Healing and Reconciliation in Rwanda' in Phil Clark and Zachary Kaufman (eds), *After Genocide: Transitional Justice, Post-Conflict Reconstruction and Reconciliation in Rwanda and Beyond* (Hurst and Co Publishers ltd 2009) 302.
170 NSGJ (note 163) 23.
171 Hollie Nyseth Brehm, Christopher Uggen and Jean-Damascene Gasanabo, 'Genocide, Justice, and Rwanda's Gacaca Courts' (2014) 30 (3) *Journal of Contemporary Criminal Justice* 333.
172 Ibid.
173 Preamble, Organic Law N0 40/2000 of 26 January 2001 Setting up Gacaca Jurisdictions and Organizing Prosecutions for Offences Constituting the Crime of Genocide or Crimes Against Humanity Committed between October 1, 1990 and December 31, 1994; NUR/CCM at page 30.
174 NSGJ (note 163).
175 Ibid., 30.
176 See for example Human Rights Watch (2004), Rwanda: Struggling to Survive. Barriers to Justice for Rape Victims in Rwanda.
177 NSGJ (note 163) 30.
178 Human Rights Watch (2004).
179 NSGJ (note 163).
180 Article 10 of the 2001 Gacaca Law.
181 See Gacaca procedure in the different Genocide Laws.
182 The 1977 Penal Code then applicable stipulated a punishment of the death penalty for aggravated murder (Articles 312 and 316).
183 See the Preambles of the Genocide Laws. They clearly mention that their aim is not only justice but also national reconciliation.
184 Usta Kaitesi, *Genocidal Gender and Sexual Violence. The Legacy of the ICTR, Rwanda's Ordinary Courts and Gacaca Courts* (Intersentia 2014) 211, 176.
185 Ibid., 212.
186 Ibid.
187 Sarah Wells, 'Gender, Sexual Violence and Prospects for Justice at the Gacaca Courts in Rwanda' (2004) 14 *Review of Law and Women's Studies* 167; Lars Waldorf, 'Mass Justice for Mass Atrocity: Rethinking Local Justice as Transitional Justice' (2006) 79 *Temple Law Review* 1; Megan M. Carpenter, 'Bare Justice: A Feminist Theory of Justice and Its Potential Application to Crimes of Sexual Violence in Post-Genocide Rwanda' (2008) 41 *Creighton Law Review* 595.
188 Sarah Wells (note 187) 188.
189 Usta Kaitesi (note 185) 208.
190 NSGJ (note 163) 271.
191 Ibid.
192 Ibid.
193 Anne-Marie De Brouwer and Etienne Ruvebana, 'The Legacy of the Gacaca Courts in Rwanda: Survivors' Views' (2013) 13 (5) *International Criminal Law Review* 937–976.
194 Sarah Wells (note 187) 192.
195 De Brouwer and Ruvebana (note 193).

196 Phil Clark, 'Bringing the Peasants Back in, Again: State Power and Local Agency in Rwanda's Gacaca Courts' (2014) 8 (2) *Journal of Eastern African Studies* 193–213.
197 NSGJ (note 163).
198 De Brouwer and Ruvebana (note 193) 954.
199 Ibid.
200 Sarah Wells (note 187) 191.
201 Usta Kaitesi (note 184) 204.
202 Ibid., 214.
203 De Brouwer and Ruvebana (note 193) 947.
204 Ibid.
205 Article 38 of the 2004 Gacaca Law.
206 Human Rights Watch, Justice Compromised: The Legacy of Rwanda's Community-Based Gacaca Courts (Human Rights Watch 31 May 2011) available at https://www.hrw.org accessed 9 November 2021.
207 Ibid.
208 See for example Articles 34, 35, 54 of the 2004 Gacaca Law; Articles 12 and 13 of the 2008 Genocide Law.
209 Cheikh Lo! *Il n'est jamais trop tard* from the album *Jamm* (World Circuit 2010). This post-independence classic by Bembeya Jazz (*Doni Doni*) was a call to honest work, building step by step, rather than to fast riches. Cheikh Lo! reimagines it here; still danceable, optimistic. He urges young Africans to restrain from taking perilous voyages to Europe. Instead, they should stay put and *petit à petit* build their countries.
210 For an exploration of Pan-Africanism since slavery see Toyin Falola and Kwame Essien (eds), *Pan-Africanism and the politics of African Citizenship and Identity* (Routledge 2013).
211 Kamari Maxine Clarke, *Affective Justice: The International Criminal Court and the Pan-Africanist Pushback* (Duke University Press 2019) 187.
212 Ibid.
213 Of Blyden, the less said the better, but for his ideas see H. R Lynch, 'Edward W. Blyden: Pioneer West African Nationalist' (1965) 6 (3) *Journal of African History* 373–388.
214 Edward W. Blyden's 1881 presidential address during the opening of the Liberia College quoted in Kamari Maxine Clarke (note 208) at 187.
215 Kamari Maxine Clarke (note 211) 186–187.
216 For an exploration of this topic see for example Kofi Kufour, *The African Human Rights System: Origin and Evolution* (Springer 2010).
217 OAU Charter. https://au.int/en/treaties/oau-charter-addis-ababa-25-may-1963 accessed 1 March 2021.
218 Ibid.
219 Constitutive Act of the African Union CAB/LEG/23.15, entered into force 26 May 2001.
220 OAU Doc OAU/CAB/LEG/67/3/Rev 5.
221 OAU Doc CAB/LEG/24.3.
222 OAU Doc CAB/LEG/153/Rev 2.
223 ACHPR/RP/XIX.
224 The first and most elaborate set of guidelines was adopted by the Commission in 1988. AFR/COM/HPR.5(IV). A second and apparently additional set of guidelines, which is much more concise, was adopted by the Commission in 1998.OAU Doc/05/27(XXIII).
225 OAU/LEG/MIN/AFCHPR/PROT (III).
226 Decision on the Draft Legal Instruments, Assembly/AU/Dec.529 (XXIII).

227 Kamari Maxine Clarke, *Affective Justice: The International Criminal Court and the Pan-Africanist Pushback* (Duke University Press 2019) 213.
228 Ibid.
229 Ibid., 177–206.
230 Article 28A Protocol on Amendments to the Protocol on the Statute of the African Court of justice and Human Rights.
231 Pauline Martini, 'The International Criminal Court versus the African Criminal Court: A Remodelling of the Principle of Complementarity as a Solution to Potential Conflicts of Jurisdiction between the Courts' (2021) 18 (5) *Journal of International Criminal Justice* 1185–1205.
232 Ibid.
233 Amnesty International, *Snapshots of Legal and Institutional Implications of the Malabo Protocol* (Amnesty International 2017).
234 Oktawian Kuc, 'The Rome Statute and Legal Limitations to the International Surrender Regime' (2012) 18 *New England Journal of International and Comparative Law* 265.
235 Ibid.
236 Kimberly Prost, 'The Surprises of Part 9 of the Rome Statute on International Cooperation and Judicial Assistance' (2018) 16 (2) *Journal of International Criminal Justice* 363–382.
237 Erik Rosenfeld, 'Application of U.S. Status of Forces Agreements to Article 98 of the Rome Statute' (2003) 2 *Washington University Global Studies Law Review* 273.
238 Ibid.
239 Ibid.
240 Amnesty International (note 233).
241 Amended ACJHR Statute Article 46A bis.
242 Kamari Maxine Clarke, *Affective Justice: The International Criminal Court and the Pan-Africanist Pushback* (Duke University Press 2019) 192.
243 For a good exploration of this case and its implications see Tanaz Moghadam, 'Revitalizing Universal Jurisdiction: Lessons from Hybrid Tribunals Applied to the Case of Hissene Habre' (2008) 39 *Columbia Human Rights Law Review* 471.
244 Bartle and the Commissioner of Police for the Metropolis and Others, Ex Parte Pinochet, R v. [1998] UKHL 41. Later affirmed in ex parte Pinochet Ugarte (No. 3) 1999 W.L.R.2 827 (1999).
245 Commission d'Enquête Nationale du Ministère Tchadien de la Justice, Les crimes et détournements de l'ex-Président Habré et de ses complices, (Éditions L'Harmattan 1993) 28 found at https://www.labaignoiredarchimede.com/livre accessed 25th June 2021.
246 Appeals Judgement *Hissein Habré Extraordinary African Chambers (EAC)* Appeals Chamber 27 April 2017.
247 Nader Iskandar Diab, 'Challenges in the Implementation of the Reparation Award against Hissein Habré: Can the Spell of Unenforceable Awards across the Globe be Broken?' (March 2018) 16 (1) *Journal of International Criminal Justice* 141–163.
248 Kamari Maxine Clarke, *Affective Justice: The International Criminal Court and the Pan-Africanist Pushback* (Duke University Press 2019) 180.
249 See in general Hartmut Behr's idea that the foundation of European epistemology has war as a template, in Hartmut Behr, *Politics of Difference: Epistemologies of Peace* (Taylor & Francis/Routledge 2014).

7 À La Fin, Le Balayeur Balayé!

The discourse begun here could not be timelier or more relevant as the debate on institutional racism and slavery legacies dominates and the conflict between the ICC and African states remains unresolved. This project has enabled me to explore the complexities of legal, political, and epistemological considerations underlying African disputes with the ICC and will enrich this research area as well as offer a potential settlement between African states and the ICC. This work will also narrow the gap in 'law authorship' because my literature review showed that although voices from 'southern' experts do exist in the so-called Third World Approaches to International Law (TWAIL), there is still, as the name suggests, a 'casting off' of this southern expertise from involvement in the authorship of ICL. Building on these alternative voices, this research has taken a unique route, combining those arguments with others that confront the biases in the criminal justice systems of the colonial state itself by applying Critical Race Theory to our discourse.

I have used my own experiences and standpoint to interrogate whether ICL is replicating the most maligned prison industrial complex exposed by social justice activists in countries like the USA as well as the racial bias exposed in the British legal system. I also wanted to divert from the practice that has meant exposing the ills of the current ICL regime without proposing an alternative. Audaciously, I suggest it is time for Africa to transit from ICC as their apex ICL court to an African court and to utilise African norms such as *Ubuntu* and formats like *Gacaca* in such a court because only in this way will Africa be a source of truly alternative/parallel global legal norms.

I indicated at the beginning that watching the Charles Taylor hearings between 2006 and 2013 raised questions in my mind not just about the power dynamics between a white bench and a black lawyer, but also about the fact that, at the time the USA and UK had invaded Iraq – leading to hundreds of thousands of lost lives because of what we know was false intelligence.[1] Neither George Bush nor Tony Blair has to date been asked to account for that war before a court of law. And therefore, the question in my mind was always why ICL was concerned with Sierra Leone and not Iraq? It is all the

DOI: 10.4324/9781003304173-7

more poignant that Tony Blair and George Bush were instrumental in bringing Charles Taylor to trial and in fact, Charles Taylor is in a British prison. More recently we see the ICC refusing to initiate any proceedings against British soldiers/leaders for war crimes committed in Iraq despite specific instances where war crimes occurred being listed. It is with these obvious contradictions in mind that I interrogated this paradox in which ICL creates 'bright' sites for the law in Africa while at the same time is seemingly blind to the prevailing 'dark' sites mentioned above. I therefore aimed to answer the following primary question: 'Is Africa a site for experimenting with new ICL doctrines?'

At the start of my research in 2016–2017, 23 cases in nine situations had been brought before the ICC and all were from Africa: all 32 individuals who had been indicted at that stage were African.[2] In a period of two years since and by April 2019, the Court had issued indictments against 45 individuals, all of them African.[3] But Africa is not the only site where 'international' types of crimes are happening. This leads to my hypothesis that Africa is being used as a 'testing site' for ICL rather than as a participant in authoring and designing ICL. To interrogate this hypothesis, I analysed the disputes between the ICC and African states[4] using a Post-Colonial and Critical Race Theory perspective. Consequently, I engaged with the secondary question of whether Africa can/should provide normative alternatives to the prevailing Eurocentric orthodoxy.

Recap

From earlier on in Chapter 2 where I explored the literature around postcolonialism, decolonisation and TWAIL, patterns were emerging that suggested most of the research has focused on International Economic Law rather than International Criminal Law although there is an emerging scholarship focusing on ICL as a continuation of the colonial and it is here that this research will have an impact on widening the pool of available literature in this field.

More telling though was the impression, better captured by Mutua's own acceptance, that there is a clear contradictoriness and ambivalence among anti-colonial and TWAIL scholars towards international law because of their tendency to regard it variously as either the problem or the solution to world's injustices.[5] Hence it was my intention in this book to expound on a proposed remedy for this coloniality, especially because such ambivalence stymies resistance/revolution and reform aimed at enhancing the equitableness of the international legal system.

In Chapter 3, I showed how ICL should always be considered together with its conjoined twin IEL because the coloniality inherent in the Rome Statute was made possible via neo-liberal orthodoxy. The neo-liberal project always leads to conflicts and hence the emerging squabble between the ICC and African states or rather the conflict between global elite and

African elite. I show that the push for African states to sign up to international human rights bodies such as the ICC was not without a colonial basis and that the subsequent fall-out exemplified by the situation in Kenya was a natural outcome of such a colonial arrangement. The link between post-colonialism and the neo-liberal drive to harmonise laws and economies is less widely discussed in existing literature but this linkage is crucial here because of my findings that, if unchallenged, the Rome Statute model reproduces racist tendencies in criminal law and, more worryingly, that the industrial complex that comes with criminal law risks mirroring slavery.

The linkage between neo-liberalism, coloniality and the ICC is relevant to discourse on African cases at the ICC because one cannot contextualise existing and future colonialism outside the prevailing neo-liberal world order. More telling though is the realisation that the Rome Statute may be a useful tool to hinder revolutions that could otherwise challenge this hegemony. In the case of Africa, the narrative of the African woman as a perpetual victim of crimes perpetrated by her brothers stops their elevation to the status of liberation icons and diminishes their leadership in future struggles while fragmenting solidarity with their brothers.

But what does this neo-liberal coloniality/enslavement look like? In Chapter 4, I detailed my findings on how iconographies from the ICC are perceived by global audiences as well as audiences from the accused's own countries and on how both the court and the accused have used such images. For example, I detail how the ICC, at least in the Kenyatta case, was naïve if not blind to political messaging and the power of courtroom appearances. In line with this, I also show the interaction between the ICC's physical architecture and the idea of the 'acting out of justice' or justice being 'seen' to be done. The Eurocentric environment in which the African trials happen is a physical expression of the 'global' populace's relationship with the ideals of justice and in my view reflects the distortion of the term 'global.' The literature reviewed on the ICC and its relationship with the African cases ignores the power messaging involved in court architecture and space utilisation, including my argument that this messaging conveys that international justice could only be served in a European city/space.

This in fact relates to ideas of who can legitimately participate in the legal arena and call the judiciary to account. What this chapter demonstrates is that the space where justice is being seen to be done should be a contested space as it reduces the African citizen to a mere spectator as far as the ICC – the sphere where their justice is supposedly being served – is concerned. The spatial and metaphysical distance between the African citizen and the ICC is exposed here because Africans become mere spectators of trials directly affecting them and there is little possibility of the African citizen participating in this arena. More tellingly, the imagery strengthens the already existing dichotomy between the criminal black man, victim black woman, and the just white people. The consequences of this dichotomy are the cases from Africa targeting black men – reproducing what is already occurring in local jurisdictions such as in the UK and USA. In relation to this idea of participatory justice, the chapter deals with how architecture affects the conditions of 'judgecraft' or projection of power. In recent times, the idea of transparency in the judicial arena has become the 'thing' to work towards and concerted efforts are made to design court houses around this view of transparent and participatory justice.

For example, to promote an idea of transparency and break from the past, glass is extensively used in the design of the Federal German Court.[6] This seems to be where the ICC's building designers sought inspiration because the ICC building is also intended to portray transparency. In another 'new beginnings' design message, the Constitutional Court in South Africa is designed to project a conception of transformative constitutionalism.[7] In my view however, this drive to present transparency means housing the court in a glass box, ironically projecting the court as fragile rather than as having the intended strength or stability. The Eurocentric design also suggests supremacy of idea(s) which ignores other thought forms including architectural influences from other corners of the world. To counter this Eurocentric law architecture, the chapter suggests looking at the example set already by *Gacaca* courts in Rwanda as an example of justice being served locally. The *Gacaca* model is suggested because, I argue, the presentation of the ICC as the place and site where all justice is served conveys an intentionally wrong impression arising out of the deliberate effort, inherited from past colonial courts, to present the 'law' as unique and as only meted out by a select few. In that sense the Court is reduced to a cabal of a few elites and therefore becomes the antithesis of resolving conflicts in the interests of a wider social justice.

In Chapter 5 we saw that most cases at the ICC so far have been from Africa which means that both the victims and the accused have been African, and mostly black Africans. Here we see the reproduction of the colonial and the racist undertones of the demarcation of Africa as where victims and perpetrators of international crimes are found, as discussed by Marti Koskenniemi and other authors. In *Bemba* we see this demarcation of civilised/barbaric in war rape prosecution and the uncomfortable links it has with previous war rape trails after World War II where the racial biases were exposed. We also see the perpetuation of the victim without agency and the infantilisation of local initiatives to find solutions fitting local circumstances which is tied in with the NGO ICL/IEL industrial complex that binds these 'sites' in a perpetual need for international interventionist agencies like the ICC. To end this white saviour complex, I suggest that we borrow from practices in social work and psychology and use holistic/therapeutic approaches to conflict situations. Such approaches however need time, commitment, local connections, and longevity, all of which are lacking in Eurocentric ICL. This approach also requires that past atrocities of colonialism and slavery are accounted for and restitution offered, which again is not forthcoming.

Victim participation is seen in the light of meanings of justice in relation to the orthodox understanding of criminal law proceedings where the prosecution provides evidence and the defendant counters that evidence. In the ICC context, I argue that the balance is tilted to the prosecution's advantage as the victim is involved in the 'evidential' stages of the process, which has an impact on fair hearing. Victim participation faces added criticisms of whether the victim could ever be without fault but also that the ICC reproduces a colonial view of the African victim with no agency of their own cementing the colonial demarcation of the saviour-victim dichotomy. As I explored in Chapter 3 this view reduces African women to victims and their places in Africa's liberation struggles are buried under the deluge of saviour rhetoric. The ICC's concentration on one individual, usually the leadership, leads to the situation where at the end, the victim does not receive justice as the real perpetrators are still free. What however cements Africa as 'the site' is that the precedent being set by the ICC using African situations is not being replicated elsewhere, including in places where atrocities are commonly reported to be occurring, for example in Palestinian territories or in Myanmar.

After exploring victim participation, I looked at plea bargains in the *Mahdi* case. First, plea bargains are seen as directly opposed to the idea of a victim-centred justice and make the ICC's impunity rhetoric seem empty, meaningless. Second, plea bargains are seen as detrimental to the black accused as they have, for example, been extensively used in the USA to commercialise law in a soft reproduction of slavery. This reproduction of slavery is also seen in the suggestion inherent in plea bargains that the law would be willing to countenance the pricing of, say, a genocide or the African body in practices reminiscent of slavery. Still in *Mahdi*, I also explored the testing of Article 8 on cultural destruction and found testing but also replication of old laws. In relation to post-colonial significance, I argue that *Mahdi* is less significant when compared to local decisions on the return of looted cultural items such as the Italian *Nostra* case where the court ordered the return the 'Venus of Cyrene' to Libya.

In Chapter 6, I explored the real possibility for alternative 'southern' norms capable of countering the Eurocentric hegemony. This is in line with my aim of propagating plurality as an alternative to the status quo and the need to look at the possibility that the south can also provide *grundnorms* that can/should be equally universal. This is because there is a need for scholars to reflect on the fact that international law has always been involved in shaping the world order and has invariably carried with it the methodology and interpretation that would provide the modalities by which such order is shaped. To think critically about international law without providing a way forward is no longer enough as an end in itself if one realises the ideological baggage discussed above. To realise the pervasive effects of international Law in everyday life, and to proceed, with the sensitivity of an ethnographer, to explore the international sites where international law is made and the local sites where international law is re-embodied and affects the lives of people may be a good reflex in interrogating where the world needs to be reshaped and the international rethought.[8]

Breaking the Shackles

I draw the conclusion that it is about time Africa does away with the ICC as a peace producing project because the peace as envisaged by a Eurocentric epistemology is built upon a concept of universal reason which may in fact contribute to, if not cause, conflict – and even war – in the first place.[9] In addition to causing wars, peace as envisaged by the ICC leads to the continued 'epistemological' colonisation of Africa and therefore an African 'born' solution to African conflicts is essential. An Africa 'owned' process that is based in Africa is necessary to avoid future reproduction of coloniality as practiced by the ICC.

Consequently, Africa's epistemology must form the foundational norm(s) for the alternative to Eurocentrism with specific norms such as *Ubuntu* and practices like *Gacaca* courts. *Ubuntu* must be embedded in Africa's current attempts to domesticate the ICL through the establishment of an African Court, as envisaged by the ACHJR. This is because, while the plan to establish an African court is a positive start, the Court's foundational norms are Eurocentric and the ACHJR completely ignores any reference to African norms. ACHJR also does not envisage use of *Gacaca* type courts which would greatly enhance peace building and bring international justice to local people. Nevertheless, I see the ACHJR as a starting point and a real opportunity to create a truly Pan-African court that tries all international crimes emanating from Africa and which can lend expertise to other regions in the future. Since the ICC's main body of work is concentrated in Africa it is logical to conclude that once the ACHJR is operational, the ICC should wind up its activities in relation to Africa, but because it has accumulated legal technologies using African bodies, it must also transfer this knowledge to African Lawyers on the continent who in turn should operationalise the ACHJR. Eventually, we should aim at having an ACHJR that has *Ubuntu* at its core and operates *Gacaca* type local courts to deal with conflicts in Africa. Through this, we will be able to reclaim the telling of our history, celebrate our mothers as the liberation icons they have always been, and throw away these white shackles.

Notes

1 Piers Robinson, 'Learning from the Chilcot Report: Propaganda, Deception and the "War on Terror"' (2017) 11 (1–2) *International Journal of Contemporary Iraqi Studies* 47–73.

2 International Criminal Court, 'Cases,' available at: https://www.icc-cpi.int/Pages/defendantswip.aspx accessed 11 April 2019.

3 Ibid.

4 Sewell Chan, 'South Africa to Withdraw from International Criminal Court' *The New York Times*, 21 October 2016.
5 Makau Mutua, 'Critical Race Theory and International Law: The View of an Insider-Outsider' (2000) 45 *Villanova Law Review* 841.
6 Thorten Bürklin, *The Federal Constitutional Court of Germany: Architecture and Jurisdiction* (Basel 2004).
7 Wessel Le Roux, 'Bridges, Clearings and Labyrinths: The Architectural Framing of Post-Apartheid Constitutionalism' (2004) 19 *Sexual Assault Prevention and Response* 629–645.
8 Andrea Bianchi, *International Law Theories; An Inquiry into Different Ways of Thinking* (Oxford University Press 2016) 226.
9 Hartmut Behr, *Politics of Difference: Epistemologies of Peace* (Taylor & Francis/ Routledge 2014).

8 Epilogue

...Le balayeur balayé
Le balayeur balayé

Arrivé comme un sauveur
Il est parti comme un voleur
Je l'avais pourtant prévenu
De la déception de mon peuple
Arrivé comme un héros
Il est reparti à zéro
Je l'avais pourtant prévenu
De la présence des vautours autour
Bye
Le balayeur balayé "[1]

Note

1 Tiken Jah Fakoly, Le Balayeur in *Françafrique* (Barclay 2002).

DOI: 10.4324/9781003304173-8

Index

Note: Page numbers followed by "n" denote endnotes.

For Product Safety Concerns and Information please contact our EU
representative GPSR@taylorandfrancis.com
Taylor & Francis Verlag GmbH, Kaufingerstraße 24, 80331 München, Germany

www.ingramcontent.com/pod-product-compliance
Ingram Content Group UK Ltd.
Pitfield, Milton Keynes, MK11 3LW, UK
UKHW020143200926
475702UK00005B/879
9781032302553